MAKING A MAN

MAKING
A MAN

Gentlemanly Appetites in the
Nineteenth-Century
British Novel

GWEN HYMAN

Ohio University Press | Athens

Ohio University Press, Athens, Ohio 45701
www.ohioswallow.com
© 2009 by Ohio University Press

Printed in the United States of America
Ohio University Press books are printed on acid-free paper ⊗ ™

16 15 14 13 12 11 10 09   5 4 3 2 1

Library of Congress Cataloging-in-Publication Data
Hyman, Gwen.
  Making a man : gentlemanly appetites in the nineteenth-century British
novel / Gwen Hyman.
    p. cm.
  Includes bibliographical references and index.
  ISBN 978-0-8214-1853-6 (hc : alk. paper) — ISBN 978-0-8214-1854-3
(pbk. : alk. paper)
  1. English fiction—19th century—History and criticism. 2. Men in literature.
3. Food habits in literature. 4. Drinking customs in literature. 5. Drug abuse
in literature. 6. Manners and customs in literature. 7. Male consumers—
Great Britain—History—19th century. 8. Men—Great Britain—Social life
and customs—19th century. I. Title.
  PR868.M45H96 2009
  823'.8093521—dc22
                                                         2009000021

For Andrew

buon appetito, amore mio

CONTENTS

ACKNOWLEDGMENTS

My most heartfelt thanks are due to Professor D. A. Miller, whose support, critical acuity, and endless patience were crucial to the genesis of this project; to Mitchell Davis for resources and directions; and to Professors William Germano, Brian Swann, and David Weir for their guidance and support. Great thanks are due as well to Andrew Carmellini, Bryna and Gerry Hyman, Samantha Heller, Julia Miele Rodas, and Catherine Siemann, without whom this work might never have arrived, cooked and plated, at the table.

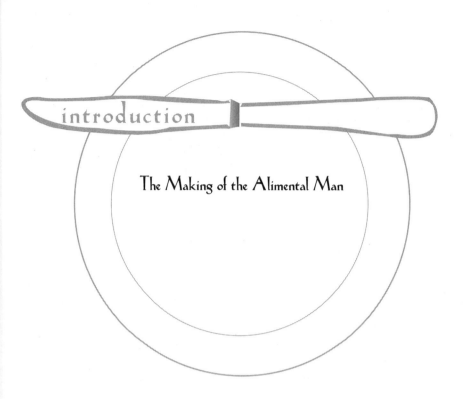

introduction

The Making of the Alimental Man

ON FALLING TO AT THE TABLE OF LITERARY ALIMENT

In Wilkie Collins's 1875 sensation novel *The Law and the Lady*, Benjamin—clerk, faithful family retainer, and most conservative and middle-class of men—finds himself faced with an uncomfortable set of questions concerning the former Valeria Brinton's new husband. Utterly unprepared for dealing with such gentlemanly unsavoriness—dead wives? poison? marriage under false names?—he attempts to calm Valeria down, to put such improbable tales aside, by turning to the simple pleasures of the table. "Suppose we get on with our dinner?" he asks wearily. "Here is a loin of mutton, my dear—an ordinary loin of mutton. Is there anything suspicious in *that?* Very well, then. Show me you have confidence in the mutton; please eat. There's the wine, again. No mystery, Valeria, in that claret—I'll take my oath it's nothing but innocent juice of the grape. If we can't believe in anything else, let's believe in juice of the grape. Your good health, my dear" (49–50).

But Benjamin's faith in the pleasures of the table is as misplaced as it is in the case of Valeria's problematic husband: in *The Law and the Lady*, as in any number of nineteenth-century British novels, confidence in mutton and claret is, in fact, an extremely complicated and nuanced proposition. As Benjamin is soon made uncomfortably aware, there is nothing overplayed about his guest's misgivings concerning her husband and his friends—the alimentary realm, so central to the construction and deconstruction of these men (and, indeed, to their dealings with our heroine), is precisely where the masquerade and mystification they trade in comes to a boil. In the gentlemanly world of *The Law and the Lady*, tea and poison are as one; champagne and biscuits hold keys to selfhood and history; and truffles stewed in Burgundy are deeply flavored with class, gender, tradition, modernity, and the performance and the creation of the self. Though Collins's novel is sensational in its engagements with food and drink, it is hardly unique in its preoccupations. In the novels of nineteenth-century Britain, when it comes to the gentlemanly table, the mutton is always deserving of suspicion; the wine is always mysterious; food and drink are always more than they appear to be.

Though eating is, as Benjamin insists, the most basic and prosaic of human operations, it is also among the most fraught: at once insistently public and intensely, intimately bodily, alimentary consumption reveals a great deal about the consumer, bringing into play the technologies, the pieties, the hierarchies, and the economies of the world in which this consumption takes place. Food, as Barbara Kirshenblatt-Gimblett puts it, is "larger than life . . . highly charged with meaning and affect" (1). Aliment serves as a potent site of revelation for a host of social, economic, and cultural issues. It is an unavoidable act, an unshakeable marker of our animal selves, which also serves to constitute us as social, transactional beings of appetite, desire, discernment, control, and culture. Aliment is an unavoidable locus of power and danger: it is the means by which the individual writes and rewrites him- or herself, the marker by which societies define themselves. As Jean-Anthelme Brillat Savarin famously wrote in his 1825 gastronomic bible, *The Physiology of Taste*, "[T]ell me what you eat, and I shall tell you who you are" (3).

In her cookbook *How to Eat*, the British food personality Nigella Lawson announces, "I have nothing to declare but my greed" (xv). This is what table and taste reveal: what we are greedy for, what we hunger for, what we cannot live without—and conversely, what we fear, that which is to be swallowed which makes us tremble. The table is a site both of great pleasure and of great fear and loathing: what we eat is, inevitably, not a part of us but a part of the world beyond and outside us, always to some degree uncontrolled, inscrutable, unknown. Food and eating are weighted with continual interdictions concerning what may and may not be considered aliment, what may or may not be eaten when and in what manner, in an endless attempt to impose the rule of law on this perpetually problematic set of substances. The table is, for the nineteenth-century literary gentleman, a key locus of socioeconomic display, a place of demonstration both of one's wealth and of one's inherent taste, fitness, and bloodlines. But at the same time, for the gentleman—always seeking place, clarity, and recuperative power— the idea of taking in the alien, outside world through aliment is fundamentally threatening.

This book is about appetite as a force that reveals the gentleman's most elemental self, even as it lays bare the layers of what Claude Lévi-Strauss would call "civilization"—the social, the political, the cultural. I turn to aliment to reveal and understand a figure who is the embodiment of power and yet hardly embodied, a figure who is much read and little looked at in Victorian literature. Tracing the construction of gentlemanliness through aliment across the nineteenth century, I interrogate class, gender, culture, and the rhetorical construction of identity. Aliment and appetite, I argue, constitute a crucial means of casting light on the shifting, elusive identity of the gentleman. By analyzing his cravings, his fastings, and his feastings, I undertake to open the literary understanding of both the gentleman and the world through which he moves, to newer, fuller, and more potent possibilities. The gentleman is a dangerous alimental force: always threatened with placelessness, he seeks to locate and mark himself through his feasting and fasting; but in doing so, he inevitably threatens to starve, to subsume, to swallow the community around him. His alimental monstrousness, then, is the nightmare of the anxious, shifting middle class.

ON IMAGINING THE ALIMENTARY

Benjamin, of course, is hardly alone in underestimating the hidden depths of aliment. Even in our own food-obsessed times, serious talk about the table as a site of sociocultural investigation is a rare dish, and hardly ever a delicious one. At a conference recently, I had lunch with a group of academics. The conversation turned to food culture—and immediately shifted to eating disorders, the disgusting problem of American gluttony, the appalling nature of high-end cuisine (foie gras! caviar!), and the virtues of veganism. The subtext of the conversation was clear: food is self-indulgent, inappropriate, decadent. Only by disciplining the appetite, by refusing luxury and pleasure in the realm of the alimentary, can we keep ourselves safe from the dangers of that which crosses the boundaries of the body in public, through the mouth, revealing our desires and our failure of control to those with whom we share the table. The solution is to put mind over matter, to equate virtue with denial: to turn away from the pleasures of the palate or at least to separate them from the serious sphere of work. When, at another conference, an organizer asked participants to be prompt for meals, explaining emphatically, "We have a lot to do, and we don't want to waste time eating," there were nods of agreement all round.

These same questions, problems, and issues make their presence known in novels, cookbooks, home health-care manuals, and gastronomic essays across the British nineteenth century. Aliment is a potent site of sociocultural construction and revelation, and food is troubling stuff. Meals are physical, temporal, and psychological spaces in which class and gender behaviors are marked and remarked upon; in which good and bad, acceptable and unacceptable, and constructive and destructive ideas and actions are negotiated through manners and etiquette as well as through the food that is taken in or refused. Meals are sites of formative rituals that, as John F. Kasson writes, "mediate between ambiguous and frequently contending realms of value. They allow participants to negotiate between various aspects of their experience and often to articulate in heightened form elements that are to some degree embattled or suppressed in everyday life" (*Rudeness and Civility*, 183). In this sense, society comes to itself through the transaction of the meal: precisely because of its insistence on form (or, equally tellingly, its insistence on the refusal of form), the rite of alimentary consumption constitutes a ground on which the sociopolitical realm is made and remade. Eating, in other words, makes culture.

And this is particularly true of eating that is done in the presence of others.

But eating is also a hazardous operation, particularly when it is done in the presence of others. If the post-Enlightenment process of coming to consciousness is the work of believing in the self as an enclosed being, an independent "I," then the necessity of eating renders that work impossible. Food penetrates the boundaries of the body, bringing the outside into that putatively contained self and reconstituting the physical being; it refuses to be kept out by the desire for control, for cleanliness, or for completeness.[1] Taken into the body across the boundary of the mouth—the most concrete site of language and speech and in this way arguably the body's most potent locus of self-construction[2]—food cannot be controlled. Indeed, as Deborah Lupton writes,

> Food is a liminal substance; it stands as a bridging substance between nature and culture, the human and the natural, the outside and the inside. . . . As the process of incorporation is inextricably linked to subjectivity it is the source of great anxiety and risk. By incorporating a food into one's body, that food is made to become self. . . . [I]f òne does not know what one is eating, one's subjectivity is called into question. It is not only the life and health of the eater that are challenged by the incorporation of food, but also that individual's place in culture. Thus the incorporation of the wrong type of substance may lead to contamination, transformation from within, a dispossession of the self. (16–17)

If alimentary consumption, as Norbert Elias posits (xii–xiii), is the most visible site of social "civilization" or self-control, it is also the realm of magical thinking, an arena in which the fantasy of self-definition may be endlessly indulged even while this fantasy is most clearly under attack. The idea that one incorporates the essence of what is ingested into oneself—for instance, that the cannibal gains the strength of his or her victim through the ritual of ingestion (Fallon and Rozin, 27)[3]—is highly potent and (in cannibal-free form) widespread. Such imagining is at work in rhetorical endeavors to endow foods with classed and gendered elements: when one swallows food at table, the logic goes, one also ingests and incorporates the sociocultural and political elements that adhere to that food. The eater is thus elevated or debased by his or her encounter with sustenance. In this sense, all food is manna: the desires and disgusts, the social narratives and self-constructions of the eater are present in the contents of the plate.

Similarly, the eating body, under social scrutiny, is constructed by means of cultural assumptions about food and eating: thinness and fatness, to choose an obvious dichotomy, are read in terms of the individual's ability to "control" his or her appetites for certain classes and types of food, and the individual is classed (and, to some degree, gendered) via this presumed relationship to food. The display of appetite or bodily control at table is interpreted as a sign and signal of the moral character, the true self, of the eater, as the marker of civilization, of an animal nature, of decadence; at the same time, aliment's invisible work inside the body marks and configures the physical self, making appetites evident, written on the skin. This sort of ocular judgment in turn works to construct aliment, lending it distinctly moral qualities. As Louis Marin has observed, "[O]ne might say that every culinary sign is Eucharistic in some sense and to some extent; or, to pursue this vein of thought one step further, one might say that all cookery involves a theological, ideological, political, and economic operation by the means of which a nonsignified edible foodstuff is transformed into a sign/body that is eaten" (121). Food is always at once definitive and excessive.

ON FOODWAYS AND FOODMEANS IN NINETEENTH-CENTURY BRITAIN

The British nineteenth century was a period of much alimentary contradiction. It was, famously, an age of conspicuous consumption in England; but it was also a time of famines and near famines,[4] a period during which social and political change were often motivated by the literal hunger of the masses. It was, for the gentle classes, a time when the rituals of the table constituted crucial signs of class,[5] but it was also a time when ladies and gentlemen lined up at the slaughterhouse to "partake of a strengthening glass of blood" (Tannahill, 292) and men of high birth marked their place through indiscriminate, inordinate consumption. Feasting marked one's wealth, but gluttony was condemned;[6] alimentary restraint was at once, in the same social circles, an indicator of want or pathology and a sign of sophistication. And concerns about what one ate, where one ate it, and with whom one ate were, as the novels of the period reveal, substantial: uncountable plot turns and revelations of character depend on the semipublic theater of meals, from the ball supper in *Pride and Prejudice* to Jane's solitary supper on the moors in *Jane Eyre* to the revelatory dinner tête-à-tête shared by Moreau and Prendick in *The Island of Dr. Moreau*. The drinking habits of the schoolboys in *Tom Brown's School Days*; Jos Sedley's outsized, childish appetites and their unfortunate effects in *Vanity Fair*; the forlorn Christmas dinner in *Small House at Allington*; the squire who eats peas on his old-fashioned knife in *Cranford*; the Earl of Mt. Severn's gout-defying suppers in *East Lynne*—all are central to the construction of gentlemanliness in the world of the novel.

Notions of when one ate and what one called one's meals were equally important. The English nineteenth century often imagined itself as a realm of speed and innovation in tension with tradition, and aliment was fundamentally imbricated in this imagining. As the focus of middle-class labor, for instance, shifted to the City, the structure and timing of meals shifted as well.[7] The substantial early dinner waned in popularity, a victim of the viccissitudes of commuting and the demands of office life; ladies' luncheons became a staple of appropriately feminine domesticity, and late dinners and teas became signs of sophistication for the rising rich. Class, gender, labor, wealth—all were marked by the timing of one's dinner, the question of supper, the presence or absence of coffee in the dining room.

The rituals of dinner were not all that became subject to change: the very nature of food was undergoing transformation as it was reconceptualized and reconstituted by industrialism, science and technology, and urbanization. Lévi-Strauss famously writes, in *The Raw and the Cooked,* of what he calls the culinary triangle: food, he posits, is uncivilized when raw; cooking—the magical transformation of food from dead animal to something else, distant from its source and impacted by technology—is the marker of civilization, while rot (food seeking to become dirt or waste) is the sign of decline, decadence, the downward spiral back to the uncivilized. The nineteenth century saw the advent of uncountable new technologies of food and drink. These included pasteurization, which allowed food to travel across time and space (obviating the need to rely on local fare), and canning, in which food arrived at locations utterly unrelated to its source, estranged from its original identity as animal or vegetable, and already more or less cooked. As Lynette Hunter notes, "Where the technology of cookery had for most people remained largely the same for several hundred years, the . . . nineteenth century saw the introduction of gas fires, gas refrigerators and cookers . . . and where marketing, preservation and conservation had been central to the housewife's work for centuries, suddenly there were commercially bottled and canned foods, and shops with unusual foreign foodstuffs, and pre-packaged foods" (57). Unsurprisingly, the reception of such fare was highly charged, demonstrating at once an infatuation with the newfangled and a distrust of the unknown. New transportation technologies meant that city dwellers could choose to eat fare grown in the countryside, instead of risking their health with, for instance, milk and meat from tired, penned, and often tubercular city-raised animals.[8] But these technologies of civilization could also be signs of the failure of transparency and coherence in the food supply, the folly of trusting to others, and the very real dangers of the modern, the new, even of technology itself. Empire and revolution overseas were also imbricated in notions of food and drink at home. English eaters (like Austen's picky Mr. Woodhouse) struggled with the implications of curries and French sauces, debated the merits of the homegrown versus the imported, chewed coca leaves or ate opium, drank port wine or coffee, or rejected the dangerous, self-altering fruits of the foreign—that is, they imbued aliment with all of the issues surrounding nationalism and Englishness. Radicals used aliment to protest colonialism, economic policies, and industrialism itself.

As knowing the source of one's food became more and more difficult, as foreign recipes and foodstuffs made their way in an everyday sense into the diet of the nation, and as food became increasingly subject to the vicissitudes and potential dangers of the free market (competition leading to adulteration to produce cheap foodstuffs, for example), anxieties about what was taken into the body became paramount. Alimentary adulteration (to make production cheaper in the open market and to make it more visually perfect and thus saleable) became rife just as alimentary hygiene became a constant topic of discussion; as food came from farther and farther afield and was presented to the consumer in forms that were more and more highly prepared, ocular proof of food safety became at once crucial and impossible to trust. In the matter of food and drink, consumers literally were unable to believe their eyes. The proliferation of trial publications concerning poisonings played on this fear. Such anxieties appear, for instance, in Collins's *Law and the Lady* in the most frightening, most domestic of alimental moments: the dutiful husband who brings a cup of tea to his suffering wife, ill in bed.

Aliment was also an important site and means of social control in the British nineteenth century. Temperance movements, the increasing popularity of coffee, the medicalization of eating and its links with hygiene movements: all were means of reshaping the body—and the body politic—in response to socioeconomic pressures and requirements. Aliment was increasingly subject to professional scrutiny, and the consuming self was increasingly pathologized, both in medical and in social terms. Foodstuffs were elevated or demonized as the notion of the self in society was endlessly rewritten, in service to competing ideologies and interests. Cookbooks, gastronomic guides, etiquette books, and medical texts proliferated: the rules shifted constantly, and notions of the appropriately feeding body were continually in flux.

Medicine, meant to cure the body of such ills and incursions, created its own set of specifically alimental anxieties. Drugs, food, and drink were conflated and confused: all were aliment in the nineteenth-century imagination. Just as arsenic and tea are mixed in *The Law and the Lady*, so too did medicalized and mind-altering substances become indistinguishable from comestibles that were more prosaic, in the absence of a bright line between them. Opium was, famously, "eaten" (that is, drunk) in laudanum form; beer soup was consumed at breakfast by industrial workers looking for something nourishing to get them through the day; cocaine was thought to be an excellent source of nutrition.[9] Nostrums, instant cures, and medical diets proliferated, complicating not only the trustworthiness of aliment and its legibility but also basic issues of control over the body. The language around drug imbibing shifted across the century, oscillating from healing to hurting, from pleasure to salvation to addiction. Indulgence, healing, nutrition, and inebriation—the substances responsible for those effects were at once healthy and fatal, longed for and interdicted in the cultural and medical imagination. Opium and cocaine were connected to imperial practices, the dangers of the foreign, the fear of degeneration, and the horrors of industrial and medical modernity at the same moment they might be viewed as cure-alls, portals to a better self, even makers of manliness.

The British nineteenth century, then, was an age of sustained and substantive fear and loathing in the arena of the alimentary. A close look at what is taken into the body and what is refused, what is served up at table and what is hoarded and eaten in secret is also, unavoidably, an exploration of politics, of economics, of foreign policy, and of the very concepts of the body, of selfhood, and of the nation during the period.

ON ALIMENT AND THE GENTLEMAN

Over the past three decades, gender scholars who focus on nineteenth-century bodies have written a great deal on women and their appetites: bingers and starvers; women who refuse meat for fear of heating the animal self and those who eat indiscriminately, hungrily, without end; women who drink and women who abstain; and women who fail to eat, by choice or by social compulsion. The appetites of working-class men have also been amply explored, as scholars seek to understand the casting of the working-man as saint or animal, ascetic or unbridled consumer. But the alimental gentleman, the upper-class man who stuffs or starves or obsesses at table, has hardly been glanced at, though his troubled and troubling relationship to food is a central concern of the novels he inhabits. My aim here is to make the gentleman visible through his alimental practices, and, thus, to come to a better understanding of the construction and implications of this paradigm-shaping figure, whose very power has led to his near-elision in the critical literature.

Gentlemanliness was a problematic concept through the nineteenth century, a slippery ranking that exceeded and bypassed all attempts to delineate it. Money played a role; so did birth and profession; so did a certain sense of character or morality or standing. But none of these markers was fixed and conclusive, and no single marker was sufficient in and of itself. As Thackeray's Clive Newcome puts it, "I can't tell you what it is, only one can't help seeing the difference. It isn't rank and that; only somehow there are some men gentlemen and some not" (quoted in Gilmour, 84). In the nineteenth century, "the nature of gentlemanliness was more anxiously debated and more variously defined than at any time before or since" (Gilmour, 2). Middle-class social and economic ambition, the protective behaviors of those with inherited positions, the increasing illegibility of class, the changing role of the gentleman in the community, and the new valences of work—all of these made gentlemanliness an increasingly fraught idea. The gentleman was a creature of his age in the most problematic of ways: a figure whose position was based at once on a myth of stability and on the economic forces that undermined it; rhetorically positioned at the center of the family and of the community but facing a looming threat of marginalization; and situated at the heart of the struggles between past and future, tradition and innovation, city and country, birthright and merit.

Gentlemanliness, then, was in flux and in dispute through the nineteenth century—and the anxiety and potential disorder that this state of affairs engendered is present in nearly every novel of the period, from the most formulaic of marriage-plot tales to the darkest of horror stories. But though he is the real center of power in virtually every nineteenth-century narrative, though the plot revolves around him (his choices and compulsions, for good or ill, regarding marriage; his money or his debts; his work in Parliament or in the civil service or in the army or in jail, or his inability or refusal to work at all; his desires, his rules, his laying down of the law or his failure to do so), the gentleman remains less than fully explored as an embodied creature. Indeed, in many novels he is barely visible, his physical self disappearing behind his manners, his words, and his actions.

But this is not the case when the gentleman sits down to eat: for this crucial literary figure, the table is a site of potent revelation. In nineteenth-century British novels, meals are highly visible rites, spaces where (even in the most proper accountings of the most proper echelons of the gentility) desire and the body are exposed. If one is constituted by what one eats, where one eats, and with whom, then the meal in nineteenth-century fiction is that rarity, at once a locus of recuperative reestablishment of socioeconomic order and a site of possibility, of social mobility, where class, gender, and position can be taken in with port wine and French or Russian service. No wonder *Emma*'s Mr. Elton gives Harriet a detailed description of his dinner at the Coles' when he should, in Emma's estimation, be courting the poor girl: he is, instead, busily courting a socially elevated vision of himself, reveling in his place at the table when he describes "the Stilton cheese, the north Wiltshire, the butter, the celery, the beet-root and all the dessert" (88–89). When he falls to at table or pushes away his plate, when he dines on health food or demands French sauces, when he feeds others on poison or dainties or old-fashioned homemade dishes, when he offers up a figurative glimpse of his glittering teeth or his growling belly, the gentleman is most fully on display, exposing the makings of his body and of his mind.

The table is the place where Dickens's Mr. Merdle works his magic, where Dorrit presides like a king or breaks down like a pauper; where Collins's Miserrimus Dexter comes to himself, cook and gentlemanly eater both, and makes his power and horror evident; where Anne Brontë's aristocratic bingers reinscribe their prerogatives on their bodies; where Austen's Mr. Woodhouse is at once most needy and childish—most superannuated—and most in control of his putative fiefdom. The table is the site of self-fashioning, a place where the gentleman remakes and rewrites himself and those who gather at his board. It is a potent site of display, of wealth, a stage on which money and power can be displayed and their lessons imbibed. The meal is a theatrical production, in which "[t]he guest is a beneficiary, a co-producer and an interpreter of the performance. . . . The organizer is a priest, the eater a communicant" (Aron, 216). Eating presents the gentleman with the imperative of performance and display even as he undertakes the most intimate and bodily of operations, and the table affords a rare opportunity to look into the body and mind of the gentleman of privilege. This is the case, too, when the alimentary consumer moves away from the table: Stoker's problem drinkers and Stevenson's solitary, alienated imbibers interrogate and perform gentlemanliness, class, and gender with every swallow.

ON MAKING A MAN

In *Making a Man*, I address the issue of the alimental gentleman in a series of novels that span the nineteenth century. I look to Mr. Woodhouse in Jane Austen's *Emma*; Arthur Huntingdon in Anne Brontë's *Tenant of Wildfell Hall*; William Dorrit and Arthur Clennam in Charles Dickens's *Little Dorrit*; Miserrimus Dexter in Wilkie Collins's *Law and the Lady*; Dr. Jekyll and Mr. Hyde in Robert Louis Stevenson's *Strange Case*; and Dracula and the band of brothers who fight him off in Bram Stoker's end-of-the-century horror story. Analyzing this pivotal figure as alimental stockpiler and uncontrolled gourmand, as feaster and faster, this book explores the ways in which food, appetite, and eating make, remake, and unmake the gentleman. Anxieties about status and place, I contend, are made strongly manifest when the gentleman sits down to eat in these texts; he is a profoundly unplaced figure, pulled apart and overwritten by technology, class movement, money, and sociocultural change. Unable to fathom himself, to understand himself, the gentleman stuffs or starves himself, feeds on health food or binges on wine or turns to more troubling, autophagic sources of nutrition to find a means to locate himself. In doing so, he inevitably threatens the health of the community that gathers at his table.

Chapter 1, "Annals of Gruel," focuses on the valetudinarian gentleman at the heart of Austen's novel *Emma*, investigating his fraught relations with food—his fixation on gruel, his obsession with food purity, and his anxious oversight of the eating habits of his neighbors—in light of early-nineteenth-century preoccupations with changing food technologies, foreign fare, food adulteration, and radical dietary theories. At the cusp of the century, Mr. Woodhouse's alimentary behavior calls into question the notion of the appropriately bounded old-fashioned gentleman: the effects of his alimentary requirements foreground the problematic ambiguities of the gentleman's role in the community, as he grapples with the implications of productivity and structure in the industrial age. Mr. Woodhouse's appetite for gruel—an appetite that foregrounds bodily disgust and class liminality, that makes manifest his mistaking of the gentleman's body and the body politic—threatens his community with stasis, impossibility, and engulfment.

Chapter 2, "'An infernal fire in my veins,'" takes up the issue of aliment as a locus and force of social control in Anne Brontë's surprisingly explicit novel of drink and its consequences, *The Tenant of Wildfell Hall*. The rhetoric of antidrinking movements and midcentury thought on alimentary discipline are crucial to the understanding of the much-vilified Arthur Huntingdon's problematic gentlemanly body as it drowns itself in drink. *Tenant*, in its anatomy of the decline and fall of a drunken husband, engages precisely with the issue of what constitutes a gentleman, literally and figuratively, in the striver's age. Here the alimentary ideologies of the middle class—and, indeed, the very construction of the middle-class body—come into direct collision with the notion of gentlemanliness as a state apart: the upper-class gentleman of leisure finds himself continually compelled to write and rewrite his class difference on his body through alimental excess, in a process that at once constitutes him and destroys him.

Chapter 3, "'By Heaven I must eat at the cost of some other man!'" looks to Dickens's voracious William Dorrit and the persistent faster and would-be moral gentleman Arthur Clennam of *Little Dorrit* to explore the issue of the self-constituting gentleman and his relationship to the social transaction and transubstantiation of the table. This novel posits an economic gentlemanliness based on acquisition and lucre and inseparable from hunger and desire—a gentlemanliness that simultaneously demands the performance of a complete obviation of want. The capitalist gentleman's appetites engulf and erase; for the gentleman who refuses appetites that swallow or starve others, the danger of self-erasure looms. But in the end, the novel offers a true commensality, a means for the gentleman to become whole through full, transactional engagement with the social realm.

Chapter 4, "An 'insatiable relish for horrors,'" focuses on Collins's ravenous, wheelchair-bound epicure, Miserrimus Dexter, in *The Law and the Lady*. Half man, half machine, and arguably at least half mad, Dexter is a howling dandy and an old-fashioned gentleman for the machine age, an industrial cyborg pinup, a connoisseur of truffles and fine wine whose other, more dreadful appetites are both signs and engines of serious monstrosity. Dexter is a complicated envisioning of the future of the wealthy gentleman: a middle-class nightmare of a corrupt and decadent gentlemanly cohort united with working-class mechanization, perpetuating itself by feeding on the heart of the social body, the True Woman. Dexter's appetites challenge the underpinnings of the social structure, the notion of advancement, and the possibility of social renewal and fecundity.

Chapter 5, "'Those appetites which I had long secretly indulged,'" explores a different sort of gentlemanly duality—that of the successful, prosperous professional gentleman. The chapter begins with an exploration of what constitutes perhaps the strangest appetite in Stevenson's much-read novella, *Strange Case of Dr. Jekyll and Mr. Hyde*: the seeming puritan Mr. Utterson's habit of drinking gin. Positing that colliding notions of gentlemanliness and professionalism create a problematic of gentlemanly place and embodiment in the late nineteenth century, the chapter looks first to gin, then to wine, and finally to Dr. Jekyll's nostrum and its real-life counterpart, cocaine. All of these, I contend, are alimental attempts to literally and figuratively fix the gentleman in place, to obviate the endless shuttling between worker and gentleman—a shuttling predicated, the novella posits, on the social imperative of striving. The true class horror of Stevenson's gothic tale, I argue, is the fear that the middle-class gentleman, as Jekyll says of Hyde, "did not even exist" (52).

Chapter 6, "'His special pabulum,'" explores the gentleman on the cusp of modernity. The vampire in Bram Stoker's *Dracula* is not the only locus of terrible appetites in this novel of overdetermined horror and indeterminate gentlemanly boundaries. Stoker's gentlemen, I argue, are estranged from themselves and the world around them by the press of technological modernity; they seek wholeness, authenticity, and connection. To find it—even as they hunt the vampire, seeking to bring clarity and order back to a corrupted England—they turn to Dracula's own "special pabulum," a substance strongly evocative of Thomas De Quincey's opium eating and medicalized morphinism—aliment formative of, irresistible to, and fatal for the end-of-the-century gentleman. But the wholeness that they crave proves to be imaginary, impossible; the thirst for place and connection leads instead to a bloody, autophagic morass sloshing beneath the skin of chivalric heroism.

The alimental gentleman is a seeker: after wholeness, after clarity, after selfhood, after place. Just as the critical reader has had difficulty distinguishing him from the world he has built in the nineteenth-century novel, so too does the gentleman seem to have trouble finding his own bodily boundaries. As his alimentary habits demonstrate—his monstrous cravings and insistent refusals; his unquenchable thirsts and finicky tastes—he continually troubles the lines between self and other, mistakes the society around him for himself, erases or engulfs. And to solve his insistent alienation from himself and from the social order, he eats, he drinks, he tries over and over again to swallow himself down in order to make himself manifest, to write himself into being.

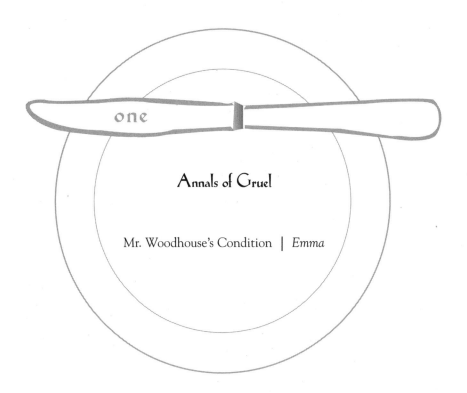

one

Annals of Gruel

Mr. Woodhouse's Condition | *Emma*

Jane Austen's *Emma* (1816) is a fertile starting point for an investigation into the alimentary construction of the nineteenth-century gentleman: this Regency-era novel is utterly preoccupied with the meals that give shape to its characters' shapeless days and the food that they swallow, refuse, discuss, and share. The novel circulates around meals, including the Coles' problematic dinner, the Westons' Christmastime feast, and the infamous Box Hill picnic. The food fetishes and aversions of the characters are detailed as scrupulously as the dinners and suppers and teas they partake in; and the most eccentrically food-obsessed of all is the eponymous heroine's father, Mr. Woodhouse.

A moneyed gentleman of leisure, preoccupied both with his own diet and with the alimentary practices of those around him, Mr. Woodhouse has

> been a valetudinarian all his life, without activity of
> mind or body[;] he was a much older man in ways than
> in years; and though everywhere beloved for the
> friendliness of his heart and his amiable temper, his

> talents could not have recommended him at any time.
> . . . His spirits required support. He was a nervous man,
> easily depressed; fond of everybody that he was used to,
> and hating to part with them; hating change of every
> kind.[1]

This kindly, genteel paterfamilias possesses "habits of gentle self-ishness and of being never able to suppose that other people could feel differently from himself" (8)—and what he generally feels is sickly. He is, in his own words, "quite an invalid, and [goes] nowhere" (209). His "tender habits" require a fire "almost every evening throughout the year" (351); his outdoor exercise is limited to two turns about the shrubbery (26); he is made ill by inclement weather (422) and, in fact, he is convinced that it is "never safe to be outdoors" (48). He is as slow and limited in thought as he is in movement (78)—cannot match his daughter "in conversation, rational or playful" (7)—and he clings to long-held beliefs and ideas with the tenacity of a child, repudiating anything that smacks of the new. An extra person at dinner has the power to make him ill (292), and the news of gypsies in the neighborhood is enough to overthrow him completely (336). And he is adamantly opposed to marriage: as "the origin of change," it is "always disagreeable" to him (7), particularly when his friends and neighbors insist on marrying strangers (177), and he is deeply distressed by the happy love matches between his elder daughter, Isabella, and John Knightley and between "poor Miss Taylor" (10) and Mr. Weston. He is saved from perpetual anxiety on the matter only by his own dimness, because, "[t]hough always objecting to every marriage that was arranged, he never suffered beforehand from the apprehension of any" (193).

The most constant of this apothecary-dependent hypochondriac's fears concern food and diet. Mr. Woodhouse has a strong belief in the variously healing and hurting qualities of food; but unlike the stereotypical gout-ridden old gentlemanly fool, he places no faith in the luxurious, rarefied food of the rich. Mr. Woodhouse is no overly nice aristocrat, no finicky lover of delicacies who finds his constitution limited to such fine fare as ortolans and foie gras. On the contrary, this wealthy gentleman's diet has a singularly plebeian cast. Emma's father's favorite dish—the food that he finds most wholesome, most satisfying, that which is most often his heart's desire—is "a nice basin of gruel" (100), preferably mixed to a careful degree of thinness by the hand of his trusted cook. Mr. Woodhouse offers "undoubting decision of its wholesomeness for every constitution, and pretty severe Phillipics upon the many houses where it was never met with tolerable" (105). He finds it a surefire cure for fatigue and other lingering maladies, recommending a bowl of the stuff to Isabella, for instance, as a palliative after her journey from London to Hartfield. Most everything else he finds too strong or too rich for his constitution, and he is continually shocked by the distressingly cavalier eating habits of other people: he cannot believe that anyone might really prefer, for instance, a slice of cake or a plate of meat to a bowl of gruel; and he "wonder[s] at [gruel] not being taken every evening by every body" (101). A culinary zealot with an ardent faith in the magical properties of his diet, he extols its benefits to everyone he encounters, and he tries valiantly to stop other people from eating food that will, he declares, surely make them ill (24). His reaction to Mrs. Weston's wedding cake (already unwholesome, as the food of that most unhealthy activity, a wedding) is illustrative:

> His own stomach could bear nothing rich, and he could never believe other people to be different from himself. What was unwholesome to him, he regarded as unfit for any body; and he had, therefore, earnestly tried to dissuade them from having any wedding-cake at all, and when that proved vain, as earnestly tried to prevent any body's eating it. He had been at the pains of consulting Mr. Perry, the apothecary, on the subject . . . [who,] upon being applied to . . . could not but acknowledge . . . that wedding-cake might certainly disagree with many—perhaps with most people, unless taken moderately. With such an opinion, in confirmation of his own, Mr. Woodhouse hoped to influence every visitor of the new-married pair; but still the cake was eaten; and there was no rest for his benevolent nerves till it was all gone (19).

Not only is the poor man tortured by the misguided congratulations of his friends on the traumatic event of his governess's marriage— he is persecuted by the widespread public evil of wedding cake! Mr. Woodhouse here seems a perfect parody of an old-fashioned gentleman, made absurd by his contact with the brave new world of the nineteenth century. Unsurprisingly, Mr. Woodhouse is often read as a useless, helpless old fool unworthy of sustained analytical attention[2] or as a feminized creature in thrall to his appetites,[3] a reading that is amply supported by his eating habits. When he does venture beyond his favorite food, Mr. Woodhouse limits himself to small servings of food grown at home and thoroughly cooked by hands he trusts: at his table, he serves apples from his own orchard baked three times over; steaks "nicely fried . . . without the smallest grease" (172); boiled pork from home-raised and home-slaughtered pigs. To drink: half-glasses of wine mixed with water. His food is bland, spiceless, and served sparingly—strongly reminiscent of the food most often prescribed to women to suppress the signs and urges of the body. Like a stereotypical lady,[4] he allows his body to control and define him: the proper care and feeding of his flesh and blood is the most important concern of every day. Like the sickly gentlewoman's body, Mr. Woodhouse's physical self is made the subject of endless self-fetishization and of extensive scopophilic preoccupation, and its vicissitudes control the social life of Highbury to an astonishing degree. Though it is never described or delineated to any significant extent, Mr. Woodhouse's body is endlessly—albeit obliquely—discussed, as residents of the neighborhood ponder, for instance, when and whether Mr. Woodhouse will venture out for a dinner visit (108); worry about the effect of the weather on his health (Mrs. Weston writes to Emma, "I felt for your father very much in the storm . . . but had the comfort of hearing last night, by Mr. Perry, that it had not made him ill" [436]); and plan activities according to his needs and demands (see, for example, the Coles' solicitude in obtaining a screen from London to shield him from drafts [207] and the Westons' anxiety to obtain his approval for the planned ball [251]).

But this "valetudinarian" is not just a mass of stereotypical feminine traits, a cross-dresser who replaces the skirt with the invalid's rug: there is a crucial difference between Mr. Woodhouse and the problematic female eater, who is thought, in the criticism, to deny herself food precisely because of her lack of authority. She wants to gain control over some small portion of her life or seeks to prove herself to be the perfect subject in a difficult and demanding world; in either case, she attempts to do so by rigorously refusing to submit to the ordinary nutritional stipulations of the body. In an alternative narrative, she starves herself out of an existence that makes no space for her.[5]

Mr. Woodhouse clearly is not this figure. He may not be the most independent, physically strong character around, but he is hardly the equivalent of a powerless woman written out of the discursive realm or reductively reinscribed in the narrow domain of the body against her will. Nor, despite his endless recourse to his vaunted illnesses, is he a man who perceives himself as marginal. He is aware of his social importance, takes pride in it, and works to make it clear to others, insisting on the importance, for instance, of his visit to Mr. Elton's bride (435); paying respects to his female guests in his courteous, chivalrous manner (294–95); beneficently sending food to his less fortunate neighbors (172); and obliquely threatening to withhold his blessing from social activities (251). This crucial difference in the realm of power means that Mr. Woodhouse and his alimentary oddities require more, not less, careful reading; his apparent allegiance to the consuming behaviors of wasting women—read in terms of his gender, his money, and his social position—becomes more, not less, complex.

Further, readings that pay scant attention to Mr. Woodhouse do a disservice to Austen's finely wrought novel: Mr. Woodhouse is, after all, the character who stands at the center of this world, the figure around whom the key events in the text pivot, including the marriage of Emma and Knightley. In this role, Mr. Woodhouse, despite his parodic function, may well be the most troubled and troubling figure in the text. It is remarkable, for instance, that the novel effectively opens with an assertion of Mr. Woodhouse's antipathy toward change (7), a statement that seems to aim directly at shutting down the discursive action of the novel before it even begins. His virulent opposition to newness persists throughout the text, as Mr. Woodhouse battles (albeit passive-aggressively) to frustrate development and action of any kind. And in the end, this seemingly ineffective, pampered old man nearly suffocates the life out of Austen's heroine, threatening her with a barren unhappily-ever-after existence as celibate parent to her own father. Mr. Woodhouse, then, must be read carefully; and such a reading requires a sustained analysis of the relationship to food and eating that occupies the center of his life. If ever Brillat-Savarin's edict were true, it is in the case of Mr. Woodhouse: aliment is the key to understanding this character and his role in the social realm of the novel.

Even so, reading from the vantage point of the twenty-first century, one might easily miss the significance of Mr. Woodhouse's alimentary conduct, viewing it as one might a contemporary manifestation of such behavior: as food phobia, as a manifestation of a sort of male anorexia born of overweening control issues, or as a comic display of health-food mania. But read in the context of the food issues of his time, this "valetudinarian" looks very different indeed: Mr. Woodhouse, after all, is a product and a part of a society in transition, and the eating habits of this English country gentleman are both material to and reflective of that society.

On the most practical level, Mr. Woodhouse's anxious monologues about food and health, his obsessive focus on the alimentary, and his insistence on eating only homegrown, homemade fare (25, 173) point toward a useful prudence at the turn of the nineteenth century, given the state of the English food supply—and his intense dislike of newness and change seems less outrageous when read in light of the alimental practices of the time. Industrial commercialism, scientific developments, and the economic exigencies of a radically changing national and international economic situation had engendered wide-ranging innovations in the preparation, distribution, and consumption of food, as well as a new attention to the effects of food on the body. But while there were many advantages to the new technologies, there were also some distinctly unfortunate consequences. The nineteenth century, for example, was the age of the invention of take-out food. By the time of *Emma*'s composition, the practice of canning foodstuffs in tinned iron containers had begun in England, and food was shipped to the mother country from all over the colonial world: inexpensive beef and condensed milk came from Australia, fancy preserved fruits and vegetables from India.[6] Canned food was marketed as purer and healthier than ordinary, unprocessed comestibles, and it garnered a large and enthusiastic audience, both among poor folk (who subsisted on cheap imported canned meat) and among the rich (who sought out hard-to-find foreign delicacies to enhance the social value of their tables).[7] But because such comestibles were prepared out of sight of the consumer—and because the new technology had some dangerous effects in the years before the development of pasteurization[8]—calls for ocular proof of the food's quality increased.

This was also the case with prepared foods on the local level. As consumers in urban environments lost access to the land and, often, to cooking facilities, they were increasingly at the mercy of shopkeepers, bakers, and cooks for the staples of their daily diet. Even putatively fresh fruits and vegetables were sold many miles from their place of origin: the growers were unknown and the hands through which the food had passed were mysterious, and so public confidence in food was substantially undermined. Urbanization, increasing industrial processing of foodstuffs, and better shipping methods led bakers to buy preground grain and publicans to serve ready-made beer, instead of preparing their wares themselves and assuming responsibility for quality control. Community oversight and control of food, then, was progressively eroded, so that people increasingly relied on the appearance of food to gauge its worth— and they sought out visual perfection to assuage their worries. But the exigencies of mass food production made this a dangerous practice. Suppliers began to doctor their fare so that it appeared to be top-grade; merchants, too, began to use increasingly sophisticated methods of food adulteration, which lent an artificial (and often dangerous) sheen to their wares, so that customers were sickened by what appeared to be perfect food. Demands for visual taintlessness, for example, helped to fuel the widespread use of alum in bread baking: the chemical helped to lighten dark bread, which was made with less highly refined (and less expensive) flours than white bread and was thought to be less pure than its pale cousin.[9]

The shortcuts and questionable practices enabled by innovation were abetted by crucial changes in the idea of government and its role vis-à-vis the marketplace. As Adam Smith's policies of supply and demand became gospel in England's houses of government, the idea of controlling the price or quality of food production came to be seen as unfair and unpalatable. For instance, the Assizes of Bread and Ale, a policy that set standard prices for these commodities, was discontinued in 1815 by a House of Commons committee. Freed from the constraints of regulation, bakers immediately began competitive price-gouging, and soon those who made bread the old-fashioned way found themselves unable to turn a profit. As a result, the use of alum as a lightener became widespread, and flours were adulterated with all manner of fillers, some indigestible and others outright poisonous. The government chose not to interfere, limiting its involvement with adulteration to those substances that were subject to import tax. The market was otherwise left to regulate itself.[10] While this sort of laissez-faire governing was certainly lucrative for the substantial segments of the gentle population that drew profits, directly or indirectly, from industrial concerns, it also bespoke a significant abdication of control in Parliament and in the marketplace, as England gave itself over to the reign of the entrepreneurial producer.

When Mr. Woodhouse contends that food produced outside the confines of his little world is dangerous, then—when he sings the praises of his homemade apple tarts and pork—he is reacting to a real problem. Food and drink suppliers, faced with the new exigencies of the marketplace and the demands of an anxious public alienated from original sources of foodstuffs, as well as by the substantial burden of duty taxes on highly popular imported goods, turned in large numbers to the dangerous shortcuts enabled by science and technology. These practices—most stunningly revealed in the pharmacist Frederick Accum's 1820 book, A *Treatise on Adulterations of Food, and Culinary Poisons*—had been an open secret at least since the turn of the century. Accum was the first to formally document public suspicions "that 'crusted old port' was new port crusted with supertartarate of potash; that pickles owed their appetizing green colour to copper; that many table wines gained their 'nutty' flavour from bitter almonds, which contained prussic acid; that the rainbow hues of London's boiled sweets were produced by the highly poisonous salts of copper and lead[;] . . . and that the rich orange rind of Gloucester cheese came from ordinary red lead" (Tannahill, 292). John Burnett notes that in 1819 alone, nearly a hundred people were convicted under the excise laws of "using *cocculus indicus* (a dangerous poison containing picrotoxin), multum, capsicum, copperas, quassia, mixed drugs, harts-horn shavings, orange powder, caraway seeds, ginger and caspicum [*sic*]: they were all employed as cheap substitutes for malt and hops, allowing beer to be diluted by giving it a false appearance of 'strength' and flavour" (74). Dutch pink and poisonous verdigris gave color to used tea leaves for resale; some two-thirds of the tea sold in England was apparently "manufactured from . . . the leaves of ash, sloe and elder . . . curled and coloured on copper plates"; and pepper was beefed up with sweepings from the warehouse floor (Burnett, 74–76).

The practice of tainting food and drink for profit was so widespread that formal guides were published for brewers and publicans who wanted to adulterate their beer, and a class of adulteration professionals came into being to meet the demand: pharmacists known as "brewers' druggists" or "bread doctors" dispensed their information and adulterants from behind the pharmacy counter (Burnett, 79–80). The bread doctors manifested a total disregard for the good of society, abusing new technologies in a single-minded pursuit of profits. In the collective imagination of an upper class that, like Mr. Woodhouse, preferred to view itself as the benevolent ruler and protector of the people and of the nation, the professional adulterer was the opportunistic capitalist, the economic adventurer prepared to subvert the social fabric in pursuit of filthy lucre.[11]

The adulterating opportunist was joined, in the popular imagination, by the foreign interloper who found his way into the homes of England through the kitchen door. Stephen Mennell and others have explored English ambivalence toward the accomplished French chefs (trained in fine French private homes and made famous in the new public restaurants of Paris) who had begun to make their influence felt in England in the early nineteenth century. With the advent of the cult of French food, the potential harm inherent in eating abroad came home, in every sense, as the foreign made its incursions into the very kitchens and dining rooms of the country. Such alimentary anxieties concerning the inscrutability and unconquerable difference of foreign fare—and the subsequent sense of invasion and loss of control over the body that its consumption implies—echoed political and social fears at a time when matters across the Channel were thought to be far from settled and the effects of the war were being felt in unemployment, unrest, and famine at home as well.[12] There were many who saw near-treason in the abandonment of traditional English culinary values and the adoption of seemingly incomprehensible French food practices, which often involved the production of dishes made inscrutable by blankets of sauce and were inevitably linked to the sophisticated horrors of the French Revolution.[13]

To a gentleman like Mr. Woodhouse—protective of his place in the social sphere and possessing a clear antipathy toward change—these new alimental poisons would appear uncontainable, impossible to catch as they wove through the digestive tracts of hapless diners and through the vital organs of the body politic itself. There was no way to be sure, when dining abroad or eating food bought in the shops and markets, whether one was being fed or poisoned. No wonder Mr. Woodhouse is "not fond of dinner-visiting" (209); no wonder he feels that his friends and family "would all be safer at home" (259). Given the circumstances, it is not surprising that a gentleman might feel threatened both on a physical and on a metaphysical level by the illegibility of food and the potential dangers it might bear, particularly given the phenomenon's connections to industrial markets and its attendant promises of class pliability. Despite the imposition of laws to shore up the position of landowners and other influential people, there was a feeling in the air that the position of the gentry was threatened—by France, by the poor, by industrialism and progress in general.[14]

In this alimental-political context, Mr. Woodhouse's love of simple food cooked thoroughly makes a certain amount of sense. Wedding cakes and other such dainties are treacherous, their antecedents veiled by layers of cookery and dressing, their bright colors and sweet flavors serving as potential markers of adulteration. Such fancy fare, taking its cues from the modern, the complex, and the trendy, speaks of the threatening unfamiliarity that lurks beyond the limits of the town—indeed, beyond the limits of the very grounds of Hartfield. Homegrown apples and home-raised pork are safe, straightforward, and unadulterated; gruel is even more unobjectionable. Such food has clear origins, hides nothing, and carries no frightening implications of danger or incursion. As Eliza Acton observed, some years later, "That which is home made can at least be relied on" (Ray, 233).

But even Mr. Woodhouse's protectionist insistence on the superior quality of his Hartfield hams and vegetables—on food grown, harvested, and cooked at home, by thoroughly known English hands—is not enough to protect him from the dangerous currents of modernity and change. In fact, his rhetoric of purity and simplicity is in itself, ironically, a harbinger of danger, enmeshing him in another, equally complicated alimentary discourse, one that takes up the issue of how food constitutes the self. And this discourse brings politics and morality into the dining room in ways that cannot fail to trouble this highly conservative gentleman.

Mr. Woodhouse, of course, is highly concerned about the effects of food on one's health, as his anxious hosting of dinner parties indicates. When the neighborhood ladies join him for an evening of cards and supper, for example,

> [s]uch another small basin of thin gruel as his own, was all that he could, with thorough self-approbation, recommend, though he might constrain himself . . . to say:
> "Mrs. Bates, let me propose your venturing on one of these eggs. An egg boiled very soft is not unwholesome. Serle understands boiling an egg better than any body. I would not recommend an egg boiled by any body else—but you need not be afraid—they are very small, you see—one of our small eggs will not hurt you. Miss Bates, let Emma help you to a *little* bit of tart—a *very* little bit. Ours are all apple tarts. You need not be afraid of unwholesome preserves here. I do not advise the custard. Mrs. Goddard, what say you to *half* a glass of wine? A *small* half glass—put into a tumbler of water? I do not think it could disagree with you." (24–25)

Such obsessive attention to aliment was not unknown in Mr. Woodhouse's day: the industrial age engendered a virtual mania about eating and health, and the drive toward control over the body through food escalated around the turn of the nineteenth century. The period saw the development of the idea of food as nutrition and the new notion of the healthy effects of alimentary restraint: "a new idea of hygiene took shape. Its principle was *reduction* (and no longer repletion); abstinence replaced universal bleeding; the ideal diet consisted of milk, fruits, fresh water" (Barthes, 68).

This notion of purity and hygiene is linked, in early nineteenth-century writings on food, to particularly anti-industrial views—ideas that seem to dovetail with Mr. Woodhouse's concerns. John Frank Newton, William Lambe, Percy Bysshe Shelley, and George Nicholson all took issue with the notion of introducing new technologies to the production of food (mass production; canning; large-scale importing and exporting; commercial meal preparation) enabled by developments in science and promoted by the exigencies of factory-based living.[15] They advocated a largely vegetarian, unrefined diet, insisting that consumption of meat was irreconcilable with bodily health. The introduction to Nicholson's book, for example, is concerned with the distinction between "simple" and "complex" foods (simple being natural and, thus, much better). Moreover, this discussion is carefully calibrated in terms of social and economic structures. The author declares that the ability to distinguish between these two alimentary categories is dependent on the class status of the potential consumer: "[T]he desire for simplicity is not shared by the working class: 'the vulgar' have 'prejudices' for bread and 'farinacea' rather than whole-grain uses of the same plants" (Morton, *Shelley*, 17).

Nicholson could easily be writing here about Mr. Woodhouse's beloved gruel: in a gesture evocative of Pierre Bourdieu, he seems to suggest that only the rich and the educated know enough to desire food that the ignorant lower classes associate blindly with famine and privation. Nicholson's move is an astonishing one, promoting the social importance of the diner through his or her ingestion of food that society at large has, until this moment, considered socially debased, so that the sustenance the poor have no choice but to depend on (meatless meals, for example) becomes a noble statement of bodily purity to which only the most cultured can aspire. So Mr. Woodhouse, with his insistence on the rare quality and purity of the gruel prepared by his own cook, his exaltation of that dish to the level of the finest fare—in fact, the best food for the constitution, in every sense, of a proper gentleman—attempts to transform this lowly dish into a sought-after rarity, and in the process reasserts his exalted class status. By eating gruel, in other words, he marks himself as a gentleman of the most educated, most knowledgeable, and most privileged type, a man who is economically and socially enabled by his position to rise above the exigencies of the industrial age, to preserve himself, sacrosanct, through the medium of carefully chosen food that he is sophisticated enough to appreciate. Gruel allows Mr. Woodhouse to position gentlemanliness as nonnegotiable, above and beyond the realm of the everyday.

But while Mr. Woodhouse's faith in the relationship between food and health—between what is taken into the body and the formation of the body itself—fits into this new science of nutrition nicely, it also associates him with the decidedly unconservative socioeconomic, artistic, and moral underpinnings explicitly linked to its ethos. Though the notion of the pure diet garnered widespread attention, it was also closely associated with radicalism. Nicholson and his compatriots took their cues from Jean-Jacques Rousseau's *Emile*, advocating a world of rule-free living and classless naturalness which was anathema to a man like Mr. Woodhouse, who declares that "it is never safe to sit out of doors" (48) and who requires a fire to tame the weather even in high summer. The desire for alimentary purity may be a wish "to retreat from the complexities of modern life to an idealized pastoral dream" (Lupton, 89) both for Mr. Woodhouse and for the food radicals; but the latter espoused a particularly overdetermined reverie. Their dietary regimens constituted a means of asserting one's philosophical opposition to industrialism by rejecting the fruits of mechanized labor; of declaring one's opposition to the slave trade by refusing to consume the taxed products of the peculiar institution;[16] of repudiating the perceived excesses of the affluent;[17] and of associating oneself with the oppressed masses. Whereas for Mr. Woodhouse, purity of eating is associated with old-fashioned safety, in the popular discourse of the day, the notion of alimentary purity was largely associated with bohemian rebels who made use of a nostalgic past in their attempts to leverage a brave new world.

Unwilling to eat beyond the bounds of his estate and risk contamination, even poisoning, from the effects of entrepreneurism and industrialism, Mr. Woodhouse is, then, equally threatened by the pure and the simple, even when such fare is rhetorically elevated. This danger permeates his world: the fatal grains of capitalism, industrialism, and radicalism infuse and infect the gentleman's physical and psychological fare, just as, in the prosaic world of the day-to-day, ordinary food may without warning become toxic, literally adulterated by slow poisons, foreign ingredients, and the vicissitudes of nature. Food, it seems, is never entirely safe, no matter how it is cleaned up and protected from the ravages of the outside world: it is always dangerous, always threatening to the notion of bodily integrity. In Mary Douglas's terms, it is continually threatening to become "dirt." Douglas famously argues in *Purity and Danger* that the autonomous self is defined and differentiated from the threatening, unbounded morass of the outside world through the creation of boundaries dividing the "clean" from the "dirty," the acceptable from the unacceptable. "[D]irt," she declares, is "matter out of place. . . . It implies . . . a set of ordered relations and a contravention of that order. . . . Dirt is the by-product of a systematic ordering and classification of matter, in so far as ordering involves rejecting inappropriate elements. . . . [P]ollution behaviour is the reaction which condemns any object or idea likely to confuse or contradict cherished classifications" (36). Food, of course, is the most dangerous kind of dirt, the most pervasive pollution, inevitably troubling the boundaries of the would-be inviolable body as it crosses the threshold of the lips, penetrating the liminal space of the mouth, bringing the outside in. It can never be made safe or pure, never be cleansed sufficiently, because it is always threatening to turn into waste (Lupton, 6) or, in Claude Lévi-Strauss's formulation, into rot (479).

Mr. Woodhouse's prescriptions and proscriptions are anxious evidence of the hazards of ingestion, because food possesses no consistent meaning. Food is unreadable and, finally, unknowable. What is safe—and valued—at one moment may be dangerous the next; the newfangled, the foreign, the technologically challenging are situated in aliment and in turn work to resituate and to destabilize the consuming body, passing the barrier of the enclosed self through the liminal space of the lips and rendering that barrier fictional, as class, industrialism, and gender slip through the lines and immerse themselves in a host striving to be complete in and of himself. Given such instability, it is no surprise that Mr. Wood-house seeks to fix the meaning of food he sees as safe, evocative of a nostalgically idealized lost time. Apprehensive about a future that threatens the situated knowledge he wishes to believe in, Mr. Woodhouse puts his faith in the homegrown, the home-cooked, the simple: in food that he imagines, utopically, to be thoroughly knowable and therefore controllable. No wonder, then, that he turns to gruel.

It seems a perfect choice. Handmade, homemade, and difficult to adulterate, gruel is also unquestionably safe from the depredations of radicalism. The food revolutionaries advocated the consumption of raw foods as a means of connecting oneself more thoroughly with an idealized notion of nature and, in this way, of opposing the perceived poisons of science and modernity; the highly cultured was anathema to them. Gruel, despite its humble associations and its simple nature, is very distant indeed from its natural state, as a recipe for the stuff from the School Board for London's *Cookery Book and General Axioms for Plain Cookery* demonstrates: "*Method.—* Have the boiling water ready in a small saucepan, add the salt and sprinkle in the oatmeal. Stir until it boils again, and *simmer very gently* about *one hour*, stirring occasionally; then strain and serve with sugar or more salt, according to taste, and a little butter if al-lowed. It is almost a jelly when cooked in this way, and most nour-ishing" (37). Thoroughly subdued by the technologies of cookery, gruel hides no nasty gastronomic surprises; straightforward and thoroughly cooked, it seems a food that remains completely under control and knowable. The consumption of gruel, redolent, as Lévi-Strauss would have it, of culture,[18] marks a crucial difference be-tween Mr. Woodhouse and the radicals. In Mr. Woodhouse's view, food must be tamed and homogenized through the process of cook-ing to make it fit for the gentlemanly table: it must be thoroughly estranged from its natural roots. He rejects, for instance, "a delicate fricassee of sweetbread and some asparagus" intended for a dinner that he is to share with Mrs. Bates, "not thinking the asparagus quite boiled enough" (329), much to the lady's disappointment. He is equally clear on his feelings concerning the raw and the cooked in the matter of apples: as Miss Bates explains to Emma, baked apples "are extremely wholesome. . . . I have so often heard Mr. Woodhouse recommend a baked apple. I believe it is the only way that Mr. Woodhouse thinks the fruit thoroughly wholesome" (237). (She adds, "[O]nly we do not have them baked more than twice, and Mr. Woodhouse made us promise to have them done three times—but Miss Woodhouse would be so good as not to mention it" [238]). In this way, Mr. Woodhouse aligns himself with mainstream culinary experts like Eliza Acton, who held that "[v]egetables when not sufficiently cooked are known to be so exceedingly unwholesome and indigestible, that the custom of serving them *crisp,* which means, in reality, only half-boiled, should be altogether disregarded when health is considered of more importance than fashion" (Ray, 140). To Mr. Woodhouse, nothing is healthier than "a nice basin of gruel."

But while technology is important in separating the privileged from the uncivilized, it should never, in Mr. Woodhouse's world, be new. Just as Mr. Woodhouse must be brought to accept change as inevitable and, in fact, as always already carried out (and therefore no longer change at all), so too does he like his food sanctioned and tamed by the contemporary world and its scientific assumptions but untouched by anything that smacks of innovation. His technologies must appear to be those of his forebears—nothing canned, needless to say, appears at his table—though they must betray little relation to the unimproved vulgarity of the natural world. Mr. Woodhouse likes his food the same way that he likes his environment: completely prepared, highly predictable, and thoroughly knowable. Gruel is this ideal incarnate.

Further, a diet of gruel promises maximum control over the physical self, minimizing the body's discordances for its owner and rendering it unobjectionable, an important concern to the proper gentleman. This is no small matter: nineteenth-century diners operated under an almost pathological fear of public alimentary upset and its obvious manifestations.[19] Cookbooks of the time are preoccupied with avoiding such potentially offense-producing ingredients as onions, garlic, and spices. Their advocacy of exhaustively boiled, plain food is in service to the ideal of the silent, odorless, thoroughly managed body. Such concerns suggest that the body might betray the inner life it hides, despite the carefully constructed and coded image of the public self, if it is not properly attended to. This is particularly problematic for the gentleman, who must be defined not by his physical attributes but by the qualities of his intellect, of his heart, and, more prosaically, of his family and of his pocketbook. It is, in a word, crass to reduce a modern nineteenth-century gentleman to his bodily components: the gentleman is ideally thought to float above corporeal concerns altogether. [20] Those whose bodies are their primary attributes are members of the lower orders for whom it is their stock-in-trade, those who are valued primarily for their labor. [21]

Mr. Woodhouse, then, uses gruel in his attempt to create a bounded, static, uncompromised, and uncompromising self: a body protected from the alimentary incursions and depredations of the industrial and scientific world, yet distanced from the uncontrollable, potentially radical implications of overly natural fare; a body that consumes only the known, the safe, the controllable, the civilized, that is never haunted by the unintended effects of foreign, undercooked, or insufficiently tamed fare. And, not content with keeping himself secure, he seeks to impose this unmoving state on all those around him.

Mr. Woodhouse enjoys playing the beneficent gentleman: finding good places for his servants, paying honors to ladies and to brides. He is concerned about his horses and his servants and is generous to a fault; his munificence extends even to the alimental, as he hosts his neighbors at table and sends food to those in need. But Mr. Woodhouse is also very much attached to holding court, to sitting in state, to being attended upon and asked after. Imagining himself to be the head of the community, he treats the neighborhood less as a collection of independent beings than as a populace of subjects reliant upon and grateful to him in varying degrees. He "was fond of society in his own way. He liked very much to have his friends come and see him; and from various united causes, from his long residence at Hartfield, and his good nature, from his fortune, his house, and his daughter, he could command the visits of his own little circle, in a great measure as he liked. . . . Not unfrequently . . . he had some of the chosen and the best to dine with him" (20). He seems to fancy himself to be very much like the feudal lords of old.

Once again, Mr. Woodhouse is very much of his time here. The nostalgic chivalric myth of origins—that is, the narrative of feudal manse and beneficent lord that offers to repair the wounds of industrialism and assuage the threats of class revolt—occupies a not-insignificant place in the nineteenth-century imagination. In this story, the gentleman of the manor, sheltered from the unpredictable life of the cities, is sustained by the produce of his lands and protected by the people whom he nurtures.[22] Mr. Woodhouse's community helps him to maintain his version of this fiction, looking to him for permission and patronage and indulging his whims and needs. The longed-for ball goes ahead only on his sufferance; the Coles send to London for a special screen to protect him from drafts before they are so bold as to invite him to dinner; and when Harriet is set upon by the gypsies, his anxiety is assuaged by the fact "that many inquiries about himself and Miss Woodhouse (for his neighbours knew that he loved to be inquired after), as well as Miss Smith, were coming in during the rest of the day" (336).

But this dream is belied by the real state of Highbury, as a look at the dining habits of its inhabitants reveals. Meals in *Emma* are almost always fraught: they are spaces of confusion and discord, of erotics and power struggles. Nearly every pivotal scene in the novel occurs across a sustenance-laden expanse. Food is clearly a highly charged commodity, the meal a political spectacle in which what is ingested through the mouth and what is vomited up verbally are equally significant. The Coles' dinner is instructive on this front. The Coles are a "very good sort of people—friendly, liberal, and unpretending; but, on the other hand . . . of low origin, in trade, and only moderately genteel" (207). Their wealth and popularity allow them to fill their dining room with the neighborhood's most exalted residents: even Emma, after a period of struggle, agrees to attend a grand dinner at their board. But the results of this social experiment are mixed at best. "The party was rather large," the narrative retails, so that "at dinner, they were too numerous for any subject of conversation to be general" (214). The subsequent social fracturing allows Emma to indulge in a dangerous flirtation with Frank Churchill and speculation about Jane Fairfax without any check from the social surveillance of others. The meal is interrupted by "the awkwardness of a rather long interval between the courses" (218), signifying a lack of proper decorum: the Coles may be able to afford the finest fare, the text implies, but they expose their status as outsiders. The meal stuffs its participants with secrets, surveillance, and plots, and their social digestion is affected for a long time after.

The social-climbing Coles are not alone in their struggles with the rituals of the table. Even meals consumed in the sanctum of Hartfield are not free from strife. At the dinner held in Mrs. Elton's honor there, for instance, Jane deals with a double assault from that redoubtable personage, who insists on taking charge both of Jane's mail and of her putative search for employment, despite Jane's heartfelt protests on both counts. Emma and Mr. Knightley disagree about Frank Churchill; the party splits in two in the drawing room, driven apart by Mrs. Elton's bad behavior toward Emma; and Mr. Weston arrives with the news of Frank's imminent return, much to Mr. Woodhouse's consternation. At the impromptu tea to which Emma invites her neighbors on a chance meeting because "she knew it was exactly the sort of visiting that would be welcome to her father" (344), Frank, still seated at the dining table, initiates the game of letter blocks that ends with Jane offended and Mr. Knightley indignant and concerned. In fact, meals are such highly combustible operations that when Emma asserts to a distraught Frank Churchill, on his arrival at Mr. Knightley's strawberry-picking party, that sitting down to supper will restore him to good temper, her naïveté is in full view. Small wonder that Mr. Woodhouse believes that "[t]he sooner every party breaks up, the better" (210); small wonder that he is of the opinion that everyone is "safer at home" (259).

It is against a backdrop of troubling meals salted with class confusion, then, that Mr. Woodhouse plays out his game of lord of the manor, seeking to stabilize and control the community through his alimental care and thus to keep it safe from the poisons and foreign fare of the threatening outside world. In using a neofeudal construct to do so, he opposes himself directly to the ways and means of the entrepreneurial/industrial economy. Gail Houston claims that the capitalist is driven by an endless desiring, a bottomless need to gorge on sustenance—as though one's body were unbounded and impossible to fill—and she suggests that the logic of capitalism demands that successful adherents to the system require that others go hungry, literally and figuratively, that some demands not be supplied, in order for the ruthless few to feed themselves. Mr. Woodhouse embodies the antithesis of this formulation. He works endlessly to deny his implication in the capitalist economy, and he makes of his alimentary habits and his care and feeding of lesser members of the community a sort of object lesson of upscale anticapitalism, positioning himself as the source of health and aliment for all. In Mr. Woodhouse's feudal dream, the sharing of food is at once confirmation of the existence of the gentleman's loyal community and an establishment of his role as powerful benefactor, as nurturer of his small world—particularly when such sharing takes place, as he prefers, at his own table, a ritual fancifully reminiscent of medieval feasts.[23]

But the enterprise of feeding others is fraught, as a supper at Hartfield with the Bateses and Mrs. Gilmour illustrates: "Upon such occasions," the narrator explains, "poor Mr. Woodhouse's feelings were in sad warfare. He loved to have the cloth laid, because it had been the fashion of his youth; but his conviction of suppers being very unwholesome made him rather sorry to see any thing put on it; and while his hospitality would have welcomed his visitors to every thing, his care for their health made him grieve that they would eat" (24). Again, when Emma leaves him with Mrs. Bates and Mrs. Goddard on the evening of the Coles' dinner, "her last pleasing duty . . . was . . . to make the two ladies all the amends in her power, by helping them to large slices of cake and full glasses of wine, for whatever unwilling self-denial [her father's] care of their constitution might have obliged them to practice during the meal.—She had provided a plentiful dinner for them; she wished she could know that they had been allowed to eat it" (213).

Like the old feudal lords, Mr. Woodhouse attempts to use the banquet to demonstrate his power, to consolidate his community and align it with himself, to demonstrate that all are (for) one and one is (for) all; but there is a signal failure in the endeavor. Mr. Woodhouse tries to control the body of the community—the body politic, as it were—in precisely the same way that he seeks to control his own body: not by feeding and nurturing it but rather by reining it in, impeding its growth, and preventing its unexpected behaviors.[24] The old style that Mr. Woodhouse craves as the sign of his stability and power comes into direct conflict with his anxieties about aliment in the industrial age, as he seeks to lay the cloth "in the style of his youth" but to dress it only in the emperor's new clothes. His is a land of want, a perpetual zone of seven thin cows and no fat ones; the company is invited to dine at the gentleman's table of abundance and is served up heaping plates of scarcity.

But this project of control is doomed to fail precisely because it depends at once on the assertion of classed difference and on the erasure of distinctions. Mr. Woodhouse's dream of an idealized feudal world is made impossible by his difficulties with boundaries and self-definitions, encapsulated in the alimentary protocols of the gentleman and those he imposes on the community. Mr. Woodhouse's boundary issues are evident everywhere. This apparent grand old man, with his "habits of gentle selfishness and of being never able to suppose that other people could feel differently from himself" (8), has the greatest difficulty in sorting out the differences and distinctions between himself and those around him. About the wedding cake, the novel explains that "[h]is own stomach could bear nothing rich, and he could never believe other people to be different from himself. What was unwholesome to him, he regarded as unfit for any body" (19). When Emma declares her intention to attend the Coles' dinner, he responds, "I am not fond of dinner-visiting. . . . No more is Emma. Late hours do not agree with us" (209), and he urges his stunningly healthy daughter to return early, telling her, "You will not like staying late. You will get very tired when tea is over. . . . [Y]ou will soon be tired. There will be a great many people talking at once. You will not like the noise" (210). In a discussion of the planned ball, Mr. Woodhouse insists that "it would be the extreme of imprudence." He goes on, "I could not bear it for Emma! Emma is not strong. She would catch a dreadful cold. So would poor little Harriet. So would you all" (249). His lamentations about "poor Isabella" (140) and "poor Miss Taylor" (9) clearly attribute his own feelings about change and abandonment to these two very happy women (as Mr. Knightley puts it, "Poor Mr. and Miss Woodhouse, if you please. I cannot possibly say 'poor Miss Taylor'" [9]). When a discussion with Isabella about the healthfulness of a trip to the seaside is angrily interrupted by John Knightley, who finds Mr. Perry's views, as recited by his father-in-law, presumptuous, the older man is "rather agitated by . . . harsh reflections on his friend Perry, to whom he had, in fact, though unconsciously, been attributing many of his own feelings and expressions" (107). Mr. Woodhouse's extraordinary empathy extends even to servants and animals: he is anxious about the feelings of James and the horses when any visit is under discussion, and while waiting for Isabella's arrival, "[h]e thought much of the evils of the journey for her, and not a little of the fatigues of his own horses and coachman" (91).

Joel Weinsheimer writes that Mr. Woodhouse's "habit of projecting himself on others . . . is the foundation of an extensive sympathy, and his errors are not those of moribund inertia but rather of a hyperactive charity. Judged by the kindness of his intentions, Mr. Woodhouse is flawless; but, by his exclusive concern with the body, his intentions are frequently misdirected" (83). But Mr. Woodhouse's tendency to displace his ideas, reactions, and emotions onto other people is more than an error of misdirection. This failure to respect the boundaries of subjectivity indicates a significant refusal of the potential individuality engendered by a capitalist economy, through which formerly nameless bodies insist on taking their place in the social fabric; Mr. Woodhouse's perseverance in performing this sort of communal self presents him not simply as a figure clinging to old-fashioned borders in an age of change but as a figure who, attempting to (re-)create such hierarchies, finds instead that he has become liminal, unbounded, unclear.

For Mr. Woodhouse, the idealized dream of a present-past is not simply a notion of a peacefully interconnected community headed by a right-ruling gentleman. Emma's father imagines himself to be not simply the man of first importance in the neighborhood but rather the embodiment, the incorporation of the town. His body is the body politic of the small nation-state of Highbury. In his view, Mr. Woodhouse's person is not simply the sacred sign of his rule but is also, in a strange sort of synecdoche, the thing to be ruled over and ministered to. His body does not merely represent the manifold bodies of the community; instead, it both incorporates and erases the corporeal status of all those around him. Mr. Woodhouse's bodily practices—indeed, his body itself—incarnate this impossible marker, attempting to have always already swallowed, digested, and become the town in all of its classes and divisions, its impurities and confusions. At the same time, Woodhouse seeks to nurture and to purify his own ascetic body, to keep it sovereign and singular as the very sign of the power that he so craves—the same vision of power that leads him to mistake others for himself.

Gruel itself—the tool that he employs to render his self and his community safe, the food that belongs neither to the radicals nor to the industrialists, the thoroughly cooked marker of uncompromisingly civilized gentlemanliness—is an equally problematic proposition. The physical properties of Mr. Woodhouse's most beloved fare are rich in confusion. Gruel is of unstable consistency, neither solid nor liquid. The texture is unsettled, capricious; heated or cooled, it changes to jelly or to thick sludge or to a sort of watery soup, never quite fixed. These qualities make gruel particularly repulsive:

> The sticky and the slimy are substances . . . that particularly threaten bodily integrity because of their ambiguity, their half-life between solids and fluids, the threat they pose of incorporating the self and dissolving boundaries. . . . Substances of such consistency are too redolent of bodily fluids deemed polluting, such as saliva, semen, feces, pus, phlegm and vomit. Such bodily fluids create anxiety because of the threat they pose to self-integrity and autonomy. Body fluids threaten to engulf, to defile; they are difficult to be rid of, they seep and infiltrate. They challenge our desire to be self-contained and self-controlled. . . . So, too, foods that are of ambiguous texture or appearance evoke disgust. (Lupton, 114–15)

Slimy food is both of and not of the body: an outside substance indicative of the inside, it refuses the boundaries of privacy, the lines of decency. No wonder, then, that others refrain from trying the restorative properties of Mr. Woodhouse's preferred meal: when her father proposes that "'we all have a little gruel,' Emma could not suppose any such thing, knowing, as she did, that both the

Mr. Knightleys were as unpersuadable on that article as herself" (100–101). Ingestion of such stuff leaves its mark on Mr. Woodhouse: though, as William Ian Miller asserts, "[f]astidiousness is a fear of disgust" (29), this particular gentleman's very fastidiousness leads him to associate himself with the liminal, the slick, the uncontrolled, with that which is beyond definition and impossible to make determinate—in other words, with the disgusting. The impulse of disgust is inextricably linked to notions of pollution and its refusal. "Disgust," Miller asserts, "evaluates (negatively) what it touches, proclaims the meanness and inferiority of its object. And by so doing it presents a nervous claim of right to be free of the dangers imposed by the proximity of the inferior. It is thus an assertion of a claim to superiority that at the same time recognizes the vulnerability of that superiority to the defiling powers of the low. The world is a dangerous place in which the polluting powers of the low are usually stronger than the purifying powers of the high" (9). If this is the case, then Mr. Woodhouse, who feels no disgust at a substance rejected by everyone around him, is inextricably associated with such low, polluting fare: he must necessarily be looked at askance by the community that is averse to his food, because if gruel is defiling, then the lover of gruel is defiled by his failure to feel the danger. Paul Rozin and April E. Fallon assert that "[d]isgust provides a powerful way to transmit cultural values"; whereas a belief in the danger of certain foods—foods that will cause direct harm to the body—requires an intellectual acceptance of faith in the specified danger (and thus may be overcome by information or experience), disgust "is more intrinsic and, hence, less subject to reversal by information or example" (33). When Mr. Woodhouse attempts to manifest his exalted role in the social sphere by controlling the aliment of others, then, urging them to follow his lead in his rejection of the delicate and the tasty in favor of this putatively healthy fare, he undercuts his influence and power by his very actions. The community's disgust undermines Mr. Woodhouse, making complete incorporation impossible. Like Miss Bates whispering to Emma about the apples baked only twice, the other characters subvert Mr. Woodhouse's feudal engulfment of them by refusing to join in his disgusting—if privileged—embodiment.

The problems with gruel hardly end there: this slippery substance is also an extremely slippery cultural construct, thickened with danger and spiced with a multiplicity of meanings. Gruel is unmistakably poverty food, and its consumption by the gentleman necessarily affects the public perception of the fundamental nature of that apparently exalted body. Mr. Woodhouse rejects the rarefied food of the typical affluent gentleman as potentially fatal fare, embedded with modernity and technology and foreignness—but the consumption of such food is precisely what marks one as a gentleman, not only because it illustrates one's class and buying power but also because it adheres to a conception of the digestive system of the upper-class body as fundamentally differently constituted from that of the inhabitants of the lower orders.

Mennell and others have noted the belief, still prevalent in Austen's day, that more than blood—actual or metaphorical—separated the rich from the poor: the lower classes were thought to have digestive systems more suited to rough, simple fare, while members of the upper echelons were literally unable to stomach the much-cooked dishes that the poor were apparently relegated to by biology as well as by economy.[25] Under the terms of this logic, gruel—the sustenance of the poor during the food riots of the eighteenth century and the near-starvation years of the early nineteenth century—should be indigestible to finely developed gentlemanly plumbing, posing a danger to the health as well as to the status of the gentleman. When this gentleman happily feasts on poverty food to preserve his fragile upper-class body, he is at the same time marking himself as not gentlemanly at all: the elevation of gruel to the level of luxury is countered and complicated by the devolution of the gentleman that its consumption entails.

And while Mr. Woodhouse may rely on gruel to control untoward expressions of the body, his dependence on this problematic food also betrays him in this arena. The bad air that Mr. Woodhouse speaks so fearfully of in his discussion of London is not limited to places or even to buildings: in the late eighteenth century and the early years of the nineteenth century, bodies also were thought to give off emanations. Scientists of the day posited that "[r]egional populations exhaled specific odors . . . as a result of the kind of food they ate" (Corbin, 39), and these distinct aromas were in turn the product of the class (in every sense) of the aliment consumed. When Mr. Woodhouse swallows his smooth, thin, well-cooked gruel, then, he must give off not the scents of purity, wealth, and gentility but the odors of want and misery.

This stench begins to point to the source of the rot in Highbury—a source ironically encapsulated and highlighted by Mr. Woodhouse's preferred historical enactment of social stability. A nostalgic, idealized version of feudalism may seem to evoke a world of order and clarity, of boundaries and proper place; but it also represents a much more destabilizing trend. Flexibility in the English class system may be traced to the royal rewriting of feudalism in the thirteenth century, when military responsibilities—and, thus, class—became based "not on blood and descent, but on landed wealth whatever its nature. . . . The long-term consequence was the formation of a much more 'open' aristocracy" (Mennell, 116). Writing of the shaky boundaries between the aristocracy and the gentry through the early nineteenth century, Mennell cites Werner Sombart's declaration, "The peculiar fact, in regard to the English gentry, is that it is utterly impossible to define its lines of demarcation, especially in relation to the stratum below" (119).

Mr. Woodhouse's qualifications are as muddy as any hinted at by Mennell: he appears to be the beneficiary of this very slipperiness. Despite his grandiose attitude, the novel reveals that the Woodhouses are only "the younger branch of a very ancient family" and their money comes not from land but from "other sources" (136), an indication that even in Hartfield, the wheels of commerce are not still: the money of the family "first in consequence" in Highbury (7) may come, the omission implies, from industry, mining, or importing.[26] The dream of the all-controlling feudal lord, then, is not only impossible but also bespeaks an unavoidable blurring of boundaries, pointing toward precisely the sort of unreadability, of potential poisoning of purity, that Mr. Woodhouse seeks to avoid. It reveals his position as intrinsically impure, marked by the flavors of industry and entrepreneurship.

Mr. Woodhouse's alimentary linking of himself with the poor undermines the position he attempts to insist on for himself, rendering impossible his claims of superiority and complicating his imagining of himself as subsuming the bodies and appetites of his putative fiefdom. By attempting to mark his body as pure through the consumption of food so highly evocative of poverty, Mr. Woodhouse ironically re-creates himself as the very unruly, untellable body he needs to define himself against, the poor body lacking the agency to make choices about what it consumes. In his ascetic pursuit of health, he aligns himself with the common, grasping body of lack, a body that otherwise seems to take up very little space—and all of that oppositional—in Austen's novel. Mr. Woodhouse may have his gruel served up on silver platters by liveried butlers, if he so chooses, but his rewriting of his favorite food is always insufficient, always incapable of fixing its meaning on its object.

Mr. Woodhouse's discourse of control over his body through diet is equally vexed: like his discussion of the safety of the fare at his table, it holds within it the seeds of its own destruction. Gruel is invalid food: the gentleman who consumes it marks himself as lacking in wholeness and physical strength, and the gentleman who consumes gruel on a daily basis indicates that the ailing state of his body is permanent, perhaps inherent. At Hartfield, invalid food—meant to repair a body that has been breached by illness, food meant to be served up in the sickroom, a space that exists only while the body within it occupies the gap between life and death—is an obscene invader of the drawing room and the dining room, where it has no place at all.

Mr. Woodhouse's endless iteration of his fears and anxieties concerning the potential depredations of the uncontrolled and uncontrollable world on his body—particularly in the area of food—reinforces this sense of himself as a helpless subject, acted upon instead of acting. This anticipation of danger is highly toxic, despite its simultaneous demonstration of his importance.[27] When Mr. Woodhouse insists on the foregrounding of his bodily needs as a marker of his power and class status, he causes his body to take center stage, so that it is endlessly, publicly discussed and rhetorically dissected. Once again, food makes the man. By denying potentially dangerous food access to his body, Mr. Woodhouse has attempted to keep himself uncontaminated—by dangerous fare, by foreign fare, by food that is poison masquerading as sustenance. But in paying such wholehearted attention to the issue, he has made himself into a sickly "valetudinarian," a man who broadcasts his state of enthrallment to the ultimately apparently uncontrollable and unpredictable dictates of his body—that is, a man who has been so infected by the threat of the dangers inherent in consumption that his sacrosanct bodily boundaries have, in the end, been entirely subjugated to them. While he strives to ensure that nothing of danger enters his mouth, Woodhouse's entire discourse—that which comes out of his mouth—is a sign of his ongoing poisoning.

Mr. Woodhouse's consumption of gruel thus suggests a disturbing alliance between the great house and the destitute cottage, between the drawing room and the sickroom. These associations threaten to place the gentleman at the edge of the community—a nonactor, a subject rather than a speaker—and create the opportunity for the unsettled figures who populate the novel to occupy positions of prime social and narrative importance. Highbury is full of upstarts, social climbers, and people of dubious backgrounds, all mixing with the gentlefolk of the place: the sons of tradesmen sit down to dinner with the scions of the oldest families; the boundaries of gentility are stretched to admit merchants and governesses; a woman born out of wedlock to unknown parents is a regular at the supper parties and teas of the first families of the town, and even at Hartfield. Highbury is a place of secrets and intrigue and dangerous incursions, and the dining tables and picnic cloths around which *Emma*'s motley crew gathers are the novel's most potent sites of revelation and complication. Young men in particular are extremely problematic creatures in Highbury, as the erotics of the marriage plot—and the potential they hold, finally, for the usurping of Mr. Woodhouse's place by marrying his daughter—revolve around figures of unrestrained appetite and foreignness who threaten to render impossible all of the stability and comfort that Mr. Woodhouse seeks. Unsurprisingly, the most problematic putatively gentlemanly characters in the text turn out to be promiscuous eaters.

Take, for instance, Mr. Elton, with his habit of eating at other people's tables whenever possible—the antithesis of careful Mr. Woodhouse. Mr. Elton is all about food, all the time. He avidly recounts the play-by-plays of the dinners he attends: when Emma contrives to let Harriet walk ahead alone with him, expecting him to use the opportunity to propose, she "experienced some disappointment when she found that he was only giving his fair companion an account of the yesterday's party at his friend Cole's, and that she was come in herself for the Stilton cheese, the north Wiltshire, the butter, the celery, the beet-root and all the dessert" (88–89). He anticipates his meals out in company just as avidly. Rushing off to the Westons' dinner party on a cold, snowy day, he observes to an astonished John Knightley, "This is quite the season indeed for friendly meetings. At Christmas every body invites their friends about them, and people think little of even the worst weather" (115); when he finds that Emma's brother-in-law never dines away from home, Mr. Elton is awash with pity. His own popularity is demonstrated by the constant invitations he receives. As Harriet declares with admiration and wonder, Mr. Elton's "company [is] so sought after, that everybody says he need not eat a single meal by himself if he does not choose it" (75).

But Harriet's enthusiastic praise is, as usual, misplaced. The ambitious Mr. Elton seems to feel that meals are sites of social mobility. With his connections in trade and his social-climbing aspirations, Mr. Elton is an upstart: as Emma reflects, his manners demonstrate "a[n] . . . error of judgment, of knowledge, of taste . . . proof . . . that he had not always lived in the best society, that with all the gentlemanliness of his address, true elegance was sometimes wanting." He is "proud, assuming, conceited; very full of his own claims, and little concerned about the feelings of others" (135). He seems to think that he can swallow class at the table, remaking himself through his appetites. But the wide-ranging tables of Highbury threaten to make the social realm as unreadable as the fancy French messes that threaten England's culinary shores. Mr. Elton fails to see this: he is not picky about what or where or with whom he eats, and he is as happy at table with the Coles as he is with the Woodhouses. His indiscriminate behavior dooms him to failure in his quest to swallow gentility along with his venison and wine.[28]

Emma's matter-of-fact suspicion that Mr. Elton "had been drinking too much of Mr. Weston's good wine" (129) when he proposes to her is telling: though he attempts to make himself gentlemanly at table, the food, like the wine, may well get the better of him. But the fact that, as the narrator notes, "Mr. Elton had only drunk wine enough to elevate his spirits, not at all to confuse his intellects" (129) is equally revelatory. In vino veritas, indeed: Mr. Elton's

misreading of his role in the social network and his failure to perceive the effects of his consuming practices are of a piece with his
hungering character, and meals are the spaces where his true nature is revealed. He knows no moderation, and so when he seeks to
take Mr. Woodhouse's place by transforming himself into the heir
to Hartfield, he trips on his own outsized appetites.[29] His marriage
to the vulgar, grasping, overdressed Augusta Hawkins, another
clear pretender to gentility, is the near-inevitable result of his
indiscriminate and uncontained consumption, paired with his appetite for advancement.[30]

In many ways, however, the most problematic eater in Highbury
is at once a foreign invader and a prodigal native: Mr. Weston's
son, Frank. An ardent eater abroad, he is the force behind much of
the confusion at meals in the novel, encouraging Emma's malicious
gossip at the Westons' and flirting with her at Box Hill, humiliat-
ing Jane with the game of blocks at the Hartfield tea. Considered
by the town to be a viable suitor for Emma, he threatens the most
serious undermining of Highbury's social order; his disturbing effects ripple through the meals at which the town's society gathers.
The difficulty in reading Frank, a font of secrets and intrigue, is tied
to the difficulty in keeping class straight in the text, and it is significant that he is both a hero (Jane's savior) and a villain (Jane's
tormentor; a potential breaker of Emma's heart). The product of
his father's indistinct station and the nouveau-riche pretensions of
his mother's family, he is energetic and driven, like a middle-class
man, but not driven to work; uncommitted to any particular place
or course of action, he is self-indulgent, ambivalent, and emotion-
ally volatile. His status as bearer of foreign ways and manners—of
an alien nature that is not understood and, though outwardly pleasant, is not to be trusted—is strongly hinted at in Mr. Knightley's
comment about Frank even before he makes his first appearance in
Highbury: "[Y]our amiable young man," he tells Emma, "can be
amiable only in French, not in English. He may be very 'amiable,'
have very good manners and be very agreeable; but he can have
no English delicacy towards the feelings of other people; nothing
really amiable about him" (148).

Frank is a figure of chaos and disorder, the man who brings the
flavor of the city to the country. When he promotes an imprudent

threat to health (that is, the idea of dancing across the corridor between two rooms) as a means of accommodating a ball in the Westons' small house, Mr. Woodhouse's condemnation seems peculiarly accurate: "That young man . . . is not quite the thing," he complains. "He has been opening the doors very often this evening, and keeping them open very inconsiderately. He does not think of the draught. I do not mean to set you against him, but indeed he is not quite the thing!" (249). There is no telling what will find its way in, once the doors are open: danger lurks abroad, and Mr. Woodhouse thoroughly understands the importance of keeping out forces that cannot be controlled once they find a way in. Yet Mr. Woodhouse's own social and bodily practices—his mistaking of his own body for the social body of the town; his grandiloquent, flawed construction of himself as the feudal lord of Highbury, the kingly body politic; his subsequent, problematic affiliation of himself with the poor, the sick, the disgusting—are precisely what lead to his subsequent opening of the paradoxically closed realm of his dinner table to those who themselves trouble boundary and category. Mr. Woodhouse's behavior creates the opportunity for the most problematic of these feasters, as Frank Churchill and Mr. Elton, potential husbands for Emma, offer to subsume Mr. Woodhouse, to swallow him whole, to stir the class status he craves into the stew of class confusion by literally taking his place.[31]

Mr. Woodhouse's efforts at control, then, ultimately result both in his centrality and in his marginalization, in his rewriting of his body and in his loss of authority over the messages that the body speaks. His belief in the all-consuming power he wields in his feudal narrative—in which he subsumes all threats emanating from other bodies and so is impermeable—leads him to create the conditions for a disorderly, conflicted metamorphic state, in which *all* boundaries become permeable: a world where a middle-class cleric can propose to the manor lord's daughter, where gentlemen dine with women of unknown birth, where the lines between city and country become confused as goods and persons move back and forth across them. If the body politic and the gentleman's body are one and the same, then the gentleman is no longer a discrete, codifiable figure, a man defined by difference in his gender and his class. He is instead a morass, a figure of disorder and chaos, an unreadable space.

But at the same time, Mr. Woodhouse is also made more powerful and more dangerous by his ability to incorporate that which the community around him rejects, while retaining his role as privileged social naysayer and imperious declarer of action and policy. In attempting to become the body and the body politic of the town, he has made himself into the figure who must be resolved for the story to move toward its conclusion. This believer in stasis, this man who can accept no change unless he has been brought to believe that it is not simply inevitable but in fact no change at all, is also the figure who perversely refuses the narrative its closure, preferring a liminal state of irresolution to a position of permanent fixity. His embodiment of that liminality makes him not conservatively central but abject: he is that which cannot be incorporated into the social body—that which, like gruel, repulses, frightens, and sickens, being both alien and like—and, because it is like as well as alien, that which cannot be labeled dirt and dismissed or refused outright.

In this way, Mr. Woodhouse infects the narrative: he is the walking dead who refuses to properly take himself away—to give up the ghost, so to speak—or to be reborn into the brave new market-suffused world.[32] Instead, he creeps through the alimentary system of the town, infecting it with his disease of ambivalence and liminality, gelling the narrative in a space between crisis and resolution. He is the force that must finally be subdued by the novel so that its narrative imperatives may be fulfilled; but he cannot simply be expelled, because he has so thoroughly contaminated the community that, like the adulterated food he fears, he has settled himself in the heart of the body politic, obscenely different and yet the same, his slow poison working its way through *Emma*'s textual veins. Instead of ridding itself of him, then, Highbury must find a way to re-place Mr. Woodhouse, to assign to him a location and a name that can be tolerated by the social fabric without engulfing it. The person to do so, it would appear, is the aptly named George Knightley, rational savior of this little corner of England.

Mr. Knightley is the novel's recuperative figure of ordered eating and provisioning, a dream figure of alimentary safety and of social and bodily integrity. Unlike Mr. Elton, Mr. Knightley is not a promiscuous eater, and he understands the safety and value of his fields and gardens; unlike Mr. Woodhouse, he is willing to venture out into the world, to open himself to both the risks and the benefits of meaningful and reciprocal engagement with the social realm. Like Emma's father, for instance, Mr. Knightley grows much of his own fare. But whereas anonymous field-workers and long-time household servants produce Mr. Woodhouse's food, reinforcing the notion of a community not of enlightened interaction but of rule and submission, Mr. Knightley works with his manager, William Larkins, and with Robert Martin to make decisions that benefit the estate, the grower, and the community. No feudal lord, Mr. Knightley is an idealized gentleman, imbricated in commerce without being lessened by it: he is a magistrate and a farmer, a thorough businessman who enters into the particulars of agriculture with his managers and tenants and animatedly discusses fields and yields with his brother. Nevertheless, as Emma says, "[y]ou might not see one in a hundred, with *gentleman* so plainly written as in Mr. Knightley" (33). In Emma's fiancé, the text offers a gentleman appropriately imbricated with the contemporary world: not a flashy city boy or an unctuous social climber but a country gentleman reinvented for the new century.

Nor is Mr. Knightley a fetishizer of his own fare. Exhibiting a complete understanding both of the business of agriculture and of the roles of the grower and the vendor, he takes a rational pride in his food as a product to be sold and shared. Mr. Knightley feeds those around him freely and generously, with no expectation of recompense or desire for gratitude: as Miss Bates says regarding his gift of apples, "He can never bear to be thanked" (245). He is a respecter of the persons and aims of all those around him. And while he understands the value of his food to both body and soul, he never imagines it to have any miraculous properties. When he sends those apples to the Bateses, for instance, he does so not to cure them or to protect them but to give pleasure and sustenance (impeding their enjoyment by no restriction on their apple cookery); when he invites his neighbors to share in his strawberries, he does so not to promote his own alimental agenda but rather in the spirit of community.

This straightforward attitude toward food and eating hardly means, however, that Mr. Knightley is unaware of the potentially vexed erotic and power dynamics of a meal: highly conscious of the dangers of alimentary promiscuity, he refuses to play the sorts of dangerous games that threaten to transform aliment into the poison of social risk. When he suggests the strawberry-gathering party at Donwell Abbey to make up for the much-delayed picnic to Box Hill, he offers an alternative to fluidity and disorder that is, in Norbert Elias's sense, highly civilized.[33] To Mrs. Elton's proposal of a gathering with "no form or parade—a sort of gipsy party . . . all out of doors—a table spread in the shade, you know. Every thing as simple and natural as possible," he responds, "My idea of the simple and natural will be to have the table spread in the dining-room. The nature and the simplicity of gentlemen and ladies, with their servants and furniture, I think is best observed by meals within doors. When you are tired of eating strawberries in the garden, there shall be cold meat in the house" (355).

While exploding the sort of pseudo-Romantic myth that Mrs. Elton finds fashionable, Mr. Knightley simultaneously acknowledges and refuses the socially destabilizing forces that underlie such discourses. The world that supports ladies and gentleman, he implies, is not natural but constructed—and that construction (with its servants and furniture) must be carefully maintained if order and right reason are to prevail. There is no safe play at looseness and gypsylike romance when actual gypsies are lurking in the woods; the social fabric is transforming under the force of a changing economic and political landscape. His comments take on particular retrospective importance in the aftermath of the Box Hill outing, the most troubled meal of all—a socially and erotically loaded al fresco collation at which Frank and Emma succeed in offending and alienating nearly everyone present, behaving as though the removal of the formal accoutrements of the genteel meal has sanctioned the removal of any check on behavior.

Mr. Knightley's pragmatism allows him to incorporate the dangerous into his vision of the town and to subdue it, just as he subdues Mrs. Elton's airy fantasies. Mr. Woodhouse, by his weakness, provides space for the ascension of the socially grasping and the culturally questionable; Mr. Knightley's strength, in contrast, allows space for a certain playful degree of looseness but effectively encloses such behavior in a social system that is elastic enough to allow for a certain degree of change without breaking apart. His guests may wear themselves out playing at a rustic strawberry hunt in his well-planted garden, but when they tire of the game they can revive themselves with straightforward English fare appropriate to the company; Mr. Knightley may make special efforts to talk to Harriet, but there is no question of him marrying her. Instead, of course, he marries Emma. The settling of their relationship appears to lead to the resolution of the problem of liminality in the text or at least to sufficient resolution to allow for narrative closure. On closer inspection, however, the story is not quite so simple.

Mr. Knightley, with becoming love and self-effacement, volunteers to give up his beloved Donwell Abbey to live with his bride and her father at Hartfield, since Emma finds it impossible to suggest to her father that she will leave him. The sacrifice is, as Emma realizes, great: "She felt that, in quitting Donwell, he must be sacrificing a great deal of independence of hours and habits; that in living constantly with her father, and in no house of his own, there would be much, very much, to be borne with" (449). Still, the task of winning Emma's father over to the idea of the marriage, even with this great concession, seems impossible. It is "a considerable shock to him, and he trie[s] earnestly to dissuade her from it" (466): faced with his distress, "his daughter's courage failed. She could not bear to see him suffering, to know him fancying himself neglected . . . she hesitated—she could not proceed" (483).

At this moment of extreme liminality—when Emma is engaged (her heart no longer virginal) but neither married nor marriageable; when the narrative, which should have been resolved twenty pages before with Mr. Knightley's proposal, is dragging itself on, straining toward a closure that Mr. Woodhouse will not allow—a saving grace appears, in the unlikely form of a poultry thief. Mrs. Weston's turkeys are stolen one night, and other houses in the neighborhood are similarly attacked. The effect on Mr. Woodhouse is serious: "Pilfering was *housebreaking* to Mr. Woodhouse's fears.—He was very uneasy" (483–84). The incursion is unbearable: a faceless stranger has penetrated the grounds of local homes and deprived them not merely of property but of the very home-grown fare that should sustain them in the battle against the dangers of the outside world. Clearly, something must be done to protect Hartfield. Accordingly, Mr. Woodhouse turns to Mr. Knightley: he believes that the younger man protects Hartfield from any incursion with his very presence. Known, clear-intentioned, and law-abiding, he is the inverse of the poultry stalker, and thus light replaces darkness, a simple equation. And so it is that Mr. Knightley is finally accepted as a son-in-law, resolving the narrative and ending the novel.

It is striking, however, that despite all his vaunted goodness—his clarity of vision, generosity, and supposed strength—Mr. Knightley does nothing to actually bring about this resolution: the novel's would-be St. George never even sets out to slay this particular dragon. Instead, *Emma*'s happily-ever-after ending is facilitated by an invasion into the safe space of the home by a shady, never-glimpsed creature who makes off with food in the dark of night: a figure who cannot be conclusively named or defined, an outsider who is not, finally, expelled from the town. The fact that it is this incursion that leads to Mr. Woodhouse's consent to the marriage implies that this apparently recuperative union rests on very shaky ground.

The dream figure of rational aliment and social clarity, then, fails in the end to triumph completely; instead, the uneasy liminality, the unresolved in-between time of Mr. Woodhouse haunts the end of the text, as Mr. Knightley leaves Donwell Abbey for Hartfield and the older man's troubling status at the center of the town is maintained. Mr. Knightley seems to function as an attempt to repair the damage Mr. Woodhouse has wrought on the figure of the gentleman. His narrative role, it appears, is to reposition the gentleman not as a creature of alimental fear and loathing, a vexed product of stunted appetites who fails to sustain himself or the community around him, but as a creature of inherence and inevitability, a figure whose appetites—social, political, erotic, and physical—are entirely within bounds, a figure who feeds others what they need without starving himself and in this way remains a vital center of the world that he inhabits. In this reverie, the gentleman's survival as an established force may be briefly threatened but is, in the end, reinforced by his emergence as an entirely fitted creature for the entrepreneurial age, embodying a rational melding of old and new.

But this attempt to rewrite the gentleman as a figure who transcends his appetites is undercut by the lurking thief, by the finicky old man, by the presence of gruel. The very invasion that imposes closure and allows stability is the sort of disruptive force that Mr. Knightley—with his distaste for Frank Churchill, his disapproval of Emma's matchmaking, and his table set indoors—has been trying to block out all along; it is (like gruel, like the old man) the undefined abject that troubles the boundaries. Closure is gained, but the perfection that is the sense of an ending remains elusive. Mr. Knightley lacks agency over the conclusion of this story he needs so badly to direct, and the liminal figures retain control over the narrative, suggesting by their very presence that inherence is mythical, that no body—physical or social—remains discrete. This is hardly the contained resolution, the rational utopia, that the idealized figure of Mr. Knightley promises. Instead, we are left with a realm that, in this ending which purports to promise a new beginning, seems to have always already been poisoned. The novel, begun with a wedding and a problematic wedding cake, closes without any reference to the breakfast feast that traditionally marks that ceremonial move into fertility and productivity; similarly, the narrative ends without a signal moment of the ascendance of appropriate gentlemanly consumption. Mr. Woodhouse's problematic gentlemanly habits have poisoned the community, and—despite the novel's perfunctory ten-line happy-ever-after summary—the town seems to have lost its appetite for growth and renewal.

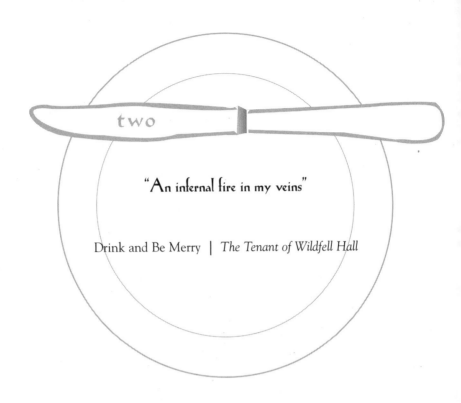

two

"An infernal fire in my veins"

Drink and Be Merry | *The Tenant of Wildfell Hall*

Anne Brontë's *Tenant of Wildfell Hall* (1848) is a novel sodden with drink. This startlingly explicit novel is a troubled and troubling anatomy of upper-crust gentlemanly drunkenness, obsessed with issues of control and productivity, of appetites and class, as they play out across the body of its prime sot, the wealthy playboy Arthur Huntingdon. Brontë's subject here is the gentleman unable to deny himself any of the pleasures of the table, the gentleman who never abstains from yet another glass, even as he suffers the ravaging consequences of his indulgences in body and mind. Inebriation was a serious preoccupation for midcentury Victorians, and *Tenant* is rife with the markers of the period's debates on the subject—but in telling her drinking tale, Brontë is doing more than simply crafting a prurient morality story meant to scare drinkers straight. Arthur's fall into the bottle is also a complicated alimentary investigation of the increasingly untenable role of the landed gentleman in the striver period; his drunken decline exposes upper-crust drunkenness not as a simple vice but as a fatally necessary behavior in the gentleman's pursuit of the ever-receding goals of self-definition and demarcation, suggesting the possibility of a radical social revisioning across that gentleman's prone, overstuffed body.

For the Victorians, drinking was a hook on which all sorts of questions about class, gender, and the body might be suspended. This was particularly true at midcentury—a time when middle-class narratives of virtuous moderation clashed with laudatory tales of social climbing, replete with conspicuous consumption. In the imagination of this period, drink and drunkenness were significant social, economic, and physical markers, at once rents in the communal fabric and longstanding signs of fellowship and community. The drunkard was a catalyst for social movement and a focus of considerable social anxiety; drunkenness—drawn as illness or weakness, self-inflicted or hereditary, curable or stoppable or preventable—served as a locus for some of the most troubling questions of the mid-Victorian age, taking up the construction or reconstruction of the social realm and the individual's place in that realm.

But even given the sustained social attention paid to drinking, Brontë's tale is remarkable for its insistently unvarnished look at gentlemanly drunkenness, a topic that was hardly the stuff of lending-library staples in its day. Narrated in a double-diary form by Gilbert Markham, a young yeoman-farmer, the novel tells the tale of a young widow (a painter with a small son and a mysterious backstory) who becomes the unexpected tenant of a long-vacant, crumbling manse in the isolated village of Linden-Car. Markham falls in love with this mysterious, romantic figure; when her affections seem to be given to another, he is consumed by violent jealousy. Eventually, Helen (who does, of course, love Gilbert truly) gives him her diary to exonerate herself. We read the diary with Markham and discover that she has abandoned a wealthy, landed husband who is very much alive. Helen is thus a criminal wife and a child kidnapper by the lights of the marital laws of her day, but the novel makes clear that her moral justification trumps any legal or social duties that may have bound her to her husband's home. Determined to protect her son from the corrupting influence of his uncontrollable father, she has flouted social approval, impoverished herself, given up her name, and hidden herself away in the countryside, fleeing a marriage destroyed and desecrated by the demon drink.

Arthur's drinking is nothing to scoff at: Huntingdon is "a drunkard who verbally abuses his wife, who prefers the companionship
of fellow . . . debauchees . . . and who feels it is his right to have
affairs with whatever pretty women come in his way" (Jackson,
199). Huntingdon is an unconstrained carouser who makes his
wife's life a misery to her as he proceeds in his career of revelry and
reaps its indigestible rewards. He spends months in town (leaving
Helen alone on their estate), indulging in "orgies" (Brontë, 206) of
drunken revelry; he brings his drinking friends home with him to
help pass the time, and takes part in drunken brawls in the drawing room (in front of the ladies) and debauches in the dining room
(in front of his small son). When he is alone at home with his
wife, he drinks himself into unconsciousness or violence. Helen's
diary is an unflinching recording of Arthur's career. She docu-
ments his transformation from an attractive, high-spirited young
lover to an abusive husband who offers to auction his wife off to
the highest bidder, flaunts his affairs with his friend's wife and with
a low-born faux governess, burns his wife's paintings, gives his tod-
dler son a taste for alcohol-fueled bacchanalias, and finally (back in
the pages of Markham's narrative) dies a slow and horrible death
of dissolution.

Tenant has generated a fair amount of critical attention in recent
years, but most of the interest surrounding the novel has focused
not on Arthur but on his long-suffering wife, Helen Huntingdon.
This tale of a woman who frees herself from the constraints of a bad
marriage and an abusive husband to find freedom and true love has
been justly celebrated for its protofeminist sensibilities: Helen
Huntingdon's famous locking of her bedroom door against her husband is often portrayed as the shot that echoed round the world of
Victorian gender politics.[1] Perhaps as a result, Huntingdon is almost always read only through his effects on his wife: his drunkenness seems to disqualify him for serious study, and he is generally
dismissed either as an enactor of excessive patriarchal authority
and droit du seigneur or as an overplayed Regency rake. But this
behavior makes him the most consistently interesting character in
the novel—far more interesting than his morally correct wife.[2] The
outré actions of the men make them compelling; when they happen to reform (as Arthur's boon companions Hattersley and Low-

borough do), they are summed up and disappear from the story. When they fail to tread the straight and narrow, however, gentlemen like Arthur Huntingdon keep a tight grasp on narrative attention—even, as with Helen's father, from beyond the grave. The devil gets all the best tunes in *Tenant*: Huntingdon is the central mover in the text, just as he is in his world of spirited ladies and boon companions, and his uncontrolled conduct and inability or unwillingness to reform provide the narrative action of the novel. The reader, granted the voyeur's view into the private heart of the gentlemanly family story, is titillated and fascinated by the debaucheries and excesses of its gentlemen—and most particularly by the bad behavior of its prime rake. His story, written in wine, makes addicts of the most abstemious of readers.

And though his behavior is almost stereotypically outrageous, Huntingdon is not simply a spoiled rich kid, a bad seed with a drinking problem. Rather, he is a figure whose complex alimental embodiment of gender and class is at once necessary to his self-perpetuation and agent of his obliteration. The most interesting question about Arthur is the simplest: why does he drink?

After all, while he is never a gentlemanly sipper, a Mr. Elton, taking "only . . . enough to elevate his spirits" (Austen, *Emma*, 131), he does not begin the narrative as a drunken wreck. When Helen marries Huntingdon, she knows that he is given to drunken revelry among his friends and associates in London: at "home— that is . . . our club," as he describes it (202), he is a prime mover at all the "orgies" (206). He makes no effort to disguise his partying from her—indeed, he seems to see it as a marker of the manly virility of his bachelor years. But in the early moments of their relationship, Huntingdon is not a drunkard: he is simply a man who likes to drink, and he seems to understand that perpetual drunkenness can only end badly. He assures Helen that though he does not "abstain like a ninny," he is no "tippler," for he "value[s] [his] comfort far too much." He adds, "I see that a man cannot give himself up to drinking without being miserable one half his days and mad the other;—besides, I like to enjoy my life at all sides and ends, which cannot be done by one that suffers himself to be the slave of a single propensity—and moreover, drinking spoils one's good looks" (207–8).[3]

Perhaps because of this consciousness of the evils of drink on his part, some critics read Huntingdon as an alcoholic in the modern sense—a tragic figure in thrall to appetites predicated on genetics and illness, for whom self-control in the matter of drinking is an illusion.[4] But while the idea of Huntingdon as a philosopher lost and found in the bottle, a rebel without a cause for the nineteenth century, is particularly attractive to a twenty-first-century readership besotted with antiheroes, it seems a stretch, according a great deal of self-awareness to a character who evinces very little of this interesting quality.[5]

More important is that this notion of Huntingdon as an alcoholic is profoundly ahistorical: our contemporary notion of drinking as an addiction out of the control of the individual was foreign to the early Victorians. In the first half of the nineteenth century, habitual drunkenness was seen as a behavioral or criminal issue inflected with ethical connotations, tied to class and dependent for its definition on widely varying community standards. The Victorian drunkard was viewed variously as viciously depraved, morally bereft, or badly socialized. Drunkards were social problems; drunkenness was nearly always tied to willfulness. And while one might certainly die from the effects of habitual intoxication, the idea of drunkenness as a disease was not widely accepted until at least the 1860s.[6]

This crucial cultural difference is predicated in part on the everyday presence of drink in the early years of the British nineteenth century, but the common consumption of alcohol was also the genesis of fierce battles over the role of drink and drunkenness in relation to the socioeconomic fabric in Brontë's day. Certainly in the 1820s, the time frame of *Tenant's* central story, England was still mired in a mild fog of intoxication—a hangover from the eighteenth century, when "[t]he traditional view of alcohol was that it was as natural and as necessary for survival as food" (Freeman, 94). Laborers and even lawyers still girded themselves for the day with a fortifying breakfast of beer soup; wine was thought to be much safer than water, especially in the cities (with good reason, given London's infamous sewage problems); and public schools served weakened "table" beer to children. Everyone drank: fine ladies and factory workers, rich and poor. Drunkenness was not particularly problematic: it was a sign of fellowship, part of the social contract. "[A]ll classes drank, often to excess, but only a few worried about it. It was a man's right to get drunk if he wanted to. Drunkenness carried no social stigma" (Shiman, 2).

Brontë's Reverend Millward, the leading light of his community, is the embodiment of this embrace of drink. As Gilbert Markham explains, "He had a laudable care for his own bodily health . . . [and] was, generally, extremely particular about what he ate and drank, though by no means abstemious, and having a mode of dietary peculiar to himself,—being a great despiser of tea and such slops, and a patron of malt liquors, bacon and eggs, ham, hung beef, and other strong meats, which . . . were maintained by him to be good and wholesome for everybody" (43). Millward declares that the supposed Helen Graham's determination to teach her four-year-old son to hate alcohol is "making a fool of the boy[:] . . . despising the gifts of providence, and teaching him to trample them under his feet": wine and spirits, Millward affirms, "are all blessings and mercies," if one knows "how to make use of them" (64). Gilbert's mother, too, affirms the widespread Regency-era belief in the fortifying, manly nature of drink: teaching little Arthur to abstain will, she declares, turn the boy into "the veriest milksop that ever was sopped!" (54). A regimen like Helen's would have been more than startling to a society that believed that beer imparted strength and that wine was a good cure-all, a necessary medicine and a crucial component of the well-bred table. In this world, the notion of the drinker as addict—victim to his appetites, helpless in the face of his compulsions—is nearly incomprehensible.

But although *Tenant* is set in the Regency era, it was written in the late 1840s, and the thinking of that period shapes the novel's attitude toward alcohol, as Gilbert's awareness of the Reverend's ridiculousness makes clear. As the Victorian era progressed, "intemperance began to be perceived as a problem. In fact all drinking was seen in a different context than formerly" (Shiman, 2). To a mid-nineteenth-century reader, Millward's views on drink—and his copious personal indulgence—would mark him as distinctly old-fashioned, an apt character for an "old-world story" (34); when he declares, as he pours himself a tall glass of Mrs. Millward's homebrewed ale, "now THIS is the thing!" (63), he is as misguided as he proves to be in lecturing Helen on morality and piety.

This sea change in attitudes toward drink and drunkenness is directly related to the new vicissitudes of high industrialism and its active remaking of the body. Work in England—even in the factories and mines that had transformed the country—had continued its subjection to the drinking culture through the early years of the century. Regular hours and regular production had remained more or less a pipe dream. Workers drank before, during, and after work, fueling their long hours and grueling labors with strengthening drafts of beer. Tipsy workers made costly and often dangerous mistakes, and production was slow. "Saint Monday"—an extra day off for carousing after the dry Sunday holiday—was widely celebrated by workers who declined to appear at work on Monday mornings, preferring to put in long hours toward the end of the week to make up for laxity at the beginning.

As factory work grew increasingly regulated and production needs changed in response to growing competition and technological changes, ambitious capitalists began to search for ways to combat these lax business practices (Schivelbusch, 148–49). By the time of *Tenant's* publication, drink-sodden England had been progressively dried out by industrialism's increasing demands for professionalism, efficiency, and productivity (Harrison, 40). Whereas drink had once been a tool used to pacify and manage workers (in the pay packet, at the company-owned pub), it was becoming an evil to be eradicated, a foe of orderly productive life. Management remade the body: owners stopped paying drink bonuses as they began demanding that workers function like machines. "Measured time, the machine, and the self were . . . the symbolically productive metaphors of the nineteenth century capitalist society. Drink and inebriety blurred time and made a mockery of its efficient 'use'" (Adler, 387–88).

Drink and drunkenness became immoral, anti-Protestant, and antisocial (Shiman, 2), a new idea most effectively broadcast by the temperance movement, which came into its own in the 1820s and '30s. In this era of sanitary commissions and other church-driven moral movements, temperance leagues were a perfect "cure" for an anti-industrial vice, combining the language of the workplace with the moral weight of the pulpit: "the movement offered a moral platform legitimating the demand for security of property, a disciplined labor force, and an expanded home market" (Adler, 386). The movement was reform minded but not revolutionary: it preached against "gin," the generic term for all hard alcohol (usually taken in cheap shots in working-class pubs),[7] but never advocated abstinence. Beer and wine were allowed, as long as moderation was observed. Prominent London churchmen and wealthy industrialists who indulged in wine and port at their own tables lent their names to the cause,[8] but the real leadership belonged to the managing classes.

Workers with an interest in "bettering" themselves found encouragement in the temperance movement, within which self-improvement through self-control was gospel: they often saw the societies as a coveted gateway to the middle class. Temperance "teas," often run by ladies, were conducted like historical- or scientific-society meetings, with great decorum and a veneer of education (Harrison, 108), and working-class member-subjects were encouraged to take productivity and gentility along with their cuppa. But while the movement was immensely socially and economically useful to its middle-class leaders, the opportunity it seemed to offer the lower orders was illusory. The temperance notion of drink and intoxication was deeply inflected by class, and the drinker urged to reform was inevitably marked as a person to whom one condescended.

Temperance leaders preached that the tendency to true drunkenness was bred in the bone. For those with the propensity, drunkenness could be avoided through moderation and care; but once a drinker had truly embarked on a career of drinking, he could not be redeemed, because the legacy carried in his blood, once taken up, could not be suppressed. The key, here as in the workplace, was gaining control over the tendency toward inebriation before it was too late. In this way, the mind could triumph over the body. The individual could win out over fate through the medium of aliment, but only to a certain degree. It was a near-article of faith that the bloodstreams of the poor were the exclusive sites of such encoding and, thus, that the poor could only be bettered to a certain degree— unlike their aspiring leaders.[9] Class was at once malleable and static: the imperative toward upward mobility among the middle classes was married to the notion of inherence among the lower classes through the device of appetite and its control.

Members of the gentry, with their putatively more rarefied blood, were excluded from the "bettering" rhetoric of the leagues, but the rise of temperance nevertheless had moral implications for their tables and their appetites. Temperance's ethos rejected drink because it was antisocial and antiproductive. Similarly, the ease-inducing—and ease-requiring—fare of the rich was increasingly perceived not only as old-fashioned but also as unproductive and (what came to the same thing) immoral as new demands for professionalism, efficiency, and productivity profoundly changed the bodily definitions of the middle class. If the workers who toiled on the factory floor were reduced, in Dickens's famous term, to "Hands," their betters in the managerial offices might be usefully imagined as disembodied heads. For the manager, the civil servant, and the barrister, professionalism—labor not of the hand but of the head—was the site of social advancement. To this end, the body had to be utterly subdued so that the mind could go about its business (Adler, 387–88). Managers and owners might have aspired, ultimately, to the luxuries of the gentle table, but they fueled their race to the top not with the heavy, brain-clogging fare of the rich—food requiring vast periods of time for preparation, ingestion, and digestion—but with breakfast on the fly, with the light City luncheon, and, in particular, with coffee.

Coffee had been popular with the rich as a breakfast drink since the eighteenth century; now, caffeinated drinks began to appear with growing regularity on the breakfast tables of the middle classes as successful professional people sought out the alimentary markers of their socioeconomic betters. Boiled drinks served as an increasingly popular alternative to plain water, still widely considered unsafe for human consumption, and they began to take the place of alcohol in many instances. In many households, coffee replaced beer soup, a popular stew of warm beer and bits of bread thought to aid growth and improve strength. As the price of coffee dropped relative to the cost of tea, coffee consumption became increasingly widespread among both managers and their workers, who often drank the brew from the new portable coffee carts stationed on city streets and outside factory doors.

For ambitious men, coffee was the perfect substitute for drink: stimulating, brain clearing, and speedy, it was "*the* beverage of the modern bourgeois age" (Schivelbusch, 38). Writing of the rise of bourgeois culture in Germany in terms applicable to midcentury England, Wolfgang Schivelbusch asserts that "coffee functioned as a historically significant drug. It spread through the body and achieved chemically and pharmacologically what rationalism and the Protestant ethic sought to fulfill spiritually and ideologically. With coffee, the principle of rationality entered human physiology, transforming it to conform with its own requirements. The result was a body which functioned in accord with the new demands—a rationalistic, middle-class, forward-looking body" (38). That most modern, most speedy of beverages did much to remake the middle-class body, bringing it rapidly out of the drunken fog into a bright new place where food and drink were salted with ethical meaning.

By outlawing certain modes of alimentation—by seeking to control the body through what was taken in and by tying this moral code explicitly to socioeconomic output—temperance rhetoric served not only to control laboring bodies but also to name any unproductively consuming body as alienated from the entire system, a relic of the past, beyond redemption. This narrative pervades the early sections of Brontë's novel, particularly in the person of Gilbert Markham. The very picture of well-directed, productive eating, Gilbert stands in sharp contrast to his neighbors. Though he is thwarted in his ambitions for a life beyond the farm by a deathbed promise to his father, his methodical approach to his work in "the improvement of agriculture" (35), his close supervision of his workers, and his valuing of productivity align him with the strivers of Brontë's age. Eschewing both luxury and self-indulgence, he fuels his daily labors of hand and of mind—for example, "breaking in the grey colt . . . directing the ploughing of the last wheat stubble . . . and carrying out a plan for the extensive and efficient draining of the low meadow-lands" (36–37)—on nothing more intoxicating than "tea, ham and toast" (39). In the matter of drink, he seems nearly abstemious, despite his argument with Helen about her plan to teach her son to hate alcohol: Gilbert is never seen to touch a drop of wine or ale. Instead, he reports on the bad drinking behavior of others, noting, for instance, the insufferable gossip

Mrs. Wilson's partiality for gin and water (she "affirmed that wine sat heavy on her stomach" [63]), just as he reports disapprovingly of his lazy brother, Fergus, who eats with great appetite while apparently never undertaking any work whatsoever.

The morally inflected middle-class imperative toward productivity and abstemious behavior that Gilbert embodies is especially problematic for the midcentury upper-crust gentleman embodied by Arthur Huntingdon—a figure more and more removed from the useful world by the advance of the business-minded striver. Whereas such a gentleman could once have been plausibly drawn as at least a putatively productive leader—benevolent owner, informed producer, capable political chief—this portrait became increasingly untenable in the popular imagination in the face of industrialism and sociopolitical changes. The image of the productive man of inherited wealth faded as the traditional activities of the English gentleman were slowly usurped by the professional classes.[10] Lawyers and bureaucrats assumed the roles that allowed city and town to function. The army and foreign services were increasingly professionalized. While the lords pondered grave issues in the Upper House, the day-to-day running of government was undertaken by a vast and ever-growing cadre of civil servants. Affairs of state and affairs of the home estate alike were most often managed by ambitious professionals.

In this new world, gentlemen like Huntingdon became utterly, strikingly unproductive. While a man of privilege might technically be a market producer (his land the site of a mine; his plantations abroad yielding spices, fruit, or tea), he was entirely estranged from the process of production. His hands were never dirtied; his brain was never taxed. He simply reaped the benefits of other people's labor. If a gentleman had no burning academic or artistic interests, what remained was not very much. There was outdoor sport (the hunt, horses); there was such indoor entertainment as billiards and amateur theatricals; there was the pursuit of ladies and the company of other gentlemen; and there was dinner. Formerly the center of his domain, the gentleman was increasingly becoming an irrelevance, a body to be kept up and cared for by legions of servants and other functionaries, removed from the business of the swift-moving century.[11] This is certainly the case with Arthur, as Helen notes:

I wish he had something to do, some useful trade or profession, or employment—anything to occupy his head
or his hands for a few hours a day, and give him something besides his own pleasure to think about. If he
would play the country gentleman, and attend to the
farm—but that he knows nothing about, and won't give
his mind to consider,—or if he would take up with some
literary study, or learn to draw or to play—as he is so
fond of music, I often try to persuade him to learn the
piano, but he is far too idle for such an undertaking: he
has no more idea of exerting himself to overcome obstacles than he has of restraining his natural appetites;
these two things are the ruin of him. (238)

Here Helen seems to look to boredom as the cause of Arthur's behavior, proposing (in good middle-class fashion) that if only he had
"something to do," her young husband would give up drink and bad
behavior at once. But the occupations that Helen proposes are, of
course, untenable for a man like Huntingdon. Reading, drawing,
and playing the piano are the occupations of ladies, and Huntingdon cannot take them up without running the risk of feminizing
himself. Conversely, he cannot "attend to the farm" without lessening his status—a dangerous proposition in the age of the striver,
when the gentleman's state suddenly required an endless and difficult process of reassertion.

Helen's diagnosis of boredom as the root of all of Huntingdon's troubles is of a piece with late eighteenth-century and early
nineteenth-century understandings of upscale overconsumption,
particularly of habitual intoxication. William Cadogan's 1771 "Dissertation on the Gout," for example, seems a textbook clinical
summary of Huntingdon's behavior with his fellows: too much
luxury and too much excess, Cadogan argues, necessarily leads to
more of the same.

Indolence, blunting all our sensations, naturally leads us
to intemperance: we want the whip and spur of luxury
to excite our jaded appetites. There is no enduring the
perpetual moping langour [sic] of indolence; we fly to

the stimulating sensualities of the table and the bottle,
friend provokes friend to exceed, and accumulate one
evil upon another; a joyous momentary relief is obtained,
to be paid for severely soon after; the next morning our
horrors increase, and in this course there is no remedy
but repetition. Thus whoever is indolent is intemperate
also, and partly from necessity. (46)

But Huntingdon's constant, excessive, and self-destructive drinking is not solely attributable to a desire to counter monotony: indeed, he drinks whether or not there is anything else to do. Rather
than being a cause in itself, his boredom is a crucial indicator of the
real motivator behind Huntingdon's drinking: it is a sign of the social and economic forces that turn the high-spirited young lover
into a serious drunkard.

While the gentleman, left with nothing to do, was vilified for
his more or less enforced leisure, his very status *as* a gentleman—
and, further, the class system itself—was under attack from the
same quarters. Even as the gentlemanly body was delineated as a
wasteful, unproductive anachronism, the striver aspired to emulate
the trappings of that body to mark his own success. The remedy for
the increasing difficulty of telling old money apart from new money
was a perpetual resetting of the requirements for genteel life (Mennell, 209): while the social climbers of the middle classes gained
money and the commodities of rarefied status, the stakes for position in terms of material possessions were necessarily and constantly
raised, so that visible signs of gentlemanliness (houses, clothing,
carriages) became increasingly unstable. Because two of the three
primary markers of heritable class—money, land, and blood—
could now be seamlessly acquired, the gentleman, to maintain his
standing, was forced to actively guard the notion that the invisible
quality that truly constituted class was bred in the bone and thus
hovered perpetually beyond the reach of the striver. This was particularly true for the landed gentleman of old wealth who was not
a member of the aristocracy: inherited titles still served as solid
class markers, but in the absence of a title, a name was no longer
sufficient. If *Tenant*'s Gilbert embodies the upwardly mobile middle-
class man, then, Huntingdon's role is to demonstrate that his is an

inborn position, that his rank is carried in his blood, unwinnable through labor and striving. At the same time that he finds himself strikingly superannuated, he must also seek constantly to differentiate himself from the forces that threaten to erase him.

Arthur's solution is to turn to the useless with a vengeance: to embrace the vision of parasitic gentlemanliness promulgated by the business-minded, temperance-inflected rhetoric of the middle class. Take, for example, Huntingdon's courtship of Helen: even in the midst of this most charged and socially difficult of operations, he can talk of nothing but gossip, drink, and triviality and can occupy himself only with petty games, mean flirtations with Annabella, and pointless pursuits (billiards, smoking). The very frivolity of such practices is important: their unproductive nature is exactly what is gentlemanly about them. Arthur's anger at Helen's destruction of his portrait is also indicative of the state of the gentleman. Though Huntingdon treats his pursuit of Helen very much as a game, he cannot allow his idolatrous image to be trifled with: his position in this narrow world as the most handsome, the most charming, and the most looked-at man in every room, the figure who is in command of everything around him (though to no apparent purpose except the gratification of his vanity), is all that is left to him.

Even Huntingdon's putatively productive activities are no more useful to society and are equally caught up in the rhetoric of empty possession: he pursues women, collecting and retailing conquests as a sign of his attractiveness and virility, the stock-in-trade that is left to him; and he brings forth a son, a child whom he seeks to train up as a man in his own pattern. In the shooting season, he "find[s] occupation in the pursuit and destruction of the partridges and pheasants" (238), which, as Helen says, "serves to get the time on . . . and gives him some better employment than the sottish indulgence of his sensual appetites" (331). But even hunting is antiproductive, the opposite of useful efficiency: it is nothing more than a mock pursuit of sustenance, a meticulously staged enactment of the stereotypical role of brutal provider (Huntingdon returns from his sport "all spattered and splashed . . . with the blood of his prey" [177]) played out on estates carefully stocked with the requisite victims. It is productive of an inassimilable overabundance, an excess of aliment that nobody particularly needs.

These activities in and of themselves are, however, insufficient
to signal Huntingdon's gentlemanliness: entirely directed outward,
dependent on the participation of others, and open to co-opting by
the striving classes in any case, these temporary antidotes fail to
constitute him, to fundamentally mark him. In the face of this failure, Brontë's gentleman of leisure is compelled, as it were, to go to
work to hold onto his place in the social order: his job is the production of his own gentlemanliness, the endless reiteration of his
own status. And because that status is an empty marker, a sign of
his social and internal barrenness, he seeks to perform his role by
filling himself with the stuff of gentlemanliness: to create a sense of
inherence by using food and drink to make himself into a man who
is indisputably a gentleman. The idea of the depraved Regency rake,
who produces nothing but destruction with his drunken binges and
his indulgence of insatiable appetites of all kinds, is precisely the
sort of image most useful to the middle-class political project of re-
fashioning the possibility of the social and excluding the privileged
from automatic power.[12] These habits of indulgence are precisely
what the gentleman seeks refuge in, reinforcing his class position
through his refusal to limit his appetites.

Aliment is the ideal means of separating himself from the striving masses, a means not only of filling himself from the inside out
with the acquirable stuff of gentlemanliness but also of demonstrating the extent of his credentials. John Burnett argues that in the
nineteenth century, "[i]n nothing was the contrast between wealth
and poverty more obvious than in food. House, dress, or manners
might still be a misleading test of income . . . but a man's dinner-
table instantly announced his standard of living to the world at
large" (71). But food demonstrates more than just income. A display of appropriate fare is a sign of an inherent understanding of
one's position in the world, of the appropriate construction of the
self vis-à-vis class position. Pierre Bourdieu writes of this phenomenon that

> [t]astes in food . . . depend on the idea each class has of
> the body and of the effects of food on the body . . . and
> on the categories it uses to evaluate these effects . . .
> which the different classes may rank in very different

ways. . . . Taste, a class culture turned into nature, that is, *embodied*, helps to shape the class body. It is an incorporated principle of classification which governs all forms of incorporation, choosing and modifying everything that the body ingests and digests and assimilates, physiologically and psychologically. It follows that the body is the most indisputable materialization of class taste. . . . It is in fact through preferences with regard to food which may be perpetuated beyond their social conditions of production . . . and also, of course, through the uses of the body in work and leisure which are bound up in them, that the class distribution of bodily properties is determined. (*Distinction*, 190)

In Brontë's day, this notion was literalized and looped: there were (as temperance rhetoric implicitly suggests) still many believers in a digestively classed universe who held that members of different genders and classes had fundamentally different constitutions and thus were able to digest different fare. The poor, for instance, were (conveniently) thought to be more capable than the rich of surviving on the rough and unpalatable food that was generally their lot;[13] similarly, the ultrarefined fare of the rich was thought to be peculiarly appropriate to rarefied bodily plumbing (Mennell, 26). The rhetoric was, of course, useful in propping up the notion of truly heritable class: this inborn bodily sumptuary code made the notion of the gentlemanly table seem inherent and thus beyond the grasp of the social climber, even when social climbing made all other markers of the upper class achievable.

Aliment, then, serves as a crucial sign of status: a clear means of displaying one's wealth and sophistication, it also seems a means of ingesting class, of swallowing the gentlemanliness one always already has whole at table and in that way making it manifest.[14] Perhaps equally important is that it facilitates the demonstration of class through particular alimentary refusal. To fill and thus to refashion the body with the fare of the striver—to value aliment that grants speed and efficiency, with its ties to the marketplace, the factory, and the City—is, for a gentleman like Huntingdon, to give in to the notion of social transformation through labor, to accept the worldview of the rising classes, to capitulate. By taking in the diet of industrialism, Arthur must in a sense deliver himself up to its ethos. To a gentleman like Arthur, such a position is impossible, intolerable: it erases his entire raison d'être, refuses the validity of his wealth and position, and insists that he earn his way in the world to justify his existence. It colludes in the notion of the man of leisure as a social parasite who needs to be repaired to fit more smoothly into a reorganized social structure based on energy, expertise, and merit rather than on tradition, blood, and privilege. For Huntingdon, ingestion of the fare endorsed by the middle class is an act of self-poisoning.

To place himself outside of the world of work, which seeks either to co-opt him or to shut him out of power entirely, Huntingdon must swallow fare that allows the gentlemanly body to insist on its validity beyond the moral strictures and social insistences of the rising classes: fare that is antiproductive, antiorderly, irrational. Indeed, to save himself, the gentleman—historically marked by his distance from the bodily, his rhetorical and social near-erasure of his physical self[15] (an ideal very much taken up, for instance, in the nearly see-through Mr. Lawrence, Helen's brother)—must re-embody the body, making himself corporeal, even grossly so, to preserve his status as a member of the elite not governed by the suppression and mechanization of the body.

Accordingly, Huntingdon turns resolutely away from the highly ordered regime of middle-class meals and the orderly body this regime is meant to produce. He spends his breakfast hours intriguing, teasing his wife, or reading his mail (or sleeps through the meal entirely); drinks coffee not in the morning to fuel his work but at noon to recover from the night before; never seems to lunch on anything at all; and regularly skips tea. Safely removed from those well-defined, productive meals, Huntingdon gorges himself at his late dinners, reinforcing his class position through his appetites. More antiproductively, he drinks. As the mad carousing, drunken wrestling, and inebriated nonsensical babbling and toasting of Huntingdon and his friends clearly demonstrate, alcohol is all about reveling in the body and refusing the tyranny of rational control.

Alcohol is a liminal food (Lupton, 31): it puts its consumer into a state not easily defined except as itself, between consciousness and unconsciousness, control and chaos. This in-between state, a source of discomfort for advocates of order and hierarchy, also subverts the mind, threatening it with the chaos of the brainless gross corpus. Rather than serving as a civilizing force, a locus of education in morals and manners, as the Victorians thought of it,[16] the table thus becomes the seat of the anticivilized, the birthplace of bad behavior. By filling his body with that which is interdicted by the industrial order, Huntingdon flouts the rules, refuses change that refuses him, feeding a social sphere that strivers like Gilbert would like to starve out of existence.

Further, alcohol leaves its mark after it has been swallowed—in drunkenness, then in the aftereffects of drunkenness, and eventually, permanently, on the face and body, "mak[ing] his eyes dull, and his face red and bloated" (330). While these marks may not be beautifying, they are visible traces of leisure, indulgence, and inherently gentlemanly appetites. In this way, they make high-class gentlemanly blood visible to the naked eye, trumpeting the drinker's difference from the pale, sharp office worker.

And so Huntingdon marks both body and behavior through drink, producing only riot and waste and thus avoiding gentlemanly obliteration. Despite his protestations, this is the case from the beginning—a fact made clear not only in his stories of London dissipation, in his flirtation with Annabella, and in the persistent rumors of his troublesome past, but also in his physicality. Helen's quiet friend Millicent, who finds him too "bold—and reckless," also objects that his "face is too red" (195), correctly reading the telltale signs where Helen sees only "a pleasant glow—a healthy freshness in his complexion, the warm, pink tint of the whole harmonizing with the deeper colour of the cheeks, exactly as it ought to do" (196).

Marriage and fatherhood drive Huntingdon further into the bottle. Adherence to the marital regime brings him closer to the social realm he must flout to maintain his status—as his friends make clear in the letters responding to his announcement of his engagement, letters full "of bitter execrations and reproaches" in which his friends "say there'll be no more fun now, no more merry days and glorious nights—and all [his] fault," for in being "the first to break up the jovial band," he has "shamefully betrayed [his] trust"

(197). Like Lowborough when he abstains from wine, Huntingdon is clearly breaking his compact with his boon companions, threatening to turn his back on their gentlemanly escapades and "reform"—that is, to bring himself into line with the prevailing social order.

As he leaves behind the utterly unencumbered life of the single man of wealth, begins to pay off his debts, and becomes a father, Huntingdon becomes at once more obviously outdated—a man of leisure stranded on his estate and choking on his idleness—and more imbricated in the useful, codified, socially structured life advocated by middle-class ideology. Though he seems, in his words to Helen during their courtship, to embrace this—he tells his fiancée that "the very idea of having [her] to care for under [his] roof would force [him] to . . . live like a Christian" and praises "the prudence and virtue [she] would instill into [his] mind by [her] wise counsels and sweet, attractive goodness" (188)—his marriage seems based on a fundamental misreading on his part: Arthur really wants a wife not to reform him but to adore him, to reaffirm his power and to demonstrate his gentlemanly badness by her very goodness, as Helen realizes. "[H]is idea of a wife," she notes, "is a thing to love one devotedly and to stay at home—to wait upon her husband, and amuse him and minister to his comfort in every way possible . . . and, when he is absent, to attend to his interests . . . and patiently wait his return; no matter how he may be occupied in the meantime" (256–57). Instead, he finds himself saddled with a wife complicit with the middle-class drive to subsume him. His "angel monitress," as he terms her (212), is, despite her gentle birth, the embodiment of the mythical middle-class True Woman, bent on saving her husband through reform: bemoaning his lack of "something to do—some useful trade, or profession, or employment," seeking "to have [his] thoughts changed . . . to think more deeply, to look farther, and aim higher" (219–20), determined to turn him, that is, into that dreaded creature: a productive member of society.

The only response for Arthur is refusal, and for Arthur, refusal is written in wine. Turning away from the middle-class myth of the sacred hearth and the angel in the house, Huntingdon flees home for his London club, a substitute "home" (202) devoted to the undermining of order and the indulgence of those appetites that the angel in the house is meant to restrain. Desecrating the hearth of home, he and his friends descend on Grass-dale to make merry, flouting the alimental rules of the social order by drinking their way through the coffee hour and disrupting and degrading the civilized, feminized rituals of tea with their drunken carousing. In all seasons and all weathers, under all circumstances, he commits himself to drunkenness. In this way, he saves himself from being entirely sidelined while avoiding usefulness and thus class eradication.

Drinking also solves the problem inherent in the purposefully purposeless life of leisure: ennui. Sober, Huntingdon is unbearably bored at home. A rainy day is enough to kill him, as Helen's description of his sorry state during their first fight makes clear:

> [P]oor Arthur was sadly at a loss for something to amuse him or to occupy his time[;] . . . had the weather at all permitted, he would doubtless have ordered his horse and set off to some distant region[;] . . . had there been a lady anywhere within reach . . . he would have . . . found employment in getting . . . a . . . flirtation with her; but being . . . entirely cut off from both these sources of diversion, his sufferings were truly deplorable. When he had done yawning over his paper and scribbling short answers to his shorter letters, he spent the remainder of the morning and the whole of the afternoon in fidgeting about from room to room, watching the clouds, cursing the rain, alternately petting, and teasing, and abusing his dogs, sometimes lounging on the sofa with a book that he could not force himself to read. (224)

No wonder that at the end of such a day, Arthur "made a long stay in the dining-room after dinner, and . . . took an unusual quantity of wine" (224). Drinking obviates the problem of boredom: his refusal of the productive, rational, and Godly order Helen represents is made manifest in "madness, folly and brutality" (354), the triumph of the irrational gross body over the mind searching for something to do. Huntingdon calls this being his "own man": his gentlemanliness demands a determined lack of control, which paradoxically is the only way to control his own life. Even when he is hung over, his painful state is not a sign of pathetic uselessness but the result of manly, worldly activity: as he boasts, "If you knew all, my girl, you'd say . . . 'What a wonder it is you can bear it so well as you do!' I've lived more in these last four months, Helen, than you have in the whole course of your existence, or will to the end of your days . . . so I must expect to pay for it in some shape" (269). His condition is a proud marker of gentlemanly prerogative: unlike a homebound woman or a workingman chained to a desk, he has the freedom and the wherewithal to plunge into excess and riot. And the effects of his excesses even serve to recast his role in his marriage, making it more amenable to his gentlemanliness: if Helen is in charity with him, she becomes his "angel" and his handmaiden, and so his power over her is reaffirmed; if she is angry, he counters by commanding and bullying, throwing books at the dog, swearing at the butler, and thus reestablishing himself as the high, manly head of the household.

This behavior is of a piece with Huntingdon's overt insistence on his masculinity as the right to do what he wants, whenever he wants. He tells Helen, for instance, "I won't be dictated to by a woman, though she be my wife" (248)—thus refusing the gendered compact of his marriage, the terms under which Helen had accepted Arthur, in which she was to play the pious reformer and he was to be the flawed man who would "do [his] utmost . . . to remember and perform the injunctions of [his] angel monitress" (212). (His initial misreading, it becomes clear, is based precisely on his assumption that it is his right to do and say whatever he wants to gratify his "manly" desires; Arthur, of course, had no intention of reforming.) On the night when he seizes Helen's diary from her and ruins her initial plans of escape, he comments, "[I]t's well . . . I wasn't overfull to-night . . . or I might have lacked the sense or the power to carry my point like a man, as I have done" (373). Manliness, it seems, is composed at least in part of always putting oneself in command, even if one has nothing to command over but one's wife; such actions reiterate the gentleman's mastery over his narrow realm at the same time that they cast gentlemanly masculinity in direct opposition to femininity and thus to social rule and order. When Annabella Lowborough leaves Grass-dale after her husband's discovery of her affair with Huntingdon, her paramour "subsequently expressed himself rather glad she was gone: 'She was so deuced imperious and exacting,' said he; 'now I shall be my own man again, and feel rather more at my ease'" (353). For Huntingdon, being one's own man is impossible within the bounds of social constraints, which are embodied in women in *Tenant;* manliness demands a determined lack of control, which paradoxically is the only way to control one's own life. As he asks his wife, apparently rhetorically, "Do you think I have nothing to do but stay at home and take care of myself like a woman?" (266).[17]

Unsurprisingly, as Helen notes, Huntingdon's "appetite for the stimulus of wine . . . increase[s] upon him" as he follows the script of upper-class gentlemanly prerogative. "It was now something more to him than an accessory to social enjoyment: it was an important source of enjoyment in itself. . . . [H]e would have made it his medicine and support, his comforter, his recreation, and his friend" (272). Huntingdon soon needs, when in his cups, to be helped up the stairs to bed. He lies insensate on the couch after his binges; then he begins to pass out on the couch during his drinking sprees. He bloats. While drinking and gorging make him gentlemanly, it seems, they also break him down.

Although there were certainly doctors in Brontë's day, generally associated with the temperance movement, who associated excessive drinking with physical and mental deterioration,[18] it is striking that only Huntingdon, of all the band of boon companions, manages to drink himself into debility. On this front, Huntingdon's role as an untitled but landed gentleman of old inherited money again comes to the fore—as does the peculiar idleness increasingly endemic to gentlemen of this particular stripe. Whereas his grandfather might have used a hearty dinner to fuel an afternoon's gentlemanly work, Huntingdon consumes vast meals to fuel nothing but leisure. The useless idle body fails to expend what it takes in; all that food and drink has nowhere to go.[19] Leisure, evoked through Huntingdon's diet, is the cause of his poisoning even as it is the mark of his status, the double-edged proof of his outsider status with reference to the marketplace. Even as it kills him, leisure demands more and creates an insatiable appetite: while Huntingdon labors to prove himself a leisured gentleman beyond the bounds of middle-class social expectations, he must also continually consume, both to re-create the states of useless inebriety or useless recovery that mark him as gentlemanly and to demonstrate his mastery even of this state. Further, a failure to endlessly enact drunkenness must be read as "reform"—that is, as capitulation, a return of the body to potential productivity, a settling of the mind in accordance with an aspirational culture—an erasure. This is why he has "an infernal fire in [his] veins, that all the waters of the ocean cannot quench" (265), why even in the depths of his illness he complains constantly of "cursed thirst" (433).

But while it is true that drink makes Huntingdon weak, tired, sickly, and cranky, this in and of itself separates him from the coffee-driven, suppressed, and repressed middle-class body. The debilitating effects of drink clarify that Arthur Huntingdon is not a productive corpus, a well-functioning mechanism subject to the tyranny of the clock. His drinking reaffirms his status: excess-driven illness, after all, is also a marker of class. Huntingdon himself, for instance, notices that "he was getting a trifle fatter . . . than was quite desirable—but that was with good living and idleness" (279). Dr. J. Edwin Danelson, a popular nineteenth-century writer-physician, noted that although "the accumulation of fat in superfluity is a disease," it was also an indicator of wealth: "It attends indolence, and excessive eating and drinking. . . . Persons of settled income, the recipients of generous annuities and the wealthy, usually are, or grow to be fleshy" (367).

Huntingdon's condition is evocative of the most famous class-marked malady to afflict the rich: gout, the disease that debilitates and finally kills Helen's dissolute uncle.[20] Since the seventeenth century, gout had been widely regarded as a manifestation of gentlemanly blood and thus as much an incontrovertible marker of class as a scourge. As George Ellwanger wrote in 1897, "From its being usually attributed to luxury and close familiarity with the rarer products of the vine, Gout is sometimes supposed . . . to be a rather desirable companion than otherwise—the acquaintance with which confers a certain title of distinction upon the possessor" (9–10). Doctors believed that the gouty gentleman overfilled his body with too much rich food and failed to eliminate it through appropriate exercise (Porter and Rousseau, 142). Huntingdon's plight is very much of a piece with this notion: stuffed to bursting with wine and excess and undisturbed by any labor except the labor of eating and drinking, his body begins to self-destruct and to shut itself down, just as the immobilized gouty gentleman's body does. Like the gouty gentleman, Huntingdon thus writes class on his body through his very incapacity, letting his rarefied bloodlines show through.

But habitual drunkenness also undermines Huntingdon's gentlemanliness, even as it demonstrates his position through the swelling immobility it brings. The playful but irresponsible young lover turns into a brutal, boorish, besotted husband who can deny himself nothing; drink makes him "sick and stupid" (291). The formerly finicky gentleman's appetites begin to coarsen in new ways. No longer limiting himself to wine, for example, he indulges in gin, the most lower-class of drinks, aligning himself with that other "leisured" class, the other site of gross corporeality, the unemployed poor.[21] By the time Helen leaves him, his appetites have become thoroughly debased, just as his taste in women has slid from Helen to Annabella Lowborough, his friend's selfish, scheming wife, to the toadying Miss Myers, the supposed governess. Each downward slip leaves him sicker, angrier, and more isolated. In this way, he is poisoned precisely by his distance from community, by the unknown that he consumes in his reckless attempt to flee the killing safety of the social order: the control that Huntingdon necessarily cedes in his quest for rule-free living and unchecked consumption helps to bring about his downfall.

In gendered terms, too, drink is Huntingdon's undoing: even as he becomes his "own man" through his "orgies," he unmans himself. Under the influence, he is far too weak to act; assaulted by the equally drunken Hattersley, "he laugh[s] and shriek[s] alarmingly" (291). The aftereffects of drink further feminize him. He becomes peevish, petty, temperamental, and cruel, a slave to his moods and passions. His "nerves [are] racked and torn to pieces" (266); "his beauty strangely diminished, his vigour and vivacity quite departed," Helen reports, "[h]e lies on the sofa nearly all day long"; he is "flushed and feverish, listless and languid" (237). His gentlemanly self-actualization through drink turns him, in other words, into the archetypal weak and emotional Victorian fainting lady.

In the last stage of his drinking career, Huntingdon is completely debilitated. He is confined to bed—the victim of a dangerous fever and internal injury from a riding accident that "would have been but trifling to a man of temperate habits" (428). He is, at last, all body: only intermittently conscious and in terrible pain, he exists only as a corpus to be fed, cooled, medicated, and soothed, and in this way he has succeeded in his project of writing himself out of the capitalist industrial striver narrative. But abandoned by friends, lovers, and all but the most vicious hired help, he has simultaneously lost any grip on rule and status. Helen returns to Arthur to nurse him, but she has no interest in reinstating him in his former sphere: she seeks, as he suspects, to reform him. She has come, she tells him, "to offer you that comfort and assistance your situation required; and . . . benefit your soul as well as your body, and awaken some sense of contrition" (430). In this endeavor she fails almost completely, despite Arthur's suffering and his manifest fear of death. To understand why Huntingdon chooses the death he dreads over sobriety, one must look closely at Helen's language and at her approach to the problem of drink. As Arthur seems to understand, Helen is now uninterested in mere temperance: instead, she seeks to feed him a new antidrink philosophy along with her cooling tonics, and in so doing, this middle-class avatar most clearly threatens to rob her husband of his remaining gentlemanly status.

As her retraining of her son makes clear, Helen has long been moving away from mere temperance and toward something more powerful. Her rhetoric, methodologies, and approaches suggest that she finds a home in the teetotal movement (though the movement, like the striver philosophy of the text in general, is contemporaneous not with the novel's fictional timing but with Brontë's day). The new antidrinking activists of the late 1830s and the 1840s were of a very different breed than the moderate temperance workers. Teetotalers were full-fledged social activists who believed that all drinking was dangerous, that alcohol was the scourge of society, and that drinkers at every level of the social ladder, of every age, from both genders, and at all stages of progress in drunkenness could be redeemed by heeding the call of reform, signing the teetotalers' pledge, and giving up drink forever. Though the teetotalers emerged from the moderate temperance movement, the split between the two groups soon became profound. Two·key ideas at the center of the teetotal movement separated it from its predecessor: the pledge of absolute abstention from alcohol and the belief that any soul desiring salvation could be saved from the demon drink. The teetotalers put their faith only in absolute abstinence—not only for reforming drunkards but also (as in the case of little Arthur) for those who were not yet drunkards but might have a propensity for drink, particularly through inheritance (Shiman, 18). Adherence to the creed meant no wine at table, no port after dinner, no alcohol for medical purposes.

And the teetotalers, who felt that no soul was beyond recall, refused to limit themselves to working-class drinkers: in direct contradiction to the temperance ethos, they insisted that anyone could potentially fall into drunkenness. Even aristocrats, they argued, could be drunkards, and even aristocrats could be reformed. Wealthy teetotalers swore to cease providing wine for their friends, to fire servants who drank, and to boycott functions at which alcohol was served—in other words, to refuse the entire network of social relations on which the upper-class economy was built. High-ranking Anglican clergymen and upscale patrons had no interest in allying themselves with a group that embraced confirmed drunkards without apology or embarrassment and preached that lords and gentlemen could be drunkards, too, effectively refusing to see innate differences between people of different classes.

Instead, nonconformist preachers and working-class speakers in the northern provinces became the teetotalers' advocates,[22] and radical politics were fused with alimentary reform. The movement became a proving ground for ambitious but poverty-stricken men, offering a genuine means of social advancement to those who were charismatic, eloquent, and energetic in their exhortations to their peers to change their world by giving up the demon drink. Teetotalers were often highly political animals, savvy social reformers who understood the potential that such a morally inflected movement held for making real change beyond the limits of its most obvious mission. Often allied with Chartists, anti–Corn Law activists, and others within the worker movements (Shiman, 32), leaders were determined to forge bonds between the middle and working classes and eventually to replace the aristocracy and the system it still putatively ran with a revolutionary democracy. "The rise of teetotalism constitute[d] a *coup* by an élite of working men allied with radicals and nonconformists . . . [and] offered the attractions of a sudden and dramatic social transformation" (Harrison, 137–38). The teetotal movement was indeed radical, and the novel's espousal of that movement is, in the context of its time, at least as shocking as its portrayal of the drunken gentleman. The most scandalous aspect of Brontë's work for her contemporaries may well have been her embrace of such socially revisionary notions through the device of her dissection of the anatomy of gentlemanly drunkenness.

There are many evocations of the movement in *Tenant*: Helen's move from a belief in moderation to an ardent advocacy of abstinence; the behavior modification she uses on her son, lacing wine and spirits with tartar emetic to instill a hatred of drink in him; her pious sermons to the bedbound Huntingdon; and in particular, her insistence that reform and forgiveness are always within the grasp of those who truly repent, an assertion that is entirely of a piece with the Methodist-inflected democratic rhetoric of the teetotalers. She finds, for instance, that her husband fears death, and she keeps that specter before him, explaining calmly, "If a consciousness of the uncertainty of life can dispose you to serious and useful thoughts, I would not deprive you of the benefit of such reflections, whether you do eventually recover or not" (434). When he asks, "Where's the use of a probationary existence, if a man may spend it as he pleases, just contrary to God's decrees, and then go to heaven with the best—if the vilest sinner may win the reward of the holiest saint, by merely repeating, 'I repent'?" she insists that "sincere" penitence may yet open the pearly gates for him (450).

Helen's insistence that the bedbound Huntingdon sign a "written agreement" (431) ceding control of their son to her before she allows him to see the child is also of a piece with the teetotaler narrative: though she creates no legally binding contract, she does evoke the pledge of abstinence that the reforming drinker was obliged to sign. The pledge was a major document, in which the sinner promised to leave the drinking world entirely, to give up pub evenings and the companionship of his friends and coworkers for the society of nondrinkers and reformed drinkers affiliated with the organizations.[23] Whereas the moderates offered talks and tracts in a sort of trickle-down theory of temperance, the teetotalers insisted on immediate, responsible involvement on the part of the reforming drinkers. The pledge was generally accompanied by a verbal confession of the signatory's drinking sins, and these often-salacious stories (ending, of course, in miraculous reform) frequently formed the basis for teetotal lectures. Though these conversion narratives were secularized, they had the hallmarks of enthusiasm and unquestioning belief; but they also bore the frisson of the forbidden, and the scandalous stories of drink and depravity that formed the core of the tales did no harm to a fledgling movement fishing for members (Harrison, 131). Of course, these stories of miraculous abstinence and hard-won reform were in themselves classed, marking the social rising of the transgressor even as they confirmed his lower status as a subject of legitimate but nonetheless prurient scopophilia.

Helen's diary is very much of a piece with this style of confessional: she offers the long, licentious, and wicked tale of the rich gentleman whose behavior cries out for reform. The errors of the drunkard, recounted in salacious detail, conform exactly to the contentions of the teetotalers concerning moderation: the drinker's appetites increase with each taste, and abstinence is manifestly the only possible refuge from the coming fall. Through the device of the confession, Helen attempts to wrest control of the narrative from her husband; in returning to him, she seeks to cap off her story with an appropriate ending and thus to give him an interiority different from the one that he attempts to create through drink.

But Huntingdon opts out of the tale: he refuses to adhere to the reform narrative, even as he undergoes the ritual trial-by-fire of his illness. "I *can't* repent," he insists; "I only fear" (450). He declares, that is, that it is impossible for him to be saved—and with good reason. By invoking the language and the methods of the teetotaling crusader in her efforts to save her husband, Helen goes far beyond the condescending class inscription that moderate temperance inevitably invokes. Instead, she threatens to imbricate him in the quasi-democratic, unapologetically meritocratic philosophy that the teetotal movement embodies. By turning him into the scopophilic subject of the mixed-class teetotaler gaze, she attempts to make him part of a world in which social climbing is made possible through moral rectitude and communal dedication—a world in which the drunkard is reformed and socially "improved" by allowing others to feed him a diet of adherence and capitulation to a vision of the larger social good, which effectively includes the eradication of class itself.

And while the teetotaler narrative seeks to subvert class through what is taken into—or refused entry to—the body, it also, ironically, confirms the notion that Huntingdon's appetites are in his blood. Drawing on the idea of inherent tendencies toward drink, the teetotalers contend that the drinker must abstain for life because every taste of alcohol is poison to him: he is portrayed as constitutionally incapable of containing his appetites. Whereas the gentleman must drink to retain his difference from the crowding middle classes, the drinker, in the teetotal ethos, must renounce the crowd by renouncing drink. The narrative creates, in effect, a new class of people, compounded from groups across the social spectrum, who opt out of the middle-class paradigm precisely by embracing it with unlimited ardor. It is, in effect, an über-strivers' realm, the antithesis of everything that Huntingdon represents. His capitulation must necessarily mean his obliteration.

This is the reason that Huntingdon turns to drink even when it is clearly lethal to him, as Helen recounts:

> [O]n finding she had covertly diluted the pale port that was brought him, he threw the bottle out of the window, swearing he would not be cheated like a baby, ordered the butler, on pain of instant dismissal, to bring a bottle of the strongest wine in the cellar, and, affirming that he should have been well long ago if he had been let to have his own way, but she wanted to keep him weak in order that she might have him under her thumb—but by the Lord Harry, he would have no more humbug—seized a glass in one hand and the bottle in the other, and never rested till he had drunk it dry. Alarming symptoms were the immediate result. . . . Every former feature of his malady had returned with augmented virulence: the slight external wound, half-

healed, had broken out afresh; internal inflammation had taken place, which might terminate fatally if not soon removed. (444–45)

The fare to which Huntingdon has turned to remake himself as a man has become entirely fatal to him: excess and drink, the crucial markers of his status, can no longer be assimilated by his body. His insides are inflamed with illness as he drops into fever. He is progressively mortified, literally and figuratively, by the aliment that has constituted him and filled him and failed to find an outlet. Helen writes that in the midst of the illness, a bleeding ordered by the doctor leaves Huntingdon "more subdued and tranquil" (433), reinforcing the notion that the trouble lies in her estranged husband's very veins. Gentlemanliness here becomes a state of atrophy: status is marked not by bloodlines but by fatally thickened blood.

By feeding him, over and over, the story of his potential reform and resurrection, Helen hopes to move Huntingdon from the realm of the abject into the position either of the living (the reformed drinker who saves his life by abstaining) or of the dead (the penitent sinner who asks forgiveness of his Maker). Instead, refusing and co-opting containment to the end, Huntingdon becomes, as Gilbert puts it, "a living corpse," progressively deprived of movement and sensation, rotting from within as his nutrient-free liquid diet embalms him alive. A more graphically abject creature cannot be imagined: he is literally the corpse that will not remove itself into death.[24] "Often," Helen recounts, "he dwelt with shuddering minuteness on the fate of his perishing clay—the slow, piecemeal dissolution already invading his frame; the shroud, the coffin, the dark, lonely grave, and all the horrors of corruption" (450). For Helen, Huntingdon is literally that which she has cast off which yet fails to part from her, that which she rejects but which is still, as she says, "a part of [her]self" (268). Huntingdon's abjection is a synecdochical evocation of the abjection of the gentleman of good blood vis-à-vis mid-nineteenth-century society: he is a creature of a past age that the present cannot seem to shake off, an embodiment of a system of position and rule that refuses to give up the ghost, so to speak, and make way for an order that values labor and merit above blood.

Helen's efforts instead nearly result in her own death, as Huntingdon seeks refuge from the horror that he sees waiting for him in the grave—erasure from the narrative—by clinging to Helen and, in effect, attempting to swallow her as the antidote to his fatal diet. "Helen, you *must* save me!" he implores (446), speaking not of his soul but of his body. As the illness progresses, his demands for her attention and care devour her, until she is, as Hattersley puts it, "worn to a shadow" (448). In his last days, Helen reports, he "clings to me with a kind of childish desperation, as if I could save him from the fate he dreads" (450). Speaking of his impending encounter with his Judgment Day, he laments, "I wish to God I could take you with me now! . . . [Y]ou should plead for me" (451). He hopes, it seems, to save himself by eating her alive, swallowing that which is marked safe but without digesting its safety himself, in the manner of the cannibalistic ideal of swallowing an opponent's strength with his flesh. By the time Huntingdon finally dies, he has "dragged her with him nearly to the portals of the grave," as Gilbert succinctly puts it (455). But his desperate attempts at autophagy as self-preservation are doomed to fail: Helen will not, cannot be absorbed into the idle gentlemanly body, despite her companionate claims to be flesh of her husband's flesh. Energetic, productive, responsible, and self-supporting, she is, for all of her wealth, a middle-class avatar. She is precisely that which threatens to blot him out, and she turns to poison in his mouth. The only escape available to Huntingdon, a creature constitutionally unable to bring his appetites into conformity with the status quo and his mind into line below God, is the closure of the grave.

His death seems to signal the end of abjection infecting the text; and, though she cannot bring her husband's story to the ending required by the teetotaler confession, Helen is able to haul the narrative back into line through other means, offering through her efforts a vision of a rightly ordered society freed from the poisonous demands of excess. While her labors on behalf of her son, for instance, are a successful enactment of the teetotaler's creed, it is in her relationship with Gilbert Markham that she most impressively takes up the narrative of forgiveness, responsibility, and reformation. In her relations with Gilbert, Helen puts Huntingdon's story to use just as the teetotalers did their members' testimonials: she first intrigues and titillates her suitor/reader (with her diary as with her person), then changes him from a violent, careless, selfish young man into a responsible, relatively self-controlled adult lover through the device of the tale of licentious abandon and its consequences. The boy who sulks and seethes, who beats Mr. Lawrence over the head with his whip handle and, in general, makes himself a misery to all around him is replaced with the rational, open-hearted man who requires only true love to render him complete. Similarly, the man "in a frenzy of ardour" who "seize[s] [Helen's] hand and would have pressed it to [his] lips," despite the fair lady's consternation—echoing both Huntingdon and Hargrave in his hungry pursuit of her (evoking Huntingdon's violent courtship, he catechizes Helen about her love for him; when she refuses to answer, he declares, "Then I will conclude you do," and when she turns away, he "[takes] her hand and fervently kisse[s] it" [123])—learns to bring his desires under control. The gentleman is constituted here precisely through the regulation of his appetites.

In this way, *Tenant* enacts a form of middle-class usurpation, suggesting that the leisured class is killing itself off with its leisured status and that to remain healthy, the body politic must excise this parasite, so that a figure more productively imbricated in society may take its place. Gilbert's status as a gentleman who is also a working farmer implies that his replacement of Huntingdon in Helen's affections—and, finally, in marriage—resuscitates gentlemanliness as a useful, socially redeemed state; his healthy appetites, predicated on productive activity and now appropriately controlled, offer a palatable counterpoint to the stuffed but never sated gent. Gilbert, the reluctant farmer who nevertheless shoulders his responsibility and provides for his family, is transformed by Helen's redemptive narrative, then rewarded for his hard work and ambition—sweetly enclosed in the sugar pill of true love and devotion—with the riches that have come to her from her no-good husband and her gout-ridden uncle.

Though Gilbert ends up a man of leisure, he is, unlike the previous owner of his money, able to use his time productively—in this case, by turning the story that the novel retails into a commodity to be consumed by his brother-in-law. And Gilbert's satisfaction with his lot hints at constitutional energies and internal resources that allow him to remain in the productive economy even in the midst of a life of leisure. He has earned his place—by fighting, like a knight-errant of old, for his lady-love and completing a voyage of enlightenment and self-discovery—and it fits him comfortably.

By removing Huntingdon from the moral sphere and relegating traditional gentlemanliness to impossible appetites, then, the novel clears a space for the productive, reformable, deserving, earning gent, thus condemning the Huntingdon-esque gentleman to extinction. The power of the cautionary confession as a socioeconomically transformative tool is made abundantly evident: a yeoman farmer becomes a new-style meritocratic landed gentleman. Though the transubstantiation is muted by Gilbert's narration of the process, it is startling in its ambition and in the possibility for the fundamental resetting of the social hierarchy that it portends.

Brontë's text, then, succeeds in its radical discourse; but the novel's revisionary work is troubled by this pilgrim's very progress. It is worth noting that Gilbert—the useful, active farmer who shoulders his responsibilities despite his inclinations in other directions—increasingly neglects his work on the farm as the narrative progresses. Helen is the catalyst for this: he leaves his fields to bring her a book in the midst of hay making, then refuses to work at all when he mistakenly believes that Helen has duped him ("I had no interest in anything now," he says [131], evoking Huntingdon). After he reads the diary and makes up with Helen, "[t]here was but little business done. . . . The farm was abandoned to the labourers, and the labourers were abandoned to their own devices" (411–12). When he is parted from his beloved, he returns to work, as Eliza notices, and as the separation stretches between Gilbert and Helen after Huntingdon's death, he becomes more and more productive.

But of course, Gilbert's marriage to the heiress makes his labors obsolete: he removes himself from the realm of fecund productivity and "bequeath[es] the farm to Fergus" (490). He lauds his brother's new interest in work, which is spurred by that erstwhile badger-baiter's desire "not only to gain [his beloved's] affection and esteem, and to obtain a fortune sufficient to enable him to aspire to her hand, but to render himself worthy of her, in his own eyes" (490). But Gilbert himself seems to have left the world of character-imparting labor far behind. A long way away from the "dusty, noisy, toiling, striving city" that his correspondent resides in (490), Gilbert has allowed the striver's age to pass him by: what he has worked for, it seems, is precisely the sort of idle gentlemanliness that he seemed at first glance to render obsolete.

In his framing letter, Gilbert describes how, ensconced in his study on a rainy day, he has "withdrawn [his] well-roasted feet from the hobs [and] wheeled round to the table" (34). Like Huntingdon before him, the once-active Mr. Markham is no longer bounding over hedges and racing up hills; in fact, like the incapacitated Huntingdon, he seems incapable of getting out of his chair. The scene calls to mind the wheeled chairs that accommodated those suffering from attacks of gout, suggesting that the overstuffed gentlemanly body may be inevitably acquired by those who seek out its place, regardless of birth. Despite the middle-class insistence on the poisonous nature of the stuff that perpetually fills Huntingdon's glass, Gilbert's stilled and idle body in the wheeled chair denotes a powerful thirst, in this striver avatar, for class, that most intoxicating, most poisonous elixir.

three

"By Heaven I must eat
at the cost of some other man!"

Gluttons and Hunger Artists | *Little Dorrit*

The texts in the previous chapters are concerned with the establishment and maintenance of inherited class status; Charles Dickens's
Little Dorrit (1857) looks at gentlemanliness from a very different
point of view. Erasing the possibility of born class entirely, *Little Dorrit* (in line with Dickens's ongoing project of social critique) posits a
gentlemanliness that is all appetite: a nightmare of capitalist getting
and spending in which class and position are predicated on a continual, monstrous swallowing of every bite of food on offer, in which
every morsel that a man consumes in pursuit of gentlemanly place
leads to the starvation of some other body. This narrative of grasping
is colluded in by those who are being starved into nothingness, precisely because it is cloaked in a story of neofeudal gentlemanly droit
du seigneur. Here the work of the gentleman is the labor of sustaining this cover story of deserving, inborn, historically continuous
gentlemanly prerogative; and since all consuming seems predicated
on this double discourse of capitalism and heritable rights, a gentleman who refuses to mouth this tale risks starving to death.

In *Little Dorrit*, as Ian Watt writes, "the attitude of the characters toward eating and drinking is deeply diagnostic" (167). The

novel begins with a signal moment of appetite that sets the terms
for gentlemanliness and aliment across the narrative. In a prison
cell in Marseilles, the murderer Rigaud and his temporary servant,
the good-hearted little Italian thief Cavalletto, while away the hours
gambling for food, thinking of food, waiting for food. The first spo-
ken words in the novel embody frustrated desire, energy, and naked
want: "Get up, pig!" Rigaud orders Cavalletto. "Don't sleep when
I am hungry!" (41). While Cavalletto is made animal in this first
phrase, it is Rigaud who "wait[s] to be fed . . . with much of the
expression of a wild beast" (41). Yet when the prisoners are fed
through the bars of their cage, the meal becomes a clear marker of
Rigaud's class status. The prison warden delivers "sausage in a vine
leaf . . . veal in savoury jelly . . . three white little loaves . . . cheese
. . . wine . . . tobacco—all for Monsieur Rigaud. Lucky bird!" as the
warden apostrophizes (43).

But though "[p]erhaps he glanced" at Rigaud's fine fare (45),
Cavalletto does not begrudge him his food, and Rigaud understands
why: as the ravenous murderer puts it, "You knew from the first moment when you saw me here, that I was a gentleman" (47). Cavalletto's response is appropriately complex: "'ALTRO!' returned John
Baptist, closing his eyes and giving his head a most vehement toss.
The word being, according to its Genoese emphasis, a confirmation, a contradiction, an assertion, a denial, a taunt, a compliment,
a joke, and fifty other things, became, in the present instance, with
a significance beyond all power of written expression, our familiar
English 'I believe you!'" (47).

Cavalletto knows his place: he takes the dregs of the wine Rigaud
offers "gratefully" (though "[i]t was no great gift, for there was mighty
little wine left" [46]); he disposes of the bottle, he lights the "master['s]" cigarette (46), he sits comfortably on the floor while Rigaud
commands the ledge with the little bit of outside light. He does all
this because, as Rigaud puts it, "A gentleman I am! A gentleman
I'll live, and a gentleman I'll die! It's my intent to be a gentleman.
It's my game. Death of my soul, I play it out wherever I go!" (48).

For Rigaud, a gentleman displays "a quick perception"; he has
"humour . . . ease . . . insinuating manners . . . a good appearance"
(402). He is a man of "fairness" and "chivalry" (49); he "do[es]
everything graciously" (819). He is "proud," and it is "also [his]

character to govern" (49). A gentleman, according to Rigaud, can-not be "a man of business" (399): he is one who is served, one who does no labor. And, of course, for Rigaud, a gentleman is one who eats well.

But this gentleman's meal is passing strange. He has used his winnings to buy a mixed-up meal of dainties and inflammatory fare: sausage (eaten for breakfast, generally highly spiced, thought to inflame the senses and to gird men for battle with the day); veal in savory jelly (expensive invalid fare: extremely nice, extremely easy to digest—often eaten by ailing old women of means); and then, of course, white bread (the bleached flour, sign of his refine-ment, removes bread from the category of staple and renders it a luxury appropriate to the bodily maintenance of a gentleman), cheese to finish the meal, wine to wash it down, and tobacco—not gentlemanly cigars but the more vulgar, new-fashioned cigarettes. The blending of breakfast and dinner; the mixed bodily messages of sickness and health, masculinity and femininity; the rough last touch of the cigarette, both modern and vulgar: Rigaud's gentle-manliness hardly seems predicated on an innate sense of what is appropriate to the gentlemanly body or on lived knowledge of how a gentleman eats. Instead, a meal seemingly intended to demon-strate that he is "a gentleman," as he repeatedly puts it (49), seems instead to show that he is anything but one.

And there is another sign that this is not a gentleman in the mode, for example, of Austen's Mr. Woodhouse: Rigaud eats rav-enously, swallowing his gorgeous repast faster than Cavalletto downs his meager loaf, and then "proceed[s] to suck his fingers as clean as he [can]" (45), ensuring that not a single morsel goes to waste. This greedy hunger of Rigaud's is not simply a product of the hardships of prison. He eats this way not only when he is in the character of an imprisoned murderer under threat of decapitation but also when he assumes the role of a poor traveler or a haughty and well-kept gent: like a wolf devouring its prey, ravenously, self-ishly, desperately. In fact, when he escapes the lynch mob and is cast out by the authorities to wander, Cain-like, it is not a mark on the forehead but the pseudonymic Blandois' ways with food that serve as the sign of the footsore traveler's true identity: at the inn where he refreshes himself in London, "[h]is greed at dinner . . .

was closely in keeping with the greed of Monsieur Rigaud at break-fast. His avaricious manner of collecting all the eatables about him, and devouring some with his eyes while devouring others with his jaws, was the same manner. . . . [W]hen he could eat no more, [he] sat sucking his delicate fingers one by one" (401–2).

Rigaud's visible, even animal hunger is, of course, problematic: the gentleman, as we have seen in chapters 1 and 2, must be care-ful to obviate need, to demonstrate his difference from the craving, striving, hungering masses. Yet in Dickens's *Little Dorrit*, the gentle-man who adheres to Rigaud's definition of the thing—a figure we might call the economic gentleman—is predicated precisely on his desire for more, on his hungers and his ability, as Rigaud would have it, to eat—and eat well—"at the cost of some other man" (171). Rigaud's dining partner at once makes this clear and reveals the re-sulting notion of gentlemanliness as performance in his approach to his own humble meal: while his "master" (41) devours a fancy meal, Cavalletto savors a bread-feast, helped along by the "old sauce" (45) provided by his knife. He explains to his cellmate, "I can cut my bread so—like a melon. Or so—like an omelette. Or so—like a fried fish. Or so—like Lyons sausage" (46). This "sauce" reveals the act of fine dining as sleight of hand that elevates some of the fare that sustains life and denigrates other food equally well equipped for the task.

Cavalletto's contented cuts with his magical knife demonstrate that all of Rigaud's fine fare merely assuages the same basic hunger that the bread will calm, a hunger shared by the gentleman and the common man alike. In doing so, Cavalletto demonstrates that fancy fare is an empty signifier: in *Little Dorrit*, food fails to make the man, because however fine the feast, hunger always lurks nearby, an extra guest at the table. Rigaud and Cavalletto between them set the terms for appetite and gentlemanliness in *Little Dorrit*. The marketplace of desire is the crucible of gentlemanliness in the novel: here class has been decoupled from blood, and what remains is a market free-for-all in which radical economic individualism is predicated on the maintenance of a dream of feudal rule and re-sponsibility. The illusion of commensality in *Little Dorrit* enables the perpetuation of a gentlemanliness that is entirely a fabric of grasping and desire. In the face of this narrative, the gentleman who refuses to feed himself by starving others—the gentleman who seeks not to grasp "the good things" (675) but to give, to nurture—is nearly starved out of existence.

The novel's hero, Arthur Clennam, is one such Rigaud-rejecting gentleman. Like Brontë's Gilbert Markham, Dickens's recuperative hero is a seeker, forced to test his mettle against a series of obstacles before he wins his true love and a life of happiness. An English mercantile exile returning to his native soil after two decades in China, Clennam is a stranger in a strange land, a man utterly without place or community. Resolved not to follow in the cold, joyless path of his mercantile, grasping parents and utterly unfamiliar with the society that he comes back to, he feels himself to be, as he tells his friend Mr. Meagles, "such a waif and stray everywhere, that [he is] likely to be drifted where any current may set" (59).

Tellingly, Clennam's new life in England begins on an empty stomach. On "a Sunday evening . . . gloomy, close, and stale" (67), Clennam sits in a desolate coffeehouse, eating nothing. The choice of venue is telling: the coffeehouse was an icon of middle-class enterprise and drive, a site that helped to organize and forward social, political, and economic movements just as its wares helped to power the Industrial Revolution. Coffeehouses had long been centers of political insurgency, public debate, and avid deal making, crucial to the rise of stockbrokers and insurance companies (Finkelstein, 36). Coffeehouses were great democratic spaces, where all classes mixed in the pursuit of business as well as pleasure (Schivelbusch, 40); they served as the community halls and power lunch spots of the rising class.

And coffee was, more than any other form of aliment, the engine of the new cult of energy and speed that had shaken Victorian England out of centuries of beer-fed lassitude (Schivelbusch, 85). It was the breakfast of champions, replacing beer soup for the worker and hot chocolate for the rich; it jump-started the 'Change and drove the driven through the day.[1] Coffee, in other words, is the alimentary force behind the mercantile England that Clennam has resolved to reject. And so, ironically, he sits at an empty table in an empty coffeehouse on the day of rest, alone and idle, unwilling to charge himself with the stuff of business, of getting and spending and striving and hoarding. No coffee—no aliment of any

kind—is consumed at Arthur Clennam's table. Instead, he feeds on
the misery of the neighborhood he sees beyond the coffeehouse
window and the terrible tyranny of the church bells, which with
each toll return him to his younger self, fed to bursting on "unser-
viceable bitterness and mortification" (68).

It is not surprising that his appetite fails to return at his mother's
house: that establishment hardly offers up alimentary nurture to its
returning son. The house still holds "empty beer-casks hoary with
cobwebs, and empty wine-bottles with fur and fungus choking up
their throats" in its bowels, as it had when Arthur left it two
decades before. "There, too, among unusual bottle-racks . . . [is] the
strong-room stored with old ledgers" (95). In place of foodstuffs and
wine to sustain the inhabitants, there are only decaying, inedible
records of purchase and sale: in this counting-house, the monetary
replaces the alimental. When a meal at last appears in the dining
room, "[t]he baking-dish [is] served up in a penitential manner on
a shrunken cloth at the end of the dining-table" (95), as though
sustenance is begrudged by the house as something shameful, to be
hidden away and swallowed quickly.

This is not to say that there is no food in the house: Clennam's
mother, long an invalid, sets great store by her alimentary rituals,
which are precise, ascetically sensual, and notably uninvalid-like.
She favors such fare as roast partridge (94), oysters (92), rusks with
butter, and a drink made with port wine (75).[2] Mrs. Clennam's meals
are reminiscent of Rigaud's strange feast: she seeks to be healed by
foods that reinforce her class status. Sitting in her crumbling home,
literally a house of business, in a neighborhood long since gone
down, Arthur's mother demands the acknowledgment of her economic gentility in every bite, eating very much like a man. Given
the implications of her fare and his decision to turn away from the
family business and its grasping ethos, it is hardly surprising when
Clennam refuses the luxurious food the servant Affery offers him:

> [She] asked him . . . would he have some supper?
> "No, Affery, no supper."
> "You shall if you like," said Affery. "There's her to-
> morrow's partridge in the larder—her first this year; say
> the word and I'll cook it."

No, he had not long dined, and could eat nothing.
"Have something to drink, then," said Affery; "you
shall have some of her bottle of port, if you like. I'll tell
Jeremiah that you ordered me to bring it you."
No; nor would he have that, either. (76)

Clennam's refusal to eat here makes excellent sense—but it is
hardly the only instance of his resolute closing of his lips. In fact,
this adamant refusal, couched in the language of a lack of appetite,
quickly becomes Clennam's signal act. Waving away Mr. Dorrit's
implied invitation to share in his paltry dinner, Clennam insists
that he will have "[n]ot a morsel" (122). In Flora's sitting room, he
is handed a crust of toast by Mr. F's aunt, who clearly expects him
to follow Flora's example and eat the crust "as a matter of business"
(590); terrified though he is of that intimidating old person, he can
do nothing but "[hold] it in his hand under the pressure of a little
embarrassment" (591), unable to eat it or to put it down (leading
that remarkable lady to announce that he has a "proud stomach"
and to prescribe "a meal of chaff" as a cure [591–92]). When Mrs.
Plornish offers him a cup of tea in return for his news of Little Dorrit, he turns her down by explaining that he is going home to dinner shortly—a remarkable excuse, suggesting that one cannot eat
with others, and thus refresh and renew oneself, because one is
going home to do so in solitude.

When Maggy and her "Little Mother" (212) appear in his rooms,
he urges food on his visitors, particularly on Little Dorrit, again and
again:[3] he "put[s] wine and cake and fruit towards her on the table"
(212) as though to compensate for "the thin worn shoes, the insufficient dress" (212). When Little Dorrit confides in him about
Flintwinch's discovery of her home, he "persuade[s] her to put some
wine to her lips, and to touch something to eat" and advises her,
"Do nothing . . . except refresh yourself with such means as there
are here. I entreat you to do that" (213). In this way, he entwines
alimental succor in his speeches and advice to her as an intimate
and yet an urgent undertaking. To relieve her of her suffering when
she asks him to refrain from giving her father money, "Clennam
made the best diversion in his power by pouring [Maggy] out a glass
of wine. . . . When she had finished . . . he charged her to load her

basket . . . with every eatable thing upon the table, and to take especial care to leave no scrap behind. Maggy's pleasure in doing this and her little mother's pleasure in seeing Maggy pleased, was as good a turn as circumstances could have given to the late con-versation" (214–15). Clennam uses food here to do all the work that he cannot: it is meant as comforter and source of succor, as rare pleasure and reassurance. But all the while that he implores Maggy and Little Dorrit to eat, he takes nothing himself; he seems unable to be satisfied unless all the food he has about him is gone before the pair departs. Imprisoned in the Marshalsea, he can force no food between his lips—not John Chivery's ham and watercress; not a drink in the tavern with the other debtors; no sustenance at all, not even tea, alone in his poor room.

Clennam's refusal to eat, then, is not predicated solely on his issues with his mother: in a novel bursting with alimental descrip-tion, he turns his head away resolutely at even the simplest fare, apparently making a fetish of fasting. But this starvation diet is not predicated on nicety or caused by a "proud stomach," nor is Clen-nam afflicted with a nineteenth-century eating disorder. Instead, his closed lips are the marker of his refusal of the poisonous fare of economic gentlemanliness. Clennam starves himself to avoid swallowing fare that will necessarily leave others to go hungry: it is the only gentlemanly model of eating on offer in the world of the novel, and he finds it impossible. His principled stand nearly leads him to disappear entirely.

The economic gentlemen who populate the novel unquestion-ably serve as cautionary figures for Clennam; the most important of these Rigaud-like figures is that other jailbird, William Dorrit, Amy's hungry father. Long confined to the Marshalsea debtors' prison, Dorrit is nevertheless no ordinary mendicant: his cultural possessions on arrival exceed the usual catalogue of debtors' attributes and de-ficiencies, and his class status has hardly been forfeited at the prison gates. He arrives "a very amiable and very helpless middle-aged gentleman . . . a shy, retiring man; well-looking, though in an ef-feminate style; with a mild voice, curling hair, and irresolute hands" (98). He has no head for business: concerning his debt, "nobody on the face of the earth could be more incapable of explaining any single item in the heap of confusion than the debtor himself" (99).

But this is not to say that Mr. Dorrit has no chips to play with: his very gentlemanliness becomes his stock in trade. As the turnkey notes, he was

> [b]rought up as a gentleman, he was, if ever a man was. Ed'cated at no end of expense. Went into the Marshal's house once to try a new piano for him. Played it, I understand, like one o'clock—beautiful! As to languages—speaks everything. We've had a Frenchman here in his time, and it's my opinion he knowed more French than the Frenchman did. We've had an Italian here in his time, and he shut *him* up in about half a minute. You'll find some characters behind other locks, I don't say you won't; but if you want the top sawyer in such respects as I've mentioned, you must come to the Marshalsea. (104)[4]

Arthur Clennam first encounters the Father of the Marshalsea in his room in the debtor's prison, sitting down to the meal that Little Dorrit prepares for him from her own uneaten dinner: in keeping with Rigaud's gentlemanly checklist, Dorrit is waited upon, though the servant is his own daughter. Despite the debased surroundings and the ignoble source of the repast, the meal is arranged with much ceremony: "[A] clean cloth was spread before him, with knife, fork, and spoon, salt-cellar, pepper-box, glass, and pewter ale-pot. Such zests as his particular little phial of cayenne pepper and his pennyworth of pickles in a saucer, were not wanting" (121). He welcomes his guest with "a wonderful air of benignity and patronage in his manner" (122); he bows, he doffs his hat, he invites Arthur to share in the meal provided by Arthur's mother's establishment. He "condescend[s] towards his brother, Frederick, as an amiable, well-meaning man; a private character, who had not arrived at distinction" (122). Here, as elsewhere, Dorrit's speech is carefully elevated, his style courtly, his pretensions to class status absolute. Arthur is "quite lost in wonder at the manner of the man" (122).[5]

At this first meal, Dorrit makes his status clear not only through the pomp and circumstance of his manner and of his dinner but also through his discussion of his usual means of obtaining his bread

and meat. Introducing the subject with a mention of his importance as "the Father of this place" (122), he explains that "it does
sometimes occur that people who come here desire to offer some
little—Testimonial. . . . [S]ometimes—hem—it takes one shape
and sometimes another; but it is generally—ha—Money" (123).
Dorrit's tale of "the gentleman who did that handsome action"
(that is, the bestowing of money) "with so much delicacy" (123)
serves to establish his gentlemanliness even as it demonstrates his
beggary. In recounting the story of the testimonial, after all, Dorrit
attests to his own worth: he is so genteel, so worthy, and so clearly
the head of the first family in the place that "[i]t very seldom happens that anybody—of any pretensions—any pretensions—comes
here without being presented to [him]" (123). His supporters become his petitioners, and his great grace in receiving them and
accepting their little gifts serves to demonstrate his high status
instead of his indigence. For Dorrit, such activities confirm his
gentlemanliness precisely because they make clear that he is supported by others. This is what makes him a gentleman: like Mr.
Woodhouse, like Arthur Huntingdon, and like Rigaud, he does not
dirty his hands with work.

It is instructive to look, for instance, at Dorrit's response to his
son's outraged behavior toward Clennam. Tip is offended at the
visitor's refusal to loan him money, which he classifies as Clennam
having not "used [him] like a gentleman" (427). The head of the
family is angered: Tip's pronouncement implies that Dorrit himself
has been treated in an ungentlemanly way. If such a person had
denied the Father of the Marshalsea an accommodation, he asks,
"Am I to be told by my own son, that I therefore received treatment not due to a gentleman, and that I—ha—I submitted to it?"
(428). For Mr. Dorrit, as for Rigaud, gentlemanliness is marked by
the ability to "eat at the cost of some other man."

William Dorrit has effectively found a new public life, a new
job, in the labor of soliciting funds from his "children," biological
and otherwise. In this life, he is neither extraneous nor idle: he works
constantly to shore up his position through carefully calibrated displays of leisure, satiation, and ease. He practices willful blindness
concerning the paid employment of his children, promenades
down the good side of the prison walk, and insists on his customs

of introduction and leave-taking, with their attendant worming-out of testimonials, for Collegians and visitors alike. And his labors pay off: the old-fashioned feudal realm that Austen's Mr. Woodhouse works so hard to recoup is here restored.

Dorrit's approach to the care and maintenance of this pseudo-feudal realm recasts the feudal order in the image of the acquisitive gentleman. Whereas Mr. Woodhouse attempts to choke everyone around him with gruel, Mr. Dorrit takes no interest in feeding others, believing that the only body that needs to be fed is his own. He is sure that the role of those around him is merely to support him openly, freely, and naturally. His benevolent alimentary gifts (particularly the great feast in the prison after his fortune is discovered) are opportunities for social display, in which the forms and toasts and grand fare are primarily meant to feed Dorrit's own image. Then, too, the laying on of such a collation confirms his distance from the Collegians who live "from hand to mouth—from the pawnbroker's hand to the day's dinner" (475), as well as his putative estrangement from hunger or even from desire—an idea central to this gentlemanly construction precisely because in the volatile world of *Little Dorrit* (like the moneyed but economically combustible world that the novel was published into),[6] hunger is an ever-present threat. This, as the swindling speculator Merdle's eventual fall makes clear, is the threat that lurks behind every bad deal, every failure, every con. It is the ultimate equalizer, the most irrefutable marker of loss of prestige, and it gives the lie to the notion that the trappings of class, the detritus of gentlemanliness, are somehow immutable and inherent.

Magical thinking is crucial to maintaining class at the table, as Dorrit realizes, particularly when the site of the repast is so problematic; the formalities and ceremonies that his meals are rife with serve to cover over need, to turn his paltry dinners into displays of excess and mastery. Hence the importance of the rituals of the gentlemanly table—the "little zests," the insistence on fine fare, and the niceties of manner that Dorrit so carefully foregrounds. Necessity is erased in the luxurious meal, as the palate is eased away from the hungering body; the economic gentleman eats to ingest and to display appropriate class values, never because he simply needs to survive. Dorrit, then, uses the rites of gentlemanly consumption to erase the possibility of want and, by extension, of the need for labor itself. The ceremonies of the table demonstrate both his accomplishment and his deserving nature: precisely because he creates such apparent distance from real want, the gentleman deserves to be supported. For these reasons, at the public dinner for the Collegians, Dorrit

> did not in person dine. . . . He . . . went about among the company, and took notice of individuals, and saw that the viands were of the quality he had ordered, and that all were served. On the whole, he was like a baron of the olden time in a rare good humour. At the conclusion of the repast, he pledged his guests in a bumper of old Madeira; and told them that he hoped they had enjoyed themselves, and what was more, that they would enjoy themselves for the rest of the evening; and that he bade them welcome. (475–76)[7]

On most occasions, however, Dorrit fails to feed others at all, instead choosing to take food from their mouths in the guise of testimonials or in the meals that he obtains from his stunted daughter. This economic gentleman justifies this behavior by approaching his gentlemanly status as a means of providing for others through the provisioning of himself: in this construction, he becomes the social body, a synecdochical representation of the community, and others are nurtured, he claims, through their feeding of him, as his relation to the testimonials makes clear.

This understanding of gentlemanliness is not limited to the Marshalsea, a fact amply demonstrated by the behavior of Mr. Dorrit's colleague in neofeudal sentimental gentlemanliness, the genteel slumlord of Bleeding Heart Yard, Christopher Casby. Like Dorrit, Casby is reliant on a distinguished appearance and an old-fashioned manner to gain his bread; like Dorrit, he has no compunctions about taking food out of the mouths of the poor to feed himself; like Dorrit, he makes excellent use of the feudal ideal of the great lord of the manor at table. Casby's well-tempered meals suggest utter conventionality and long adherence to prosperous convention. His table is covered with an abundance of plain, simple, homegrown fare. There are no strange dishes obscured by thick French sauces here, no imported delicacies or dangerous undercooked vegetables or piles of costly sugared fruits (see chapter 1): the food—not trendy, like the fare of the nouveaux riches; not overly fine, like the fancy dishes of Society—suggests an old-money affiliation, a sense of continued place and tradition that is Englishness itself. Casby's style of eating is as old-fashioned, in Dorrit's neofeudal sense, as the fare at his table, at which "[t]he last of the Patriarchs . . . dispose[s] of an immense quantity of food with the benignity of a good soul who [is] feeding some one else" (199). This striking image recurs later in the novel:

> The Patriarchal state . . . was . . . particularly serene that evening. . . . Everybody else within the bills of mortality was hot; but the Patriarch was perfectly cool. Everybody was thirsty, and the Patriarch was drinking. There was a fragrance of limes or lemons about him; and he made a drink of golden sherry, which shone in a large tumbler as if he were drinking the evening sunshine. . . . [H]e had a radiant appearance of having in his extensive benevolence made the drink for the human species, while he himself wanted nothing but his own milk of human kindness. (866)[8]

When he feeds himself "with the benignity of a good soul who [is] feeding someone else," Casby consumes for all of those who are hungry, who are thirsty, who require.[9] Mr. Casby, like Mr. Dorrit, portrays himself as the sum total of the community. He is the collective body, carefully maintained through appropriate care and feeding, and so the actual bodies of the people whom he is benevolent enough to represent, like Mr. Dorrit's subjects, must make sacrifices to keep him in good working order. And like Mr. Dorrit, Mr. Casby feels that he is doing the best for all by doing well for himself, as his dealings with his agent Mr. Pancks makes clear: "Bleeding Heart Yard had been harrowed by Mr Pancks, and cropped by Mr Casby. . . . Mr Pancks had taken all the drudgery and all the dirt of the business as his share; Mr Casby had taken all the profits, all the ethereal vapour, and all the moonshine, as *his* share; and, in the form of words which that benevolent beamer generally employed on Saturday evenings, when he twirled his fat thumbs after striking the week's balance, 'everything had been sat-isfactory to all parties—all parties—satisfactory, sir, to all parties'" (865). Casby, like Dorrit, is, in his own view, the body politic, the community in synecdoche: for these unfatherly fathers, the gentle-man is not merely representative of but in fact constituted by and constitutive of his people. When these men parade among their subjects, they play at beneficent lordship, assuming the role of the great man who sheds sunshine and wisdom with every nod and acknowledgment, who seems to distribute sustenance through his very presence. But in each case, the largesse on offer is a nutrient-free feast, a beautifully dressed table devoid of actual sustenance. This is the generosity, the pseudofeudal benevolence that Mr. Casby and Mr. Dorrit practice.[10] Both offer up junk food, empty calories that make one feel full and fat without nourishing the body: they are, as Pancks terms his Proprietor, "sugary swindler[s]" (868), "sweet as honey" but bad for the teeth and bones and stomach, made up of slow bodily poisons.[11]

Like Dorrit's subjects, Casby's constituents are literally constitu-tive of the Patriarch: to use Dickens's famous term from *Hard Times* for the drudges of industry, they are Hands (83), and the product is the gentleman himself. True, the ironically named Bleeding Hearts, like their impecunious brothers-in-arms in the Marshalsea, are thought to be remarkably incapable of manufacturing anything at all: in fact, lack of work is "the general misfortune of Bleeding Heart Yard. From time to time there were public complaints . . . of labour being scarce . . . but Bleeding Heart Yard . . . was never the better for the demand" (179). But it is not entirely the case that the unemployed residents produce nothing. When Casby sends Pancks to collect the rents, his evocative term is "to squeeze": the bodies of the tenants are, so to speak, wrung dry so that the Patri-arch can benefit from the sweat of their brows and the blood in their veins. This is the most obvious form of production; in this sense, the tenants are an actual part of the product. They are not only the bodies on behalf of whom the Patriarch feeds, not only the bodies that labor to produce his sustenance, but also the food itself: the "golden sherry" with which the Patriarch refreshes himself, the mutton and apple pie on which he sustains himself.[12] The yard becomes a factory whose sole product, generated endlessly, is Casby.

But this "sugary swindler" is constituted by more than just squeezing: his visual marking as an old-fashioned gentleman also prompts Casby-production. The Bleeding Hearts, with their great respect for "the long, grey, silken locks, and the broad-brimmed hat" (869), help to manufacture the olden-days myth that dresses the rapacious capitalist body and renders it, in a word, gentlemanly. When they agree that "if a gentleman with that head of hair and them eyes took his rents into his own hands, ma'am, there would be none of this worriting and wearing, and things would be very different" (325); when they turn admiring eyes on Mr. Casby and honor his great perceived benevolence; when they take part in the imaginative exercise of alienating his economic depredations from his persona, they construct Mr. Casby as the great lord of Bleeding Heart Yard, the hero of their economic romance.

Similarly, the Marshalsea, home to those who have set the mechanics of getting and spending awry by spending too much while not getting enough, is also the site of production, the birthplace, so to speak, of its own Father, created from the alms that they stint themselves to provide. When the Marshalsea residents present their visitors to Mr. Dorrit, when newcomers are brought to make his acquaintance on arrival, and when those leaving the jail put coins under their Father's door on parting, long before the ceremonies of the testimonials are established, they help to create the Father, writing his gentlemanly story. "It is often said," Amy Dorrit tells Arthur, "that [Mr. Dorrit's] manners are a true gentleman's, and quite a study. I see none like them in that place, but he is admitted to be superior to all the rest. This is quite as much why they make him presents, as because they know him to be needy" (137). The impoverished, perpetually unemployed Plornish lauds Dorrit: "'[T]here's manners! There's polish! There's a gentleman to have run to seed in the Marshalsea Jail! Why, perhaps you were not aware,' said Plornish . . . speaking with a perverse admiration . . . 'not aware that Miss Dorrit and her sister dursn't let him know that they work for a living. No!' said Plornish . . . with a ridiculous triumph. . . . 'Dursn't let him know it, they dursn't!'" (180). No wonder that "[t]he more Fatherly he grew as to the Marshalsea, and the more dependent he became on the contributions of his chang-ing family, the greater stand he made by his forlorn gentility" (113).

Dorrit and Casby, then, both reference an imaginary olden-days, neofeudal model of gentlemanly behavior, in which the gentleman is the center of the community and is sustained by the people whom he in turn helps to sustain. Each gentleman does so as a means of surviving in the world of getting and spending without having to resort to labor. But these gentlemanly men are hardly natural-born gentlemen like Arthur Huntingdon, struggling to mark themselves as outsiders to the striver realm; nor, like Mr. Woodhouse, are they truly old-fashioned men, attempting to main-tain class by keeping the world at bay. Casby, after all, is simply "Old Christopher Casby, formerly Town-agent to Lord Decimus Tite Barnacle" (187), revealed, in the end, through Pancks's impro-vised barbering and haberdashery, as a "bare-polled, goggle-eyed, big-headed lumbering personage . . . not in the least impressive, not in the least venerable" (872), a staring, heavy-footed English-man who has, on the evidence, helped himself to one too many good dinners. Dorrit, too, is made of the most ordinary Englishness. As Ferdinand Barnacle points out at Mr. Merdle's table—devour-ing Dorrit and his reputation as he devours the latest French dish—Dorrit (no longer an inmate of the Marshalsea but having become a man of means) had been "a partner in a house in some large way—spirits, or buttons, or wine, or blacking, or oatmeal, or woollen, or pork, or hooks and eyes, or iron, or treacle, or shoes, or something or other that was wanted for troops, or seamen, or some-body—and the house burst" (620).

Indeed, despite the fare on their tables, these gentlemen are made not of leisure but of mercantile labor. Though Casby seems removed from the details of filthy lucre, in his bottle-green coat and his list shoes, he is all business: his agent dines with him every night (and tends to his daughter on his behalf); the work of elicit-ing rents goes on in part beneath his old-fashioned, unchanging roof; and he is in the habit of receiving debtors in his private sitting room. He does not go out to work, because he is the sum total of his work and thus can never leave it behind. This is true as well for Dorrit, whose distance from the world means that his feudal rela-tionship with his constituents is the ruling order of the community:

his entire existence is predicated on the project of acquisition. Dorrit and Casby are no more and no less than every other Englishman, because while they feed on those around them, they fail to digest their best bits into something greater. Each man has ingested the lifeblood of others in his attempt to shore up his gentlemanliness; in doing so, he must to some degree make himself of them, eliding the boundaries even as he creates them.

The same is true of every economic gentleman in Dickens's novel. The need to swallow the poor to sustain the project of richness may be thought of as the core of this sort of gentlemanliness and thus functions as a crucial destabilizing force that keeps alive the ever-looming possibility of descent, of slipping down through the ranks to the level of those whose neediness has been ingested by the gentleman with their blood and sweat. Those who swallow the hunger of others find that it becomes a part of themselves. As Paul Rozin and April Fallon note, cannibalism is predicated, in part, on the idea of acquiring the attributes, the essence, of the eaten (27). But in this case, the gentlemanly devourer swallows not strength but weakness, poverty, and need. These become his own.

A similar problem appears in the Merdle sections of the novel, which are stuffed with descriptions of gatherings around magnificent tables laden with fine fare. Note, for instance, the description of the dinner that is the occasion for the great conference between Mr. Merdle and Lord Decimus Barnacle: "It was a dinner to provoke an appetite. . . . The rarest dishes, sumptuously cooked and sumptuously served; the choicest fruits; the most exquisite wines; marvels of workmanship in gold and silver, china and glass; innumerable things delicious to the senses of taste, smell and sight, were insinuated into its composition. O, what a wonderful man, this Merdle, what a great man, what a master man, how blessedly and enviably endowed—in one word, what a rich man!" (618). The performance of the meal is conflated with essential substance, as though Merdle's status and all of his riches, like Casby's sunshine, are taken in by mouth. Here the feudal myth is rewritten as capitalist fairy tale. Merdle's guests stuff themselves at his dinners as though they can fill themselves with class and with riches through old sherry and fine meals, but the real delicacies here are radical individualism and selfishness: the aim, at Merdle's table, is for each guest to get as much as he or she can, and the lord to whom Society pledges its allegiance is "the man who could have any one he chose to dine with him, and who had made the money" (673). The feast thus serves only to reveal the grasping, self-interested nature of its partakers, as the men's money-seeking conferences with Merdle after dinner demonstrate: "[S]o many of the magnates had something to say to Mr Merdle that he held little levees by the side-board, and checked them off as they went out at the door" (296). Despite its trappings and ceremony, then, the meal reveals itself as being, at bottom, all about hunger and appetite.

The table is thus a site of revelation of the emptiness of class, even as it is a place where class is established and marked. While Dickens's economic gentleman seeks to fill himself with class at the haute board, his very need, his hunger, also demonstrates his affinity with the low. However it may be dressed up or sweetened, eating links the very poorest with the most wealthy and privileged. The most refined, cultured, and moneyed gentleman sitting down to the most lavish meal that money can buy cannot avoid his own appetites. When he picks up his fork, only the contents of his plate and, perhaps, his table manners mark the differences between himself and the lowest street urchin—or prisoner—swallowing his bread and butter.

This paradox shows through in the very rituals of dinner. As Dorrit talks during his first meal in the company of Arthur, for example, "though he had finished his supper, he was nervously going about his plate with his knife and fork, as if some of it were still before him" (124). Emily Hoffman argues that "Dorrit's nervous gestures . . . illuminate his own lack of abundance—his empty plate—and therefore his incapacity as a host" (26). Despite his ceremonies and fine phrasings, Dorrit has allowed the spectre of hunger to intrude on the meal: in making manifest his need, he strips the niceties from his supper and allows its insufficiency to stand forth.

The trick, then, is to cover over want, as Casby does so well; but Mr. Dorrit finds it impossible to maintain a smooth gentlemanly façade at table precisely because he understands hunger. Mr. Dorrit, to his own regret, reads aliment very clearly, forced by circumstances to acknowledge its hidden purpose of nourishing the body.

For this reason, his fetishization of aliment as a marker of class fails continually, even as he feeds himself on the strength of the performance of such fetishization, which is his bread and butter. In the world of class as it is so clearly delineated by Rigaud, anyone who knows what it is to starve cannot be a convincing gentleman.

For Dorrit, class is an endless, rapacious appetite for more: his constant fear that he will not have enough to maintain his status drives him into an endless glut of consumption. This overbearing, unappeasable need to fill himself with the stuff of gentlemanliness and, in this way, to hide the need for the very hunger that drives him is manifested itself in serious alimental monstrosity. Not only does Dorrit see no difficulty in taking the coins of the poverty-stricken debtors around him to fill his belly with meat and drink and little luxuries, but he also has no qualms about taking food from the mouths of his own children. In fact, this willingness to swallow the sustenance that should be theirs—in particular, to literally stunt his daughter's growth even as he stunts her life by making her his servant and caretaker—both defines his gentlemanly paradigm and reveals its ravenous, self-swallowing nature.

This is illuminated most clearly at another Marshalsea collation, the meal at which Little Dorrit soothes her father's anger after she foils his attempt to sell her off, more or less literally, to John Chivery. Irate at the failure of his stratagem; angry, perhaps, at himself for contemplating such a thing; Dorrit breaks down at table, first behaving angrily with his dinner ("laying down his knife and fork with a noise, taking things up sharply, biting at his bread as if he were offended with it" [272]), then pushing his plate away, like a petulant child who refuses to eat when crossed. He calls himself "[a] poor prisoner, fed on alms and broken victuals; a squalid, disgraced wretch" (272), as indeed he is—thus demonstrating that he possesses a distinct awareness of the emperor-without-clothes fate that looms if his ceremonies and privileges and fine airs are stripped away. Having taken his feeding habits a step too far, he has lost his appetite as he has lost his self-respect, exposing even to himself the animal greed at the heart of his social self-construction. The fine gentleman sustained by ceremony and by the "zests" (121) provided by his "petitioners" is stripped away to reveal the prison-house creature, the monster who feeds himself on the degraded and degrading flesh and blood of other prisoners and, most terrible of all, on the flesh and blood of his own children.

In this moment, the first of two significant breakdowns suffered at the dinner table, he is eventually brought back to calm by his daughter, who "comfort[s] her father's wasted heart upon her inno-cent breast, and turn[s] it to a fountain of love and fidelity that never ran dry or waned through all his years of famine" (274). The episode evokes the story of Roman Charity, the tale of the daugh-ter who suckles her father in prison to prevent him from starving. The scene seems written for maudlin sentiment; however, for Dickens's audience, the reverberations must have been horrifying. For the nineteenth-century reader, the notion "[t]hat parent should batten on child . . . was appalling, *contra naturam*. And that . . . powerful members of society in a responsible parental re-lation to the rest should claim sustenance rather than offer it, should act as wolves rather than as shepherds, should constitute a parasitic burden upon the poor and powerless, was similarly intol-erable" (Meisel, 305–6).

In this crucial scene, then, the façade of the benevolent gentle-man, the "Father of the place," falls to the ground entirely; in its place, we are left with an image of anthropophagy and, in fact, of autophagy, in which the gentleman-parasite feeds not merely on the tenantry, as Casby does, but also on the flesh of his own flesh. At this moment, in the privacy of his room with the daughter he so depends on, Dorrit is faced with the horror of his situation; though in the end it is resolved exactly as it is created—the "poor prisoner" is sustained and revivified in his gentlemanliness by the body and the blood of the daughter—it also reveals a significant fis-sure in Dorrit's construction of gentlemanliness. The two versions of gentlemanliness that Mr. Dorrit carries about with him collide most violently here: Dorrit's role as a gentleman, as he understands it, is to swallow all around him to sustain himself, but ironically, this feeding obliterates the claims to family that are crucial to his maintenance of patriarchal gentlemanliness. He cannot be, he sees (however briefly), the benevolent father and the sucking vampire at the same time, cannot feed his child by feeding off of her. He un-derstands simultaneously that his actions are wrong and that they are what preserve him in the face of poverty: he cannot be both at

once, and yet he must, or else be neither and thus yield himself
to his situation (just as his weak brother Frederick has done), give
way, fall.

Nor is the problem resolved by wealth. Dorrit, once he has
come into his fortune, no longer needs his daughter to "help him
to his supper and his rest," since, as she well knows, "[i]f Mr. Dorrit had wanted supper, there was an Italian cook and there was a
Swiss confectioner, who must have put on caps as high as the
Pope's Mitre, and have performed the mysteries of Alchemists in a
copper-saucepaned laboratory below, before he could have got it"
(668–69). But this is not to say that he has got over the problem of
feeding on his children. He tells Amy, for instance, that the "responsibility imposed upon [her] by [her] position . . . is to develop
that position" by contracting, as her sister Fanny has done, "a
marriage, eminently calculated to extend the basis of our—ha—
connection, and to—hum—consolidate our social relations" (669).
Amy's response is telling: she "entertain[s] no harder reflection . . .
than that he now saw everything through their wealth, and through
the care he always had upon him that they should continue rich, and
grow richer" (670). In his grand Italian villa, as in the Marshalsea,
the father—having become rich and materially comfortable—still
seeks to feed off his daughter, desiring to swallow prestige and ever
more cash through her marital sale. His rapacious appetite is driven
by the fear that there is never enough to maintain or display one's
status: what he seeks to swallow is gentlemanliness itself. There is
no cure for Dorrit's devouring affliction.

In the end, Dorrit fails to storm the bastion of Society not because he lacks the right stuff—he has mien, he has money, he is, in
effect, a gentleman, to paraphrase Rigaud—but because he cannot
believe in his façade, cannot stop himself from knowing the truth
about his hunger. His elaborate plans, his grand palace, his extensive visiting, his connection to Merdle, and even the first taste of
the splendid offerings of Mrs. General, gained through a kiss of her
hand (a taste that "may be conjectured to have been a rather bony
kiss of a cosmetic flavour" [707]), fail to suppress his undeniable appetites. In fact, his gains seem to bring on his hunger, as though the
prospect of the obliteration of need draws out his striver's nature
instead of sating it. Knowing hunger in every way—physical hunger,

the hunger of desire for what one cannot have, and particularly the hunger for status, place, and solidity—Mr. Dorrit remains rapacious yet becomes thinner and thinner, less and less substantial. By the time he sits down to dinner at Mrs. Merdle's table, he appears "shrunken and old" (707): he is wasting away in the midst of plenty, unable to fill himself, to satisfy the gaping hole within that is always growing, always demanding more, always presenting the spectre of the empty belly.

In this new life, in which he remains driven to acquire yet finds himself with nothing to do—no need to grow richer from the labors of others or to sustain himself by feeding on others—William Dorrit is able to do nothing except present himself as a fait accompli, and so he is lost. No wonder he tells his daughter (imagining himself not at his in-law Mrs. Merdle's glittering board but at the head of a table of Marshalsea newcomers in the Snuggery, soliciting testimonials), "I don't feel quite myself" (708). This dream of ease and riches can never be enough for his striver's soul; he is driven, as his breakdown at Society's most esteemed table makes clear, by want, suffering, and making do. This, it turns out, is the reality of economic gentlemanliness, which is beggary.

When he lies on his deathbed insisting on the "pawning" of his rings and trinkets, it is, then, hardly surprising that he "appear[s] to consider it the equivalent of making the most methodical and provident arrangements" (712). In fact, this is the most selfless act that this father has performed, stemming as it seems to from a real concern about the welfare of his family after his looming death. In this way, he is indeed restored to himself and thus restored to usefulness (however feigned): the gentlemanly laborer has reasserted himself and can thus eat his dainties without guilt. In his own mind, he is the clever, prudent provider. In this ironically false moment, the two sides of Mr. Dorrit's much-vaunted gentlemanliness have finally come together, as economic acquisition and moral clarity combine to create an illusory future for the actual family that is the gentleman's most important marker.

Dorrit's death is hardly redemptive, however: just as his hallucinatory provisions fail to create stability for his family, so too does his passing fail to obliterate the economic gentleman's all-consuming appetites from the text. But his decline and fall—like

Merdle's suicide, like Casby's de-hatting—does make space for other, less rapacious forms of gentlemanliness. If the economic gentleman is a monster here, the hero of the piece—the knight in armor, brandishing a sword—is that unhungry gentleman, Arthur Clennam.

In light of the consuming behaviors of the economic gentleman, after all, Clennam's fasting makes a certain amount of sense: it is the sign of his guilt at his perceived unlooked-for participation in and benefit from the rituals of this gentlemanly dinner. Surrounded by gluttonous consumers, Clennam is painfully aware of the effects of such eating and drinking on the bodies of those who cannot eat and drink: every bite that is swallowed, it seems, causes someone else to starve. His suspicion of the guilty sources of his parents' money feeds this assumption; so does his witnessing of Mr. Dorrit's problematic meal, as well as his presence at Mr. Casby's well-laden table, supplied by the poor of Bleeding Heart Yard with whom he has just become acquainted. Appalled by such self-serving desire, Arthur concludes that all indulgences of appetite are wrong. Accordingly, he gives up his own appetites and seeks to disappear entirely. He simply refuses to eat.[13]

Moreover, where Dorrit consumes, Clennam divests: from his earliest days in London, he sets out to feed others on the limited bounty he has amassed. He attempts to nourish Little Dorrit with actual food as well as with sustenance of a less literal sort; he "accommodates" her father, supplying that gentleman's table; and he creates a job at his factory for Cavalletto, who has no means of buying bread. But this provisioning of his makeshift community is no mere altruism on Clennam's part. Arthur is driven by guilt: he is convinced that his family shelters a guilty secret, most likely as a result of his parents' economic greed, which has caused others to suffer and go hungry.[14] By nourishing others, Clennam hopes to erase what he sees as his culpable indebtedness to the world. The source of this belief and of Clennam's sense of himself as at once a repository of that guilt and a potential site, through self-sacrifice, of its obviation becomes clear early in the novel, as the newly returned Arthur stands in his mother's "spare, meagre" dining room (71), unchanged since his childhood. Despite its nominal title, the room is not a promising place for meals:

The Plagues of Egypt, much the dimmer for the fly and
smoke plagues of London, were framed and glazed
upon the walls. There was the old cellaret with nothing
in it, lined with lead, like a sort of coffin in compart-
ments; there was the old dark closet, also with nothing
in it, of which he had been many a time the sole contents, in days of punishment, when he had regarded it
as the veritable entrance to that bourne to which the
tract had found him galloping. There was the large,
hard-featured clock on the sideboard, which he used
to see bending its figured brows upon him with a savage joy when he was behind-hand with his lessons, and
which, when it was wound up once a week with an iron
handle, used to sound as if it were growling in ferocious
anticipation of the miseries into which it would bring
him. (72)

Nothing to satiate and fuel the body here except the body itself:
the only edible matter in this dining room is, it seems, Arthur, or
his remembered child-self, stored away in the closet like so much
salted meat. The suggestion of parental cannibalism implied by the
ghostly presence of young Arthur in the closet aligns not only with
Dorrit's Roman Daughter tendencies but also with the text's later
discoveries concerning Arthur's vexed position in the family. Born
not to his nominal mother but to the woman his father had loved,
he is at once treasured by the harshly pious Mrs. Clennam as a
retributive prize and scorned as the product of a hated alliance. His
parents feed on their child to sustain their rigid relations with one
another, keeping him in the closet as both necessary ration and
self-indulgent luxury; they sustain him on the scraps of their bitterness and hatred, so that he becomes the endlessly renewable fatted
calf for their sacrificial altar in a sickening cycle of psychological
and narrative anthropophagy.

It is in keeping with his upbringing, with his image of himself in
the dining room closet, that Clennam seeks to feed others while
taking in nothing at all. Food, he is convinced, is poisonous, necessarily holding within it more of what he seeks to obviate: for this
gentleman, eating without causing suffering is impossible.

Those few occasions on which Clennam, relaxing his rigid hold on his principles, agrees to consume aliment serve only to reinforce this belief: he is inevitably betrayed by his tentative appetites. Arthur first sits down to dinner at Mr. Meagles's table, for instance, after an hour or so of turning over the question of "[w]hether he should allow himself to fall in love with Pet" (239), the Meagles's beautiful daughter. That meal in the Meagles's snug cottage is re-laxed, friendly, and devoid of ceremony. The food is not discussed; friends and common experiences constitute the real, nutritive ele-ments of the meal. This "very pleasant" meal (239), constitutive as it is of community, industry, and rational consumption (it is after this meal that Arthur speaks to Mr. Meagles about becoming part-ner to the inventor Daniel Doyce), is, however, soon overwritten by the unhappy breakfast and still more unhappy dinner that take place after Henry Gowan's arrival. Arthur will clearly be forced to repudiate his sexual appetites—forced, that is, to give up Pet. Gowan, the interloper who seeks to cadge what he can both in terms of food and in more problematic terms, ensures that the ease and comfort—the nourishment to body and soul—of the previous day are eradicated by his selfish, grasping appetites. When Gowan in-troduces Young Barnacle, activating Mr. Meagles's social-climbing instincts, the ruin is complete: "All the natural charm of the pre-vious day was gone. The eaters of the dinner, like the dinner itself, were lukewarm, insipid, overdone" (252). The meal, in short, be-comes unhappily like any other; the Elysium of the Meagles's little cottage is erased, and Arthur is once more left unable to swallow. Here begins the chain of events that leads to his repudiation of sexual appetite, his symbolic self-death.

On the only occasion on which Arthur actually admits his hunger to another, the results are considerably worse. After refusing to eat with the Plornishes, he uncharacteristically invites Pancks to dine, at the same time revealing his need: "If you will come home with me . . . and will share what dinner or supper there is," he says, "it will be next door to an act of charity; for I am weary and out of sorts to-night" (637). While Pancks's "works" are "oiled" by "[a] dinner of soup and a pigeon-pie, served on a little round table be-fore the fire, and flavoured with a bottle of good wine" (638) (a straightforward, old-fashioned meal without ceremony, served in a manner conducive to comfort), Arthur is not actually seen to eat anything. But he does smoke a pipe—for this abstemious man, a serious act of feeding. His unceremonious ease in front of the fire with Pancks leads him to talk of his personal perplexities regarding his mother's secret and to take advice from his companion. The return on his unaccustomed personal and alimentary openness is, however, not a good one: at this meal, Pancks "[gives] out the dangerous infection with which he [is] laden" (640), that is, the infection of Merdleness. He advises his friend,

> I don't say anything of your making yourself poor to repair a wrong you never committed. That's you. A man must be himself. But I say this, fearing you may want money to save your own blood from exposure and disgrace—make as much as you can! . . . Be as rich as you can, sir. . . . Be as rich as you honestly can. It's your duty. Not for your sake, but for the sake of others. . . . Poor Mr. Doyce . . . depends upon you. Your relative depends upon you. You don't know what depends upon you. . . . Why should you leave all the gains to the gluttons, knaves and imposters? Why should you leave all the gains that are to be got to my proprietor and the like of him? Yet you're always doing it. When I say you, I mean such men as you. . . . Therefore I say . . . "Go in and win!" (642)

So Clennam, seduced by Pancks's rhetoric of the selfless duty to do good by doing well on behalf of others, sets out to win. He invests the profits of Doyce & Clennam in Mr. Merdle's empty enterprises, and when the crash comes, he finds that he has "ruined [his] partner" (778). This time, Arthur's withdrawal—from engagement with the world, as from the table—is considerably more profound.

For the gentleman, there seems to be no way to avoid eating "at the cost of some other man." And so Arthur Clennam, painfully aware of the dark underbelly of the marketplace, puts himself back on a starvation diet. Convinced that all gentlemanly eating is gluttonous economic rapaciousness, Arthur seems equally convinced that all aliment must turn to economic poison in his mouth. Unable to see another way of eating, he gives it up entirely. Clennam is convinced that he can expiate his imagined inherited sins only by starving himself out of existence, by becoming, literally and figuratively, no body instead of an overconsuming, ravenous gentlemanly body dictated by economics. In depriving himself of sustenance, he is engaging in the best behavior he knows—even though it is behavior that threatens to obliterate him.

In resolving to close his lips against all sustenance, he adheres to the crucial gentlemanly concept that the Victorians refer to as disinterestedness. Robin Gilmour sees this notion as the heart of the gentlemanly ideal: it is "[t]he belief that a man's ultimate loyalty ought to be to something larger than his own pocket . . . an ideal intellectual and moral independence climbing above the pull of 'interest' and dogma" (96). Certainly, this notion appears to encapsulate all that seems admirable in Arthur's character: he is no slave to money, puts the needs of others before himself, and insists on his independence from the ingrained systems of thought and behavior espoused by the less appealing characters around him. This is, let us not forget, the man who, in service to others, makes his quiet, stubborn way into the Circumlocution Office and, as the monocled Young Barnacle recalls, "said he wanted to know, you know! Pervaded our Department—without an appointment—and said he wanted to know!" (252). Indeed, Arthur seems to present himself as a model of disinterestedness in his early conversations with Little Dorrit: after his first visit to her family in the Marshalsea, he tells her, "What I have seen here, in this short time, had greatly increased my heartfelt wish to be a friend to you. It would recompense me for much disappointment if I could hope to gain your confidence" (126).

In this way, Arthur seems to seek to create a gentlemanliness based on right living and morality, in direct opposition to the economic gentlemanliness so problematically embodied by Dorrit and his ilk. But his refusal of appetite, cast as generosity and self-sacrifice, obscures a more subtle form of self-interest no less intense than that espoused by the more overtly economically driven gentlemen: self-starvation as a means of preserving oneself apart. As Gilmour writes on John Henry Newman's *Idea of a University*, the "gentlemanly stance was a refuge from commitment, from the prospect of surrendering oneself to the transforming power of sex or politics or religion, and so losing the self-conscious inner poise that made life possible" (91). In other words, the disinterested gentleman, while writing himself a rhetoric of morally noble living, in fact preserves himself in amber, so to speak, by refusing to swallow the fare of the world. This self-protective stance is evident in our hero's actions. Convinced of his inherited guilt (that is, the guilt of having more than others), he is sure that the meal, that crucible of social relations, will reveal his true core, the rancid flavor of corruption that he fears lurks within himself.

This, tellingly, is also the mark of another purported gentlemanly abstainer: Mr. Merdle, the "master-mind of the age" (765), that great feeder of Society. Merdle is "the most disinterested of men—did everything for Society, and got as little for himself out of all his gain and care, as a man might" (293). Much of what he does is manifested in the fine dinners that he gives for Society—dinners at which he swallows virtually nothing. At the first great feast at his table, "Mr Merdle's own share of the repast might have been paid for with eighteenpence" (295–96), and at the great Merdle-Barnacle summit dinner, "[h]e took his usual poor eighteenpenny-worth in his usual indigestive way" (618). He seems to require nothing, to desire nothing, to be, in point of fact, like Clennam, no body at all.[15] As he tells his wife, he is nothing more than "a benefactor to Society . . . a person who provides it with all sorts of expensive things to eat and drink and look at" (447).

But Merdle's is not genuine benevolence, nor is his abstaining done in the interests of anyone but himself. Merdle is well aware of the dangers of self-revelation that eating holds; he thoroughly understands that the way in which the diner approaches his food speaks volumes about his self-imagining and his position in the world. In Merdle's case, refraining from food at table constitutes a canny move: his identity as a swindler (albeit a swindler whose felonious grasping at what he calls "good things" [675] is for the putative benefit of Society) is hidden beneath the mask of the self-sacrificer, the man who gives up everything, even bodily health, for the sake of the maintenance of the social order. Merdle is, of course, the greatest striver of all: his goal is to obscure his appetites behind a screen of self-abnegation, to gain all by appearing to give up all and thus to distance himself from the image of the grasping, devouring economic gentleman, even as he devours all of England. This behavior is extremely effective: Mr. Merdle is read by all around him as a man who has ruined his digestion through hard, self-sacrificing work and is wasting away. In the hours before he kills himself, Fanny lectures him about the necessity, for a man of his importance, of keeping up his strength with regular meals: "Having so much to do, Mr Merdle, loss of appetite is a serious thing with you, and you must have it seen to. You must not be ill," she says (764).

But while he seems to consume nothing, Merdle actually swells with his secret intake, his swindler's candy, made of that which he takes in from the besotted investors and would-be investors who invoke his name as though it were money itself. In death, he is stunningly revealed as a "heavily made man, with an obtuse head, and coarse, mean, common features" (771), a man who has grown fat on the proceeds of his nebulous, imaginary labors. Like Casby and Dorrit, he feeds off the lifeblood of others to sustain himself. Like Casby and Dorrit, he is constituted by what he takes in: the nutrition-free fare that he swallows is the greed of those around him.[16] It acts as a poison in his system, making him chronically ill, so that, despite Physician's assertion that "[h]e has the constitution of a rhinoceros, the digestion of an ostrich" (299), he can digest none of the "good things" (675) with which he supplies his table.

This is why Merdle is perpetually perceived, by those around him, as suffering from some mysterious internal ailment: he is so completely constituted by this poison that it shows through in his very skin. He is visually "a little dyspeptic," as Dorrit notices (674). At the first meeting between Dorrit and his newly minted in-law, "[t]here were black traces on [Merdle's] lips where they met, as if a little train of gunpowder had been fired there; and he looked like a man who, if his natural temperament had been quicker, would have been very feverish" (674). And because Merdle does not merely feed but is fed upon, the poison of greed returns to the bodies whence it came.[17]

Clearly, then, demonstrations of disinterest and self-sacrifice are not to be trusted. Even as gluttony is condemned by the novel, self-starvation is retailed not as noble sacrifice but as self-protection and selfishness. But though Clennam's fall is caused most directly by Merdle's death, it is also the demise of that singular figure that brings about the possibility of renewal in *Little Dorrit*. While all of England feeds on Merdle, there is no hope of change; but with the Great Man exposed, with the poison draining from the system of the body politic, there is, finally, space for healthier fare.

Not that our protagonist immediately grasps this opportunity. Instead, he wastes away at a record pace. His starvation diet, unlike Merdle's self-seeking version, is a sure-fire reducer: Arthur grows so narratively thin that he threatens to disappear from the story entirely. His attempt to create a moral gentlemanliness entirely divorced from the self-seeking economies of the putative gentlemen around him fails utterly. Instead, in that most selfish of all Christian sins, he seems to be swallowing nothing but his inevitable demise. Our brave hero threatens to arrest the quest narrative—and thus the movement of the novel—as he rots away in the Marshalsea prison, no longer merely unwilling but actually unable to swallow any sustenance at all.

Entombed in William Dorrit's old prison room, he is, in stark contrast to his predecessor, unable to accept the bounty offered up by others (a meal from John Chivery; a basket of food from the Plornishes), though the offerings are motivated not by the sort of neofeudal construction of the world retailed by his predecessor but by real regard and concern for Arthur. He can see no difference, it seems, between Dorrit's endlessly solicited testimonials and these anxiously proffered offerings of food. To Arthur, being fed by others is in and of itself problematic, a manifestation of selfishness that he cannot countenance, in line with that expressed by the economic gentlemen whose realm he has rejected. Instead, he turns inward, refusing literal and figurative admittance to those who would offer him succor.

Ironically, in pursuing this path, Clennam returns to the religious starvation diet of his childhood. His self-denying ethos is in line with what Norman Vance describes as "the withdrawn, ascetic spirituality commended by the leaders of the Oxford Movement . . . [which] stress[ed] the total depravity of ordinary human nature and the necessity for holy contempt of the world" (30). The Evangelicals of Arthur's day, like the Oxford Tractarians of Dickens's,[18] strongly advocated the rigorous suppression of human appetites and desires: "sublime disdain for man's sinful physical nature" (Vance, 32) and the promotion of fasting (Vance, 35) are commonplaces in Tractarian writings. The unbending religion of Arthur's mother is clearly aligned with the beliefs and practices of the Tractarians. And Arthur's attempt to obliterate the self through an ascetic denial of all appetites—and thus to purify himself of the untoward, unproductive, and exploitative appetites he sees indulged everywhere around him—is in the tradition of the Oxford Movement.

Like the ascetic Tractarians, Clennam seeks to erase the worldly and the bodily; his retreat, however, is not to the godly but, rather, to the vexed inner vicinities of his own mind. As Vance points out, for mainstream Protestants, "[i]t was a common objection that mortification of the flesh and other [Tractarian] religious observances were often ultimately selfish will-worship . . . a deliberate attempt to win to heaven by one's own efforts and by 'meretricious formalism' rather than through Christ" (39). In this common reading of Tractarian doctrine, reserving the self through asceticism is wrong because its innate selfishness runs counter to a sense of community endeavor: one must take part in the world and take the world into oneself to build a strong body politic. If this communal body is not fed appropriately, it will wither away, just as Arthur's body threatens to do.

At the same time, this apparent retreat from the world may also be read as a highly modern move. In his essay "On the Civilizing of Appetite," Stephen Mennell theorizes that in Western cultures, the notion of voluntarily restraining one's appetites has developed through a confluence of economic, political, and social changes, including the easing of consistent widespread hunger and the subsequent breakdown of firm class distinctions between those who possess the means to feast and those who do not (326–27). Self-restraint thus increasingly becomes a mark of refinement, wealth, and class, a sign of protomodern sophistication and distance from physical need; Arthur's extreme self-restraint, with its intense inward turn, may thus be read as a most radical form of modern-style individualism. Despite his work at feeding others, then, Arthur finds himself acting out the effects of the gluttonous gentlemanly appetite: like the economic gentleman, he starves his community by fetishizing his body.

The moral implications of Clennam's behavior in terms of its impact on others are made clear by a most unlikely source. Young John Chivery, the turnkey's son who loves Amy Dorrit, generously takes on the maintenance and feeding of his rival despite his anger toward Clennam. "If it's not a liberty," he asks him,

> "how long may it be your intentions, sir to go without eating and drinking?"
>
> "I have not felt the want of anything yet," returned Clennam. "I have no appetite just now."
>
> "The more reason why you should take some support, sir," urged Young John. "If you find yourself going on sitting here for hours and hours partaking of no refreshment because you have no appetite, why then you should and must partake of refreshment without an appetite. I'm going to have tea in my own apartment. If it's not a liberty, please to come and take a cup." (790)

Young John's offer constitutes one of the few instances of generous, meaningful commensality in the text: though he resents Clennam as a rival, he goes to some trouble to feed him. But despite Young John's care in putting together an appetizing meal for Arthur—he leaves the prison and returns with "fresh butter in a cabbage leaf, some thin slices of boiled ham in another cabbage leaf, and a little basket of water-cresses and salad herbs"—Clennam cannot eat: "The ham sickened him, the bread seemed to turn to sand in his mouth. He could force nothing upon himself but a cup of tea" (791). Young John points out that if Clennam cannot eat for himself, he should at least attempt to eat for "some one else's" sake (Chivery means Amy Dorrit's, of course). "Truly," Arthur answers, "I don't know for whose" (793). The moment reveals the selfishness at the heart of Clennam's self-denial, as well as his lack of understanding of the true benevolence involved in preserving community by preserving the self. Whereas Arthur, the putative gentleman, seeks to remove himself from the world, Young John, the turnkey's son with his ridiculous affectations, understands the difference between the inward slant of self-abnegation and the real generosity of selflessness.

Arthur's trial by fire—his immersion in the prison, his isolation, and his literal fever—at length brings this truth home to him. "Light of head with want of sleep and want of food (his appetite, and even his sense of taste, having forsaken him)" (824), Arthur is completely broken down, his self ironically laid bare not by eating but by refusing to eat. He is, at long last, ready to be fed—that is, to admit weakness, to be helped, and to reenter the world. Tellingly, the sustenance he takes first is both metaphorical and highly suggestive. When Little Dorrit returns to him, she is shocked at his illness. "[D]rawing an arm softly round his neck," she "laid his head upon her bosom, put a hand upon his head, and resting her cheek upon that hand, nursed him as lovingly, and GOD knows as innocently, as she had nursed her father in that room when she had been but a baby, needing all the care from others that she took of them" (825).

Little Dorrit is no longer the exploited, overburdened daughter, fed upon by the ravening, unnatural father. She has become "something more womanly than when she had gone away, and the ripening touch of the Italian sun was visible upon her face" (826). The problematic figure of the father has been replaced by the lover whom she has chosen, in a relationship offering considerably greater possibilities of reciprocity. That lover, in turn, is nurtured by the child transformed into a mother/lover (truly the "little mother" [210], as Maggy would have it), at once returning him to babyhood (and thus allowing him a fresh start, a new beginning) and reestablishing him as a sexual and thus a productive being.[19] Both Arthur and Little Dorrit are thus redeemed and restored by this rewriting of the Roman Daughter scene. It is the beginning of his entry into the communal realm and a striking first instance of Arthur feeding others by allowing himself to be fed.

Next, the attention of the narrative turns to the actual food that Amy and Maggy bring Clennam: fresh, straightforward market fare, cooling jellies, wine and water, and, of course, chicken—this last evocative of the "Chicking" that brought Maggy back to life in the hospital (143) and has fed her imagination ever since as the magical cure to all illness, physical or otherwise. Arthur at last swallows sustenance, however scanty, drinking when Little Dorrit puts a glass of something restorative to his lips. Returned to the realm of desire by her presence, he is able to take in the world by mouth, to live. Reaching true selflessness by allowing himself to be loved and cared for, he eats.

In eating, he gives up both his radical, hypermodern individualism and his nostalgic ascetic rigor. In return, he gains community. Horrified by the monstrous appetites of the economic gentlemen around him yet irrevocably tied to the world of business; convinced of the destructive, self-serving nature of working for gain yet well aware of the debilitating effects of poverty, Arthur Clennam has sought to solve the social dilemmas of the market system by withdrawing from it entirely. But food also serves as the marker of the impossibility of Arthur's move, demanding, by its public and transactional and unavoidable nature, a constant acknowledgment and declaration of desire, a constant move toward fulfilling desire that will only be born anew. Hunger, it seems, is both problematic and necessary; it is the impetus that drives the marketplace, and the marketplace itself, the novel suggests, is not inherently bad in its appetites. Shared for the purpose of the sustenance of all (as it is, for instance, at the Meagles' table before the advent of Gowan and Young Barnacle; as it is at the Ruggs', at the dinner where the plot in favor of Little Dorrit is furthered), food never turns toxic in the mouth in *Little Dorrit*. The systems of the body politic, like the human body, depend on desire, acquisition, and exchange.[20] Only when its participants take sustenance out of the mouths of others do things fall apart.

By refusing to swallow, Clennam has shut himself off from the transactional, transubstantiative nature of feasting. When he agrees to open his lips, he at once admits the necessity of appetite and gives up on the seductive notion of the sacrosanct, inviolable self. This notion of reciprocity marks the crucial difference from economic gentlemanliness: the system of petitioning and benevolence, in line with the olden-days dream of the feudal, is intimately tied to patronage and thus must necessarily withhold true sustenance both from the putative provider of benevolence and from the recipient. For Arthur, the natural cycle of birth and death—of feeding and being fed—reasserts itself as the basis for community.

Tellingly, Arthur here returns to the scant optimism of his youth: nature, the text reveals, was his only "mother" in this respect, giving him "hopeful promises . . . playful fancies . . . the harvests of tenderness and humility that lie hidden in the early-fostered seeds of the imagination . . . the oaks of retreat from blighting winds, that have the germs of their strong roots in nursery acorns" (884).

In fact, a crucial moment of Arthur's reestablishment in the world—the moment at which Little Dorrit reveals the loss of her fortune, which removes her from the sphere of economics and clears the way for the couple's marriage and reentrance into the world—takes place on "a healthy autumn day," on which the prisoner is "weak but otherwise restored." It is a day when "the golden fields had been reaped and ploughed again, when the summer fruits had ripened and waned, when the green perspectives of hops had been laid low by the busy pickers, when the apples clustering in the orchards were russet, and the berries of the mountain ash were crimson among the yellowing foliage" (883). This natural bounty, harvested by the activity of usefully employed people, is, of course, absent in the "changeless and barren" (883) Marshalsea; but Little Dorrit brings the natural world into the prison in her voice as she reads to Clennam, giving him refreshment and renewal. This renewal is not the rebirth of spring but the labor-intensive, more mature liberality of the autumn crop: there is nothing easy or naïve about this construction of nature, but it promises sustained nutrition for the body and mind and carries Arthur far from the burning lassitude of summer, that period of indolence and want of energy that is reminiscent here of the prison, of the stagnation and waste of Society, of the home in which Arthur was raised, of the opening moments of the novel, set in the barren, dislocated wastes of Marseilles.[21] Little Dorrit, then, helps Arthur to reenter the natural cycles of the world, to escape from the prison-house of ascetic denial just as she helps him to escape from the Marshalsea, to return to the realm of fecundity, of bounty, and of possibility.

Having dismissed money entirely as a source of meaningful or stable class affiliation, the novel here returns to the notion of character in its construction of class, a notion diametrically opposed to the self-centered radical individualism of the protomodern economic gentleman. In leaving Arthur, newly emerged from the crypt of the prison, as the last gentleman standing, so to speak, the novel retools ideals to which characters such as Casby and Dorrit pay lip service to hide their rapacious natures, recasting such notions as viable social values. Arthur is a gentleman because he is, in a word, benevolent. But his gentlemanliness can be assumed only in conjunction with others: alone, he wastes away in his ascetic isolation.

Class, in this new sense, is not merely the ability and the willingness to set a fine table for others; it is also the ability and willingness to sit at the feast, to eat and drink with others, to reveal the self in the world, and to acknowledge the leveling power of hunger and its insistence on the equality of bodies. The novel offers up, in the place of Dorrit and his ilk, a vision of gentlemanliness predicated on useful engagement with a world that is, for better or for worse, always already a marketplace. The moral gentlemanly body may be read as another synecdochical construction, though with a difference that sets it apart from the Casbyian and Dorritian models: instead of simply swallowing the whole, the gentlemanly body becomes a communal body. In opening itself up, this gentlemanly body creates a contingent self, a transactional self in the terms of business, a messy and shifting self that is a body politic in every possible way. Traditional notions of class are thus effectively erased.

In this way, *Little Dorrit* is a novel ending not, as it has often been read, in capitulation or in tears but in a notably unstable and tentative but nonetheless flourishing vision of community life. *Little Dorrit* has repeatedly been described as one of Dickens's darkest efforts: the novel, many critics contend, manifests an abandonment of the notion of redemption, a cry of despair for the apparently dwindling possibilities of meaningful social reform, an indictment of the hopelessness and credulousness of the masses who suffer the most under the tyranny of the class system.[22] But such dark and dismal readings of the social realm in *Little Dorrit* miss the sense of possibility that floats beneath the surface of the novel, ultimately resulting in a complex conclusion embracing at once the brave new world of midcentury industrialism and the idea of the renunciation of capital, the notion of progress and the mythical ideal of the gentlemanly leader, realized not through an unthinking acceptance or rejection of industrialism or mercantilism but through a tenuously calibrated notion of reciprocity and transactional community. *Little*

Dorrit reimagines the public realm as a cooperative society headed by a gentleman, a society that is aligned (uncomfortably but productively) with the marketplace even as it reestablishes hierarchies based not on wealth but on that fragile quality, character. This carefully cultivated utopian capitalist optimism, this dream of a newborn Englishness led by a newly made gentleman, is what makes the novel both compelling and politically fraught.

And this, in turn, is what the novel's remarkable and much-reviled ending reveals. The sense of rebirth in this moment is palpable. Arthur's visitors have left him on the afternoon before the wedding, "[a]nd the day ended, and the night ended, and the morning came" (893), the narrative clearly echoing the biblical resonances of Genesis. Rigaud's letter, that last link with an exploitative and unproductive past, is burnt; the wedding takes place, witnessed by many friends; and then Arthur and Little Dorrit

> paused for a moment on the steps of the portico, looking at the fresh perspective of the street in the autumn morning sun's bright rays, and then went down. Went down into a modest life of usefulness and happiness. . . . They went quietly down into the roaring streets, inseparable and blessed; and as they passed along in sunshine and in shade, the noisy and the eager, and the arrogant and the froward and the vain, fretted and chafed, and made their usual uproar. (894–95)

The conclusion of the novel, in fact, offers Arthur the only complete integration that he has found anywhere in the text. Having left behind the self-denying persona he constructed to defend himself against the world—having ceased to feed on himself—Arthur emerges as a new kind of ideal gentleman. He is reborn as an Adam for a new age, not secluded from the world by grand dinners and great fortunes but instead immersed in it, drawing sustenance from it while he provides it with succor. He is, indeed, "happy and useful" in his new life, in which he and Little Dorrit are "inseparable and blessed": in reaching beyond the self, he has become complete. Needing a modicum of money to sustain themselves, and yet separated from the grasping impulse, Clennam and Little Dorrit are both of and apart from the marketplace, engaged in a transactional communal life that effectively overwrites the problematic exploitative version promoted by the economic gentleman.

Instead of subordinating themselves to the putative members of the ruling class who have misled the novel's London world, Arthur and Little Dorrit have effectively replaced them: the fall of the houses of Clennam and Merdle (literal and figurative), the death of Mr. Dorrit, the unmaking of the Patriarch, and, most suggestively, the live burial of Rigaud have cleared the way for new blood. Activity becomes crucial: "Against the artificiality of stasis and fixed identity are the images of road and street, into which, appropriately, Clennam and Little Dorrit descend. . . . Change, which is movement in time . . . becomes essential to whatever possibilities the austere world of *Little Dorrit* will allow" (Levine, 17).

This is not to say that the old forces of stasis have been removed; the Barnacles toil on, Fanny and Mrs. Merdle battle it out, "the arrogant and the froward and the vain" go on as usual. But just as the Circumlocution Office has become irrelevant to Daniel Doyce, who has circumvented it by gaining honor and just reward abroad, so too have the creaky workings of Society become beside the point. Its acolytes are left to run themselves on into obsolescence or redundancy if they so choose, but Arthur and Little Dorrit's union, and their entry into the world as rationally producing and consuming beings, illustrates the loss of control that these representatives of traditional sources of power have undergone.

Aliment, then, serves as political barometer and social prod, revealing the vacancy of the extant social contract and positing a hopeful, if conflicted, vision for a future free both of bingeing and of starving. It is a tentative and messy but nonetheless optimistic vision of a world in which the perceived stranglehold of the rich on England has been, if not broken, at least eased enough to allow breathing room. Not exactly a landscape of revolution or a middle-class Elysium, the London that Dickens leaves his readers with is nonetheless a place where class has begun to be reimagined—and the connection between food and the gentleman is both a key marker of and a mover in that reimagining. The novel's ending suggests a rational utopia: the possibility of a union of business and human concern, a marketplace—since there will inevitably be marketplaces—of true production, in which workers are no longer alienated from the products of their labor, in which a move is made toward sharing the "good things." Arthur Clennam is freed by rational productive labor tied to meaningful human benefit, returning to the world in the capacity of business partner to Doyce, husband to Amy, and in the course of time, father. In this way, the community, led by one who unites business and humanity in his very being, the child of the artist and the businessman, can maneuver around the forces of economic gentlemanliness—"the noisy and the eager, and the arrogant and the froward and the vain"—and carry on.

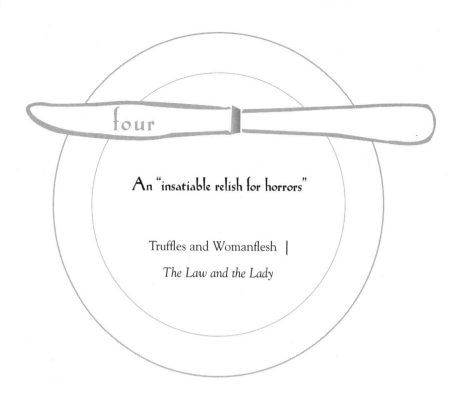

four

An "insatiable relish for horrors"

Truffles and Womanflesh |

The Law and the Lady

Wilkie Collins's *Law and the Lady* (1875) is suffused to choking with food: the novel is a fabric of secret repasts and indigestible meals, of monstrous appetites and unswallowable flavors. The novel's greatest problem eater is surely one of the most striking gentlemen in nineteenth-century literature: Miserrimus Dexter, a legless, truffle-cooking, Burgundy-drinking, physically abusive, lascivious madman with the handsome face and flowing hair of a Romantic poet, the hands of a woman, and the frilled dress of an aristocrat from the previous century. A tale-spinning shape-shifter who makes his way through the world variously in a wheeled chair, on his belly like a snake, or head over heels, tumbling down the room at break-neck speed in an activity he calls "Dexter's Leapfrog," he is the pivot on which Collins's strange murder-mystery/love story/detective fiction turns. And he is not a man to be trifled with: at once degenerative and forward-looking, aristocratic and labor-driven, Dexter is a hybrid monster of gentlemanliness with "an insatiable relish for horrors" and a highly refined anthropophagous appetite. In Dexter—half man, half machine, and at least half mad—Collins has created a Gothic monster for the machine age. A figure of great nostalgia

who is physically imbricated in the speedy, uncontrollable industrial world he seems to reject, Dexter threatens not only to shut
down or swallow the gentlefolk around him, relegating them to the
stasis of a present-past, but also, boundary-less, to swallow the striving middle class whole.

The Law and the Lady tells the story of our narrator Valeria's discovery that her new husband, the old-money gentleman of leisure
Eustace Macallan, has married her under a false name. When she
confronts him, he refuses to explain and begs his wife to stop prying: "[I]f you stir a step further in this matter," he declares, "there
is an end of your happiness for the rest of your life!" Naturally,
Valeria finds it necessary to stir a step or two further. She turns detective and discovers the truth: Eustace Macallan's first wife, Sara,
died of arsenic poisoning and Eustace was tried for her murder. The
verdict was "Not Proven," a damning compromise decision allowed
under a quirk of Scottish law. Mortified at Valeria's discovery,
Eustace runs away from his new wife. Determined to clear his
name, Valeria turns detective, searching for the true history of Sara
Macallan's death.

She begins her search for exculpatory evidence with the aptly
named Miserrimus Dexter, Eustace's old friend and a witness for
him at trial. Dexter enters the novel with a sensational courtroom appearance:

> Gliding, self-propelled in his chair on wheels . . . a
> strange and startling creature—literally the half of a
> man—revealed himself. . . . A coverlid, which had been
> thrown over his chair, had fallen off. . . . The loss of it
> exposed to the public curiosity the head, the arms, and
> the trunk of a living human being: absolutely deprived
> of the lower limbs. To make this deformity all the more
> striking and all the more terrible, the victim of it was—
> as to his face and his body—an unusually handsome,
> and an unusually well-made man. His long silky hair, of
> a bright and beautiful chestnut color, fell over shoulders
> that were the perfection of strength and grace. His face
> was bright with vivacity and intelligence. His large,
> clear blue eyes, and his long, delicate white hands, were

like the eyes and hands of a beautiful woman. He would
have looked effeminate, but for the manly proportions
of his throat and chest: aided in their effect by his flowing beard and long moustache, of a lighter chestnut
shade than the colour of his hair. Never had a magnificent head and body been more hopelessly ill-bestowed
than in this instance! Never had Nature committed a
more careless or a more cruel mistake than in the making of this man! (173)

Dexter seems a sad victim of nature's folly—a freak of nature,[1] a
gentleman utterly bound by his body, fated to be looked at not as a
man of power but as a victim, a failure of old-fashioned bloodlines.
But Dexter's singular physical state is a source not only of weakness
but also of power. The strange, boundary-crossing nature of this
power is made manifest in one of the novel's strangest meals: an
afternoon collation cooked and served in Dexter's drawing room by
the "strange and startling creature" himself.

The meal takes place during Valeria's second visit to Dexter at
his crumbling mansion. When Valeria explains to Dexter that she
hopes he will help her to clear Eustace's name and acknowledges
that she "suspect[s] somebody" (242) in the matter of Sara's death,
her host is laid low by the revelation. He asks her to leave him alone
for a few minutes, explaining, "Any reference to events at Gleninch
excites and shakes me. I shall be fit for it again, if you will kindly
give me a few minutes to myself" (242). Valeria, of course, complies.
When her host summons her to return, she discovers that "this most
multiform of living beings" (244) has transformed himself:

> His eyes sparkled with good humour; his cheeks were
> flushing under a new excitement of some sort. Even his
> dress had undergone alteration since I had seen it last.
> He now wore an extemporised cap of white paper; his
> ruffles were tucked up; a clean apron was thrown over
> the seagreen coverlid. He backed his chair before me,
> bowing and smiling; and waved me to a seat with the
> grace of a dancing-master, chastened by the dignity of a
> lord in waiting.

"I am going to cook," he announced, with the most engaging simplicity. "We both stand in need of refreshment, before we return to the serious business of our interview." (244)

Dexter leads Valeria to a tiny kitchen, hidden away behind a curtain; here he takes a jar of truffles from a cupboard and announces that he will serve them "stewed in Burgundy" (246) for his guest. Turning his chair toward the stove after a long speech to his guest, he begins to cook.

The scene is remarkable in any number of ways: the fact of the kitchen itself, Dexter's extraordinary costume, the decision of this gentleman to cook at all, and the contents of the meal all give the moment the quality of a fever dream. The substance of Dexter's meal seems at first to be as rarefied as Mr. Woodhouse's dinner of gruel is debased, and in this way it marks Dexter's gentlemanliness, much like Arthur Huntingdon's fatal gentlemanly fare.[2] It is tempting, in fact, to understand Dexter as a man who sets out to reingest and reiterate his status as a man of class through rarefied food. Here, after all, is the man who drinks only Clos Vougeot, "the King of Burgundies" (244) (which are in turn collectively "the King of Wines")—a particularly expensive luxury in an age when imported wines were taxed according to their relative strength, so that champagne was cheap to import while fortified wines were very expensive (Drummond and Wilbraham, 339). Truffles, of course, were "extremely dear" (Freeman, 73), so costly that they graced only the tables of the very rich. Clearly, this is food that marks the host as privileged indeed. His choice of aliment, then, gives the impression that Dexter seeks to swallow status at table.

This idea of the assumption of class through aliment is, too, taken up in Dexter's behavior. His reverential attitude toward cookery transforms it from labor to a rarefied, serious, worthwhile gentlemanly employment: he "plunge[s] into profound reflection at the sight of" the truffles; he says to Valeria, as he lights the gas, "'Forgive me if I observe the most absolute silence . . . dating from the moment when I take this in my hand. . . . Properly pursued, the Art of Cookery allows of no divided attention,' he continue[s] gravely. 'In that observation you will find the reason why no woman ever has reached, or ever will reach, the highest distinction as a cook'" (246). Dexter clearly is not a worker like his doglike, half-witted devoted servant, Ariel, who produces only plain joints, sustaining life in the most prosaic way. Instead, he is an accomplished artist who cooks not in the kitchen belowstairs but in the drawing room, and his culinary abilities are directly related to—indeed, grow directly out of—his gentlemanliness.

The contents of the meal at once reinforce Dexter's status and ensure that Valeria feels his alimentary superiority: he casts himself as a man belonging to an unquestionably elevated realm who condescends toward his visitor, marking her as a distinctly lesser light (not unlike a Casby or a Woodhouse). To the uninitiated, truffles—among the most esoteric of luxury foods—are, as Valeria makes clear, not only inscrutable but also fundamentally unappealing. When Dexter first produces them from a mysterious black bottle by means of an evil-sounding spike, she sees "some little irregularly formed black objects[,] . . . occult substances, of uninviting appearance" (245). When she asks him, "'What are those things, Mr Dexter? and are we really going to eat them?'" her host's response is appropriately amazed: "'Where is our boasted progress?' he crie[s]. 'What is education but a name? Here is a cultivated person who doesn't know Truffles when she sees them!'" (245). Valeria's lack of sophistication, he implies, is breathtaking. "'Look at it; meditate over it,'" he directs her sternly (246).

When he presents the finished product, his tone is equally unmistakable: "'Compose yourself, Mrs Valeria,' he said. 'This is an epoch in your life. Your first Truffle! Don't touch it with the knife. Use the fork alone. And—pardon me; this is most important—eat slowly'" (248). Valeria, it seems, must be taught not only to recognize but also to eat and to appreciate truffles appropriately. The value of this delicacy is created not through its intrinsic appeal, through any unalloyed pleasure of the palate, but rather through discourse. One must be a person not only of means and of inherent class but also of discernment—a person who is knowledgeable, aware, and moving in the right circles—to recognize and properly esteem a food so sublimely incomprehensible in appearance and flavor, a food that, Valeria "humbly" notes, "might have been familiar enough to a woman accustomed to the luxurious tables of the rich; but which were a new revelation to a person like myself, who had led a simple country life in the house of a clergyman with small means" (245). In this way, truffles perform Dexter's class work on Valeria, establishing him as unquestionably a man of power, knowledge, and refinement—a gentleman born, a gentleman at table, a gentleman even when he stands before his doll's kitchen.

Not incidentally, truffles are also helpful in asserting Dexter's gendered status: the fare that he serves up—rich, strongly flavored, and redolent of wine—is hardly appropriate for a ladylike appetite. Dexter's truffles are unequivocally the sort of food that feeds masculine power.[3] The reason for this alimentary flexing may seem readily apparent. Dexter, after all, clearly has some obstacles to overcome in the performance of his gender, given his physical embodiment. Unsurprisingly, this "half of a man" is often read as a perfect embodiment of Lacanian theory, a man for whom the fulfillment of desire is perpetually deferred, whose profound lack of the phallus is literally written on the body. Numerous critics have read Dexter as little more than a foil for the novel's protofeminist heroine, a cross-gendered or degendered gentleman who serves only to emphasize Valeria's strength. Kate E. Brown, for instance, describes Dexter succinctly as "the least eligible bachelor in Victorian fiction." She asserts that Dexter, "[i]nsistently heterosexual yet singularly ill equipped for conjugal duties, equally dexterous and sinister . . . embodies both masculine beauty and a perfect absence of masculinity. In this light, it is hardly without irony that he prefers to be called Master: the mastery that Dexter claims is inevitably exposed as a fantasy by the limits of his body" (6).[4] Never, it appears, was lack more clearly incorporated—never was the castrated gentleman, the ineffectual anachronism of the strivers' age, better delineated.

But the overt sense of performativity that Dexter brings to his cookery belies his belief in the notion that aliment has the power to constitute the self. His costume, his lightning shifts in mood and character, and his overwrought speeches give the impression that Dexter's labors in the kitchen are a sort of set piece, a performance in which he does not truly believe. The kitchen resembles a child's playhouse: here are "a neat little gas stove for cooking[,] [d]rawers and cupboards, plates, dishes, and saucepans . . . all on a miniature scale, all scrupulously bright and clean" (245). Dexter's flourish of welcome, as he draws the curtains, has the touch of the performer about it: "Welcome to the kitchen!" he cries, as he draws "out of a recess in the wall a marble slab which served as a table" (245). This seems more like a space for make-believe, a stage set, than a real kitchen (like, for instance, the "bleak and barren" version [228] belowstairs in Dexter's home, where Ariel produces her boiled joints of meat).

Then there are the rituals by which Dexter declares himself to be abiding in his cookery. He announces to his guest, "You see me in my cook's dress—forgive it. There is a form in these things. I am a great stickler for forms" (244). But Dexter's "form" is completely different from the clear social rules demonstrated, for example, by Major Fitz-David's easy hospitality or by the straightforward, everyday nature of a meal at Benjamin's table. In an era of conspicuous consumption, the proper meal of gentlefolk (crafted, of course, by servants and professional chefs) is an affair of many courses and many dishes; the sort of "refreshment" that Dexter proposes arrives most often in the form of tea and its standard accessories.[5] But what Dexter offers up is hardly tea and rusks and butter: "truffles. . . . stewed in Burgundy" (246) are not exactly light, ladylike fare. In fact, Dexter's alimental rituals seem to follow no clear structures or forms whatsoever: the repast he offers Valeria is not a proper meal at all, consisting as it does of only a single, incomplete course[6] and occurring as it does at an odd hour in the middle of the afternoon, neither luncheon nor teatime nor dinnertime. Dexter's insistence on form, in light of this "meal" that lacks virtually every marker of that highly codified social operation, appears quixotic, eccentric; his behavior betrays the fact that this "refreshment" is an invented structure, following no necessary rules of gentlemanly behavior.

Dexter's enthusiastic production of truffles stewed in Burgundy, then, despite his "linger[ing] and languish[ing] over" his meal (248), seems nothing more than another element in a set he has constructed—an idea that he gestures toward in his reply to Valeria's letter after her conversation with Lady Clarinda, one of the Macallans' houseguests on the night Sara died. Aware that Lady Clarinda's story has revealed the falsity of his accusation of Mrs. Beauly (another guest, and the woman Eustace had declared his love for) in Sara's murder, Dexter ironically gestures toward this exposure when, in promising to rebut Lady Clarinda's accusations, he writes, "I await the honour and the happiness of your visit. Send me word by telegraph, whether you would like Truffles again, or whether you would prefer something simpler and lighter—say that incomparable French dish, Pig's Eyelids and Tamarinds. Believe me always your ally and admirer, your poet and cook" (270). Truffles, it seems, are as illusory as this invented French dish, the desire for them equally nonsensical, equally rooted in a desire for the impossible, the make-believe. His mischievous dismissal of the meal that he has made such a fuss over reveals that Dexter places very little value on the fare that he seemed to exalt so; clearly, the truffles are not the important food, the fare that Dexter is willing to pursue at any cost. And, in fact, he produces this questionable feast not for his own sustenance but for that of his guest. When Valeria tells him that she has never tasted truffles, for instance, he replies, "'You shall eat it, Mrs Valeria, stewed in Burgundy!' He [lights] the gas for cooking, with the air of a man who was about to offer [her] an inestimable proof of his good will" (246). But this is no innocent act of alimental generosity.

To understand Dexter's meal and its aims—his lack of alimentary need for this performative fare, his real object of consumption—it is important to understand his strange gentlemanly body. A repeated slippage in his portrayal signals the power and danger that the legless Dexter embodies. In his initial entry into the text, the boundaries between the wheelchair and the man are shaky: whether "self-propelled" (173) refers to the organic, upper-body Dexter alone or to the combined wheelchair-and-man frame is unclear. When he leaves the stand, "[t]he chair on wheels glide[s] away, with the half-man in it" (179); the narrative shifts between giving agency to the man in the chair and giving precedence to the chair that carries the man. Valeria's first direct encounter with Dexter entails an elaboration of this slippage. She reports that a "high chair on wheels moved by . . . carrying a shadowy figure with floating hair, and arms furiously raised and lowered, working the machinery that propelled the chair" (206). The sentence seems deliberately confusing: the "arms" may belong either to the chair or to the man carried inside it; the chair appears at first to move of its own volition, bearing its load, and only later is the man introduced.

Valeria goes on to describe how the man "swept past me, on his rumbling and whistling wheels"; how "the chair rushed out of sight." Apparently giving up on sorting out man and machinery, she continues, "[T]he strident wheels turned at the far end of the room. . . . The fantastic and frightful apparition, man and machinery blended in one—the new Centaur, half man, half chair—flew by me again" (206). And when Dexter catches sight of Valeria and her mother-in-law in the doorway, "[t]he wheelchair stopped with a shock . . . altered its course, and flew at us with the rush of a wild animal" (207). During Valeria's second visit, the wheelchair seems to be the sum total of the man. "The wheeled chair advanced to meet me," she recalls, "so slowly and so softly that I hardly knew it again. Miserrimus Dexter held out his hand" (231–32).

Dexter himself offers no correctives: speaking through the testimony of a sheriff's officer in the trial transcript, he reinforces this confusion. As the deputy, Isaiah Schoolcraft, recalls for the court, he had been frustrated in his attempts to search a drawer in Eustace's room by the man he refers to as "the crippled gentleman" (144), who had blocked the table in question with his chair. "Finding there was no moving him by fair means," Schoolcraft explains, "I took his chair and pulled it away. . . . The crippled gentleman flew into a furious rage with me for presuming to touch his chair. 'My chair is Me,' he said: 'how dare you lay hands on Me?'" (145). In this way, Dexter claims the sacred privilege of a gentleman— that is, the right not to be touched by one's inferiors without one's express permission—for the wood-and-steel machine that is his lower half.

Rather than a pathetic figure incapacitated by his weak body, a being defined by lack, Dexter is a creature of excessiveness, of power and horror derived not from his missing limbs but from his imbrication of the industrial machinery of the chair into his very self; he finds potency in his truncated physical form. And he exploits his bodily difference at key moments in the text, using his legless state to his advantage as he hops and slides, for instance, through Eustace's sleeping household, secretly amassing a store of illicit knowledge on its inhabitants in the service of his pursuit of

Sara Macallan's affections (because Dexter, it turns out, was in love with Eustace's unloved wife and had offered to run away with her). As he recounts for Valeria, he "drops noiselessly from his chair, on to his hands; lies flat on the floor"; and watches the goings-on in hallways and bedrooms from the cracks at the bottom of doorways "like a cat at a mousehole" (254). Wanting a better view, "he pops his head out of his door, down on the floor where nobody would think of looking for him" (254). He "hop[s] on his hands" (254) and "slid[es] down the stairs" (255), he says, in pursuit of Mrs. Beauly. Dexter, then, uses his body to accomplish what ordinary humans cannot. Far from limiting or inhibiting him, his legless state seems to render him uncontainable, unstoppable.

And he revels in his difference, finding a visceral, explosive pleasure—even a *jouissance*—in his physicality. The game of "Dexter's Leapfrog" that so unnerves Valeria is one sign of this pleasure: "Hopping down the room," she relates, "he overthrew . . . all the smaller and lighter chairs. . . . [H]e turned . . . encouraged himself with a scream of triumph, and leapt rapidly over chair after chair, on his hands—his limbless body, now thrown back from the shoulders, and now thrown forward to keep the balance, in a manner at once wonderful and horrible to behold" (259). Valeria's first view of him, thundering up and down the room in the person of dead heroes of the past, is equally evocative:

> "I am Napoleon at the sunrise of Austerlitz!" shouted the man in the chair as he swept past me, on his rumbling and whistling wheels. . . . "I give the word; and thrones rock, and kings fall, and nations tremble, and men by the tens of thousands fight and bleed and die!" The chair rushed out of sight, and the shouting man in it became another hero. "I am Nelson!" the ringing voice cried now. "I am leading the flight at Trafalgar. I issue my commands, prophetically conscious of victory and death. I see my own apotheosis—my public funeral, my nation's tears, my burial in the glorious church. The ages remember me, and the poets sing my praise in immortal verse!" The strident wheels turned at the far end of the room, and came back. The fantastic and frightful appari-

tion . . . flew by me again in the dying light. "I am
Shakespere!" cried the frantic creature, now. "I am writing 'Lear,' the tragedy of tragedies. Ancients and mod-
erns, I am the poet who towers over them all. Light!
light! The lines flow out like lava from the eruption of
my volcanic mind. Light! light! for the poet of all time
to write the words that live for ever!" He ground and
tore his way back towards the middle of the room. (207)

Dexter appears full to overflowing with power: he is a mass-producing
creature, turning out ideas and words and identities as rapidly as he
thunders up and down the room on his wheels. This amalgamation
of chair and man is not simply a suturing or confusion of physical
boundaries but a luxuriant denial of the existence of such barriers
between man and machine.

And Dexter is not just a Victorian protorobot. His visceral and
emotional nature is much in evidence as well, and it is not confined to the organic body or mind: the chair rushes about "like a
wild animal," invested with the wills and desires of the animal-
man. Those desires include a considerable sexual appetite, particularly for Valeria. Dexter studies her figure and tells her about it; he
gets too close; he touches her. Finally, Dexter loses control: "He
caught my hand in his, and devoured it with kisses. His lips burnt
me like fire. He twisted himself suddenly in the chair, and wound
his arm round my waist. In the terror and indignation of the moment, vainly struggling with him, I cried out for help" (299).

Obviously, despite his physical disabilities, his almost textbook
Lacanian lack, this man does not consider himself a eunuch. And
his desire is not limited to Valeria: before Sara's marriage to Eustace, the lawyer Mr. Playmore exclaims, "Miserrimus Dexter asked
her—deformed as he was, seriously asked her—to be his wife" (278).

Dexter's physical attempt on Valeria, his insinuating questions, his examination of her figure, and his proposals to Sara all
demonstrate his belief in himself as emphatically male and emphatically entitled; they also speak to his emotional life, his sense
of himself as a gentleman of standing and worth. As he tells Valeria, speaking of Eustace's ability to attract the women in whom
Dexter is also interested:

There are some men whom the women all like; and there are other men whom the women never care for. Without the least reason for it in either case. The one man is just as good as the other; just as handsome, as agreeable, as honourable, and as high in rank as the other. And yet, for Number One, they will go through fire and water; and for Number Two, they won't so much as turn their heads to look at him. Why? They don't know themselves. . . . Is there a physical reason for it? Is there some potent magnetic emanation from Number One, which Number Two doesn't possess? I must investigate this when I have the time, and when I find myself in the humour. (238)

To understand these tangled threads, it is instructive to turn to economic history: this ravenous, useless gentleman is of a piece with the socioeconomic climate into which *The Law and the Lady* emerged. Collins's novel was published serially in the *Graphic* in 1874, in the early moments of a period that the Victorians would come to call the Great Depression of 1873–96.[7] The tough times were fueled in part by industrial competition from overseas, particularly from Germany and America, where newer, more efficient factories and machines were outstripping the gains of the cradle of industry; by England's outdated tariff policies; and by widespread English speculation both in shaky domestic ventures and in the very overseas concerns that were creating problems for the nation's industrial areas. The gentle classes were hit hard: during the Great Depression, many of those at the top of the social heap began a slide from power and ease that was to continue, virtually unabated, well past the end of the century. Agriculture, the mainstay of the landed economy, began to encounter stiff competition from overseas, and the value of land began to plummet. The great estates began the breaking-up that would soon become wholesale selling-off. At the same time, the striver fortunes that had been made by industrialists during the boom years were joined by the hefty incomes of the City men, and together this nouveau-riche class began to seriously rival and indeed surpass the inherited wealth of the gentry. Men and women of leisure and their compatriots in genteel employment might be forgiven for looking to the future with alarm.[8]

But the times were hardly easy for much of the middle class. Though in the long view the Great Depression may have ushered in an era of great middle-class power and prosperity, in the short run, the social and economic upheaval it engendered was a decidedly mixed blessing. Certainly, opportunities opened up for the striving classes when the stratified social order began to break down: mobility was easier than in the past, and bold entrepreneurship could be very rewarding. But as the rich found themselves with less and less disposable income and as the poor (often laid off from factory jobs because of upstart overseas competition or unable to turn a profit on rented land) found their incomes ever more unreliable, much of the middle class "suffered an 'income squeeze' during the price, rent and profit slump," as Richard Tames puts it (32). Trade-unionism and demands for universal suffrage swept the country, bringing a heady sense of power to the working classes and to women but complicating matters for managers and owners; the public imagination was seized with images of rack and ruin, and middle-class literary voices were quick to blame the upper classes. The standard specimen of the middle class was imagined as energetic, enterprising, and independent, ready to take over the helm of society from the superannuated gentleman; the gentleman was presented (in more or less veiled and more or less vicious depictions) as useless, unproductive, and out of touch, a Dorrit-esque parasitic anachronism waiting to die out.[9]

Collins's Major Fitz-David seems a model for such gentlemanliness: with his taste for the ladies, his dyed hair, and his little dinners, he is an antiquated emblem of depravity and luxury, entirely removed from the world of work, an antiquated gentlemanly type who swallows those who help him to preserve the last remnants of gentlemanly rule. Eustace, too, seems a throwback, a would-be chivalric gentleman grasping at Romantic despair, a useless creature who wanders through his own story like a ghost. But Miserrimus Dexter is a different sort of fellow: in him, the superannuated gentleman is bulked up with some new high-energy fare. This is not to say that the old-fashioned—even the anachronistic—is left behind in Dexter. On the contrary, in many ways he is a self-conscious avatar of venerable gentlemanly tradition who declares himself a defender of all that is vanishing in the machine age, a stalwart supporter of tradition and nostalgia. His quixotic stance is apparent in Valeria's first view of his home. She describes his suburban neighborhood:

> I saw the half-completed foundations of new houses in their first stage of existence. . . . In front of us . . . rose a black mass which gradually resolved itself . . . into a long, low, and ancient house. . . . "There is one of his madnesses!" [Mrs. Macallan] said. "The speculators in this new neighbourhood have offered him, I don't know how many thousand pounds for the ground the house stands on. It was originally the manor-house of the district. Dexter purchased it . . . in one of his freaks of fancy. He has no old family associations with the place; the walls are all but tumbling about his ears; and the money offered would really be of use to him. But, no! He refused the proposal of the enterprising speculators, by letter, in these words: 'My house is a standing monument of the picturesque and beautiful, amid the mean, dishonest, and grovelling constructions of a mean, dishonest, and grovelling age. I keep my house, gentlemen, as a useful lesson to you. Look at it, while you are building round me—and blush, if you can, for your own work.'" (202–3)

Here is Dexter in his character as champion of a vanishing age of beauty and refinement; here is Dexter in serious opposition to the ready-made, the mass-produced, the hallmarks of the industrial. Much of his behavior tends to reinforce this impression of old-fashioned, chivalrous gentlemanliness in direct and defiant opposition to the new. He plays "the ancient harp of the pictured Muses and the legendary Welsh Bards" (219); he wears "lace ruffles at the ends of his sleeves, in the fashion of the last century" (213); and he asserts, referring to his gold bangles and his quilted silk jacket, that "[e]xcept in this ignoble and material nineteenth century, men have always worn precious stuffs and beautiful colours. . . . I despise the brutish contempt for beauty and the mean dread of expense which degrade a gentleman's costume to black cloth, and limit a gentleman's ornaments to a finger ring, in the age I live in" (232). He paints; he composes; he pursues, in a word, the life of a refined man of leisure, borrowing self-consciously from a host of traditions and fashions dating from classical antiquity forward.

His description of himself as melancholic is of a piece with this self-presentation. The term occurs more than once: he tells Valeria, for instance, "This is one of my melancholy days. Tears rise unbidden to my eyes. I sigh and sorrow over myself; I languish for pity. Just think what I am! A poor solitary creature, cursed with a frightful deformity. How pitiable! how dreadful! My affectionate heart—wasted. . . . Sad! sad! sad! Please pity me! . . . Pretty Mrs. Valeria, say you pity me!" (232). His language conjures up an image of an old-fashioned, neo-Romantic character, a Byron out of step with the world and in thrall to his own oversensitive soul.[10]

But while Dexter creates a sense of himself as an old-fashioned man of ease and leisure, an outdated artiste in thrall to his passions, he is also a creature of uncontained energy who brings his time-honored affectations with him into a realm of speed, as Valeria's first encounter with him makes clear. Here old and new, past and present come together in the rush of the wheels as Dexter rockets down the room, embodying historical figures while he drives himself along at breakneck speed on his mechanical appendages. He imagines himself as a leader of fighting men, a figure of power and brute strength, a man who makes his mark on the world. The mass-productive force embodied in his metal wheels allows him to embody and then discard his imagined personae, one after another, simulating their strength and authority with the exhilarating pace and motion that his mechanical lower half allows. The violent, aggressive language often used to describe Dexter's movements suggests that the mechanized essence of speed and raw power that is part of the chair-as-machine is also a part of Dexter himself, and his actions underscore this sense of inherent industrial strength, speed, and repetition, as he enacts the unstoppable revolutions, the tireless, staccato essence of mechanization. When Dexter's "immense imagination is at work," when his "brains are boiling in [his] head," as he puts it (204), when he barrels, unstoppable, up and down the room on his rattling wheels or takes on the spirits of great old heroes, he is an engine, a device of overwhelming output.

And because the chair is not simply a removable appendage, nor yet an isolable part of Dexter, but, rather, is intrinsic to him, his power and danger are not erased when he chooses to slip from his seat and make his way through the world without benefit of wheels. Whether careening down his room on his hands, knocking over the furniture, in "Dexter's Leapfrog" (259) or creeping about on his belly like that other, mythically unpopular legless creature, Dexter makes powerful and effective use of his physical form, manipulating what the world sees as a physical limitation into a tool to open doors that ordinary humans cannot pass through. In Dexter, the markers of the machine—raw force, speed and endless motion, fitness for the task to which it is assigned and for which it is constructed—are melded with the intelligence, the courtliness, and the selfishness of the gentleman. Dexter's power lies in his ability to wed the best stereotypical attributes of his declining class—the ability to command, the rhetorical gifts, and the long memory of and respect for a tradition of rule—with the key factors that have enriched the middle class at an astounding rate: that is, energy, efficiency, and, in every sense, industry. As such, he is an answer to the encroaching ambitions of the striving class and a reversal of the paradigm of upward mobility that it adheres to; he turns the familiar trend of middle-class movement toward the manners and habits of the traditional upper class on its head by positing an upper class striving toward the marketplace and factory-floor accomplishments of its inferiors.[11] He is an embodiment of the possibility of reinvention and thus of a new type of survival for the old order.

Dexter, then, may be fruitfully read not as a mistake, a freak of nature, but as the Next Big Thing, a gentlemanly prototype for a new era. Dexter is a possibility for a new model, a gentleman who retains the power and privilege of the old order but is entirely imbricated with the rush of the world. He is a monster of modernity, celebrating the mechanical, the artificial, and the mass-produced and rewriting it as natural. And it is precisely his strange melding of old and new, of gentlemanly behaviors and rushing wheels, that renders him so magnificently excessive. He is, as Mrs. Macallan says of his behavior at the trial, "just like himself—a mixture of the strangest and the most opposite qualities" (199). He is a flashy, futuristic model, a paradigm for the vicissitudes of modernity—a gentleman, that is, for the machine age.[12]

Dexter, then, is less a "crippled gentleman" than he is a nineteenth-century cyborg: a creature in whom the technologies of his time are completely and inextricably imbricated, a figure without limits, in whom there are no clear boundaries between the technological and the "natural." In his strange melding of steel and flesh, spokes and sinews; in his merging of the speed and power of the machine and the rarefied airs of the man of good birth, Dexter links the energy of the industrial age with the resources, the accomplishments, and above all the discursive codes that mark the more leisured and leisurely echelons. Dexter, despite his strangeness, is unquestionably a gentleman: a man of family, of means and leisure, deferred to by social inferiors, indulged and tolerated as only a person with standing can be. But the key marker of Dexter's class is his talk. His fluency, his ease with the idiom and tone of his class, and most important, his endless verbal iterations of himself as a person of gentility place Dexter in the discourse of rank. Because this discourse demands a subordination of the body, Dexter can, in effect, efface his difference: since the gentleman's value does not rest in his ability to do bodily labor, he may not be evaluated as the sum of his physical parts but instead must be judged on the basis of his social skills, his charm, his cleverness. As long as he can talk the talk, Dexter may be a "madman," as Eustace's mother calls him, but he cannot, in polite society, be a freak.

But precisely for this reason, Dexter's gentlemanly position demands a constant stream of talk, just as Arthur Huntingdon's requires a constant infusion of drink; when he stops speaking, only the visual remains. So, like any well-designed machine, he manufactures; his product is words. Dexter is endlessly turning phrases and telling tales; embroidering, inflating, narrating; lecturing, cajoling, explaining. Ironically, impossibly, the man-machine actualizes his gentlemanly status through his staccato mass-production of language. This birthing of gentlemanliness through the gritty works of the industrial floor is not the only class paradox that Dexter embodies: his power and status are actualized through his bodily incorporation of the laboring classes. Like a magical Marxist invention, he is, in and of himself, both owner and worker, at once the means of production, the proprietor, and the mechanic who runs the switches and engines. In his manipulation of the levers of his chair, Dexter is a laborer, a man literally compelled to perform work of the hand to make his way through the world. And in the construction of his steel wheels, Dexter is, equally literally, a product of the invisible hands of labor.

By naturalizing the chair into his body, Dexter enacts the drama at the heart of capitalism, estranging the workers from their product and the product from its origins while insisting on the power, danger, and dynamism of the machine world that has produced it. By incorporating the chair into itself, making it part of a self-run system, Dexter's body also elides the working "Hands" who ensure that the machine—and thus the system of industrial production itself—runs smoothly, working its levers and oiling its joints. At the same time, his gift for selling his rhetoric and his energetic strivings in that endeavor make him an excellent iteration of the middle-class entrepreneur. In this way, Dexter safeguards his gentlemanly status by bringing the marketplace into the drawing room: by exchanging the product he manufactures, his endlessly produced rhetoric, for social currency, he maintains his role as a bona fide member of the privileged class.

This amalgamation of the classes in Dexter's body is the most potent site of his monstrosity: he overturns the familiar notion that the middle class adopts the manners of its betters, positing instead an upper class striving to usurp the skills of the marketplace and the factory floor. In this, his monstrous body—differently abled, indeed—is utterly of a piece with the socioeconomic anxieties of his time. Donna Haraway famously describes the cyborg as "a condensed image of both imagination and material reality, the two joined centers structuring any possibility of historical transformation" (150). Dexter is precisely such a joining of material reality and imagination; a site of political contestation; a locus of crucial historical metamorphosis. He is, in other words, a monster for his time.

A utopian rewriting of the capitalist paradigm, Dexter is product and producer, owner and laborer, all in one, with no class conflict to disrupt production. He is thus a nightmare vision of the future for the middle class: a specter of a society in which the middle class is entirely elided. In this dream-story, it is the entrepreneur, not the aristocrat, who wakes up one morning to find himself an endangered species, pushed to the sidelines by an evolutionary prototype particularly fitted for survival in a new era. In a text replete with the language of Darwin's brave new science, Dexter celebrates the mechanical, the artificial, the mass-produced and rewrites it as a natural order. He is a gentlemanly adaptation for the machine age, spectacularly well adapted to his world. Bearing the attributes of a potential überclass under his skin and in his blood, Dexter is a new Frankenstein's monster built from the charnel house of the gentle classes, bolted together with the miraculous new rivets and screws of the factory; a promising monster, at once pointing to the decline of the gentleman and figuring his potential triumphant evolution.

This potential is encapsulated neatly in Dexter's singular collection. Even given the mania for collecting that marks the Victorian era, Dexter's treasures are extraordinary. In Dexter's drawing-room kitchen, Valeria finds an

> insatiable relish for horrors. . . . The photographs hanging on the wall, represented the various forms of madness taken from the life. The plaster casts ranged on the shelf opposite, were casts (after death) of the heads of famous murderers. A frightful little skeleton of a woman hung in a cupboard, behind a glazed door, with this cynical inscription placed above the skull—"Behold the scaffolding on which beauty is built!" In a corresponding cupboard, with the door wide open, there hung in loose folds a shirt (as I took it to be) of chamois leather. Touching it . . . I disarranged the folds, and disclosed a ticket pinned among them, describing the thing in these horrid lines:—"Skin of a French Marquis, tanned in the Revolution of Ninety Three. Who says the nobility are not good for something? They make good leather." (247–48)

This collection of the macabre is, in one sense, a museum of human extinction, a pseudogentlemanly collection of specimens of human failure and foolishness. Stored on shelves and in cupboards like so many dry goods (like, in fact, the truffles), Dexter's "horrors" stand as evidence of his "insatiable" appetites and their potential effects: the failed human, it seems, is preserved in order to be endlessly fed upon by him in his machine-dream state, and the empty shells are left behind to mark the feast. In this sense, his stores emphasize Dexter's status as a future-creature, a gentleman for a new age— and the danger that he poses for the outdated members of the gentle classes who have not adapted.

But clearly Dexter feeds on that which is proximate to himself, even as he marks its difference. The death-casts of murderers, after all, might easily represent Dexter in his guilty relation to Sara; the photos of madness correspond to the popular view of Dexter, the "latent insanity" that Mr. Playmore's doctor diagnoses (281). They stand like trophies of the hunt or like preserved *tête de veau*, waiting for consumption. The woman's skeleton demonstrates both Dexter's disdain for female preoccupations with appearance and his narcissistic, gender-bending nature; the skeleton, stripped of the body's essence, stands as a collection of bones, the leftovers of his feeding. And the skin of the nobleman is particularly revealing. Clearly, the nobleman's uselessness (except as "good leather") stands in stark contrast to Dexter: if the nobleman is the outdated version, the model that has not adapted to the future and cannot move on, Dexter, the industrial gentleman with the spinning wheels and the need for speed, is his opposite number. But at the same time, the skin has an almost tangible use to Dexter, who dresses himself, literally and figuratively, in the clothes of the turn-of-the-century aesthete, with his frilled sleeves, his harp, and his poetry, in this way perpetuating this old-fashioned notion of gentlemanliness together with new-fangled mechanization. Using the magical thinking of cannibalism,[13] he has taken on the powers of those whom he has consumed and swallowed. In this way, he is able to embody both the past and the future of gentlemanliness. Dexter, then, reveals himself here as a consumer of the human itself. With the bad grace of a conquering power, he attributes this aliment to the past, displaying it in his museum of failed humanness, but at the same time, this strange fare is the stores he keeps in his cupboards and on his shelves, his emergency rations, that which constitutes him.

But Dexter's delicate balance—between sanity and madness, between gentleman and machine—requires an even more complex alimentary regimen. Both his gentlemanly self and his energetic, high-flying industrial self must be appropriately nourished, and these dry stores are insufficient for the purpose. In this sense, Sara is, in many ways, Dexter's perfect meal. Where Eustace sees an unlovable plain woman who serves only to feed his self-pity and his sense of chivalric martyrdom, Dexter sees a woman who possesses the ideal combination of ingredients to keep his powers balanced. Sara is, first, the consummate romantic, living her life in a cloud of excessive feeling: the abject lover, the runaway, the pining, neglected wife, she is as "sad" (232) as Dexter himself. Her nurse reports that she is "a great hand at composing poetry . . . of the dismal kind; despairing about herself, and wondering why she had ever been born, and nonsense like that" (130–31). Sara's poetic temperament provides sustenance for Dexter's gentlemanly nature: in her, he finds a potent source for his own melancholy, crucial in maintaining his class stature. In his romantic pursuit of the lady, he enacts his masculinity, following the dictates of courtly love to great dramatic effect for himself; even her refusal of his hand in marriage is food for Dexter's melancholy gentlemanly self, helping him to cast himself as the abject lover who pines for his beloved, even as he feasts on her misery.

Dexter's body helps him to live out that role even as it gives him special access to his beloved. He asks her for the key to the door between her bedroom and the little study, for instance, explaining, "With my infirmity, I may not be able to profit by the first opportunity of visiting you here, unobserved; I must be able to choose my own time and my own way of getting to you secretly" (389). In this way, he circumvents every basic rule of propriety, casting himself as the stealthy lover with special right of entry to his lady's boudoir. Sara's acceptance of his reasoning obviates her refusal of him as a lover, in terms of the story he seeks to feed himself. At the same time, however, Dexter's pursuit of Sara affords a meal for his speedier self. To capture his prey, Dexter relies on precisely those abilities that mark his difference from the merely human man—his speed, his preternatural agility when moving about on his hands, his size, and his flexible, adaptable corpus.

Sara proves willing to swallow the fare that Dexter offers—the truth about her husband's feelings for her, as detailed in his stolen diary—despite her loathing toward him. She feels akin to Dexter: as she writes in her suicide note, "No other feeling than compassion for deformed persons has ever entered my mind. I have, indeed, almost a fellow-feeling for them; being that next worst thing myself to a deformity—a plain woman" (388). Motivated by her intense jealousy and her insecurities, she yields to the "temptation" (388) Dexter offers, feeding avidly on his desires, his duplicity, and his envy.

This is crucial to Dexter's self-fashioning: he needs to fatten Sara up with that which is found only in himself. Marked as excessive and only proximately human by his speeding wheels, Dexter seeks not to eat his way out of his difference but to sustain it, in productive tension with his gentlemanliness, through a carefully balanced diet consisting of the humanness to which he is both the same and alien and of the difference that marks him as a future-creature. Accordingly, Dexter, at once anthropophagic and autophagic, seeks to devour those who have already fed on him and are thus made like to him—that is, he seeks to rejuvenate himself by consuming in others that which makes him himself, but to do so he must, like the vampire who seeks a mate, first infuse others with this essence.[14]

But Dexter's avidity ruins his meal for him. Overcome by his hunger for Sara, he fails to see that she has swallowed a fatal dose of his bitter betrayal and that this fare has only strengthened her appetites for Eustace and the domestic gentlemanly world that he represents for her. Dexter's alienation and his desire for revenge are the delicacies she consumes along with the contents of the diary; the bitter almond of the arsenic is merely an actualization of that unappetizing repast.

Faced with the knowledge of her husband's indifference, she has only two alternatives: to submit to Dexter's feeding, to allow him to gorge himself on her, to become, through this symbiotic meal, as "deformed" as Dexter himself, regardless of her decision concerning his anticipated elopement—or to refuse his meal by following the narrative of spurned love to its logical conclusion and bringing on her own death. By turning to this desperate narrative, she insists on playing out her story not as the ugly and unlovable wife but as the romantic, self-denying woman who will give up even her own life for the happiness of the man she loves. As she writes, "I have already sacrificed everything but my life to my love for you. Now I know that my love is not returned, the last sacrifice left is easy" (391). Her admission makes her sadness, her loneliness, and her neglect at her husband's hands readily apparent. Her suicide serves, in other words, to safeguard her both from the narrative of the grasping, pathetic wife as albatross around the stoic husband's neck—that is, the meal that Eustace has turned her into—and from the role that Dexter has prepared for her as the passionate creature who flees beyond the dictates and limits of ordinary society with her lover, fed to repletion on his irresistible estrangement.

Dexter's hunger for Sara hardly ends with her death, as his recounting of the night of her death makes clear: "All through that horrible night I was awake: watching my opportunity until I found my way to her! I got into the room, and took my last leave of the cold remains of the angel whom I loved. I cried over her. I kissed her, for the first and last time. I stole one little lock of her hair. I have worn it ever since; I have kissed it night and day" (298). Valeria dwells on the horror of the moment: "I saw again the ghastly scene in the death-chamber—the deformed creature crying over the corpse, in the stillness of the first dark hours of the new day" (304). The image is striking: the monster hovering over his victim, the vampire, that only proximately human creature, ravening on his prey.

After Sara's death, Dexter attempts to feed himself on memory, replaying his loss as he kisses the lock of hair he has stolen from her corpse, drawing out the last drops of sustenance. But he requires some other, more nutritious means of maintaining himself; though the memory of Sara can feed his gentlemanly melancholy, reinforcing him as an upscale, well-born outsider in the manner of the Byron-esque poets, it cannot nourish his future-half, the portion of Dexter that provides—and requires—energy and movement and force, the part that promises to sustain him.

Dexter, then, prefers to feed on those whose blood runs warm in their veins; he is less a vampire in this sense than a species of parasite, stealing the essence of his host. In this, as in the nature of his alimental cravings, Dexter is not alone: gentlemanliness affiliated with birth in *The Law and the Lady* is invariably marked by an engagement, with or without a struggle, with the eating of women. Major Fitz-David, for instance, despite the mutual antipathy he shares with Dexter, is an unabashed swallower of the feminine. Clearly "a gentleman by birth and breeding" (19), as Valeria's Uncle Starkweather puts it, Major Fitz-David bears a gentlemanly character that may be summed up by the contents of a drawer that Valeria comes across in her search of his drawing room: "a loose bundle of ornamental cards, each containing the list of dishes at past banquets given, or attended, by the Major, in London and Paris . . . a box full of delicately tinted quill pens (evidently a lady's gift) . . . a quantity of old invitation cards . . . some dog's-eared French plays and books of the opera . . . a pocket-corkscrew, a bundle of cigarettes, and a bunch of rusty keys . . . a passport, a set of luggage labels, a broken silver snuff-box, two cigar-cases, and a torn map of Rome" (78). No wonder Valeria concludes, as she puts it, that there is "[n]othing anywhere to interest *me*" (78): the sort of idle, restless gentleman, occupied by luxury and distraction, represented by this collection is the antithesis of the useful, rational middle class that she represents.

The major is an ineffective, superannuated gentleman who has turned entirely away from the world, leaving behind all engagement with the busy, the practical, and the useful. Even his title seems fanciful, almost imaginary: the only scar that the major carries is a bullet wound, which, he says, was "[n]ot received in the service of my country—oh, dear no! Received in the service of a much-injured lady, at the hands of her scoundrel of a husband, in a duel abroad" (71). The detritus of his career ("his sword and pistols, his epaulettes, his sash, and other minor accoutrements" [88–89]) lies forgotten in a bottom cupboard. Major Fitz-David is entirely preoccupied with the maintenance of a personal façade attractive enough to win over "the ladies" he so actively adores (61). Valeria's description of him is telling: "[H]e was like a finely-preserved gentleman of (say) sixty years old; little and lean, and chiefly remarkable by the extraordinary length of his nose. After this feature, I noticed, next, his beautiful brown wig; his sparkling little grey eyes; his rosy complexion; his short military whiskers, dyed to match his wig; his white teeth and his winning smile; his smart

blue frock-coat, with a camellia in the button-hole; and his splendid ring—a ruby, flashing on his little finger as he courteously signed
me to take a chair" (59–60).

Largely constructed by technology and art, Major Fitz-David is
a fabric of courtliness, graciousness, and gorgeousness, a dandy par
excellence. Like Dexter, he is a great believer in the power of
clothing.[15] He resembles Dexter, too, in his marked attention to
and desire for women; and he is willing to direct an enormous
amount of energy and resources toward pleasing them. As he tells
Valeria, "I study everything that can make me useful or agreeable
towards your enchanting sex" (194). The major has learned about
old lace; he collects cameos, ivory carvings, and silks. He has
launched two erstwhile divas and is hard at work on the third, footing the substantial bills for a thorough education in the mysteries
of the operatic world. He has paid off the debts of a number of his
lady-friends; he has even sold off his country estate in order to provide the ladies with ready cash. And he declares, "I don't regret it.
If I had another estate, I have no doubt it would go the same way.
Your adorable sex has made its pretty playthings of my life, my
time, and my money—and welcome!" (71).

Though the major—unlike self-willed, imperious Dexter—is
willing to woo and propitiate the women he encounters in any way
within his power, he puts particular stock in food and drink. When
Valeria approaches the delicate topic of her husband's past, for instance, he turns immediately to sustenance to help himself out of
this sticky situation, much as his legless counterpart does. He offers
Valeria tea to counter her suggestion that there is "some dreadful
mystery in [Eustace's] past life" (62); he proposes "a little dinner"
to be got up on her behalf (69) and questions her repeatedly on her
preferences for the soup course to distract her from the issue at
hand. When she threatens to faint, he offers her "a tiny bottle of
champagne" that he has "had bottled expressly for the ladies" and
"a plate-full of delicate little sugared biscuits" that "come to [him]
direct from Paris" (74)—the provisions proof in themselves of the
major's belief in the power of food in his dealings with women.
When Valeria notes his startled response at her discovery of the
shattered vase (80) and again when she catches him spying on her
(83), he rallies by offering her more champagne. When Valeria

refuses to be dissuaded from her quest to meet Dexter, the major responds with another "little dinner," at which she might be introduced to his legless friend, adding, "I will shut myself up this evening, and approach the question of dinner with my cook" (193). Like Dexter, he treats the food served to Valeria with ceremonial reverence and an apparent belief in its rhetorically transformative qualities: Valeria recalls that when the major lunched at Benjamin's board, "[h]e led me to the table and filled my plate and my glass, with the air of a man who considered himself to be engaged in one of the most important occupations of his life" (190).

The major's constant proposals of food and drink summon up the image of a fetishist who gains his pleasure from watching women eat—but his interactions evoke another, more disturbing possibility and align him once again with "that crack-brained personage" (193), as he calls Mr. Dexter. On Valeria's first meeting with the major, for example, she recalls that he "took [her] hand, and lifted [her] glove to his lips, as if that glove was the most delicious luxury the world could produce" (60); when she tries to take her hand back from his grasp, he entreats her, "Lend me—I wish I could say give me—this pretty hand. I am such an admirer of pretty hands" (61). In discussing his plans for the dinner party, he refers to his new acquaintance as "my sweet friend" (61). He kisses his would-be diva's hand "as devotedly as he had kissed [Valeria's]" (64); before he leaves Valeria to her search, he lifts her "hand to his lips" (75). Once again, when he prepares to leave Benjamin's luncheon table, Valeria notes that the "modern Don Juan" (189) "took [her] hand, and looked at it critically, with his head a little on one side. 'A delicious hand,' he said; 'you don't mind my looking at it, you don't mind my kissing it—do you? A delicious hand is one of my weaknesses'" (194). At the dinner he finally hosts for Valeria, the major is "always kissing [his female guests'] hands, always luring [them] to indulge in dainty dishes and drinks, always making love" (262).

In this last instance, the major's two alimentary activities come together most clearly: while Major Fitz-David feeds the ladies, he is also busily feeding upon them. Despite his self-consciously chivalric behavior, he is a devourer, and he relies on this monstrous ingestion to maintain himself in his gentlemanly persona. The major depicts woman-eating as his most appropriate occupation, an act he performs in service to his gentlemanly role; he transforms courtly behavior and polite attention into occasions for tasting and sipping.

Like Dexter's cookery, the Major's ravening is designed to assuage his own sociocultural nutritional needs. The major seeks in his "ladies" their essence or identity, as he perceives it: youth, beauty, charm, ease, and leisure, the elements that he desires the most for himself, the elements that mark his pointless, useless gentlemanly status. But he is unwilling to trust entirely to appearances in this respect, knowing, as he does so intimately, how exteriors might be constructed. So, like Dexter, to ensure that he eats exactly what he needs, he feeds his ladies himself, fattening them up on champagne and biscuits and other fine fare redolent of luxurious comfort and extravagance, of expensive self-indulgence. Sturdy everyday fare has no place at the Major's table.

Major Fitz-David's ravening is made most explicit in the singular book that Valeria discovers during her search, which holds, to her "unutterable amazement and disgust . . . locks of hair let neatly into the centre of each page—with inscriptions beneath, which proved them to be love-tokens from various ladies, who had touched the Major's heart at different periods of his life. The inscriptions . . . [were] devoted to . . . reminding the Major of the dates at which his various attachments had come to an untimely end" (87). Here are the romantic, overplayed leftovers of Major Fitz-David's many meals. These captive remainders, carefully preserved on pages "of the finest vellum" (87), drive home the implications of the major's sugar-coated appetites: the contents of the book are not just overblown memorials to lost loves but pieces of the women he has romantically devoured, Dorian Gray–like relics that help him to preserve his own image of youth and beauty. But the major's acts of devouring constitute a sort of symbiotic relationship: his ladyfriends gain a great deal in exchange for opening a figurative vein for their patron. Not so for Dexter's victims, as that other relic, the locket holding hair cut from Sara's corpse, makes abundantly clear.

Gentlemanly ravening is everywhere in *The Law and the Lady*: even the ineffectual Eustace Macallan finds himself consuming the women around him, despite his best intentions. Eustace's public behavior in the matter of his first wife is gentlemanly in the most disinterested sense.[16] When he unwittingly arouses strong feelings in Sara as a guest in her aunt and uncle's home, he leaves immediately, despite the serious injuries that have extended his stay. When she runs off to the city in pursuit of him, turning up in his rooms unannounced, he attempts to hide her—and when she is discovered in his bedroom, he saves her reputation by marrying her. As a dutiful and well-meaning if unloving husband, he attempts to maintain a civil and smooth-running family circle. His declaration of innocence sums up his position: "I asked my wife no questions about the use of the arsenic," he writes; "I implicitly believed what she told me. . . . I assert positively, that I lived on friendly terms with my wife; allowing, of course, for the little occasional disagreements and misunderstandings of married life. Any sense of disappointment, in connexion with my marriage, which I might have felt privately, I conceived it to be my duty, as a husband and a gentleman, to conceal from my wife" (151).

But this sort of magnificent sacrifice is not sufficient in the matter of burying the gentleman's problematic appetites; nor is it a complete portrait of Eustace's motives and actions. His diary reveals that his marriage to Sara, undertaken after his beloved Mrs. Beauly's engagement, was motivated by his despair and his sense of his own uselessness: "My prospects were closed; my hope had ended. I had not an aspiration left; I had no necessity to stimulate me to take refuge in work. A chivalrous action, an exertion of noble self-denial, seemed to be all that was left to me, all that I was fit for" (162). Eustace, like Arthur Huntingdon—like William Dorrit in his wealth—finds himself superannuated, without position, a gentleman bereft of purpose. Economically removed from the need to work and culturally removed from the possibility of aspiration, he believes, like Arthur Clennam, that he can find direction for himself only by denying himself—that is, by imitating a sort of mythically chivalric gentleman. But in order to do so, he feeds on Sara, sustaining himself both on her hopeless love for him and on his own sacrifice.

According to Eustace's private writings, he believes it generosity to avoid Sara as much as possible, gentlemanly beneficence to ignore her: "The effort of my life is *not* to notice her, in anything she does or says," he writes in his diary (163). But his effort to hold himself apart is not an act of sustenance for others through self-denial; rather, it is a different sort of fatal feeding, in which his victim—the woman he apparently intends to save—wastes away on his indigestible dietary regimen. As Sara's suicide letter reveals, Eustace's inability to pretend love and desire for her has been rich fare for her, an endless meal of unhappiness and jealousy. This undigested and indigestible food, in turn, has led her to swallow literal poison in a quixotic bid to make herself more attractive: as she writes, she has asked Eustace to buy the arsenic "to try if I could not improve my ugly complexion—not from any vain feeling of mine: only to make myself look better and more lovable in your eyes" (392). When she consumes the diary, she discovers that Eustace loves her even less than she has thought, and that his heart belongs to another woman. It is this bitter fare that leads her to down that other, more tangible toxin: "The poison . . . might have failed to improve my complexion," she writes. "It will not fail to relieve you of your ugly wife" (392).

Still longing to be succored and sustained by Eustace despite her suicide plans, she silently gives him a second and even a third chance to redeem himself when he brings her fare to be taken by mouth. When he arrives with her medicine after she has swallowed the first dose of arsenic, she writes, "I thought to myself, 'If he looks at me kindly, I will confess what I have done, and let him save my life.' You never looked at me at all. You only looked at the medicine" (393). Of her decision to take the second, fatal dose, she recounts,

> I determined to give myself a last chance of life. That is to say, I determined to offer you a last opportunity of treating me kindly. I asked you to get me a cup of tea. If, in paying me this little attention, you only encouraged me by one fond word or one fond look, I resolved not to take the second dose of poison.
>
> You obeyed my wishes, but you were not kind. You gave me my tea, Eustace, as if you were giving a drink to your dog. And then you wondered, in a languid way (thinking, I suppose, of Mrs Beauly all the time), at my dropping the cup in handing it back to you. . . . You politely hoped, before you went away, that the tea

would do me good—and, oh God, you could not even
look at me when you said that! You looked at the broken bits of the tea-cup.

The instant you were out of the room I took the poison—a double dose this time. (393–94)

Though Eustace offers Sara a great deal to chew on, he fails to feed
her any sort of real nourishment: he shares nothing meaningful or
positive with her, even at her lonely board in her sickbed, though
he goes through the motions of solicitude. Eustace at bottom seeks
to feed only himself; but by gnawing on his melancholy and his lost
love, he produces a meal of dregs—the bitter flavors of disappointment, disillusionment, and loss—which he serves to Sara with her
tea and her medicine. And while he imagines that he feeds only on
himself, eating away at himself in overblown language ("I must suffer and submit. Oh, Helena! Helena!" [162]), he fails to realize that
he is also ravening on his wife—that he devours Sara, transforming
her into an unlovable harridan through his neglect, to assuage his
appetite for melodrama and self-pity.

In feeding on these women, then, the gentlemen who populate
Collins's novel seek to renew and re-create themselves: their victims provide them with the narrative qualities that they need to
maintain themselves, echoes of their own traits and complemen-
tary signs of their conceptualization of their classed and gendered
roles. In this way, the gentlemanly figure may, so to speak, live forever, a creature of ease and leisure and chivalry, utterly distinct
from any social, political, or economic imputations of gentlemanliness. This barren self-perpetuation, generating nothing but more
uselessness and more appetites, appears to be the fate of heritable
gentlemanliness; it is a fate that is only partially ameliorated in the
novel's closing pages. The once-powerful figure of the gentleman
seems reduced to maintaining himself by consuming others; and
his prey is found at the very heart of the sociocultural domestic
scene. He creeps into the drawing room—or, like the spider and
the fly, invites the innocent into his parlor, there to disarm her,
ensnare her, and, he hopes, devour her.[17]

But Dexter has different aims with his specialized diet: he
promises, with his steel wheels and his kitchen full of horrors and

truffles, to swallow down old-fashioned gentlemanliness entirely, regenerating it as a piece of his speedy, forward-moving, linguistically productive monstrous machine-self. When he meets Valeria, he seems to think that he has found an ideal source of nutrition. The second Mrs. Eustace—a self-described lady and the energetic middle-class daughter of a businessman, a serious romantic with a strong logical, innovative streak—appeals to both sides of Dexter, combining old with new, gentility with ingenuity, energy, strength, and imbrication in the world. This is the reason that Dexter pursues Valeria with such avidity, the reason that he seeks her out, over and over again, despite his fears about her pursuit of the story of Sara's death.

Dexter's attempted consumption of Valeria is evident in several moments in the text. In Collins's gentlemanly monster, the metaphoric relationship between sex and food is literalized: Dexter seeks not to penetrate Valeria but to enwrap her and swallow her, snakelike. He devours her with his eyes, scrutinizing her body without compunction (234–35) and telling her about it. When Valeria evinces sympathy for his sufferings in regard to his loss of Sara, he crosses the line of propriety completely: "He caught my hand in his, and devoured it with kisses. His lips burnt me like fire. He twisted himself suddenly in the chair, and wound his arm round my waist" (299), she recalls.

When Dexter attacks Valeria, he seems, literally and figuratively, to attempt to devour her, like a python squeezing its prey to death as it delivers a kiss of death, a kiss that is also a swallowing. And on Valeria's return from abroad, "[h]is eyes fastened on [her] with a fierce, devouring delight" (326). Approaching her, "'Your hand, Light of my Life!' he murmured in his gentlest tones. 'Your hand— only to show that you have forgiven me!' I gave him my hand. 'One?' he whispered, entreatingly. 'Only one?' He kissed my hand once, respectfully—and dropped it with a heavy sigh" (328). Like a drinker who cannot stop at just one, Dexter finds that he cannot hide his cravings for Valeria; at this late date, he drops even the pretense of benevolent mastery, allowing his hunger to define him.

His need for her substance is clearest in the final scene in his drawing room, when he begs her, as he prepares to launch on his last story, to turn "'[y]our face a little more this way. . . . Let me find my inspiration in your eyes. Let me feed my hungry admiration on your form. Come! have one little pitying smile left for the man whose happiness you have wrecked. Thank you. Light of my Life, thank you!' He kissed his hand to me, and threw himself back luxuriously in his chair" (338). Dexter clearly seeks to feed on Valeria as a means of "find[ing] his inspiration"—of moving ahead, continuing to invent, continuing, that is, to be an innovating future-creature. At the same time, he sucks the marrow from the discourse of her rejection of his advances, casting her as the cruel lady who spurns the artistic, romantic gentleman's advances and so gives him the gift of art, albeit art dedicated to his sorrows. In this way, he draws both past and present from her, rewriting her in his own image despite herself in order to swallow her down and reconnect with his image of himself.

But Valeria is not, as it turns out, the perfect fare for Dexter: though she provides him with food for melancholy, she lacks the sense of refinement and class—the true ladyhood Sara possessed— that would allow him to vitamin up his gentlemanly, leisurely, self-indulgent self. As a meal, then, she is singularly imbalanced: too much protein, not enough sugar. To make her suited to his dietary needs, Dexter must, so to speak, fatten her up. This is why he feeds her truffles in Burgundy.

Dexter's attitude summons up the false benevolence of a Casby or a Woodhouse, predicated as it is on patronization masking greedy desire. "Make the most of one of the few first sensations in the life, which has no ingredient of disappointment lurking under the surface," he tells her (246). He gives her "a smile of benevolent interest" (248) as he serves up her meal, as though he is feeding her a substance that will impart gentility, through its very essence, to her sadly middle-class self. Dexter's method of obtaining that which he desires, then, is predicated on feeding Valeria what he perceives she is deficient in, at the same moment that he wishes her to feel his superiority over her; he wishes to draw her close through her ingestion of fare that stands in stark cultural counterpoint to her self-sufficient, energetic self-construction. Valeria is relegated to the position of the lesser party, the one who embodies lack. But he takes care to ensure that a sense of possibility remains. By feeding her truffles, Dexter benevolently implies, he can feed her the missing elements of class that she so clearly requires—but only if she accepts him unquestioningly as her guide through this alimentary world and only if she follows his rules concerning forks and knives. In other words, he uses truffles to make her more like himself.

Dexter realizes that although food in and of itself has no intrinsic ability to create class and gender status, it certainly possesses rhetorical class and gender values that are imparted to those who partake of food in the presence of others. His description of Ariel's cookery is in line with this thinking: "Plain joints!" he exclaims. "Bah! A man who eats a plain joint is only one remove from a cannibal—or a butcher" (245). Butchers and cannibals are the same, in Dexter's view: they are those who eat food whose greatest marker is its state of undress. A plain joint, he seems to assert, lacks the sanctity and the ceremony of gentlemanly food; the person who eats such prosaic fare gains no rhetorical power from his or her meal. Louis Marin's *Food for Thought* takes up this issue in a discussion of the fairy tale "The Sleeping Beauty of the Forest." Analyzing the passionate alimentary desire of an ogre queen for her human daughter-in-law and her mostly human grandchildren, Marin looks in particular at the ogre's request for her victims to be prepared in Sauce Robert. Explaining that the headwaiter substitutes first a lamb, then a goat, then a doe for the human victims, concealing them beneath the sauce, Marin writes,

> What becomes manifest . . . is the importance of the culinary sign par excellence: the sauce . . . for it is prima facie the sauce that makes it possible to mediate between fresh human meat and fresh animal meat. . . . [T]he cultural sign of cooking (Robert sauce) transcends the opposition between human meat and animal meat. It renders both the former and the latter unrecognizable. . . . [T]he sign transsignifies, rather than transubstantiates. It transforms both what is inedible according to social prohibition, as well as what is edible according to the rules governing culture, into a prepared dish that is ready to be eaten. (145)

The dressing of the food, then, is what creates the dish in the mind of the consumer, transforming it not necessarily into culture, as

Claude Lévi-Strauss maintains, but into the desired. The plain joint, like the cannibalistic meal, bears no such transformation: it is meat as meat, undressed. As such, it is completely undesirable in terms of its cultural transformative potential. Dexter's performative approach to the cooking and eating of truffles, in contrast, is designed to impart a dressed-up sense of class. His alimentary rituals, like his "profound reflection" (245) and his "linger[ing] and languish[ing]" (248), make this delicacy not merely luxurious but sacred. His insistence on the exclusion of knives, like his unhurried savoring of the dish, separates the truffle (and the person who consumes it) from appetite and hunger altogether,[18] inscribing it as a food valued in part for its very lack of necessity and thus for its power to transform. Such veneration means that the truffle is not eaten like an ordinary food at all: it is not a necessity or even a "refreshment" but something entirely extraneous, something not required—or even desired—by the body. When Dexter announces to Valeria that her "first Truffle" (248) heralds a new "epoch in [her] life," he implies that these little black lumps are magic apples that can deliver class through their ingestion—but only if their mysteries are appropriately venerated.

Truffles, then, serve not only to make Valeria subject to Dexter but also to make her more fit for him: that is, proximate to him. He seeks, so to speak, to fatten her up on the elements she lacks, so that his consumption of her will be easier and smoother. Dexter uses his food to reconstitute Valeria as he would like her to be, urging her to feed on himself and his attributes by reinscribing aliment in his image, so that she becomes more easily digestible. He suggests that his fare holds within it the sort of dietary elements that Valeria is deficient in: luxury, ease, sophistication. But the eating of truffles also threatens to impart to Valeria his less desirable qualities. Inscrutable and unpalatable to the gastronomically uneducated, truffles bear a distinct resemblance to Dexter: these uncultivable "foreign luxuries," as Valeria describes them (246),[19] are alien in every way, barely proximate to the ordinary Englishperson's understanding of a vegetable.

This desire to impart his problematic attributes to Valeria is also evident when Dexter shares his wine with her. Clos Vougeot, as an expensive imported luxury, is representative of Dexter's status.

Moreover, the wine is unquestionably evocative of that other "purple red liquor" (244): its sacramental and vampiric connotations are evident, particularly when Dexter drinks the wine from "a goblet of ancient Venetian glass" (244), lending a sense of ceremonial sacredness to the operation of imbibing. When Dexter urges Valeria to drink with him—"I have been taking some wine. Please sanction that proceeding by taking some wine too"—and she complies (244), she swallows class, drinking, as it were, the blood of Dexter's gentlemanliness, in this way making herself both ripe for and vulnerable to him; and she makes herself like to him, vampire-like, by sharing in his blood-red libation. "I quite agreed with him; I thought it delicious," she recounts (244) of this subtle, potentially fatal alimentary seduction, one that threatens to place her beyond the pale, in league with and in thrall to the only proximately human Dexter. The truffles stewed in Burgundy that Dexter serves Valeria constitute the perfect meal in this way. The Sauce Robert in this instance is the marker of everything that the middle-class Valeria lacks: a sense of classed history, of elevation beyond the everyday, of rarity; a sense of belonging to that which has passed, that which is seductively foreign. And the dish is also the blood of Dexter's blood, the flesh of his flesh.

There are moments when Valeria, like Sara before her, appears to be willing to swallow what Dexter has to offer, blinded by her appetites to his project of making her fit for his consumption. She is, it is true, utterly uninterested in the meal of class that Dexter serves her: faced with truffles stewed in Burgundy, she thinks "the new vegetable a great deal too rich, and, in other respects, quite unworthy of the fuss that had been made about it" (248). The middle-class woman clearly wants no part of such indulgent, leisurely stuff. But she does manifest a serious appetite for some of Dexter's more esoteric fare. When he tells her that though he "hungered and thirsted to [Mrs. Beauly] in the hangman's hands," "Mrs. Borgia-Beauly" may only be caught by "a woman who can watch her with the patience of a tigress in a state of starvation—" "Say a woman like Me! . . . I am ready to try," Valeria interrupts (252). Here Valeria takes on the most dangerous of Dexter's traits: though she has rejected his meal of class, she is willing to swallow whole his cannibalistic tendencies—to drink down his wine—in order to hurt her rival. Like Sara, she is conquered by jealousy. She seems to have completely given herself up to the meal of revenge that Dexter offers her, and he behaves as though his prey is within reach: at Valeria's declaration of intent, "[h]is eyes glitter[]" and "his teeth show[] themselves viciously under his moustache" (252) as his monstrous desires surface. When Valeria reaffirms her intent, pledging to make her discoveries at Major Fitz-David's dinner (thus undermining both the communal, social nature of the shared meal and the major's circumspect aim of feeding on "the ladies" himself), Dexter invites her to "drink to the hanging of Mrs Beauly, in another bottle of Burgundy!" (259).

But Valeria, coming to her senses and recognizing, albeit belatedly, the monstrousness of the fare that he offers to share with her, turns him down: "I seized desperately on the first excuse that occurred to me for getting away from him," she recalls (260). Her subsequent discoveries about Dexter's past make her lose her appetite for his dangerous fare. When she returns from Scotland, it is clear that Valeria has begun to understand the true nutritional content of this very curious cook's rhetorically fraught food and his sanguineous wine. Dexter's attempt to "devour" her in Benjamin's library (299) frees her from the last of her dangerous cravings.

Unable to feed on what he requires to keep himself going, Dexter deteriorates. The "balance" that Mr. Playmore's psychiatric report speaks of (282) is lost: deprived of the mixed diet of gentility and energy that allow him to maintain his equilibrium and unable to snare Valeria in order to perpetuate himself through vampiric feeding and transubstantiation, Dexter swings dangerously from one extreme to the other. No longer an integrated body, he is by turns a gentleman and an industrial machine, fading into lassitude only to recover himself in tremendous productive bursts of rhetoric. After Valeria's repulse of Dexter, he leaves Benjamin's house no more than a "cripple" (299), a "deformed creature held to [the gardener's] bosom, like a woman sheltering a child" (300). Rather than a speedy, forward-looking creature of power, a gentleman for the machine age, he has become regressive, careening back to a mindless, careless childlike state. His last appearance, on Valeria's return from Europe, amply demonstrates his inability to maintain himself without appropriate sustenance:

His features were pinched and worn; the whole face seemed to have wasted strangely in substance and size. . . . The softness in his eyes was gone. Blood-red veins were intertwined all over them now; they were set in a piteous and vacant stare. His once firm hands looked withered; they trembled as they lay on the coverlid. The paleness of his face . . . had a sodden and sickly look—the fine outline was gone. The multitudinous little wrinkles at the corners of his eyes had deepened. His head sank into his shoulders when he leaned forward in his chair. Years appeared to have passed over him, instead of months. (329)

Dexter, in other words, has become old.[20] The superannuated gentleman is asserting himself over the rushing wheels of the future-man. Deprived of a source of fuel for his machine-self, Dexter is fading rapidly away; he falls asleep over his harp (334); he seems barely able to move his chair up and down the room, stopping, finally, "for want of breath." As he explains to Valeria, "I'm out of practice. . . . I hadn't the heart to make the wheels roar, and the floor tremble, while you were away" (335). His modern-mechanical self has slowed to a crawl, deprived of the fare that allows it to rattle and roll. He is reduced to bringing together his industrial power and his gentlemanly mastery in distinctly sustenance-free endeavors, playing with his food, so to speak, as he uses aliment to discipline Ariel, a pale and unpalatable substitute for Valeria. Instead of feeding Ariel as he feeds his other victims, he withholds sustenance, using her honest animal hunger as a demonstration exercise for his much-reduced powers. Valeria stumbles on Dexter engaged in this singularly heartless amusement:

The unfortunate Ariel was standing before a table, with a dish of little cakes placed in front of her. Round each of her wrists was tied a string, the free end of which (at a distance of a few yards) was held in Miserrimus Dexter's hands. "Try again, my beauty!" I heard him say. . . . "Take a cake." At the word of command, Ariel submissively stretched out one arm towards the dish. Just as

> she touched a cake with the tips of her fingers, her hand
> was jerked away by a pull at the string, so savagely cruel
> in the nimble and devilish violence of it, that I felt in-
> clined to snatch Benjamin's cane out of his hand, and
> break it over Miserrimus Dexter's back. (326)

Clearly, Dexter has no real desire to feed on his devoted Ariel: utterly bereft of class, undesirable, and without power, she lacks
anything that he requires to sustain himself. Instead, he both amuses
himself and demonstrates his control over her by depriving her
even of the sugary empty calories offered by the cakes. When he finally gives up his game, at Valeria's command, he orders Ariel to
"'[t]ake the cakes' . . . in his most imperial manner" (327), under-
lining the fact that there is no "form" necessary in Ariel's alimentary practices. Ceremony, ritual, the rhetorical transubstantiation
of food into class that mark the meal of truffles: all are absent as
Ariel, a creature of base animal appetites, claims her prize (when
Dexter begins to speak, "Ariel, silently devouring her cakes, crouched
on a stool at 'the Master's' feet, and looked up at him like a faithful dog" [328]). Her combination of animal appetites and clumsy
ineptness is the antithesis of his self-conception, and its display,
under Dexter's hands, is intended to deny that self-conception's
visible dissolution, however crudely.

Indeed, Dexter loses all interest in Ariel as soon as his real prey
appears. He protests that his torture of his servant cousin is what
Valeria's absence "reduced [him] to" (322), making clear that Ariel
is the food that he plays with, an unwanted starvation diet, while
he waits for the real thing. He begs for a bite of that long-denied
meal immediately ("One? . . . only one?" [328]), despite past
events, despite Benjamin's presence in the guise, as Dexter ironically puts it, of "Retributive Justice" (327). But the real thing is
now indisputably beyond his reach, and Dexter can only feed on
himself, turning to the wine that he attempted to feed Valeria as
the sign and signal of his own essence. That quasi-sacramental
liquid has some power to refresh and sustain Dexter, to make him
"quite [him]self again" (244), as he puts it; but it bears too much of
the gentlemanly past-creature, not enough of the future-creature.
The wine stimulates Dexter to display his class and his mastery—

in the kitchen, and in his last story-telling attempts. But its inspiration is deceptive, as it lends him the appearance of regained fortitude without the underpinnings of innovation or strength. Drawn from within, not without, composed entirely of luxury and leisure, and utterly distant from the world of industry and energy,[21] Clos Vougeot has only limited power to delay the inevitable shutdown that Dexter's starvation diet has imposed on him.

In his last desperate moments of lucidity, when all of his diversions and arts have failed to reassert the imperious, artistic gentleman who can control and direct the levers and engines of his machine-self, he manages to use his wine to fend off his fate temporarily. "That's what I want, Valeria, to set my invention alight and flaming in my head," he cries. "Glasses for everybody! Honour to the King of the Vintages—the Royal Clos Vougeot!" (336). Even at this late date, he attempts to shape and control others through his control over their aliment, "forc[ing]" Valeria, Benjamin, and Ariel to share in the dangerous sacrament with him (336). As the wine takes effect (Valeria sees "the colour rising in his face . . . the bright intelligence flashing again in his eyes" [336]), he makes a final attempt to raven on Valeria. "Let me feed my hungry admiration on your form" (338), he demands, as payment for his story.

But Valeria remains an unobtainable meal, and the starvation diet that his speedy self has endured continues unrelieved. Deprived of sustenance, Dexter's spinning industrial works spin themselves out in one last burst of activity, disgorging flowing spools of discourse that tell, in their disjointed way, the story, the bolus, that he has been unable to digest since that fateful night in Sara's room. At the end of his tale, "there was one long, deep, wearily-drawn breath. Then, nothing but a mute vacant face turned up to the ceiling, with eyes that looked blindly, with lips parted in a senseless, changeless grin. Nemesis at last! The foretold doom had fallen on him. The night had come" (346). Emptied of fuel, he stops running; the old-fashioned gentlemanly self has fallen into the somnolence of superannuation, and the works of the machine-self have closed down permanently. He is left only with base animal appetites, unredeemed by any sauce; as the gardener reports to Valeria, "He showed an animal interest in his meals, and a greedy animal enjoyment of eating and drinking as much as he could get—and that was all" (350). The body, unguided by the discernment and intelligence of the gentleman, becomes no more than a collection of animal appetites, and the rushing wheels, deprived of direction, provide nothing more than an insatiable desire for more, the worst manifestation of industrial capitalism.

Dexter's gentlemanly self—the creature of endless leisure and ease, the figure of authority and accustomed rule—regenerates itself in his last moments, fed perhaps by the lassitude of his life in the asylum. Tellingly, Dexter first recognizes Ariel, that faithful but nutrition-free figure, and then asks, once again, for Valeria, perhaps still hoping to sustain himself through her. But this final request for the meal that might have saved him is far too late, and Dexter's past-self reasserts itself once and for all. "Before the messenger could be despatched, he said, with a touch of his old self-importance, 'Silence, all of you! My brains are weary; I am going to sleep.' He closed his eyes in slumber, and never woke again" (407).

Dexter's terrible appetites, then, are vanquished, as indeed they must be, in this middle-class fairy tale. He seeks, after all, to perpetuate himself at the cost of the nation, feeding on the regenerative heart of the social by ravening on his female victims; he is even more potent a force than the other gentlemen in the text, craving not simply the stuff of upper-class life but the force at the center of the middle-class world, the reinvented, energetic true woman. As Franco Moretti writes, "The modern monsters . . . threaten to live for ever, and to conquer the world. For this reason they must be killed" (85). Dexter becomes, in the end, one of the spectacles he harbors in his closet, a member of the freak show of the useless extinct.

If the middle-class fairy tale is to end appropriately, after all, Valeria must prevail: Dexter's hideous gentlemanly appetites must be replaced with more wholesome eating. And, indeed, it seems as if this promises to be the case. The major, after all, is reduced to a harmless old man by his marriage to the ambitious Miss Hoighty (408), and Eustace, chastened by his feverish trial-by-fire, seems ready to reform his alimental practices. Valeria's description of her reunion with him is telling: "He was too weak, poor fellow, even to raise his head from the pillow. I knelt down at the bedside and kissed him. His languid weary eyes kindled with a new life, as my lips touched his" (372). Where Dexter's burning kisses and the Major's unctuously gallant petting are aimed at devouring Valeria, the lady's kisses for her husband give sustenance, and the taste of his wife seems to bring Eustace back to life. When Eustace agrees to let Valeria decide when to share her information on Sara's death with him, she says, "We sealed our compact with a kiss" (384): the husband and wife (like Amy Dorrit and Arthur Clennam) are finally on equal ground, feeding and feeding from one another in a relationship that is appropriately symbiotic.

It seems, then, that the fairy tale is complete: the ravenous, ravening Miserrimus Dexter has been supplanted by this other, more palatable model, this other, more sustainable and reproducible figure who brings together gentility and middle-class energy in her person and, potentially, in her son. But the ending of the novel remains ambiguous and fraught: like Austen and Brontë, Collins finds that the overwhelming, problematic appetites of his gentlemen cannot be easily resolved by a liberal dose of happily-ever-after. Instead, the reader is left with the strange scene that takes place in Valeria's bedroom (replacing Sara's), where she lies with her infant son. Waiting for Eustace to make his decision about reading Sara's suicide letter, she is restless, moving that problematic document about, until "an odd fancy strikes" her. She "lift[s] up one of the baby's hands, and put[s] the letter under it—and so associate[s] that dreadful record of sin and misery with something innocent and pretty that seems to hallow and purify it" (411).

In this way, the child—the product of this mix of old and new, of upper-class and middle-class traits—inherits the tangled web of secrets that Valeria has unearthed. The letter that is placed under his hand preserves the legacy of Dexter, the monster who has died out and yet who, assuredly, lives on through Sara's letter; and it serves as a testament to the descent of gentlemanliness into cannibalism and of the failure of communion at the gentlemanly board, embodied in Eustace's behavior toward his unfortunate first wife. Yet the combination that produced him—the potentially productive, not monstrous, mixing of the middle and upper classes—may indeed provide the power needed to "hallow and purify" this problematic birthright. Created from Valeria's love and her well-placed, well-used energy and ingenuity, the child, it is to be hoped, also embodies Eustace's best qualities, as they are in evidence in this final scene: chivalry, love, and a disinterestedness informed by generosity.

But the ambivalence of the final scene remains, the conclusion at best incomplete, the sense of a happy ending withheld. Faced at last with his decision, Eustace "lifts the baby's little pink hand to his lips. For a while, he waits so, in sad and secret communion with himself. . . . With a heavy sigh, he lays the child's hand back again on the sealed letter; and, by that one little action, says (as if in words) to his son—'I leave it to You!'" (412–13). The troubled and troubling appetite of the gentleman remains in evidence. Even as he seeks to do right both by Valeria and by Sara's memory (412), Eustace once again turns his appetites inward, "in sad and secret communion with himself," summoning up the shadow of his would-be self-feeding during his marriage to Sara. But instead of confining that feast to his body, he feeds simultaneously on his child. The baby, produced not through the vampirelike feeding and reinscription of the self on others that Dexter attempted but through the sexual nourishment of the marriage bed, becomes a source of sustenance and a repository for it, as Eustace stands with the child's hand to his lips. But the child is also blood of Eustace's blood, flesh of his flesh; he is the product of the self that Eustace seeks continually to feed on and the feminine other that Eustace seems unable to prevent himself from devouring, and in this sense Eustace simply reprises his untoward alimentary behaviors at this moment of potential renewal.

"And so it ended!" Valeria writes, closing her narrative with a plea for understanding for "the follies and errors of [her] husband's life" (413). But closure has been denied; clarity has been elided. The monstrous appetite that the novel assigns to gentlemanliness may have been vanquished by middle-class industry and ingenuity; but it may also live on, closing off possibilities of rejuvenation and renewal through its endless anthropophagic cravings. As he stands beside the marriage bed, holding his baby in his arms, then, Eustace, not Valeria, has supplanted Dexter, for good or for ill; he remains at the very heart of the English social world, taking his meals, for good or for ill, at the font of productivity and possibility.

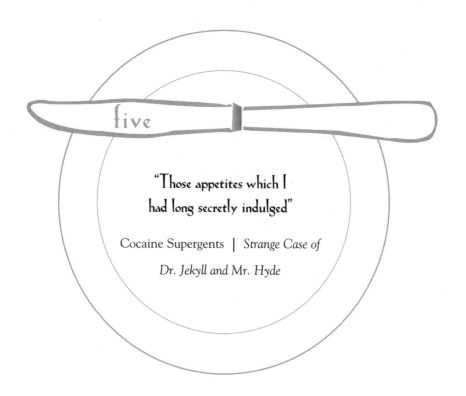

five

"Those appetites which I
had long secretly indulged"

Cocaine Supergents | *Strange Case of
Dr. Jekyll and Mr. Hyde*

Robert Louis Stevenson's *Strange Case of Dr. Jekyll and Mr. Hyde* (1886) is all about aliment: Dr. Jekyll's transformative draught is perhaps the century's most complicated homebrew, a potent mixture of identity, consumption, the body, and selfhood. But Dr. Jekyll is not the novella's only problem drinker. The lawyer Mr. Utterson's strange solitary drinking practice, too, takes up fundamental issues of class and gentlemanliness, and, in particular, the question of the place of the working gentleman in late-nineteenth-century society. In *Dr. Jekyll and Mr. Hyde*, the monstrous combination of Miserrimus Dexter is reversed, so that the gentleman splits entirely in two. When Dr. Jekyll's mixture is read in light of Mr. Utterson's libation, *Dr. Jekyll and Mr. Hyde* opens itself to a reading of class panic enacted through alimental construction of the gentlemanly body—a panic arising from speculation that the gentlemanly professional, like Mr. Hyde, does "not even exist" (52).

Though we view the novella's action through Mr. Utterson's eyes, our introduction to him is hardly a moment of readerly identification with a comfortable stand-in. He is a man of a rugged countenance, that was never lighted by a smile; cold, scanty and embarrassed in discourse; backward in sentiment; lean, long, dusty, dreary and yet somehow lovable. At friendly meetings, and when the wine was to his taste, something eminently human beaconed from his eye; something indeed which never found its way into his talk, but which spoke not only in these silent symbols of the after-dinner face, but more often and loudly in the acts of his life. He was austere with himself; drank gin when he was alone, to mortify a taste for vintages; and though he enjoyed the theatre, had not crossed the doors of one for twenty years. But he had an approved tolerance for others; sometimes wondering, almost with envy, at the high pressure of spirits involved in their misdeeds; and in any extremity inclined to help rather than to reprove. "I incline to Cain's heresy," he used to say quaintly: "I let my brother go to the devil in his own way." In this character, it was frequently his fortune to be the last reputable acquaintance and the last good influence in the lives of down-going men. And to such as these, so long as they came about his chambers, he never marked a shade of change in his demeanor. (7)

So the story of Dr. Jekyll and Mr. Hyde begins: not with the horror of the monstrous Hyde but with this man of business, apparently unremarkable but for his puritanical way with his own appetites and his tolerance for the hungers and weaknesses of others. It is an introduction that is often skipped quickly over—a pathway, merely, to Stevenson's real story, to the tale that Utterson's cousin Enfield retails of the trampling of the little girl, the dilapidated doorway, the bribe, the strange man. Our narrator is dry and professional; trustworthy with secrets (though not particularly interested in the entrustment of souls); a jealous, repressed middle-class watcher of society from the margins; a quiet shade, a gray-flannel-suit-wearer, a silent, anonymous walker in London's streets. If this first chapter is the "Story of the Door," as its title announces, then Utterson appears to be little more than a "door" to the real action and the real characters. He is a voyeur, a window, a space allowing a view.[1]

But there are notes in this description that resonate oddly. While the lawyer's "envy" of the lost souls he meets is perhaps understandable—clearly, his appetites are not absent, merely curtailed by his puritanical turn—his practice of drinking gin "to mortify a taste for vintages" is less easily explained. To the twenty-first-century reader, the passage may appear to speak simply to the lawyer's desire to tame or shame his appetite for luxuries: Mr. Utterson avoids fine wines, one might reason, just as he avoids the theatre, because he sees both the activity and, more important, his enjoyment of the activity as sinful. Certainly, many contemporary critics have read Mr. Utterson in this way.[2] But to a nineteenth-century reader, the idea of the dry lawyer drinking gin alone in his own dining room must have been jarring. Some fifty years into the full-blown power of the Victorian temperance and teetotal movements, the associations and affiliations of gin would have been instantly clear to Stevenson's audience—and the strange implications immediately conjured by this first page of his *Strange Case* would have been troubling indeed.

Gin, after all (as I discuss in chapter 2), was hardly a value-free potation. Gin was the generic name for hard alcohol, and it was a substance not generally found in a respectable gentleman's home (Harrison, 69): it was meant only for getting drunk, whether consumed in low working-class spirit pubs or in the new "Gin Palaces" (Dillon, 292), fancy drinking-places that took their cues from other Victorian pleasure palaces and amusements—though they were hardly family-friendly in this case. Gin was tied to all sorts of bad behavior, including chronic joblessness, domestic violence, and public disturbances. This was the stuff that temperance pamphlets and *Punch* cartoons were made of: it was the fuel for abusive, uneducated, and uncouth lower-class men who took the stuff (often made of the vilest ingredients) in cheap shots. In the popular imagination, drinkers consumed shot after shot, until they were blind drunk (often literally) and dead broke, and then, if they were able, rolled home to beat their wives and children. The cautionary tales were legion: gin drinking led to unemployment, debt, sickness, madness, blindness, rack and ruin, and eventually death (inevitably producing widows and orphans to be thrown out on the streets, destitute). An inebriate's taste for "vintages" was to be "mortified" with prayer, abstinence, and testifying, not with this utterly bodily, anti-industrial, anticapitalist liquor. Gin drinking, in other words, was the absolute antithesis of gentlemanly consuming.

This is not to say that gin drinking was limited absolutely to the lower classes. As we have seen, very privileged, high-born men like Brontë's Arthur Huntingdon sometimes drank gin—but they did so to flout society's conventions, to demonstrate the freedoms from social expectation gifted them by their class, not to "mortify" themselves or their bodies. This is precisely the sort of slumming behavior that might be expected of the "down-going men" who "came about [Utterson's] chambers," particularly given the "high pressure of spirits" they engaged in: gin sublimated the mind to the body, undermined the middle-class imperative for good order and good government, and refused the rules of law and the clock upon which bourgeois Victorian society was rhetorically built. It was the sort of behavior that dissolute young men were expected to grow out of before it killed them.

This great social ill had, unsurprisingly, become the primary focus of the antidrink movement in the latter part of the century. Gin was totally unacceptable not only to teetotalers but also to moderate temperance folk: it was the point of no return, the inevitable site of the drinker's downfall. Patrick Dillon notes that the "Gin Craze" in the early part of the century was "soon followed" by a "Gin Panic" (232). Antispirits societies spread across England and Scotland, and well into the final third of the century, "through interminable feuds, mergers and divisions, children's rallies and temperance tracts, marches and fund-raising events, campaigns in Parliament and thunderous sermons from the pulpit . . . the panic about drink would run uncontrolled" (Dillon, 232). Often church-affiliated and always preoccupied with the suppression of uncontrolled appetites and desires, temperance seems precisely the sort of social engine that a man like Utterson would endorse.[3] Indeed, Utterson's Sunday behavior—his joyless perambulations with his cousin, his sober meditation over a religious text—seems perfectly calculated to evoke the hard edge of temperance, even of teetotaling.[4]

His habit, then, seems bizarrely inappropriate for this "austere" and "dusty" lawyer—and hardly a prescription for success in suppressing untoward appetites (see chapter 4). When read in light of the strange case of class and gentlemanliness in Stevenson's novella, it helps us to unlock not only the unspeaking character of Utterson but also the secrets of Dr. Jekyll and Mr. Hyde. Utterson's ritual is the marker of the true class horror of the story: the fear that as individuals and a class, appropriately placed and ordered, the bourgeoisie, as Jekyll says of Hyde, "did not even exist" (52).

As Andrew Smith and others have noted, Stevenson's novella is very much a story about the horrors of the prosperous middle ranks of the gentle classes. This is where Utterson and his friends place themselves: they are gentlemanly in their rituals, their public faces, and their behavior. Theirs is a world of prosperity, comprising good houses, good servants, and good wine. They draw on the privileged, long-term connections created by wealth: Utterson and Lanyon, for instance, are "old friends, old mates both at school and at college" (13). Lanyon owns a house in Cavendish Square, guarded by a "solemn butler" (13), and keeps a carriage. Jekyll was "born . . . to a large fortune" (47), possesses a home with "a great air of wealth and comfort" (18), and employs a full staff of servants to run his bachelor household. The men meet at "pleasant dinners," often hosted by Jekyll, that are attended by "intelligent, reputable men . . . all judges of good wine" (19). They may not be aristocrats or landed gentry, but they are educated, privileged, and insulated from the basic wants of the body, partakers in and appreciators of fine dinners and fine libations.

But these men are also creatures of labor of the head, charter members of the professional middle class. Unlike, for example, the putatively working men who populate *Little Dorrit*—identified by their professions but largely concerned, like the Barnacles, with "how not to do it" while eating well at the tables of others—Stevenson's professional gentlemen are entirely imbricated in their work. "Mr. Utterson the lawyer" (7) in particular is made entirely of his career, which forms not only his behavior but also his very body. He is "a man of a rugged countenance . . . lean, long, dusty, dreary" (7): a creature of labor, he bears a face that suggests the wear and tear of a working life and a body that enfolds the very detritus of his law books. If the task of the man of the rising middle class is to separate himself from his work, to achieve upward mobility, to pass as a man born to leisure, then Utterson has always already failed: his labor (like Arthur Huntingdon's leisure in *Tenant*) is written on his countenance, grossly evident, sign and signal of his fitness not for the drawing room or the dining room (he is "embarrassed in discourse") but for the courtroom and the law chambers.

Utterson's accustomed practices affirm this idea. The "last reputable acquaintance and the last good influence in the lives of down-going men" is visited by these reprobates at "his chambers" (7). The text seems to suggest that his living space and his working space are one and that he receives his friends as clients, or his clients as friends—that business and pleasure are inseparable. Utterson does not actually live "in chambers," but we see very little of his "bachelor house" beyond his "business room," which he visits on a Sunday—instead of keeping the Sabbath by sitting over "a volume of dry divinity," as is his wont—to study Dr. Jekyll's will (12). The line between business life and private life is indistinct: to Utterson, work seems to be truly Godly, just as well suited for the Lord's Day as a book of sermons.

Other gentlemanly houses likewise embody the problem of work and gentlemanliness. Utterson's old school chum and confidant, "the great Dr. Lanyon," lives in "Cavendish Square, that citadel of medicine," where he both "receive[s] his crowding patients" and sits "alone over his wine" (13); when Hyde appears to reveal his secret to Lanyon, he "[creeps] into [Lanyon's] house" (47), which serves as both consulting room and a receiving room for friends. The house of Utterson's "friend the doctor" (18) Jekyll seems old-fashioned and genteel: the place "[wears] an air of wealth and comfort." Its most celebrated feature is "a large, low-roofed, comfortable hall, paved with flags, warmed (after the fashion of a country house) by a bright, open fire, and furnished with costly cabinets of oak"—an old-fashioned, manorial room that Utterson finds "the pleasantest . . . in London" (18). But Jekyll's is also the only house "still occupied entire" on a street of "ancient, handsome houses, now for the most part decayed from their high estate and let in flats and chambers to all sorts and conditions of men: map-engravers, architects, shady lawyers and the agents of obscure enterprises" (17–18).

Jekyll's home is the last bastion of domesticity in a square of houses transformed from their long-ago function of sheltering and protecting families of wealth and gentility—families removed, that is, from the world of work—to awkward work spaces, compromised by their history of domesticity but lacking any domestic use whatsoever. In this context, Jekyll's house feels less like a gentleman's home than like a theme park: a relic, or a simulacrum, of genteel London life. The problem is further articulated by the house's history: hardly inherited as an old family possession, Jekyll's house was "bought" by the doctor "from the heirs of a celebrated surgeon" (25), and his predecessors' labors are evident. Confusion reigns within the walls of the residence:

> Down by the kitchen offices and across a yard which had once been a garden [was] a building which was indifferently known as the laboratory or the dissecting rooms. . . . [T]he block at the bottom of the garden . . . [was a] dingy windowless structure . . . [with a] theatre, once crowded with eager students and now lying gaunt and silent, the tables laden with chemical apparatus. . . . [T]he doctor's cabinet . . . was a large room, fitted round with glass presses, furnished, among other things, with a cheval-glass and a business table, and looking out upon the court by three dusty windows barred with iron. The fire burned in the grate; a lamp was set lighted on the chimney shelf. (25)

Here the personal and the working worlds come together: chemistry, biology, and business, along with the private realm of hearth and home. Later, when Utterson breaks into the cabinet, he finds "a good fire glowing and chattering on the hearth, the kettle singing its thin strain, a drawer or two open, papers neatly set forth on the business table, and nearer the fire, the things laid out for tea; the quietest room, you would have said, and, but for the glazed presses full of chemicals, the most commonplace that night in London" (39).

This is the domestic made uncanny, undone by business, commerce, the world. The realm of work is not in any meaningful way bounded from the domestic sphere in *Dr. Jekyll and Mr. Hyde*; nor is it mitigated by the presence of wives or mothers or children in the home, that is, by the possibility of healthy reproduction, the notion of moving on beyond the business world.[5] Utterson, passing through Jekyll's kitchen, notes that "the fire was out and the beetles were leaping on the floor" (34). No sustenance comes from this kitchen; the hearth warms no hands, heats no good things; beetles, creatures of rot and death, leap on the floor, the very image of Mary Douglas's "dirt"—that is, "matter out of place," the disgusting presence of disgusting creatures where they should not be.[6] It is the familiar made strange indeed.

The barren kitchen is an important sign of the state of gentlemanliness in *Dr. Jekyll and Mr. Hyde*. As we have seen elsewhere, Victorian novels often take great pleasure in recounting the bounties (or the scarcities) of the table; but Stevenson offers no paeans to oysters or roast meats, no philosophizing on the merits of gruel or truffles, no descriptions of food of any kind. At their fine dinners, Utterson and his friends seem only to drink. Lanyon, encountered at his dining table, sits "alone over his wine" (13). Henry Jekyll, giver of "pleasant dinners" (19), can only "make a feint at breakfast" (54). Utterson may sit down to table, but he is rarely seen to eat; he confronts his Sunday dinner, for example, "without relish" (12). Where in *Little Dorrit*, Arthur Clennam refuses food; in *Tenant*, Arthur Huntingdon bloats even as he loses his appetite at his own groaning board; and in *Emma*, Mr. Woodhouse fetishizes his simple fare, turning away from the food of the world—here, food simply disappears.

The only meal actually consumed in all of the novella, in fact, is the breakfast the lawyer "hurrie[s] through" (22) while a policeman waits to accompany him to identify the body of Sir Danvers Carew, the fine old gentleman murdered in the street by Hyde. Here the ascetic lawyer seems to grasp at the law: to insist on ritual in the face of an incomprehensible dissolution of the social order. Called not to witness a will but to look at a body—to stand visual sentinel to the death of a figure marking the apex, the success, of gentlemanly structure and clarity—he sits down to the meal with which professionals are expected to fuel their days, and he does not stir without that important nutrition in his system. He is, so to speak, full when he stands before Sir Danvers's body—full of lawyerly propriety, utterly constituted, by his collation, of the well-ordered professional world; and in and of himself a bulwark against the chaos the murder seems to portend.

Professionalism is, in fact, the reason for the invisibility of meals in the text. If, as Marianna Adler suggests, the Victorian striver must subdue the body in order to successfully let the mind go about its business undistracted, in this way distancing himself from the bodily laborer of the lower classes (387–88), then meals are about efficiency, keeping the corpus in good order so that the brain may labor unimpeded. Mr. Utterson eats breakfast before viewing Sir Danvers's body not only because the marking of the ritual helps him to create the illusion of sense and order where these valuable commodities have disappeared but also because an infusion of an early, businesslike breakfast, that most middle class of meals, will provide him with the energy, the mental and physical fuel, that he needs to face the professional task at hand. But where, in *The Law and the Lady*, Dexter's fuel is the women he desires, the nature of Mr. Utterson's fuel is so unimportant that its incorporation is barely glanced at, because to do otherwise would be to acknowledge the needs of the body, and this, of course, is impossible: the well-ordered professional gentleman has no bodily needs or desires, because he is a structure only of labor and striving of the mind. If food is simply fuel, then there is no need, no possibility, for commensality or even for alimentary pleasure. Like secrets, like money, it is simply socked away until it is needed to drive the Pancks-like engine.

This diet seems entirely appropriate to the striver: as many critics have noted, the Victorian middle-class ethos is, of course, taken up with the notion of the value of work. The well-regulated middle-class man, manager of people and money and production, is held up as the epitome of proper living; the middle-class man's morality, his church, and his labor of the mind are inseparable. Work, that is, makes the man. But this invisible worker's diet is also insufficient for the striving professional gentleman; and the erasure of the body that it enables is undercut, even reversed, precisely by the aspirations that are the striver's most important fuel. The striver, after all, seeks class mobility. To pass, that is, to live as a man of privilege, he must, of course, give up work, must devote himself to leisure—but by doing this, he violates his moral code, that which forms the basis for body and mind, since men of leisure, this narrative insists, are useless creatures, antiworkers, parasites on the body of the nation, feeding off the labor of others.[7] As we have seen elsewhere, the gentleman of leisure is always, inevitably, constituted by his appetites; it is his foregrounding of his bodily needs and desires that marks his class, albeit in problematic ways. If this is the place to which the professional gentleman aspires, then, his ascension must necessarily erase him by making the body visible. The middle class in the novella, in other words, is always moving toward self-obliteration, because its very reason for being is aspirational. Like Mr. Hyde, hidden away in the body of the gentlemanly Dr. Jekyll, it, too, does "not even exist."

The gentlemen who populate the novel, then, are unwieldy monsters: workers aspiring to leisure but unable to live in it; men of taste and money, striving to be productive even as their hard work undermines their gentlemanly status. It is here that the anxiety undergirding *Dr. Jekyll and Mr. Hyde* is found. The horror of the novella lives in the untenable, unlivable place where the belief in labor as a social good and the belief in leisure as the ultimate personal and social achievement clash in the very impossibility of the middle class itself.

This is why Mr. Utterson drinks "gin when he [is] alone" (7): he hopes to give himself a place from which to aspire. Gin drinking is as low as anything can be. It is utterly, grossly corporeal, removed from the pleasures of palate and education and concerned only with the immediate effects of itself: of drunkenness, of unreflection, of the subsuming of mind by body. It is the opposite of the striver ethos. Utterson seeks to make himself lower not to mark his freedom from social constraints, as Arthur Huntingdon does in *Tenant*, but to create social order. Utterson's gin drinking is not an act of self-destruction in the way that Huntingdon's life in the bottle clearly is. By affiliating his drinking with his austere and clearly unenjoyable Sunday ritual (at the end of which "he would go soberly and gratefully to bed" [12]—the gratitude being, apparently, for the end of his dull Sunday as much as it is for God's grace), the text strongly suggests that Utterson believes his private tipple is a necessary if unpleasant medicine, good for what ails him, rather than an indulgence. His is the dilemma of the middle-class man: that there is, in Gertrude Stein's famous phrase, "no there there" (289). There is only the low to be parted from and the aspirational high to be sought. In the middle class, one is always either going up or going down. By defying the moral code of the middle class, Utterson paradoxically allows himself to remain within that code; by mortifying the mind and the appetite—for good things, for the good life—he gives himself somewhere to go, something to prove, to which he can aspire. By forcing himself backward, he allows himself to continue to evolve, albeit in a manner that is, like the class system itself, entirely constructed. To Mr. Utterson, gin is class medicine, a dose to restore him, literally and figuratively.

This is not to say that there is no connection between Huntingdon and Utterson; there is one, and it is telling, as the lawyer's affiliation for "down-going men" makes clear. His aims and theirs, after all, are at bottom the same: to create class by dropping down to the bottom of the social heap. But whereas Huntingdon and his band of brothers (and perhaps the down-going men) drink constantly to mark inherent gentlemanliness on the body, Utterson drinks to counter the effects of gentlemanliness achieved through striving: to mortify the body, to keep it still, and so to give himself somewhere to strive from. Utterson's reliance on gin also suggests that the self is formed through what is taken in—that the constitution of selfhood is neither intrinsic nor static but is instead created, maintained, and altered through a transactional relationship with the outside world contained in comestibles. In other words, to paraphrase Jean Anthelme Brillat-Savarin, aliment makes the man. This idea implicitly refutes the notion of class as inherent to the body, a physiological state of being. It is an idea crucial to the middle-class notion of the self-made man: the striver must believe that blood is not the determining factor for selfhood, that anyone with the appropriate will to power can succeed.

Utterson does, certainly, inscribe himself through drink. But whereas *Tenant*'s Huntingdon wears his drink on his body and Collins's industrial monster, Dexter, marks his alimental proclivities in ruffles and steel wheels, in the case of the lawyer, gin seems to leave no trace on his dusty corpus at all. Rather, the drinking of gin allows Utterson to preserve his workaday, striving physical appearance instead of undermining it—and in this, his outer body's aspect is as much a deceptive shelter as his friend Dr. Jekyll's is for Mr. Hyde, allowing no access to what goes on beneath.

This is of a piece with the notion of the enclosed body in the late nineteenth century. Claudia Benthien claims that the notion of skin, of the boundary of the body, changed profoundly in this period. In earlier times, she argues, "skin was understood less as a wall in which closable windows and doors were embedded and more as a kind of porous tissue that could potentially have an opening anywhere" (40). Late nineteenth-century medical practices, however, altered this notion of the body, constructing an interior medical self that was closed off. Whereas the older model of the body posited danger on the inside, "it was the threat of external things that posed a potential threat to the body. . . . [H]ealth was protected by shuttering it against potential external dangers of infection" (42). The self is locked away, inside a protective shell. In *Dr. Jekyll and Mr. Hyde*, then, what is taken in by mouth may constitute the body—but that marking is not always written on the skin. Instead, it can be hidden beneath, flowing in the blood, constituting a self that is not accessible from the outside, so that coherence and clarity are defeated.

Fittingly, the aliment that the professional gentlemen of *Dr. Jekyll and Mr. Hyde* do share, on occasion, is a substance imaginatively linked to that self-making, invisibly marking blood, one that penetrates the skin, so to speak, overcoming the enclosed self and allowing for gentlemanly communion and commensality, albeit briefly. The "friendly gatherings" in which Utterson and his compatriots take part are all about class—about the transformation from worker to man of leisure, the direction in which these engines are set to move—and as a result, fuel is the furthest thing from the minds of the partakers. Instead, they make a meal of a substance that offers transformation, the magical, Eucharistic thinking of the swallowing of class: wine.

For the gentlemen of the *Strange Case*, wine is very different from food. Wine allows "something eminently human [to] beacon[] from [the] eye" when it is "to [the] taste" of the drinkers (7); the men are "all judges of good wine" (19), and a dinner at which it is featured is always "friendly" (7) and "pleasant" (9). Utterson's in-

terlude with his clerk, Guest, also shares much of the transubstantive potential of these gatherings. Mr. Utterson

> sat on one side of his own hearth, with Mr. Guest . . .
> upon the other, and midway between, at a nicely calcu-
> lated distance from the fire, a bottle of a particular old
> wine that had long dwelt unsunned in the foundations
> of his house. The fog still slept on the wing above the
> drowned city, where the damps glimmered like carbun-
> cles; and through the muffle and smother of these fallen
> clouds, the procession of the town's life was still rolling
> in through the great arteries with a sound as of a mighty
> wind. But the room was gay with firelight. In the bottle
> the acids were long ago resolved; the imperial dye had
> softened with time, as the colour grows richer in stained
> windows; and the glow of hot autumn afternoons on hill-
> side vineyards, was ready to be set free and to disperse
> the fogs of London. Insensibly, the lawyer melted. (27)

The moment encapsulates the importance of wine to the gentlemen of the *Strange Case*. Here is a substance with a pedigree, a "particular old" bottle in which "the acids were long ago resolved"—in
which, that is, the strife of production and commerce have disappeared with time, leaving only the palatable, easily swallowed flavors of long-accomplished goals. This is reinforced by the proof of
discernment that Utterson evinces here: he is "particular" about
his wine, which rests "at a nicely calculated distance from the fire."
Similarly, "the imperial dye [has] softened with time, as the colour
grows richer in stained windows"—that is, the unpleasant aspects
of rule and gentlemanly order have faded away, leaving only the
pleasing patina and the association with stained glass, with its al-
lusions to church, godliness, and right rule of the most pleasant
sort. It embodies an always-already naturalized flavor of leisure, of
ease, of rightful place at the top of the social order, beyond work of
the hand or work of the head—a flavor "ready to be set free and
to disperse the fogs of London," that is, to rid the atmosphere of
the sickly, expensive flavors of the striving life, of industrialism as
social engine.

Wine removes the men of *Dr. Jekyll and Mr. Hyde* from the realm of the striver and allows them to have always already arrived, beyond the reach of the reforming, classed language of temperance, to which Utterson makes himself implicitly available with his secret drinking.[8] The properties of wine are here diametrically opposed to those of Utterson's secret beverage. An anticapitalist drink in its antisocial and anti-self-control properties, gin is nevertheless the outcome of capitalism: imagined as entirely manufactured, a simulacrum, that is, an industrial/chemical compound meant to act on the body, it reduces the drinker to a body, to a faceless drunkard. Wine, in contrast, is anti-industrial, anticapitalist. It is not manufactured but grown, cultivated, crafted, made by hand; the more expensive the bottle, the more likely it is to be artisanal, named, a creation of individuals. Wine is not commercial (taken in public, in gin palaces or pubs) but residential (both in the sense of where it is consumed and in the sense of being constructive of the private realm, as Utterson's "particular bottle" lies in the foundations of his house). Whereas gin is all about the industrial city, wine is about escape from that place, about private spaces and connoisseurship, about Romantic-style anti-industrial paeans to simpler lives in simpler places, like the sunny southland conjured up by Utterson's bottle. And, of course, where gin mortifies— keeping the self at a low level, that is, always already defined— wine "melt[s]."

By drinking wine, the lawyer is able to achieve, albeit temporarily, the gentlemanly state—that is, to leave the mechanized nature of his professional-industrial life behind, to become flesh and blood, to taste, to feel. Wine is transformative, transubstantive, capable of overcoming the alienation of industrialism, of producing "friendly" commensality and community. It allows Mr. Utterson to "melt," to reach out to other human beings as a social creature. Wine, in *Dr. Jekyll and Mr. Hyde,* is the Eucharistic site of communion between men, literally bringing them back from the undead, vampiric state of class incoherence and warming the blood in their veins. Drink makes the man: if gentlemanliness has long been associated with blood, then wine, here, is the lifeblood of gentlemanliness. Drinking mellowed old wine at once demonstrates a taste for the sophisticated and suggests, so to speak, a transfusion, a remaking of the body—of the self—as gentlemanly through what is taken in by mouth. Taste, class, and discernment at once mark and make the gentleman. This is why "something eminently human beacon[s] from [Utterson's] eye," the pathway to the soul, when "[a]t friendly meetings . . . the wine [is] to his taste" (7). The machine-man striver is made human by wine, by the dream of class placement and always-already achievement it offers.

But though wine is very much associated with discernment (Jekyll's "pleasant dinners" are attended by "old cronies, all intelligent, reputable men and all judges of good wine" [19]; the libation must be "to his taste" before Utterson's humanity emerges) and their appreciation of and desire for wine seems to constitute these men as gentlemen, it remains problematic, precisely *because* wine "melts" the self. A taste for "good wine" may be about the mind (discernment), but it is also about the body (that is, about appetite), which is precisely why Mr. Utterson's taste for vintages requires mortification. The transubstantiation that wine performs is not only intellectual or emotional but also physical: the body ceases to be a machine and begins to be "human." Wine melts the boundaries of these men at "friendly gatherings," taking them beyond the social rules, beyond mechanization. If "something human beacon[s] from [the] eye" in the presence of wine, this very beaconing indicates a breaking down of body boundaries, an instance of permeability that is antidefinitive. In this way, wine suggests that not only striving but also gentlemanliness itself is antidefinitive, placeless—that is, not only that there is nowhere to go but down but also that downward movement is a given. If gentlemanliness is constituted through wine (if this is the only possibility of commensality, community, belonging) but wine also melts the boundaries of the body and makes the discrete self impossible, then the dream of arrival is necessarily impossible, holding within itself the seeds of its own destruction.

Commensality, too, proves to be an elusive dream. The middle-class work imperative is about individualism, about making one's way in the world; suppression and mechanization constitute at once a moral code and a business requirement. Drinking together, taking wine at table, is about reversing that process by creating community. Unsurprisingly, this, like other iterations of gentlemanliness we have seen, is a construction deeply steeped in nostalgia: the friends' old school ties, Jekyll's olden-days house, and the very act of sitting over a well-aged bottle of wine evoke notions of old-fashioned, historically continuous, in-the-blood gentlemanliness. This is an impossible dream, of course—as the very consumption of wine *as* the stuff of gentlemanliness makes clear—and though "something human" may "beacon" from Utterson's eye when "the wine is to his taste" in the company of his peers, there is no evidence that true connections occur. The schism between Jekyll and Lanyon, apparently unknown or misunderstood by Utterson for some time, calls up the solipsistic nature of gentlemanly existence here, as does the faceless nature of the other gentlemen in attendance at Jekyll's "pleasant dinners" and indeed the puzzle of Utterson's Sunday perambulations with his cousin Enfield, to whom he has nothing to say. These successful strivers may want to form community and may think that their act of pouring and drinking together creates it—but in the end, everything "looks like Queer Street" (11), and so everyone is alone, unbothered by questions, "allowed to go to the devil in his own way," and unsaved by true connection.

The melting performed by the wine, then, is more problematic than otherwise, dissolving body boundaries but not creating a coherent class identity in exchange: an older iteration of the self, wine posits an always already unbounded gentlemanly body, connected by near-visible blood to others, but this is impossible in the machine age. This is why Utterson's friends, at the end of their dinners, "liked to sit awhile in his unobtrusive company, practising for solitude, sobering their minds in the man's rich silence, after the expense and strain of gaiety" (19). Utterson's mortification preserves some of the automaton nature, the enclosed physical shell, that the professional gentlemen require to go back out into the world of getting and spending, of striving ever upwards. When he takes his leave, they are themselves again, literally and figuratively.

And, of course, as Austen's Mr. Woodhouse has amply demonstrated, wine, like all aliment, can never be completely controlled when it originates beyond the bounds of one's own estates. The world, as it is swallowed, is not pure, not legible, and its effects on the body are similarly tainted. In *Dr. Jekyll and Mr. Hyde*, that tainting lies in the wine's handling. In the case of the "particular" bottle of wine resting before the lawyer's fire, for instance, the wine's foreign origins may be a source of the problem—its sacred warmth hiding a Gothic southern European tendency—but the house also plays a role. The wine has long lived in the "foundations" of Utterson's home—that is, it is imbricated with himself, with what makes him, which is business. It is made of work, and here it is also a lubricant to work—in other words, it is associated with the endless appetites of capitalism and the striver—and in this sense calls up its bloody nature not as a filler of veins but as an occasion of the drinking down of figurative lifeblood. Utterson's drinking is intended as a means of "fish[ing] for" the "advice" from his clerk that he "long[s]" for in the matter of Hyde (25). It is, in other words, not actually an idyll of gentlemanly leisure but a front for business.

The myth of capitalism is, it seems, given life in these solitary, wine-drinking men, who are fathers to no one, sons to no one, husbands to no one—managers to the core, producers of nothing, consumers of the fruits of alienated work of the hand of unseen others who enable their wealth. The point is driven home when Guest, an expert on handwriting, takes a look at Hyde's note in comparison to one from Jekyll: it is "[o]nly an invitation to dinner," yet it seems to prove that "Henry Jekyll forge[s] for a murderer!" (28). The Eucharistic becomes the cannibalistic: the ritual that transforms the wine is revealed as a cover for a rapacious and bloody appetite, deeply associated at once with the rituals of dinner and with work.

This, in fact, is the meal most often taken by the gentlemen (a meal reminiscent of Sara Macallan's autophagic repasts): Mr. Utterson sits over a collation for which he has little "relish" after his discussion with Enfield regarding the story of a door, instead chewing over the puzzle of the problematic Edward Hyde. Dr. Lanyon receives Jekyll's strange letter while at dinner and rises "from table" (43) to carry out his friend's request. Jekyll tells Utterson that he has received the news of Sir Danvers's murder during his morning meal: "They were crying it in the square. . . . I heard them in my dining room" (25). Secrets, mysteries, horror, murder: all are taken in at table by our efficient, business-like gentlemen. And, as we shall see when we turn more fully to Hyde, this psychic meal has a distinctly fleshly, autophagic flavor.

Neither gin nor wine, then, can fix Utterson in place, that is, give him a class status that is clear and cogent and can be occupied. And it is precisely because both wine and gin fail to constitute selfhood in a coherent, meaningful way that Jekyll turns to drugs.

Like Utterson, Jekyll seeks to fix the problem of placelessness through what is taken in: to reshape himself through aliment. In some ways, Jekyll's drug is akin to Utterson's gin: like that debased drink, its aim is a literal "mortification" of the social man.[9] But unlike Utterson, Jekyll does not seek to affiliate himself with the low and, thus, to find space for himself to evolve and aspire. Rather, he makes use of science in an attempt to put himself beyond the impossible bind of the class system entirely. He seeks utter selflessness, remove: to be placed in and of himself, not through social marking. Jekyll's concoction is the product of hard work of the mind, the progressive alchemy of medicine. Speedy, scientific, and ingenious, it is a uniquely middle-class means of reaching inside the self; yet in its antiproductivity, its antisocial nature, it is the opposite of all that is middle class. It is, in many ways, the essence of modernity that Jekyll is swallowing.

Like Utterson, Dr. Jekyll seems inherently class-conflicted. He is "a large, well-made, smooth-faced man of fifty, with something of a slyish cast perhaps, but every mark of capacity and kindness" (19)—that is, he is at once both high and low, inherently gentlemanly and physically degenerative. His "slyness" denotes something hidden away beneath the skin; the language is immediately evocative of the descriptions of Jews in London at the time, who were thought to have a "sly cast" indicative of degeneration, a sign of the untrustworthy, corrupting nature hidden beneath an apparently "white" exterior.[10] This early reference to the dangers of "passing" at once presages what will soon be revealed by the text and indicates, in its very ordinariness and in the text's simultaneous generosity to Jekyll ("every mark of capacity and kindness"), an unstated problem in the very heart of gentlemanliness that is glanced away from by narrator and characters alike. Jekyll himself notes, in his statement, that his hand is "professional in shape and size . . . large, firm, white and comely" (54). His body, in other words, reveals his biological turn toward middle-class, "professional" work of the mind: "white" because of his indoor labor

and "firm" to denote character requisite to the true middle-class
gentleman—though also "large" and "comely" like a well-fed upper-
class man.

Jekyll is more placeless than either Utterson or Lanyon. "[B]orn
. . . to a large fortune, endowed besides with excellent parts, inclined by nature to industry, fond of the respect of the wise and
good among [his] fellow-men" (47), he is a strange brew, a mixture
of striver and upper-class gentleman of leisure, and he is unable to
reconcile these competing identities. Utterson's cure is impossible
for him, because he finds "a certain impatient gaiety of disposition
. . . hard to reconcile with [his] imperious desire to carry [his] head
high, and wear a more than commonly grave countenance before
the public" (47–48). In other words, gin fails him: Jekyll's taste for
the low, the bodily, only emphasizes his internal division and, thus,
the space in between his "low" self and his "high" self, the liminal
space he actually inhabits. Driven by "an almost morbid sense of
shame" and "the exacting nature of [his] aspirations"—that is, re-
spectively, the trait most strongly inculcated in the lower classes by
the reformers and the trait most typical of the striver—he seeks relief from this fact: "I was no more myself when I laid aside restraint
and plunged in shame, than when I laboured, in the eye of the day,
at the furtherance of knowledge or the relief of sorrow and suffering" (48). It is clear to Jekyll that he is never entirely "himself." He
is always betwixt and between, straining upward with ambition and
a profound sense of shame, or leaning downward with a great
hunger to indulge his bodily appetites. In both cases, the cause is
the placelessness, the emptiness of the middle ground. Son of industry, gentleman and grubber in the dirt of science, he is everywhere and nowhere.

Jekyll's aim of reconciling himself is the driving force of his experiments. He relates, in his "Full Statement of the Case," that he
has been "committed to a profound duplicity of life" (48): determined to become "honourable and distinguished" but afflicted with
"a certain impatient gaiety of disposition" (47), he has for years
"concealed [his] pleasures" (48) to present a coherent, entirely "honourable" face to the world. He finds, in the course of his scientific
studies, that this divide is utterly embodied: reasoning from his
own case, he discovers "that man is not truly one, but truly two"

(48). He discovers that he is dual: "[I]f I could rightly be said to be either, it was only because I was radically both." This sense of naturalized division provides him no solace, however. He dreams "of the separation of these elements," concluding, "If each, I told myself, could but be housed in separate identities, life would be relieved of all that was unbearable" (49).

Martin Tropp claims that Hyde's behavior "all may stem from his over-riding purpose, to assert the power of his will. . . . Jekyll's experiments demonstrate his belief that to control his will means he can reshape his body" (122–23). Indeed, as Jekyll recounts, "I began to perceive . . . the trembling immateriality, the mist-like transience, of this seemingly so solid body in which we walk attired. . . . I not only recognised my natural body for the mere aura and effulgence of certain of the powers that made up my spirit but managed to compound a drug by which these powers should be dethroned from their supremacy" (49). But what Jekyll seeks is not merely the middle-class dream of subduing the body through aliment so that the mind could go about its business. In the face of the impossibility of class that he embodies, Jekyll seeks to create wholeness, a complete and coherent self, by, paradoxically, effecting a split; and the division he proposes is not simply goodness from badness, high from low. Instead, he proposes a full separation of the mechanized, gentlemanly working self from the upscale gentleman of leisure—the gin drinker versus the wine drinker.

Fittingly, Jekyll's professional self—the investigative, problem-solving, aspirational side of him, hungering for fame and respect—finds a cure for his self-division in the realm of modernity and science. When Jekyll swallows the potion for the first time, as he recounts, "I came to myself as if out of a great sickness. There was something strange in my sensations, something indescribably new and, from its very novelty, incredibly sweet. I felt younger, lighter, happier in body; within I was conscious of a heady recklessness" (50). The drug seems to have cured his malaise; though his physical body is shrunken under its influence and he detects something seriously malign in the face he sees in the mirror, he seems, at first, to have indeed found wholeness through division. The drug appears to solve the problem of the "incoherency in [his] life," as Jekyll puts it (52): it seems to provide Jekyll with that elusive quality, place. The doctor, gazing at his new second self in the mirror, asserts, "This, too, was myself. It seemed natural and human. In my eyes it bore a livelier image of the spirit, it seemed more express and single, than the imperfect and divided countenance, I had been hitherto accustomed to call mine" (51).

The being he calls forth is a creature utterly devoted to self-indulgence, a selfish being bent only on pleasure, however he may define it. Jekyll, by contrast—the man who is resuscitated every time Hyde takes the drug—may be found "quietly at home, trimming the midnight lamp in his study" (53). As Jekyll explains his dilemma when faced with the need to eliminate one or the other of his selves: "To cast in my lot with Jekyll, was to die to those appetites which I had long secretly indulged and had of late begun to pamper. To cast it in with Hyde, was to die to a thousand interests and aspirations" (55). Hyde plays; Jekyll works. Hyde is the man of leisure, Jekyll the driven professional. And the drug seems to enable both.

Jekyll's drug, then, seems, for a time at least, a miraculous and magical cure for the impossible state of the professional gentleman. In this, it is hardly a project only of imagination, a purely literal medicine for social ills. In its attributes, its marvelous transformative possibilities, and in the potential it offers for an ambitious doctor, it evokes one of the most popular palliatives of the 1880s: cocaine. Speedy, refined, work-inducing, medically sophisticated, transformative, and utterly modern, cocaine was a bellwether for its time, for good and for ill; and its echo in the novella does much to explain and to place the behavior of both Dr. Jekyll and Mr. Hyde as gentlemen of appetite. If, to paraphrase Wolfgang Schivelbusch, coffee was *the* drug of bourgeois capitalist industrialism,[11] then cocaine was arguably the drug of choice for the dawning of the modern age of the individual in Britain.

Much has been made of Stevenson's putative cocaine use, particularly during the composition of *Dr. Jekyll and Mr. Hyde*,[12] but the implications of the drug's echoes in the text go far beyond the biographical. Coca, of course, was hardly new to England: the plant, and stories of its miraculous properties, had been imported to Europe from South America since the sixteenth century.[13] Steven Karch notes that "[s]uch claims . . . were taken quite seriously, and they were firmly lodged in the public's consciousness. In the nineteenth century, letters to the editors of the *Lancet* and the *British Medical Journal*, from military surgeons and team physicians, described how coca chewing could be used as a way to decrease thirst and increase endurance" (30). The stories told of indigenous workers undertaking backbreaking labor—digging pits, hauling gear, hiking up mountains—for days on end with little or no food, drink, or rest, sustained only by the coca leaves they chewed constantly.[14]

But though cocaine was isolated from coca by Albert Niemann in 1859[15] and the stuff quickly became popular as a key ingredient in patent medicines,[16] cocaine was not embraced by the medical community until considerably later in the century. Cocaine was difficult to isolate and expensive, and debate continued over its efficacy[17] and its safety[18] into the early 1880s.

But this lukewarm reception among members of the medical establishment began to change with the publication of an essay on cocaine written by a young Viennese neurologist named Sigmund Freud. In early 1884, Freud, desperate to make an impact on his profession (and to earn enough money to marry his fiancée), ordered a small sample of cocaine from the Merck Company in Germany, the principal refiner and supplier of cocaine in Europe, and began experimenting with it—primarily on himself. He quickly became enamored of the white powder, extolling its effects and benefits (and its apparent total lack of negative effects or drawbacks)[19] in an essay entitled "Uber Coca," published in July 1884.[20]

Freud's essay (a combination literature review and first-person account) extols the energy that cocaine produces in the consumer, its pleasurable effects, its positive impact on digestion, its potential in cases of wasting diseases, and (most important for the medical community) its apparent ability to cure morphine habituation without ill effect. As I discuss in chapter 6, chronic morphine inebriation was seen as a problem across all strata of society, but it was perceived as a full-fledged epidemic occurring, ironically, among doctors in particular in the last two decades of the nineteenth century. The idea that cocaine could offer a cure with no apparent downside was greeted with great attention by the medical community. Published well over a year before *Dr. Jekyll and Mr. Hyde* was composed, "Uber Coca" received widespread attention in the medical world and beyond; responses and reprints and Freud's follow-up essays were widely circulated and much discussed. Freud published at least two more essays on the subject before the fall of 1885, when *Dr. Jekyll and Mr. Hyde* was composed, extolling the virtues of cocaine and downplaying its unfortunate effects. His work was promoted by Merck, which was eager to find buyers for its expensive powder, and was widely disseminated.

There are clearly many similarities between Jekyll's drug and cocaine: the physical appearance of his "simple, crystalline salt of a white colour" (43), the invigorating effects. Like Freud, Jekyll obtains his "salt" from a professional outfit, "a firm of wholesale chemists" (50), rather than from a local shop; like Freud, he takes his mixture as a draft. And Jekyll, like Freud, experiences immediate effects from the drug: Jekyll feels "younger, lighter, happier in body"; similarly, Freud, in "Uber Coca," notes that "[a] few minutes after taking cocaine, one experiences a sudden exhilaration and feeling of lightness. . . . After a few minutes the actual cocaine euphoria began" (58).

Freud, like Jekyll, believed that his drug could resolve the traumas of self-division in the industrial age. In "Uber Coca," he notes that cocaine has "been prescribed for the most diverse kinds of psychic debility—hysteria, hypochondria, melancholic inhibition, stupor, and similar maladies. . . . Mantegazza praises coca as being almost universally effective in improving those functional disorders which we now group together under the name of neurasthenia; Fliessburg reports excellent results from the use of coca in cases of 'nervous prostration'; and according to Caldwell, it is the best tonic for hysteria" (64–65). In "On the General Effect of Cocaine," an influential lecture[21] that Freud delivered at the Physiological Club on March 3 and at the Psychiatrische Verein (Psychiatric Society) in Vienna on March 5, 1885, he returned to this notion. "Psychiatry," he argues, "is rich in drugs that can subdue over-stimulated nervous activity but deficient in agents that can heighten the performance of the depressed nervous system. It is natural, therefore, that we should think of making use of the effects of cocaine . . . in the form of illnesses that we interpret as states of weakness and depression of the nervous system. . . . [C]ocaine has been used . . . against hysteria, hypochondria, etc., and there is no shortage of reports of individual cures obtained with it" (116–17).

And the divided self is not simply soothed through the application of Freudian cocaine: it is resolved, made whole through its division. Both Jekyll's confusion between self and other—his recognition of himself in his new form and, in true abject fashion, Hyde's failure to part from Jekyll—and his dream of completeness resonate with Freud's work. Freud wrote of cocaine,

> The psychic effect . . . consists of exhilaration and lasting euphoria, which does not differ in any way from the normal euphoria of a healthy person. The feeling of excitement which accompanies stimulus by alcohol is completely lacking; the characteristic urge for immediate activity which alcohol produces is also absent. . . . One is simply normal, and soon finds it difficult to believe that one is under the influence of any drug at all.
>
> This gives the impression that the mood induced by coca in such doses is due not so much to direct stimulation as to the disappearance of elements in one's general state of well-being which cause depression. One may perhaps assume that the euphoria resulting from good health is also nothing more than the normal condition of a well-nourished cerebral cortex which "is not conscious" of the organs of the body to which it belongs. ("Uber Coca," 60)

For Freud, then, the cocaine state is the normal state of being: far from narcotizing or transforming the user, the drug instead brings the user into himself, makes the self clear, free of the detritus of depression and the worries of life. The parallels to Jekyll and his desire for a drug that would absolve him of his sense of self-division are readily apparent: "This, too, was [him]self" (51). For Jekyll, division is obviated: the radically alienated self is made coherent, no longer always straining toward its other.

Freud returned to the notion of the apparently unchanged self in "On the General Effect of Cocaine." He describes the results of his experiments:

[I]f [a small] dose of cocaine hydrochloride is taken by a subject whose general health is impaired by fatigue or hunger[,] [a]fter a short time . . . he feels as though he had been raised to the full height of intellectual and bodily vigor, in a state of euphoria, which is distinguished from the euphoria after consumption of alcohol by the absence of any feeling of alteration[.] . . . [T]he absence of signs that could distinguish the state from the normal euphoria of good health makes it . . . likely that we will underestimate it. As soon as the contrast between the present state and the state before the ingestion of co-caine is forgotten, it is difficult to believe that one is under the influence of a foreign agent, and yet one is very profoundly altered for four to five hours, since so long as the effects of the drug persist, one can perform mental and physical work with great endurance, and the otherwise urgent needs of rest, food, and sleep are thrust aside, as it were. (114)

The state of normality that Freud saw during cocaine use, then, is of a particular kind: it is the normality of the worker. Again and again, Freud returned to the theme of labor. In the addendum to the essay, he notes that despite individual differences in reactions to cocaine, "an increased capacity for work seems to me to be a common symptom of the coca effect" (107–8). Cocaine enhances the ability to labor without creating new appetites: its appetite-suppressing powers seemed to suggest that the drug could enable work and obviate the need to eat without bringing on a wasting of the body.[22] And though Freud cited many stories of enhanced physical strength and endurance from the literature, the drug's effect on the brain was what he found most interesting. In "Uber Coca," he asserts that "[l]ong-lasting, intensive mental or physical work can be performed without fatigue," but although he "tested this effect of coca, which wards off hunger, sleep, and fatigue and steels one to intellectual effort, some dozen times on [him]self," he undertook "no opportunity to engage in physical work" (60). Cocaine is truly a modern drug: better than caffeine, better than nicotine, it focuses and stimulates the mind, subdues the body, and lets the user get on with his work. As Freud notes; "coca . . . steels one to intellectual effort" (60).

It is precisely in the arena of labor of the head that "[o]ne is simply normal"—that is, one is able to be one's working self. In one fell swoop, Freud rewrote this medico-cultural phenomenon not simply as a palliative or a cure-all for the aches and pains of the modern world but as a means of accessing the true working state of the late-Victorian professional gentleman. The drug is a perfect enabler of modernity. For an unplaced gentleman like Jekyll, a man who was "born . . . to a large fortune" but is "inclined by nature to industry" (47)—a man who has guests wait in an old-fashioned drawing room while he spends his time in a laboratory out back— cocaine seems to offer a palliative, a naturalization, a means of becoming whole by becoming wholly composed of and wholly dedicated to labor. For Jekyll, through the drug, work becomes a natural state of being, instead of a way station or a stage or a means to an end. Whereas Utterson must labor, despite his bodily markings, to be made of labor, Jekyll becomes utterly made of work.

Cocaine, then, seemed capable of making the body magically efficient, turning it into a true tool of the mind, completely under control—and thus allowing a radical but effective separation of body and mind, in which the thinking self remained "human" while the body became a machine. It held the promise, in other words, of solving the gentleman's dilemma—the cocaine-imbibing gentleman could strive while having arrived, could literally exist in two places, two classes, at once.

The story of the professional Jekyll, then, is clear. And what of Hyde? To understand the monster produced by the split, one might productively return to the potion. Beside the powder in the drawer, Lanyon tells us, is a "phial . . . about half-full of a blood-red liquor, which was highly pungent to the sense of smell and seemed to me to contain phosphorus and some volatile ether" (43), as well as some other ingredients, unfamiliar even to an old medical hand like Lanyon. When Hyde sets out to mix the potion in Lanyon's presence, he asks his fellow doctor for "a graduated glass" (46), in this way indicating that his proceedings are wholly scientific—of a piece with the nature of his white powder. But what happens next gives the lie to that idea, even before he drinks the potion and "melt[s]" into Jekyll: "He . . . measured out a few minims of the red tincture and added one of the powders. The mixture, which was at first of a reddish hue, began, in proportion as the crystals melted, to brighten in colour, to effervesce audibly, and to throw off small fumes of vapour. Suddenly and at the same moment, the ebullition ceased and the compound changed to a dark purple, which faded again more slowly to a watery green" (46).

His salt may be modern, but Jekyll's mixture seems the opposite of forward-looking. Based in a "blood-red liquor," evocative of gentlemanly wine and of drinks that are more vampiric, it bubbles, throws off smoke, and changes color twice—first to a royal purple, then to a witchy green. The potion is pure magic, a throwback to England's pre-Christian traditions, to sorcery and Merlin and the search for the philosopher's stone, for the elixir of life. And these throwback evocations, in turn, call up not the modern world of science but a different nineteenth-century movement, awash in nostalgia, the Gothic, a longing for authenticity and magic and truth—a longing often made manifest precisely through the use of drugs.[23]

Jekyll's medical interests, as he puts it, are "wholly towards the mystic and the transcendental" (48)—that is, toward the Romantic. His first transformation, he says, includes "a grinding in the bones . . . and a horror of the spirit that cannot be exceeded at the hour of birth or death. Then . . . I came to myself as if out of a great sickness. . . . I felt younger, lighter, happier in body" (50). The grinding of bones, as though Jekyll is moving into the marrow of his own body; the evocation of birth agonies and of escape from the "great sickness" of the world; the advent of the younger self: all seem to suggest that Jekyll has discovered a truer self, that his quest is nostalgic for some precivilized, Rosseauian state of being. His experience in taking the drug and his interest in these less definable aspects of medicine evoke the opium travels of the Romantics—the voyages into the self in an attempt not to find clarity, a true self appropriately bounded and defined, but rather to discover the unbounded innocent, the pre-Fallen (see chapter 6). This evocation is both magical and horrifying: Judith Halberstam, writing of the final discovery of the body in Jekyll's cabinet, argues that "Poole's inability to identify the 'thing' in the laboratory as other than 'not-Jekyll' suggests that Hyde cannot be classified, he has no place in the order and history of things" (67).

But Hyde is not simply the abject unbounded: he is, rather, a figure precisely for gentlemanly achievement as it is defined in Stevenson's late-century text. In describing the transformation from Hyde to Jekyll, Lanyon writes, "the features seemed to melt and alter" (47). Lanyon's language echoes Utterson's own transformation under the influence: sitting with Guest before the fire with his good wine, "insensibly, the lawyer melt[s]" (27). The olden-days magical elixir, then, may be a product of science—but what it evokes is wine. This is fitting, because Hyde is the embodiment, in Jekyll, of the gentleman complete. If, in the worker-gentleman split, the white powder is Jekyll's natural fare, then surely wine is the aliment best suited to Hyde.

Look, for instance, to the description of his apartments in the low regions of Soho. Mr. Utterson, searching for the murderer of Sir Danvers Carew with Inspector Newcomen of Scotland Yard, finds the rooms "furnished with luxury and good taste. A closet was filled with wine; the plate was of silver, the napery elegant; a good picture hung up on the walls . . . and the carpets were of many plies and agreeable in color" (24). Thomas L. Reed claims that Hyde's rooms are an anomaly, a glitch in the text: these digs, he argues, are more fitting for Jekyll than they are for Hyde. But it is Jekyll, not Hyde, who is the worker bee; Hyde, not Jekyll, who is the creature of upscale appetites. Reed suggests, further, that Stevenson's novella is a fabric of antidrink rhetoric; to this end, he reads the closetful of wine in Hyde's rooms as a sign of his inebriation problem—an argument that Lisa Butler also takes up. But while Jekyll certainly seems to grow addicted to his drug,[24] Hyde's closet of wine is much more evocative of Utterson's cellar, that much-fetishized bottle, the very stuff of gentlemanliness. As is the case with Miserrimus Dexter in *The Law and the Lady*, who keeps the tanned skin of an aristocrat in a closet in his little kitchen, the presence of the wine—like the picture, the good napery, and the fine carpets—demonstrates Hyde's class. He is not simply "troglodytic" (17), as Utterson terms him: if he is a throwback, it is less in the usual degenerative sense than in a sense tied precisely to nostalgia for and insistence on class power and prerogative. Hyde, with his gentlemanly rooms beneath the rough skin of Soho, his rakelike indulgence in low pursuits, and his exultation in his bad behavior, is Jekyll's true gentlemanly self. He is, in a sense, *Tenant's* Arthur Huntingdon, taken in elixir form.

It is not surprising, then, that Hyde drinks wine: if he is the embodiment of the upper-class roué, unconstrained by the requirements of work, driven to mark his freedoms through his behavior, and dedicated to an always-already notion of class and place, then wine is what reaffirms his status in every sense. As Jekyll, under the influence, the doctor is entirely modern: he is speedy, he is placed, he is clarity itself. And where his cocainelike "salt" suppresses Jekyll's body and turns him into the perfect worker, the potion—of wine, of blood, of magic, of olden-days evocations—brings Hyde's physical self to the forefront. Unlike Dexter, who is high and low at once, Hyde is a creature of complete and radical division. But, like Dexter, Hyde is a creature of distinctly autophageous appetites.

For Hyde, as for Utterson, gentlemanliness is rarefied, a flavor much to be savored and hoarded, an intoxicant without equal, speaking to the discernment of the drinker. But whereas for Utterson, wine is Eucharistic, for Hyde, this is not the case. If Hyde is the upper-class self literalized and embodied, then his nutrition, too, must be made literal and bodily. Like Dexter, Woodhouse, and Huntingdon, Hyde cannot swallow that which is alien to him: he cannot embody striver appetites but instead seeks only to swallow himself down. His appetite is limited to that which falls within his own purview. Hyde's taste for "blood-red liquor[s]," then, goes beyond the Eucharistic, the representational: he wants to taste the thing itself. If, for instance, Sir Danvers Carew is the ultimate gentleman, then he is precisely what Hyde craves; Hyde desires not to be like him but to be him, to take him in, to incorporate him.

The language in which Jekyll/Hyde recalls the Carew murder in his "Full Statement of the Case" is telling in this respect: "With a transport of glee," he writes, "I mauled the unresisting body, tasting delight from every blow" (56). The scene is most often read as a coded event of violent homosexual appetite, the murder depicted (most cogently by Elaine Showalter in *Sexual Anarchy*) either as a homosexual rape or as an attack that is the product of homosexual panic. Denise Gigante sees Hyde's cravings as metaphoric in precisely this sense. Writing of the displaced appetites for vampirism and cannibalism which, she argues, characterize much Romantic writing (and which speaks to a displacement of interdicted desire), she notes in passing that "[h]is uncontrollable appetites define the monstrous Hyde. . . . Jekyll is the quintessence of the unmarried, middle-class connoisseur . . . whose closest companions are other unmarried bachelors, and Hyde is a monster by virtue of his lack of restraint, especially in 'those appetites which [Jekyll] had long secretly indulged' and to which by the end of the novel he instinctively returns 'with a greedy gusto'" (138). But the language of the text here, while richly available to such readings, is also the language of *actual* alimental appetite.

Carew is "an aged and beautiful gentleman . . . with a very pretty manner of politeness" whose face "seemed to breathe . . . an innocent and old-world kindness of disposition, yet with something high, too, as of a well-founded self-content" (21). He seems completely unlike the "pale and dwarfish" Hyde—who gives "an impression of deformity," has "a displeasing smile," conducts himself "with a sort of murderous mixture of timidity and boldness," and inspires "disgust, loathing and fear" (17)—in every seeming particular. Yet it is not Carew's differences from his attacker but his similarities that drive the attack. As Showalter and others suggest, there are indications that Sir Danvers is hiding a secret, a split self, so to speak—a low life, hinted at by his presence in the street during the deserted night hours and the very fact that he "bow[s] and accost[s]" Hyde in the street at that hour (21). Indeed, the fact that he has a letter addressed to Utterson in his pocket when he is found is hardly a sign of his good character, given Utterson's predilection for "down-going men." He is, then, fitting food for Hyde—utterly gentlemanly, and perhaps also like to Hyde in his secret self. By devouring his interlocutor, Hyde seeks to preserve himself by taking in only that which is like, that which reinforces and rewrites himself. If, as Maggie Lane and others have noted, the logic of cannibalism is the logic of taking in the power of the other, of subsuming the other in the self, then here, the power that Hyde seeks is the power of himself, externalized and then returned to the internal realm. The "love that dare not speak its name," indeed.[25]

Many critics have argued that *Dr. Jekyll and Mr. Hyde* is a novella horrified by the possibility of atavism. But Hyde's horror is less that he is devolved than that he is the embodiment of the upper-class gentleman. If he is savage, he is so because the drug reveals what is hidden behind the mask of class, what is left behind when work is removed: a bloody appetite for the self. It is this that predicates meat, savagery, hungers, horror: not an atavistic return but the putative pinnacle of civilization, the state which the striver aspires to but can never comfortably achieve without leaving himself behind. In Hyde, that magical act of leaving behind is complete: the gentleman, embodied in him, has nothing to reach for, no reason to strive. He need only continually reinscribe himself in order to mark himself, to rebirth himself, and he does so by eating the rich—those who are akin to his only-consuming, never-producing self.

In his "Full Statement," the doctor notes that "Jekyll (who was composite) . . . with a greedy gusto, projected and shared in the pleasures and adventures of Hyde" (55); on the day of his "fall," his sudden transformation in Regent's Park, he sits, as Jekyll, "the animal within [him] licking the chops of memory" of his behavior when he is Hyde (58). It is no surprise that the "composite" Jekyll, the powder-driven worker machine, shares in Hyde's appetites, even as Jekyll disavows Hyde's behavior; it is no surprise, ultimately, that Hyde overtakes Jekyll. After all, the professional's position in the class system demands exactly this. Aspiration drives the workers in the text, providing the only rationale for labor of the mind. Jekyll is no exception to this. When he first takes the potion, he tells us, Hyde is produced because his "virtue slumbered" while his "evil" side, "kept awake by ambition, was alert and swift to seize the occasion" (52). Ambition is the force that, at bottom, compels Jekyll: he is "fond of the respect of the wise and good among [his] fellow-men" and seeks "an honourable and distinguished future" (47); his split self is unbearable to him because he cannot "reconcile" his "impatient gaiety of disposition" with his "imperious desire to carry [his] head high" (47–48). He is driven, he says, by "the exacting nature of [his] aspirations" (48).

In this sense, Jekyll is exactly like Utterson, with his gin drinking: as a professional, Jekyll requires and is made of the aspirational, even as he attempts to live in the prosperous always-already space of gentlemanly arrival, to protect his Huntingdon-esque gentlemanly nature with appropriate care and feeding. This is the source of his prosperous impossibility, of the agonizing self-divide he calls the "profound duplicity of life" (48).

It is inevitable, then, that Jekyll shares in Hyde's pleasures with "a greedy gusto": the working self is, by definition, the aspiring self. Where other gentlemen sit with Utterson, relearning sobriety and re-establishing the boundaries of themselves, in order to return to their professional, machine-dream selves after indulging in the "melting" that gentlemanly commensality offers, Hyde need only "escape into" his laboratory door . . . mix and swallow the draught . . . and Edward Hyde would pass away like the stain of breath upon a mirror; and there in his stead, quietly at home, trimming the midnight lamp in his study, would be Henry Jekyll" (52–53). Hyde truly "[does] not even exist" (52): he is the revelation of the true nature not of the old-fashioned aristocracy but of the professional class itself. No wonder Jekyll transforms into Hyde precisely when he gloats over his active good works in tandem with his exploits as Hyde. These hypocritical good works are revealed as merely autophagic fuel for the machine, which in turn enables and creates the monstrous, autophagic appetite that is Hyde.

Linda Dryden suggests that "Stevenson was a writer on the brink of modernism" (75). Indeed, Henry Jekyll is a character faced with the promise and the horrors of the modern. Jekyll looks into the abyss of the empty self and the impossible social sphere. Driven by a nostalgia for an imagined past clarity and order embodied in his olden-days hall that is predicated, ironically, on the impossibility both of the class system itself and of the middle-class project of rejecting that system while finding a place, he turns to the übermodern realm of science to find a means of restoring himself. But he fails, of course. It is telling that, when Utterson discovers the body, "the strong smell of kernels that hung upon the air" signals to Utterson that he is "looking on the body of a self-destroyer" (39). Hyde dies by taking cyanide, which, of course, smells of bitter almonds: food and drug, aliment and poison shade into one another. Hyde's use of cyanide evokes stories, relatively common in the period, of poisoning and murder connected to adulterated foodstuffs. The death of the monster, then, evokes anxieties about legibility and coherence, about place and knowledge and power and clarity.

But the death is also a success for the self-divided Dr. Jekyll and Mr. Hyde. Hyde, it is true, is a relic in his own home: like the skin of the aristocrat hanging in Dexter's kitchen, he is no more than an empty shell of gentlemanly horror in his own cannibal closet. But in swallowing his last dose, Jekyll finally achieves a state that is complete, that cannot be intruded upon, compromised, or reversed. His body entirely disappeared, it is Jekyll, finally, who "does not even exist," who has withdrawn entirely from the social into the safety of the self, swallowed whole in a last autophagic act which stops the cycle of class and allows him, finally, to stand still: a perfect modern act of self-creation.

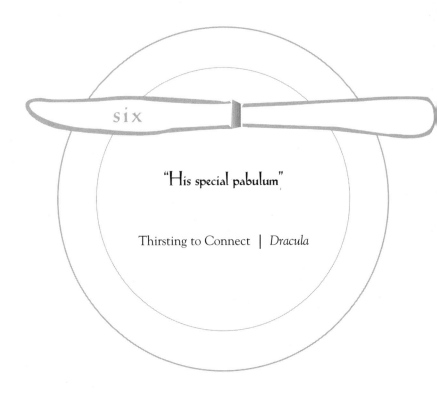

six

"His special pabulum"

Thirsting to Connect | *Dracula*

Bram Stoker's *Dracula* (1897), like Stevenson's *Dr. Jekyll and Mr. Hyde*, is a monster story very much concerned with gentlemanly doctors and their habits of self-prescription. At the same moment that Dracula is making his way to Carfax Abbey to take up residence, Dr. John Seward, the young director of an asylum for the genteel insane located just next door to the ruined abbey, sits alone in his room, thinking about the failure of his marriage proposal to the beautiful Lucy Westenra. Speaking into his phonographic diary, Seward reflects, "I am weary tonight and low in spirits. I cannot but think of Lucy, and how different things might have been. If I don't sleep at once, chloral, the modern Morpheus—$C_2HCl_3O-H_2O$! I must be careful not to let it grow into a habit. No, I shall take none tonight! I have thought of Lucy, and I shall not dishonour her by mixing the two. If need be, tonight shall be sleepless" (97).

Like Henry Jekyll, John Seward turns to a drug to heal himself—but where Jekyll seeks a radical split, a division between his leisurely self and his professional identity, Seward longs for wholeness, communion, an integrated selfhood. And though he posits a synthetic medicine as his cure—thus proposing that, like Jekyll, he can heal himself through his professional gentlemanly ambitions—what he really craves is a much more organic compound, one that provides not obliteration but a Romantic wholeness, an escape from the alienated modern world into the real. But this quest brings some serious complications to Seward's gentlemanly, chivalrous pursuit of Dracula. His "modern Morpheus," it turns out, is very much akin to the count's libation—and Seward, a warrior for gentlemanly clarity and order in his vampire hunting, is also a seeker after the engulfing morass offered by the vampire's fang. He is not alone in this: in *Dracula*, the gentlemanly hunger and the aristocratic, atavistic, monstrously hungry hunted are not so very different after all.

Dracula is very much preoccupied with the problem of modern isolation and the desire for wholeness and connection—a problem predicated in part on the status of gentlemanly class at the end of the century. The novel's monster is, famously, an aristocrat of the stereotypical first water: the scion of a family that has long ruled Transylvania, he is titled, moneyed, equipped with a tradition of rule and power. And, like the stereotypical aristocrat (in particular at the end of the century), Dracula feeds off the members of the middle class: he is "a filthy leech" (53), engorged with the blood of others who attacks the True Women of the text to sap healthy reproduction and instead produce legions of undead servants who will do his bidding. He attempts, that is, to use the technologies and professional abilities of the middle class to his advantage (just as he hires Jonathan, sucks what he can from him—language skills, lawyerly knowledge—and then locks him away in the castle to die) in order to obviate the middle class entirely, fashioning a world of masters and slaves. As he tells the men, "Your girls that you all love are mine already; and through them you and others shall yet be mine—my creatures, to do my bidding and to be my jackals when I want to feed" (267).

Dracula is, too, a Jekyll-and-Hyde creature of high and low: at the same time that he embodies the highly sophisticated (even oversophisticated and decadent) upper class, he is also a throwback, degenerated, atavistic, "a criminal and of criminal type," as "Nordau and Lombroso would so classify him" (Stoker, 296). Jonathan's first description of Dracula reveals both tendencies. Though the solicitor's host seems "courtly" (22) and is possessed of a "lofty domed forehead" (23) and hands that "seemed rather white and fine" (24), on close inspection, Count Dracula gives rather a different bodily impression:

> His face was a strong—a very strong—aquiline, with [a] high bridge of the thin nose and peculiarly arched nostrils; with . . . hair growing scantily round the temples, but profusely elsewhere. His eyebrows were very massive, almost meeting over the nose, and with bushy hair that seemed to curl in its own profusion. The mouth, so far as I could see it under the heavy moustache, was fixed and rather cruel-looking, with peculiarly sharp white teeth; these protruded over the lips, whose remarkable ruddiness showed astonishing vitality in a man of his years. . . . [H]is ears were . . . at the tops extremely pointed. . . . [H]is hands . . . were rather coarse—broad, with squat fingers. Strange to say, there were hairs at the centre of the palm. The nails were long and fine, and cut to a sharp point. As the Count leaned over me and his hands touched me, I could not repress a shudder. It may have been that his breath was rank, but a horrible feeling of nausea came over me. (23–24)

The Count, then, embodies in one physical entity what Jekyll and Hyde embody in their two split selves, one inside of the other: he may be refined, gentlemanly, and aristocratic, but up close, he has the hairy palms of a self-abuser, the aquiline nose that betrays the stereotypical passing Jew,[1] and the sharp nails and pointed ears and (of course) the fangs of a predatory animal. He is high and low at once, not made whole by separation as Jekyll and Hyde aspire to be but, like Miserrimus Dexter, made monstrous through integration. The classed nature of his dual self, too, is clear: his body, up close, evokes the degenerative tendencies of the working class in the middle-class imagination.

Dracula is, certainly, a worker: when Jonathan enters the castle, he recalls in his journal, Dracula "took my luggage; he had carried it in before I could forestall him," claiming, "[I]t is late, and my people are not available" (22). In subsequent days, Jonathan becomes aware that there are no "people" to do the work: he "found [Dracula] making the bed . . . [and] later . . . saw him through the chink of the hinges of the door laying the table in the dining room. . . . [H]e does himself all these menial offices" (32). Dracula clearly labors at the lowest, dirtiest servant jobs. When he shakes Jonathan's hand, "[t]he strength of the handshake was so much akin to that . . . [of] the driver" that Jonathan wonders whether "it were not the same person" (22). Here the parasitic aristocrat and the lazy, equally parasitic lower orders are linked, obviating the need for the hard-working, entrepreneurial-class gentleman.

This link is repeated in Dracula's alliance with the Szgany men, who cart his boxes around, collude in Jonathan's confinement (they hand his smuggled letter over to the Count) and, in the final confrontation between the Band of Light and the monster, fight fiercely on the vampire's behalf: menial laborers, servants for hire, they are also serfs loyal to their undead master, in a literalization of the feudal nightmare Mr. Woodhouse evokes at the beginning of the century. This alliance is also made manifest in the implied connection between Dracula and the English carters who take over the Szganys' transportation duties in London—working men remarkable mostly for their prominent, endless thirst, a thirst they seek relief from through the economic support of the novel's middle-class gentlemen. Though the seemingly endless dry mouth of these characters is predicated on humorous good-fellowship (the carters attacked by the madman Renfield outside Dr. Seward's asylum give "as [a] reason for their defeat the extraordinary state of drouth to which they had been reduced by the dusty nature of their occupation and the reprehensible distance from the scene of their labours of any place of public entertainment" and require "a stiff glass of grog, or rather more of the same" to set things right [142–43], Seward's deputy explains with a virtual wink), its insistent repetition also speaks to a strong connection between worker and aristocrat, feudal lord and loyal servant.

Similarly, the men who unload the count's cargo from the ship tell Jonathan Harker, who seeks information about where Dracula has hidden the boxes of earth that are his sanctuary, that moving the boxes was "dry work" (201). Jonathan soon finds this thirst resident everywhere that Dracula's boxes have been handled: at King's Cross station, though "[t]he opportunities of acquiring an abnormal thirst had been . . . limited" by the fact that the boxes were only tallied by the workers in question, "a noble use of them had, however, been made, and . . . [Jonathan] was compelled to deal with the result in an *ex post facto* manner"; and at Carter Paterson's office, the laborers responsible for the delivery of the boxes to Carfax "were able to supplement" the written record of the job "with a few details . . . connected almost solely with the dusty nature of the job, and of the consequent thirst engendered in the operations" (201).

The repetition of the notion of thirst implicitly links the carters and workers to the vampire, and the fact that every man so afflicted has handled Dracula's coffins of earth implies that these Everyman working-class Englishmen have caught the dread disease—that is, that Jonathan's vision of the vampire preying on London's "teeming millions" (53) has already become reality or, as a more troubling possibility, that the monster's kind are already extant there. Both the workingman's dry mouth and its link to the vampire's thirst are made explicit in Van Helsing's narration of his conversation with the men of the ship *Czarina Catherine,* bound for Varna, on which Dracula has booked passage for his boxes (and thus, at a bargain steerage rate, for himself). Van Helsing and Quincey "ask many men who are rough and hot" for information and conclude that "these be better fellows . . . when they have been no more thirsty. They say much of blood and bloom" (276) in their telling of their captain's dealings with a "tall man, thin and pale":

> [T]he captain tell him that he had better be quick—
> with blood—for that his ship will leave the place—of
> blood—before the turn of the tide—with blood. . . .
> Final the captain, more red than ever, and in more
> tongues, tell him that he doesn't want no Frenchmen—
> with bloom upon them and also with blood—in his
> ship—with blood on her also. . . . No one knew where
> he went "or bloomin' well cared," as they said, for they
> had something else to think of—well with blood again.

. . . [T]he captain . . . wished that he and his box—old
and with much bloom and blood—were in hell. But the
thin man did not be offend. . . . My friends of the thirst
and the language that was of bloom and blood laughed.
(276–77)

Van Helsing's apparently imperfect English makes things perfectly
clear: thirst and blood are intimately linked, at least in the case of
men of the working class. *Bloom* is the appropriate word for the
vampire, who grows younger and more flourishing as he feeds on
his victims; the city, the tide, and the boxes are certainly "with
blood," and the vampire does indeed belong "in hell." But the
workingmen "of the thirst and the language that was of bloom and
blood" seem to share indiscriminately in the vampire's appetites, as
does the increasingly red-faced captain.

Philip Holden argues that while the workers' thirst is akin to
the vampire's—is, in fact, tied to the vampire's money lust—
"[t]he extremes of a decadent, parasitic aristocratic body, and a
degenerate, equally parasitic proletariat one bracket a healthy
bourgeois body, its integrity maintained by work and disciplined
consumption" (479). But as I discuss in reference to *Dr. Jekyll and
Mr. Hyde*, the combination of high and low tends to result not in
opportunity and safety for the middle classes but in their obviation.
In the case of *Dracula*, the gentlemen of the middle ranks who fight
the vampire are fighting for their classed lives: they are being
squeezed, in a manner evocative of Mr. Casby with the residents of
Bleeding Heart Yard, until they give up their possessions—their
money, their knowledge, and their technology—even as they are
being devoured.

The gentlemen seem to oppose this devouring with their bravery, their chivalry, combined with a modern ability to make use of
science and technology. They possess what Van Helsing calls "the
power of combination—a power denied to the vampire kind," the
"resources of science," and "self-devotion in a cause, and an end
to achieve which is not a selfish one" (210). They seem to reach
across class barriers: the Band of Light is figured as a utopian collection of gentlemen from across the gentlemanly sphere, comprising the self-made striver; the educated, well-born doctor (Lucy

says he is "an excellent *parti*, being handsome, well off, and of good birth . . . and really clever" [56]); the aristocrat; and the brave adventurer.[2] In contrast to *Dr. Jekyll and Mr. Hyde*, in which gentlemanly combination is an elusive dream, here it is the key to fighting the vampire.[3] Each member of the group brings special strengths and skills to the task: in their pursuit of the monster, it becomes clear that the power of the individual is not highly prized. Alone, each is in danger of dying a "calf's" death, as Jonathan, trapped in Castle Dracula, puts it (49), of becoming an ignoble victim of the vampire's superior strength and power; together, they can face the monster head-on (as they do in London) and force the blood-drinking bully to back down. The gentlemen will use the old and the new—ambition and old money, resourcefulness and titles, education and street smarts, plus bravery, intelligence, and true hearts—to defeat the force of evil, the monstrous, overdetermined body in which the superannuated, degenerate, parasitic aristocrat and the worker are combined. Their collaboration seems a victory for science, for community, and for the forward-thinking man.

The gentlemen of the Band of Light, then, seem to resolve all of the difficulties and struggles of gentlemanliness and identity that I have parsed through texts spanning the century, proposing to eliminate the parasitic upper classes and remake the world in the image of middle-class energy, initiative, and good government, coupled with old-fashioned chivalric heroism. Together, they will fight the antiprogressive monster, the force of stasis and alienation who offers not rebirth, newness, or movement but only unnatural reproduction of the feudal model. In contrast, the vampire seems to be Mr. Woodhouse, Mr. Casby, Mr. Dorrit re-embodied: his disgusting appetites overpower the world through which he moves, allowing him to perpetuate an allochronistic olden-days realm of absolute rule. Jonathan's position in Castle Dracula, for instance, makes the threat clear. Shut away from the world, forced to send out false letters of return home and reunion to Mina and Mr. Hawkins, alone for hours every day, and physically incapable of leaving the castle, he is the princess locked in the tower, waiting for a rescue that never comes.

But things are not this simple: easy opposition, in this overdetermined text, is always undercut. In this case, for instance, though the vampire issues the invitation, he does not compel Jonathan to enter the castle: he simply stands aside at his front door, telling Jonathan, "Welcome to my house! Enter freely and of your own free will!" (22). It is work that takes Jonathan to his tower room in the castle: as the solicitor states, in response to the Transylvanian innkeeper's wife's pleas for him to delay his trip, "[T]here was business to be done, and I could allow nothing to interfere with it . . . my duty was imperative, and I must go" (13). His professional responsibilities are what lead Jonathan to follow the Count's directive, writing to Mr. Hawkins to tell Hawkins that Jonathan will stay in Castle Dracula for a full month: "It was Mr Hawkins's interest, not mine, and I had to think of him, not myself" (37). Technology, modernity, work, and social and economic advancement: all of these take Jonathan to this place of stasis, in which the middle-class professional is a font to be squeezed of knowledge and then devoured whole. The struggle the gentlemen undergo to find their footing against the class-split monster—to find place for themselves—results neither from the vampire's predations nor from a threat emanating from the lower classes but from the professionalization of the gentlemanly classes.

This problem is figured in appetite. Philip Holdén argues that when the members of the middle class eat, "the solidity of food is seen as fortifying the body" and "[c]onsumption of cooked food becomes a cultural act inscribing the solidity of bourgeois identity against the rawness of blood . . . and, presumably, the rancidity of beer" (479). But the novel includes few moments of commensality. The group does take "a sort of perfunctory supper together" that "cheer[s] [them] all up somewhat" after the vampire's last attack on Mina and the subsequent events, and though Seward guesses that "[i]t was, perhaps, the mere animal heat of food to hungry people" that creates good feeling, the act of eating together seems important: "[T]he sense of companionship may have helped us . . . [for] we were all less miserable, and saw the morrow as not altogether without hope" (268). But this is a rare instance of healthy appetite replacing the monstrous appetite of the vampire in the text. Even of here, the food (invisible, to the reader—there is no luxuriating over fine fare or gruel here) seems less important than the horrors the members of the Band of Light chew over at table: they tell

Mina the story of their encounter with Dracula in the London house as they eat, and when she stands to speak to them, insisting on Christian charity for the vampire, they look on her awareness of "the red scar on her forehead" "with grinding of [their] teeth" (268). In most cases, shared meals simply disappear, are passed over without comment. Mina notes, for instance, that the group gathers in Dr. Seward's study for their lecture on vampirism "two hours after dinner, which had been at six o'clock" (208), allowing the collation to slip away between her visit to Renfield and this moment.

Commensality, then, fails: where in *Little Dorrit*, for instance, community can be rebuilt at the table through the rational sharing of food and drink, here no shared communion is possible. Arthur Clennam's dream of starving the body to save it from imbrication in the neofeudal capitalist economy of feasting at the cost of others is here complete: in *Dracula*'s England, gentlemen are only seen to sit down to table together as a narrative device meant to get to the next important moment of talk or action. Eating together is a moment to be skipped over, bearing no importance. Whereas we have seen elsewhere a Mr. Elton-esque dwelling on the moment of consuming and the stuff to be consumed—be it wine or truffles or gruel or lemonade—here, as in *Dr. Jekyll and Mr. Hyde*, the matter of the table disappears.

This erasure of healthy eating is predicated not on the presence of the vampire (indeed, it is only once he has broached the barriers of the group's asylum-home that the group sits down to table together) but on the replacement of the physical, the bodily, with the endless narrative of professional work. Whereas in *Dr. Jekyll and Mr. Hyde* the gentleman worker at once strives for leisure and embodies his work, here the professional seeks at once to escape the world of work for a space of connection and to disappear inside it. Certainly, work seems to engulf these gentlemen: Jonathan, the newly minted solicitor, goes to Transylvania to do his "duty" (13) to business, money, industry, and advancement. Dr. Seward turns to labor to cure his ills: after his "rebuff" by Lucy, experiencing an "[e]bb tide in appetite" and unable to sleep, he turns to his professional obligations to settle his mind and suppress his body. "I have a sort of empty feeling; nothing in the world seems of sufficient importance to be worth the doing," he notes. "As I knew that the only cure for this sort of thing was work, I went down amongst the patients" (61). Squeezed dry between the devouring, parasitic aristocrat—a creature of sensibility and "love" (43), of history and courtliness and place—and the endlessly thirsty, insistently embodied parasitic worker, the middle-class gentleman finds himself without structure, without location, except in the world of work, of logic and science and law. The realm of emotion and the body belongs elsewhere; what remains, the work these men undertake to make themselves—like Jonathan's shorthand diary—is "nineteenth century up-to-date with a vengeance" (40), but it holds within it no nutritional possibilities. By taking on work, they take on only the state of the "patients": that is, madness.

The "empty feeling" Seward experiences seems to be the ordinary state of being for the gentlemen of this text—gentlemen who live in a world in which individuality, selfhood, and narrative coherence have been obviated in favor of technology, repetition, simulacra, the machine. In a novel in which nearly all of the narrative voices sound alike; in which bodies, names, and tendencies double and redouble (John Seward and Jonathan Harker; Mina and Lucy; even Van Helsing and Dracula); and in which experiences are, in a peculiarly cinematic move, played and replayed (the three proposals; the four transfusions; Lucy's two walks), the idea of individuality, of finding place and selfhood, seems nearly impossible. Differentiation fails. It is no wonder Lucy tells Mina that Dr. Seward "would just *do for you*, if you were not already engaged to Jonathan" (56): one will "do" as well as the next because, as Lucy discovers, it can be difficult to tell the difference between one man and another. This repeated repetition, speaking as it does to the proliferation of Baudrillardian simulacra, implies the impossibility, in such simulacra-as-characters, of interiority, meaning, connection.

This state of the simulacrum—an "empty feeling," a hollow core, beneath the surface of the skin—is the state of modernity in the novel. The solipsistic, isolating nature of the modern is readily apparent. Letters and telegrams cross one another, are misdelivered, or fail (Van Helsing's telegram to Seward concerning the care of Lucy arrives too late; Mina's letter to Lucy is delivered after her death). The act of telling is repeatedly frustrated or fragmented.

Characters fail to listen to one another, hearing instead only external social mores or pieties: Mina cannot understand Lucy's fractured narration of her night with the Count; Seward cannot comprehend Van Helsing's assessment of vampire-Lucy; Renfield's pleas for his own removal, a means of saving Mina from the vampire, go unheeded; and Mina is shut out of the men's confidence by her gendered role.

In the face of this isolation, the gentlemen attempt to make sense by speaking to themselves, narrating their experience to externalize it, observe it, shine the light of science on it and bring it into order. Though he purports to keep his records for Mina, for example, in Jonathan's repeated recourse to the diary as a place to find clarity in Castle Dracula it is evident that he is talking to himself, attempting to retain control by narrating his own circumstances. "Let me be prosaic so far as facts can be; it will help me to bear up, and imagination must not run riot with me," Jonathan writes early in his ordeal (30). As the Count's plans become clearer, Jonathan writes, "Let me begin with facts—bare, meagre facts, verified by books and figures, and of which there can be no doubt. I must not confuse them with experiences which will have to rest on my own observation or my memory of them" (35–36). Jonathan's trust in himself is already obliterated; he turns to his diary as though it were a second self, as though the recording of information could distance it from his "observation" and recast it as clarity and order. As he notes later, "The habit of entering accurately must help to soothe me" (41). Accuracy, indeed: Jonathan records dates, places, and times, like the professional he is, attempting to make sense of the world through his notes, kept in shorthand, the written language of his business. But his work fails him: faced with the horror of the castle, his only "hope" is that he "be not mad" (41). And it is in part his alienation, his failure to find another human being with whom he can verify his existence and his knowledge, that drives him mad: "If there were any one to talk to I could bear it, but there is no one" (30).

Seward, another of the text's central diarists, also tries to create coherence, meaning, and clarity through self-narration, making use of technology to do so: he keeps his diary on wax phonograph cylinders, literally talking to himself, in the absence of a confidant, to ease his mind and keep his records. Denied the longed-for cure for his isolation, the idealized balm of love and marriage, by Lucy's rejection of his suit, he seeks wholeness through his dictation of his inner self into the waiting ear of the phonograph, replacing the human with the technological. By doing so, he hopes, like Jekyll and Hyde, to displace the desiring self: Seward tries to cure his inability to eat or sleep, to forget about Lucy, by creating a mechanical second self made entirely of the reasoning professional mind. But this self-narration, too, fails. The phonographic recording cannot resolve his alienation or explain him to himself: it can only record and thus make manifest his failure to understand himself.

Love—that is, the transcendence of the self through union with another—is a principal preoccupation of the novel, a means of escaping from this "empty" existence, in which labor seems the only space of narrative yet leads only to miscomprehension, disorder, and madness. But love is continually put off, and its lack creates serious misery. Jonathan and Mina, engaged to be married but separated by the demands of business, long for reunion and marriage, but their communication is frustrated and then stopped up completely by the vampire's machinations. John Seward, Quincey Morris, and Arthur Holmwood all propose to Lucy, and neither of her two rejected suitors takes her negative response lightly: Morris faces a "lonely walk between this and Kingdom Come" (60), while Seward is "broken-hearted" (58). And whereas in *Dr. Jekyll and Mr. Hyde* the home is a barren place devoid of women and children, in *Dracula* the women become fare for the vampire, not helpmeets but reproductive slaves who fail to keep hearth and home pure and safe from the world, so that healthy reproduction and progress are not absent but entirely corrupted. It is telling that (in contrast to *Little Dorrit* and *Dr. Jekyll and Mr. Hyde*, in which the world of work and the world of home often overlap or collide, so that the domestic and the professional are insoluble) here home and work both are located in the alienist's asylum.

This is the environment in which Seward, lonely and defeated, turns to chloral hydrate. Here the gentleman's "[e]bb tide in appetite" (61) is overcome, as the physician—fittingly, a doctor whose work is the healing of the "alienated," those who are strangers to themselves and to the world—seeks to heal himself of his alienation through the escape into sleep that chloral offers. A synthetic hyp-notic, popular as a sleeping aid in the 1880s, chloral hydrate seems a logical cure for what ails Stoker's gentleman. Entirely created in the laboratory, it offers professional control over the alienated mind, a sanctioned, professional, scientific cure for the failure to make sense, to only connect, to find place. Seward's self-prescription of chloral is a profoundly modern cure for the ailment of gentlemanly modernity. Looking to the body as a foreign thing to be scrutinized, ordered, and repaired, rather than as an intrinsic part of the self, his medicine offers oblivion, forgetfulness, to solve the problem of the end-of-the-century gentleman: the longing for place and connec-tion in a world bereft of meaning. The drug will complete Arthur Clennam's starvation diet, going one better than Jekyll's potion by erasing self-knowledge entirely.

Unfortunately for Seward, science has already failed him, as his self-admonishments make clear: "I must be careful not to let it grow into a habit," he tells himself. "No, I shall take none tonight! I have thought of Lucy, and I shall not dishonour her by mixing the two" (97). This is not the language of a drug offering a haven of nothingness, an erasure of desire: it is the language of addiction, of wanting, of an uncontrollable growth in need and neediness. This would hardly have been surprising to Stoker's readers: chloral's addictive properties were well known by the time of *Dracula*'s pub-lication.[4] And Dr. Seward is not unlike other gentlemanly chloral inebriates, as a description in the *Quarterly Journal of Inebriety* in January 1880 attests:

> A . . . class of men who became habituated to the use of chloral are men of extremely nervous and excitable temperament. . . . What to other men is passing annoy-ance, thrown off with the next step, is to these men a worry and anxiety of hours. They are over-susceptible of what is said of them, and of their work, however good their work may be. They are too elated when praised, and too depressed when not praised or dispraised . . . they take all their cares and anxieties into bed with them, in the liveliest state of perturbation. Unable in this condition to sleep . . . they resort to the use of . . .

chloral hydrate. They begin with a moderate dose, increase the dose as occasion seems to demand, and at last, in what they consider a safe and moderate system of employing it, they depend on the narcotic for their falsified repose. (53–54)

The chloral habituate, then, is not complete in and of himself but is, instead, estranged from himself and as a result is uneasy in his own skin, overanxious about what others think of him, constructed through external eyes. This is certainly the case with Seward, who is offended even when the asylum inmate Renfield—a man he considers to be mad—fails to accord him the proper respect. As he recounts, "[Renfield's] attitude to me was the same as that to the attendant; in his sublime self-feeling the difference between myself and attendant seemed to him as nothing. . . . [H]e will soon think that he himself is God. These infinitesimal distinctions between man and man are too paltry for an Omnipotent Being. How these madmen give themselves away! The real God taketh heed lest a sparrow fall; but the God created from human vanity sees no difference between an eagle and a sparrow" (96).

The longing that Seward's compound creates, then, is precisely what Jekyll's potion takes up: aspiration, ambition, and hunger for place. Certainly Seward is a seeker after greatness, as his thinking on the subject of Renfield elsewhere makes clear. When his patient's "zoophagous" (71) method of offering flies to spiders and spiders to birds as a means of storing up lives for his ultimate consumption becomes clear, the alienist muses to himself:

What would have been his later steps? It would almost be worth while to complete the experiment. It might be done if there were only a sufficient cause. Men sneered at vivisection, and yet look at its results today! Why not advance science in its most difficult and vital aspect—the knowledge of the brain? Had I even the secret of one such mind—did I hold the key to the fancy of even one lunatic—I might advance my own branch of science to a pitch compared with which Burdon-Sanderson's psychology or Ferrier's brain-knowledge would be as nothing. If only there were a sufficient cause! I must not think too much of this, or I may be tempted; a good cause might turn the scale with me, for may not I too be of an exceptional brain, congenitally? (71)

The passage is remarkable in its clinical bloodthirstiness. "Completing the experiment," of course, involves allowing Renfield to eat his way all the way up the food chain—presumably ending with a human life—and then killing him and dissecting his brain (or perhaps, given the reference to vivisection, attempting to do so while he is alive). The purpose is to gain renown for Seward's own "exceptional brain," which he explicitly refers to here in tandem with that of the madman: science is simply a means to an end, which is fame and fortune. In other words, Seward, too, seeks to live forever—if not in the body, then in reputation; and if not through the literal consumption of "lives," then through a displaced, medicalized act of cannibal consumption.

Seward, then, seems professionally driven to acquire the eternal life offered by fame—an immortality he seems willing to pay for with lives that are less worthwhile than his own, lives he counts not as human but as cases—that is, as meat for his professional table. In this, Seward echoes Mr. Utterson: entirely made of work, he is nevertheless a striver despite himself, unable to avoid grasping for greatness, for mastery. And in *Dracula*, the bearer of the name "master" (26) is the vampire himself, the "noble" (26) figure who occupies the space of always-already-arrived gentlemanliness of leisure.

This longing in Seward for a distinctly vampiric "mastery" is not limited to his dealings with Renfield. Seward is the lover who "play[ed] with a lancet" during his proposal to Lucy, "in a way that made [her] nearly scream" (58). In diagnosing Lucy, he is pleased to be "actually able to test the quality of her blood": Lucy cuts her hand on a window, which "gave [him] an evident chance. . . . [He] secured a few drops of the blood" (105). Van Helsing's telegram in response to Arthur's plea, through Seward, for help with Lucy reads, in part, "Tell your friend that when that time you suck from my wound so swiftly the poison of the gangrene from that knife that our other friend, too nervous, let slip, you did more for him when he wants my aids and you call for them than all his great fortune could do . . . it is to you that I come" (106). The connection between the transfusions and the vampiric, of course, is clear. Even his depiction of Renfield's death holds the echo of the vampire: Seward tells of the madman "lying . . . in a glittering pool of blood" (241), a description that seems to evoke visual pleasure, temptation. Like jewels, like rubies, like the red eyes of the vampire, the blood glitters; it calls.

The connection between Seward's medical practices and the interdicted, uncontrollable appetite for the wine of endless gentlemanly life becomes clear when Seward offers a sleeping draught to Mina, to counter the "bad dreams" she suffers as she sleeps alone in her bedroom at the lunatic asylum. Shut out of the men's plans—"a bitter pill for me to swallow," as she puts it (214)—she has been made victim to the vampire, in an attack she records in her diary but refuses to name or acknowledge as real, even to herself. "I must be careful of such dreams," she writes, "for they would unseat one's reason if there were too much of them" (228). Unable to speak the truth of her attack (it is madness), she asks Dr. Seward for a "sleeping draught" (228): protection, through oblivion, from dreaming. But the vampire's most horrific access of her is predicated precisely on her consumption of the preparation the doctor proffers. The drug helps her not to protect herself but, rather, to shut off her social and moral boundaries, so that, when the vampire "placed his reeking lips upon my throat," as she recalls, "strangely enough, I did not want to hinder him" (249).

Alienated from herself (she wishes herself "Good night" [228] in her diary, as though speaking to a stranger) and alienated from community, husband, and safety by the drug-state of the medical modern, she is utterly open to Dracula's appetites.[5] Seward's professional ministrations, then, rather than bringing light to the dark places of body and mind, have led to a complete breakdown of order and clarity, to a violation of the novel's saving angel, a desecration of the marriage bed, a subversion of gentlemanly rights and responsibilities, and an introduction of a terrible liminality.

This liminality marks the medical endeavor in the text; the obviation of boundary in pursuit of place and clarity is the sign of the gentleman-seeker here. This pursuit is marked not in the failed escape of chloral hydrate but in a different drug, suggested by Seward even as he looks to his synthetic would-be salvation. His paean to chloral, after all, refers to the drug as "the modern Morpheus," not as Hypnos: as the god, that is, not of unconscious sleep but of dreams (a longing echoed by Mina's request for "a little opiate of some kind" [228]). Though Seward claims to long for unconsciousness, for temporary oblivion, what he actually seeks is something very different: escape from loneliness and isolation into a realm of imagination, possibility, and connection. Seward, the gentlemanly alienist alone in his room, seeks to heal himself by finding a deep and authentic "I" beneath the proliferating simulacra of the modern industrial world. To do so, he turns to Morpheus's namesake, that nineteenth-century new god of dreams, morphine. And it is this taste, this longing, that unites the gentleman and the vampire. Morphinism, opium eating, gentlemanliness, dreaming: these are linked in troubling ways throughout the text, always with the shadow of the vampire falling across the page.

Opium was, of course, an exceedingly common drug. It had been widely used in Britain for centuries as a cure for a host of diseases and as a palliative for aches and pains. Through the nineteenth century, opium was taken in nostrums and patent medicines as well as in home cures like poppy-head tea (Jay, 66), derived from British-grown poppies. Griffith Edwards claims that "between 1830 and 1860, the average inhabitant of the British Isles consumed annually 127 standard therapeutic doses of opium" (103). Doctors, pharmacists, and ordinary people relied on opium as a ubiquitous cure-all for a wide range of physical maladies. Opium found its way into elixirs, mixes, medicines, and tonics, pervading the English body and turning the clear day of bourgeois industrialism into dreamy night.

Morphine (refined opium) was the drug of the professional man—and, in particular, of the doctor. Though morphine was isolated in 1806, its use was rare before reliable injection drug methods became available at midcentury.[6] It became immensely popular among doctors, who "welcomed it as the new panacea which would relieve pain quickly and easily with no deleterious side effects"

(Parsinnen, 79). Doctors concerned about opium habituation and overuse imagined that intravenous morphine would solve the problem, given the efficacy of much smaller doses of the opiate in this form. But it soon became clear that this view was very much mistaken. The results of the doctors' error fell most heavily on doctors themselves.

The notion of morphine as a highly habit-forming substance was popularized in particular by Edward Levinstein's *Die Morphiumscucht*, or *Morbid Craving for Morphia*, first published in English in 1878. As discussion of the phenomenon spread, a consensus grew that medical men were both at fault for most cases of morphine addiction—because morphine was almost always first administered by a physician—and, as a group, most likely to suffer chronic morphine inebriation. The American doctor J. B. Mattison, writing in the *Medical Record* in 1883, asserted that "physicians form a large proportion of opium habitués in general, and the great majority of any professional class" (621). "As to why so many opium habitués are recruited from the ranks of our profession," he continued,

> the physician's calling involving, as it often does, especial inroads on his mental and physical well-being, exposes him more than any other to the various influences which stand as factors in the etiology of this disease. . . . [S]ome form of neurotic disorder . . . leads the list. . . . [T]he opinion of a medical gentleman—who, some years ago, was under our care, and who afterward gave . . . a most graphic recital of his experience—may be of interest. "I proclaim it as my sincere belief that any physician afflicted with neurotic disease of marked severity, and who has in his possession a hypodermic syringe and Magendie's solution, is bound to become, sooner or later, if he tampers at all with the potent and fascinating alleviative, an opium habitué. . . . This overmastering palliative creates such a confident, serene, and devil-may-care assurance that one does not for once think of the final result. The sweetness of such harmony can never give way to monotony." (621–22)

Like chloral inebriation, then, morphine addiction was thought to be widespread among those who were most pressed by modern life: the professionals who dirtied their hands with alienation, who felt pressured to relieve the pressures of life for others, who searched for clarity and order in a world in which these qualities were perceived as increasingly difficult to find. In his 1902 *Morphinism and Narcomanias from Other Drugs*, Thomas Davison Crothers writes that "morphinism as a disease is due in a large measure to modern civilization, associated with the rapid exhaustion following changes of life and living; also from absence of nerve rest, and the continual strain upon the organization in its effort to become adapted to a new environment. . . . The impression once made of rest and removal of suffering is rarely effaced, and the desire to resort to the remedy again under stress is so great as to be irresistible" (32–33). The "irresistible" temptation of morphine for a gentleman like Seward, then, is clear: it offers relief from the press of the modern, "harmony" in a time of alienation. Whereas chloral hydrate promises obliteration of the self, morphine goes one better, offering wholeness and meaningful healing.

Morphine, of course, was administered via a needle,[7] and the needle, of course, connects both the drug and the doctor to the vampire. The morphine needle, like the vampire's fang, penetrates the boundaries of the enclosed modern body (see chapter 5). The needle injects healing, wholeness, and ease into the unknown morass, the unreadable self beneath the skin. Like the vampire's fang, it brings dreams. In this sense, while the doctor displays vampiric tendencies and an appetite for blood as a drug, the vampire may be said to embody the medical professional, offering sleep, dreams, "something very sweet and very bitter" (94) to his "patients."

But Seward is not the only gentleman in *Dracula* to long for Morpheus, and the drug's connection to the vampire goes far beyond the needle. The text's greatest dreamer is Jonathan Harker, who spends much of his trip to Transylvania in a sort of dream state seemingly induced by the evocatively red substances he consumes. Jonathan experiences "queer dreams" courtesy of the paprika, the "thirsty" red substance he consumes on the road to Castle Dracula, a substance whose power cannot be assuaged by "all the water in [his] carafe" (10). A little later, he recounts the contents of his dinner—meat with more paprika, plus wine, "Golden Mediasch, which produces a queer sting on the tongue, which is, however not disagreeable"—"lest who reads [about his experiences] may fancy that [he] dined too well before [he] left Bistritz" (13) and thus merely dreamed the tale of his midnight ride through the mountains. The red wine, productive not of satiation but of more thirst ("a queer sting on the tongue"), might certainly be blamed for such dreams. That trip seems "like a sort of awful nightmare" (19), and his arrival at the castle, too, is "like a horrible nightmare" (21). The endless voyaging through the night; the wolves, the blue lights, and the periodic disappearances of the coachman; Jonathan's strange host, with his nocturnal habits and his unwillingness to eat with Harker (who consumes two glasses of "old Tokay," suggestively sanguine fine wine); the ruined castle—it all has the feel of a gauzy nightmare that cannot quite be woken from.

Under the circumstances, Harker might be expected to be wary of bringing on more bad dreams—or of losing hold of his waking self at all. Instead, he appears, like Dr. Seward, to long for an internal nightscape: he continues to drink the wine of the country and to eat paprika even after he has drawn connections between his consumption and his "dreaming." And at Castle Dracula, he seems to look beyond the ordinary pleasures of the foreign table for his dreamy fix. When the Count warns him against falling asleep outside of Jonathan's own rooms in the castle, a practice that will result in "bad dreams for those who sleep unwisely" (38), he deliberately and with "pleasure" (41) disobeys, luxuriating in the prospect of sleeping and dreaming in the ancient drawing room he discovers. "[A] soft quietude come[s] over" him (40) in this room in which "the old centuries had, and have powers of their own which mere modernity cannot kill" (41). The new nightmare produced by his nap is the advent of the female vampires. When the seeming young ladies appear, he recounts, "I thought . . . that I must be dreaming when I saw them" (41–42). And when the blonde vampire bends to his neck, Jonathan recalls, "I closed my eyes in a languorous ecstasy and waited—waited with beating heart" (43). His pleasure in the "dream," and in the seduction that it portends, is pointed to over and over: Jonathan's desire to be "kissed" by the blonde vampire is readily apparent, his understanding of the druglike effects of the kiss implicit, his willingness to "dream" obvious.

In *Emperors of Dreams*, Mike Jay writes of the state of the un-accustomed opium user: the drug's "effects seep into the conscious-ness slowly: a relaxation and physical heaviness, a falling away of anxiety, a sense of timeless and profound contentment. . . . [I]t insulates you from the outside world, lending you an inner warmth and languorous euphoria. . . . As you drift into sleep you're swal-lowed up by a world of beneficent dreams, vivid and exquisite, and sleep is deep and restorative" (53). This is almost precisely the lan-guage of Jonathan's recounting of his eventful evening with the female vampires.[8] Nor is this Jonathan's only opium dream: while waiting at the window for Dracula's lizardlike return up the wall, Jonathan watches "some quaint little specks floating in the rays of the moonlight." He recalls his sensations: "I watched them with a sense of soothing, and a sort of calm stole over me. . . . I felt myself struggling to awake to some call of my instincts; nay, my very soul was struggling, and my half-remembered sensibilities were striving to answer the call. I was becoming hypnotized!" (48). So, Thomas De Quincey says in *Confessions of an English Opium-Eater*, the opium eater "lies under the weight of incubus and night-mare. . . . [H]e would lay down his life if he might but get up and walk; but he is powerless as an infant, and cannot even attempt to rise" (74).

Dracula is sodden with De Quincean opium-eating references. Besides the naming of the adventurer Quincey Morris, there is the narrative itself: told nearly entirely through diaries and letters, the text, like De Quincey's work, is one long "confession" of a struggle with terrible, irresistible appetites. It is a fabric of secrets and inner-most thoughts revealed (for instance, of his attraction to the fe-male vampires, Jonathan writes, "It is not good to note this down, lest some day it should meet Mina's eyes and cause her pain; but it is the truth" [42]). As Peter K. Garrett notes, the narrative struc-ture of *Dracula*, and, indeed, the building of knowledge through conversation on the part of the protagonists, constitutes an access-ing of the unconscious (69); and the unconscious mind, De Quincey posits throughout his work, is the true source, the font of selfhood and authenticity accessible through the opium dream. De Quincey's nar-rative is, too, a striver's story, in which the narrator is transformed from a starving boy in the streets of London to an educated gentle-man of leisure in a tranquil cottage, with his wife and children about him—all while under the influence (and arguably due to the transformative power) of opium.[9]

De Quincean echoes are readily apparent in Jonathan's adven-ture. Harker lies in an old-fashioned drawing room where, he imag-ines, "of old[,] ladies had sat and sung and lived sweet lives whilst their gentle breasts were sad for their menfolk away in the midst of remorseless war" (Stoker, 41); and, indeed, such ladies appear, in undead form. The scene evokes De Quincey's recurring dreams of "a crowd of ladies," of which he wrote, "And I heard it said, or I said to myself, 'these are English ladies from the unhappy times of Charles I. These are the wives and the daughters of those who . . . met . . . in the field of battle . . . and washed away in blood the memory of ancient friendship.'—The ladies danced, and looked as lovely as the court of George IV. Yet I knew, even in my dream, that they had been in the grave for two centuries" (De Quincey, 77–78). Jonathan's lack of clarity about whether he has dreamed the encounter takes up De Quincey's note that, as he became in-creasingly habituated to opium, "a sympathy seemed to arise be-tween the waking and the dreaming states in one point—that whatsoever [he] happened to call up and to trace by a voluntary act upon the darkness was very apt to transfer itself to [his] dreams" (De Quincey, 75).

Jonathan's Transylvanian dreamscape also evokes the interior journeying in which De Quincey's *Confessions* famously indulges. The drug's mind-altering qualities, as is well-known, made it par-ticularly attractive to many Romantic radicals seeking a pathway to deeper consciousness;[10] but it was De Quincey's exploration of his opium dreams, first fictionalized and narrated in *Confessions* in 1821, that most strongly impacted the rhetorical notion of the drug across the nineteenth century. De Quincey's characterization of opium as a pathway to the real self, paired with the development of large-scale opium production in the colonized subcontinent, produced an understanding of opium as an Orientalized path out of the ordinary and into the exotic. The East, understood through the racialized language of colonialism as an allochronistic space, "out of time" with the age in which it existed and closer to the depths of the human past, was also imagined as a foreign and troubling but nonetheless compelling site of an authenticity prior to and beyond Christianity and the West. As De Quincey writes, "The mere antiquity of Asiatic things, and of their institutions, histories, modes of faith, &c. is so impressive, that to me the vast age of the race and name overpowers the sense of youth in the individual. A young Chinese seems to me an antediluvian man renewed" (81).

De Quincey's belief in the drug as a means of finding the true or inner self is well known. Of his first adventures in opium, he wrote, only partly hyperbolically, "Good heavens! what a revulsion! What an upheaving, from its lowest depths, of the inner spirit! what an apocalypse of the world within me!" (44). This early section of his work, "The Pleasures of Opium," portrays this inward journey as entirely positive: "[T]he opium eater . . . feels that the diviner part of his nature is paramount; that is, the moral affections are in a state of cloudless serenity; and over all is the great light of the majestic intellect" (47). In this telling, the true self is discovered, unearthed, within the skin and the mind of the seeker, aided by his drinking of the Morpheus-invoking drug.

Unquestionably, Dracula is an excellent site of such Oriental-ized longing for connection and authenticity.[11] Birthed from the allochronistic past-world of Transylvania, he is the synthesis of aristocrat and Rousseauian, unfallen Natural Man. He is one with his past, undifferentiated—his ancestors and himself in one (he has, of course, never undergone Jacques Lacan's mirror stage as a vampire). He is at once present in the world and utterly oceanic, unestranged from himself. And though the vampire's method of producing hideous progeny has been read as a figure for industrial capitalism run rampant,[12] Dracula's "special pabulum" (211) also offers the possibility of authenticity, of access to the self: it is an embodiment of complete connection, a doorway to a way of being that is all-encompassing.

By breaching the skin, the vampire seems to reveal blood as a direct link to a consciousness that transcends boundaries. The vampire's drink taps into a vast collective unconscious, an atavistic hive mind that is all sense-memory. The ritual, self-swallowing, self-creating nature of blood drinking allows for the symbiosis, the synthesis longed for by the men in their search for love in the

novel, as Dracula and the vampire women make clear. When he
prevents them from "kissing" Jonathan, the women taunt Dracula,
crying, "'You yourself never loved; you never love!' . . . [to which]
the Count . . . [says] in a soft whisper:—'Yes, I too can love; you
yourselves can tell it from the past'" (43). Here love conquers all.
In *Dracula*, blood-drinking is a literal return to the pre-Fallen
realm of immortality, defeating the actual and metaphorical death
of the solipsistic modern world, the radically individualized interiority that the modern world reifies, by making the boundaries of
the physical body disappear even as they seem to be retained. The
aristocrat, then, seems to embody precisely that which the striving
professional seeks: wholeness, connection, selfhood. And the narrative of opium, of morphine, of the fang, of the East connects it to
the scientific, the colonial, and the modern.

In this light, Jonathan's disobedience of Dracula's rules against
falling asleep outside of his rooms can be recast. Jonathan recalls
that "[t]he Count's warning came into [his] mind" when he found
himself feeling "sleepy" in the ancient drawing room at Castle
Dracula, but he takes "pleasure in disobeying" the warning: "The
sense of sleep was upon me, and with it the obstinacy which sleep
brings as outrider. The soft moonlight soothed, and the wide expanse without gave a sense of freedom which refreshed me. . . .
[U]nthinking of and uncaring for the dust, [I] composed myself for
sleep" (41). The petulant child, careless of his safety despite all
that he has experienced, here becomes the seeker after experience,
the opium novice prying open the doors of consciousness and
connection, just as Jonathan has prised open the jammed-up door
of the drawing room.

In his thirsty desire to dream, his uncanny half-recognition of
the blonde vampire who attempts to feed on him ("I seemed somehow to know her face," he recounts, "and to know it in connection
with some dreamy fear" [42]), Jonathan seems to be retreating into
the very source not only of his Freudian subconscious but also of a
collective unconscious, taking up the Romantic notion of opium
eating as a means of discovering the true state of consciousness before and beyond the alienation of the modern world. The repeated
invocations of a misty past knowledge and the moves into the allochronistic past-present of the foreign East evoke a seeking for a

buried, more authentic or original self—pre-civilized, pre-Fallen, unmodern. The idea that this deeper selfhood is accessed through the vampire bite suggests the opposite of modern individualism, the self-made man, middle-class ambition: rather, it suggests that like calls to like, that Jonathan and the vampires are the same beneath the skin. Jonathan's half-recollection of the blonde vampire offers the possibility, in the vampire's bite, of an oceanic oneness, a collective wholeness, a return to a Romantic, longed-for self, before experience, alienation, and the modern. Jonathan's retreat into the dream of the past, the mixing of "pleasures" and "pains" in his experience with the vampire, and his longing for the blonde vampire to "kiss [him] with her red lips" (42) all become sign and signal of his De Quincean pursuit of wholeness, authenticity, and class.

But the selfhood that Jonathan seeks seems very much taken up with class: he thinks about wealthy ladies awaiting the return of their brave and chivalrous men. This is the narrative Jonathan is pursuing when he makes his way to Castle Dracula: the gentlemanly orphan, without blood or money, craves completeness and the clarity of an ordered story, of place, in this imagined long-ago notion of upper-class gentility. A true believer in the striver narrative, he is convinced that this dream can be achieved through acquisition, through what is taken into the body: paprika, Golden Mediasch, the "kiss" he seeks from the female vampire. The opium dream seems to promise such order and clarity: as De Quincey writes, "[O]pium . . . introduces among [the mental faculties] the most exquisite order, legislation, and harmony. . . . [C]ommunicates serenity and equipoise to all the faculties, active or passive: and with respect to the temper and moral feelings in general, it gives simply that sort of vital warmth which is approved by the judgment" (46). The vampire, too, promises a space of completion and order: where Jekyll and Hyde divide the professional and the leisurely bodies between them, Dracula combines both. Like Dexter, he is an adaptation for his age: the needle contained in his very body, the stuff of tranquility in his fangs and in his veins. He is the professional and the aristocrat in one.

Though Jonathan experiences "a horrible feeling of nausea" (24) in the presence of this uncanny monster, he remains seduced by the fulfillment the Count seems to offer. Like any inebriate who has not studied his teetotal literature, Jonathan thinks that a single taste (displaced to the body of the blonde vampire) will hardly kill him. But Jonathan underestimates the power and danger of aliment, forgetting that in remaking the man in its image, it moves beyond the consumer's control, bringing all of its implications and flavors to bear; in a similar way, just as he only sees the hair on the palms of Dracula's "fine" hands up close, so too does he mistake the patina of always-already class arrival for a through-and-through sense of self, meaning, place, complete integration. And the substance in which he seeks this ideal state, of course, is, like the vampire himself, an unstable marker, a difficult read, and a site of both "longing," in Jonathan's words, and "deadly fear" (52).

Opium, after all, was hardly an unproblematic substance at the end of the nineteenth century. Anxieties about opium initially circulated around the threat of foreign invasion. Though opium was commonly used both as a home remedy and as a medical cure even late in the century, it was also complicated—seen at once as cure and as scourge, affiliated with medical and moral degeneration and the influx of the foreign even as it kept its place in medicine cabinets and kitchen cupboards as a benign, all-purpose palliative, suitable for children's elixirs and everyday consumption.[13] Medical feeling about opium and morphine and moral opposition to opium at home and abroad in the wake of the Opium Wars, combined with anti-Eastern and anti-immigrant feeling, created a groundswell of support for the antiopium movement.[14]

Anxieties over opium (in particular, over the proliferation of opium dens) were also related to a small but highly publicized influx of Chinese immigrants to London.[15] Rhetoric on the subject was suffused in Orientalist stereotyping and fed a sense that the influx of aliens was the harbinger of a revenge narrative related to the Opium Wars.[16] Sensational opium-den narratives proliferated in newspapers and in novels, and an Oriental "enemy" was invented "who could be expected to use subtle and evil means to gain the field" (Milligan, *Pleasures*, 85). In London's East End, stories suggested, drooping, incapacitated Englishmen of all stripes were lured into the dens by voracious Easterners bent on transforming them into mindless, degraded inebriates. The literature of morphinism and opium inebriation reads much like Jonathan's fear of the vampire preying on London's "teeming millions," creating "a new and ever-widening circle of semi-demons to batten on the helpless" (Stoker, 53–54). And while anxieties about the effects of opium on the working classes (and, thus, on industry) were widespread, gentlemen were not exempt from this narrative.[17] Opium retained its reputation as a drug capable of opening the doors of perception—but the result was thought to be not De Quincey-esque "pleasure" but soul-sucking "pain."

This notion of opium is clearly evoked by Dracula, the shape-shifting, allochronistic invader from a land that time seems to have forgotten—the place where the trains do not run, a country of soil soaked with the blood of ancient wars. Dracula seems a perfect purveyor of opium: when he slices open a vein "with his long sharp nails" (252), he evokes the racist stereotype of the inscrutable Eastern drug addict/potentate, an Eastern invader floating somewhere between life and death, toxic. When the Count creates a psychic link with Mina through her consumption of his blood, he moves toward a communal, transcendent self, not limited by body boundaries, even as he evokes the specter of the invading Asiatic hordes, "turning" Englishmen and, in particular, Englishwomen into opium inebriates and eventually into ersatz Chinese.[18]

Then, too, Dracula's method of attack evokes the morphinism panic of the end of the century. Crothers wrote about the increased potency of morphine via the needle: referring to De Quincey's famous claim of consuming a quart of opium in a single day, he argued that, if De Quincey "[h]ad . . . used morphin with the needle, the quantity required would have been less, but he never could have abandoned it" (33). He added, "[t]he fascination of the needle is profound and wide-ranging. . . . [T]here is a certain contagion associated with the prick of the needle, and the restful calm which follows is both physiologic and psychic in its effect. It is now well recognized that there is a needle mania . . . likely to occur in neurotics" (Crothers, 34). The needle itself is seen as addictive; Crothers's *Morphinism and Narcomanias* contains stories of patients so addicted to injection that they display none of the symptoms of withdrawal when their morphine is replaced with water, though they suffer acutely when denied their injection (38).

Like the dreams he retails, the vampire, then, is addictive in and of himself: he offers an impossible, magical monstrosity, a class placement that realigns the professional and the aristocrat, combining them in a single body and thus not obliterating but reifying the middle-class man and his boundary-breaking technology—a Darwinian adaptation indeed. Crothers writes, "Neurasthenia and cerebrasthenia are new differentiations of nervous defects incident to the times; and morphin is the new solace which gives temporary relief and conceals the real condition while intensifying and increasing it" (Crothers, 33). The drug of the vampire, then, offers solace from the madness of loss of place, loss of identity, and modern solipsism. But its effects are temporary and illusory: it does not solve this alienation in the age of the simulacrum but simply covers it over, as Dracula's method of reproduction makes clear.

Jonathan learns his lesson and attempts to kick the habit (marrying his sweetheart in his hospital bed, handing over the narrative of his adventures to Mina, and attempting, without even the aid of chloral hydrate, to forget). But long before he arrives at Castle Dracula, it is already too late for his fellow vampire-fighters. Jonathan is, after all, not the text's only gentlemanly traveler—nor is Transylvania the novel's only foreign travel destination. Seward, Arthur, and Quincey, old friends as they are, have ranged much farther afield together, and the vampiric seeking after wholeness that lurks beneath the surface of Jonathan's apparently businesslike quest is figured here, infecting, shaping, and addicting them long before they meet again in Lucy's drawing room. This becomes clear in Quincey Morris's letter to Arthur, a note of reconciliation after the results of the men's proposals to Lucy become clear. Morris writes,

> We've told yarns by the camp-fire in the prairies; and dressed one another's wounds after trying a landing at the Marquesas; and drunk healths on the shore of Titicaca. There are more yarns to be told, and other wounds to be healed, and another health to be drunk. Won't you let this be at my camp-fire tomorrow night? . . . There will only be one other, our dear old pal at the Korea, Jack Seward. He's coming, too, and we both

> want to mingle our weeps over the wine-cup, and to drink a health with all our hearts to the happiest man in all the wide world, who has won the noblest heart that God has made and the best worth winning. We promise you a hearty welcome, and a loving greeting, and a health as true as your own right hand. We shall both swear to leave you at home if you drink too deep to a certain pair of eyes. (62)

Voyaging abroad seems, for these brave, adventuring gentlemen, to be about forging and testing one's manhood: going into battle, sacrificing oneself for one's compatriots, and being physically brave, manly, generous, and loyal. Here one of the primary questions that haunts the issue of gentlemanliness—is it acquired or inherent?—is symbolically put to rest as, following the old chivalric tradition, our gents go abroad to find out who they are, both creating themselves through experience and discovering themselves as themselves. They rewrite themselves here as old-fashioned heroes, knights in shining armor bearing their standards as they ride out against their foes. Quincey posits the adventuring life the men have shared—a life lived not at a civilized table but around a Rousseauian campfire—as an occasion of deep bonding, of becoming one with one another, so to speak, even as it is also a process of remaking the self, that is, forging oneself through adversity, and of discovering one's mettle by discovering what lies within, bringing that internal self (buried, in ordinary circumstances, under the dressings of civilization) to the forefront. Connection, here, seems to be located between men and signified through a longed-for commensality absent elsewhere in the text: though Arthur has won Lucy, Quincey implies, the result of the contest is not particularly productive of alienation from one another, because these bonds between men are endlessly renewable and speak of real knowledge of one another. These ties of real love, he suggests, offer a meaningful overcoming of the solipsistic boundaries of modernity.

Philip Holden argues that "[w]hen fluids are associated with middle-class identity, they have a restorative function" (479). But Quincey's proposal of "mingl[ing] our weeps over the wine-cup" to "drink a health with all our hearts" is hardly restorative in the usual sense of things. The act connects drinking with autophagy, though here it is not blood but another bodily fluid that the men down to recenter their gentlemanly, masculine selfhood—and it is not Lucy's fluids they seek to consume but their own. I am not suggesting, as Christopher Craft and others do, that Stoker is queering the text here: rather, I am positing that, having failed in their quest for love from Lucy—having found only division and alienation there, as is apparent to Quincey and Seward and will soon become clear to poor Arthur—they have turned back to one another, determined to heal themselves by finding themselves through a ritual of auto-phagic drink, which, as with Utterson's wine, "melts" the barriers between them and allows true commensality. Drinking healths, then, is an act of taking in the collective and the individual body, of drinking oneself and one's compatriots—of drinking down gentle-manliness itself. The gentlemen's appetite is not only for the "health" of a "certain pair of eyes" but also for the life of their own veins: that is, for the vampire's elixir.

This transformative draft has the ability to obviate boundaries, to bring the men together, and to create a sense of shared purpose and understanding that overcomes modernity, solipsism, and even time and space. Arthur's response to Quincey's letter is simple and direct: "Count me in every time. I bear messages which will make both your ears tingle" (62). Communication is not obviated by so-cial nicety or failures of language here: the message is clear. It is de-livered by telegram, demonstrating that this fellowship overcomes even technology (in a rare occasion of functioning telegrams in the text). Here, the construction of the gentlemanly hero requires mul-tiplicity, an elision of class lines, of nationalities, even of bodies. The insistent individualism of gentlemanliness—the troubled and troubling narrative of making one's way or protecting one's pre-rogative, of naming and transforming and finding place for the self, even if that process involves a narrative of bodily elision or era-sure—is here cast aside. In the last years of the century, amid anxi-eties over economic and colonial decline at the end of empire, over fears of degeneration and immigration, these gentlemen bring to-gether the language and the aims of the chivalric individual hero (men who set out to save their women, who "did dare much," as Jonathan concludes the narrative, "for [Mina's] sake" [327]) with the act of subsuming the self, of finding a universal, undifferentiated, anticlassed, antigentlemanly Romantic wholeness through the medium of the vampire's bite, of the blood, of the drug of dreaming. The notion of seeking after selfhood is at once located in the physical self and placed in the metaphysical realm, in the transubstantive act of overcoming the physical boundaries of the skin, the linguistic and psychological and sociocultural boundaries of the modern, to reach, in the allochronistic outer world far from England, a sense of connection and universal selfhood.

But—like opium, like morphine—the wholeness the men seek brings both "pleasure" and "pain." Quincey's reference to the idea that the men have "drunk healths," for instance, evokes at once the good-fellowship of the gentlemanly board and Renfield's biblical mantra, "[T]he blood is the life!" (130). It also presages Lucy's ordeal, in which the vampire will literally drink her health away. The echo locates these gentlemen, too, as possessors of vampiric appetite—that is, an appetite for connection, for love.[19] Then, too, when he refers to drinking "healths on the shores of Titicaca," the American adventurer speaks of the land of the Incas, famous from travelers' letters for their blood-sacrifice rituals, often associated with vampiric and cannibalistic practices. The association gains resonance when it echoes in Quincey's reaction to Lucy's vampirized condition: "I have not seen anything pulled down so quick," he muses, "since I was on the Pampas and had a mare . . . go to grass all in a night. One of those big bats that they call vampires had got at her in the night, and, what with his gorge and the vein left open, there wasn't enough blood in her to let her stand up" (138). If South America is a place where vampirism is at home, then the men's presence there raises the possibility of vampiric opening— an idea perhaps reinforced by South America's reputation in the period as the home of strange plants and drugs, as a site of European exploration of new ways of approaching the body and self (see chapter 5).

When Quincey mentions "the Korea," he presumably refers to an American assault on Korea carried out in 1871 in retaliation for the Korean destruction of an American ship, the *General Sherman*.[20] Accounts of the assault dwell on the difficulty the Americans experienced in understanding the traditions and cultural expectations of the residents of the "Hermit Kingdom" (the *General Sherman* was destroyed because its captain, avid to trade with the closed nation, insisted on traveling upriver and docking, against the express orders of the Emperor). The East, the story suggests—the source of opium, of the vampiric—is indeed inscrutable and treacherous; the trade disputes evoke the Opium War battles, and the men's presence there suggests a potentially fatal—or engulfing—set of misreadings very similar to those that Jonathan performs in Transylvania. What the men long for may, in fact, be the unreadable, the unknowable.

The reference to Korea marks a voyage, if not to China then to an Asia that, in the nineteenth-century English mind, was largely undifferentiated by precise geography. This evocation sheds light on the implications of the men's "mingling." In "The Pleasures of Opium," De Quincey speaks to childhood memories as the foundation of his opium dreams; but in the book's second section, "The Pains of Opium," childhood fades away, to be replaced by terrifying creatures and images from the imagined primordial soup of Asia and Africa. In *Pleasures and Pains*, Milligan argues that "De Quincey's opium dreams are so torturous precisely because they erode the desired division between self and other even in the otherwise presumably inviolate sanctum of individual consciousness" (47). De Quincey claimed Asia as "the cradle of the human race" (80), and saw the region as the source and site of "swarming" humanity (81); Milligan posits that while De Quincey protested his utter difference from Asia, insisting on the basis of his dreams only in himself and his personal past, he also implicitly acknowledged the presence of Asia—that is, the inscrutable, ancient self-other that is the long-ago origin to which, in his narrative, opium allows access—in the self. The opium-eater, Milligan writes, "is 'transported into Asiatic scenes' without leaving his English cottage, and his identity ultimately disintegrates as he lies 'confounded with all unutterably slimy things, amongst reeds and Nilotic mud'" (47). In eating opium, the eater swallows the other who is the self before the self, subsuming himself in a collective unconscious that is terrifyingly undifferentiated.

Blood—like its stand-ins (opium, tears)—is a source of originary humanness, and so the gentleman's appetite for the stuff is inevitably also an appetite for losing the self, dissolving into the mass. Unlike chloral hydrate, which gives wholeness through erasure, the vampire's libation—what the men seek in their Eastern travels, in their cup of "weeps"—makes class, gender, selfhood, gentlemanliness impossible, even as it allows "mingling," that is, combination, commensality, and love: hence the horror the men harbor for the vampire but also the longing for what he has.

The notion of the other who is the self in the most gentlemanly, most class- and gender-defined and bloodiest of ways is taken up in *Dracula*'s suggestion of modern simulacra, positing that individuality and self-definition are impossible, in its intimations that everyone is always already the same beneath the skin. The recurrences of names, the voices that are all the same, the repetition of action, of intention, of desire among the men—most tellingly, the shared desire for Lucy and the subsequent commingling of blood in her veins—all may suggest the machine-dream repetition of industrial modernity and technology, but they also imply a serious lack of differentiation. And the gentlemen's thirst, of course, reconstitutes the question of bloodlines in this regard. Whereas in *Dr. Jekyll and Mr. Hyde* wine is Eucharistic but blood constitutes the real thing (the stuff of gentlemanliness), in *Dracula* the very circulation of blood at once gives the stuff inherence—it is the site of the "Nilotic," the originary human, the aristocrat's beverage of choice—and makes it all the same, erasing class differentiation entirely.[21] The idea that blood can be passed around, can move from one body to the next as a means of reconstituting that body, makes impossible the notion of class, of place, and, indeed, of inherent selfhood tied to the body.

Count Dracula himself can be read, in some senses, as a blending of the gentlemen who seek to destroy him. Like Arthur, he is of proud old family and wealth; like Quincey, he is physically brave and strong; like Seward, he is fascinated by knowledge and likes to use his brain to control others; and like Jonathan, he seeks to move onward and upward, to explore new worlds, to make a memo of what he is seeing, to taste—he is thirsty. He is a palimpsest of the men, the thing itself, the state of wholeness that they seek through fellowship, through consumption, through true love. The clarity of gentlemanly blood here becomes (in the vampire's body) literally and figuratively impossible, unreadable. Purity and order, Dracula insists, are impossible: the pursuit of wholeness takes the seeker into the realm of the pre-Fallen not in the Adamic, idealized sense but in terms of the degenerated, the prelinguistic, the "Nilotic mud" of human experience. If he is a monstrous compendium—modern technology and the ancient, professional and aristocrat and worker in one—he is also blended, indivisible, a shape-shifter, a morass. Whereas Dexter requires balance between his aristocratic, melancholy self and his steel wheels, with Dracula no such thing is possible: the threads are entirely intertwined, the sinews and the steel grown together.

The circulation of blood also enables a dissolution of boundary between the metaphoric and the actual: if, as we have seen elsewhere, gentlemanly selfhood is always figured—by its presence, by its absence, or by its appetites—in blood and if, as in *Jekyll and Hyde*, drinking is a Eucharistic activity, then here "weeps" become blood, blood and wine are interchangeable, the unfathomable insides become that which is taken in by mouth. The notion of human blood as essence overwhelms the idea of blood as inert bodily substance: there is a visceral sense that drinking blood is drinking the self. Disgust—so strongly present in *Dracula*, as in Jonathan's description of the count as a "leech" in his coffin (53) and in Mina's declaration of herself as "Unclean! Unclean!" (248)—is tied to the monstrous appetite for that which belongs inside the body.[22] As Deborah Lupton observes, "bodily fluids create anxiety because of the threat they pose to self-integrity and autonomy. Body fluids threaten to engulf, to defile; they are difficult to be rid of, they seep and infiltrate. They challenge our desire to be self-contained and self-controlled" (114–15).

Dracula is literally filled with the stuff of disgust—the most problematic of bodily fluids, that which sits at the nexus of the sacred and the profane. The literal lines between one body and another are refused, disappear. In Michel Bakhtin's sense, Dracula, like Mr. Woodhouse, that other disgusting would-be feudal lord, is "grotesque" (26): unclosed, unlimited, unrestrained, and unseparate from the world around him, sending his effluvia outward instead of keeping it decently in check. So, too, are the vampire's gentlemanly antagonists—who drink one another's healths, fill

Lucy's body promiscuously with their blood, drink each other down, and actively seek to rub out the boundaries between self and self as they pursue wholeness.

The disgust and horror revealed by the search for the authentic oceanic is present too, in Quincey's reference to "dress[ing] one another's wounds after trying a landing at the Marquesas." Consisting of a group of French Polynesian islands in the middle of the Pacific Ocean, the Marquesas were well known in the late nineteenth century: Herman Melville set his 1846 novel *Typee* there, and Paul Gauguin lived out the last years of his life in the Marquesas. Alone in the middle of nowhere, the islands were often figured as throwback places, out of time—a dreamworld of the primitive. Opium was a part of that narrative. It was everywhere in the Marquesas, taken there by the colonialist endeavors that enabled the imagined incursion of the in-creeping Orientalist nightmare that London so feared. The stories of the Marquesas that were told in England evoked not Romantic oneness but the dissolution of order, the threat of criminality and degeneration—a threat echoed by Jonathan's appetites for Transylvanian delicacies, by the men's drink of bodily liquid, and by Mina's triumphant diagnosis of Dracula himself as a "criminal type" (296). In his *In the South Seas*,[23] Robert Louis Stevenson writes of crime and prison in the Marquesas:

> The main occasion of . . . thefts is the new vice of opium-eating. "Here nobody ever works, and all eat opium," said a gendarme; and Ah Fu knew a woman who ate a dollar's worth in a day. The successful thief will . . . produce a big lump of opium, and retire to the bush to eat and sleep it off. A trader, who did not sell opium . . . said . . . "The natives only work to buy it. . . . [O]pium is the currency of this country."
>
> [A prisoner] . . . lost patience while [a] Chinese opium-seller was being examined in his presence. "Of course he sold me opium!" he broke out; "all the Chinese here sell opium. It was only to buy opium that I stole; it is only to buy opium that anybody steals. And what you ought to do is to let no opium come here, and no Chinamen." (60–61)

Opium—retailed by these same Orientalized, irresistible Asian brokers—here creates appetite and need, even as it erases labor, advancement, and possibility. Though it is tempting to imagine that this opium effect is more profound on minds thought to be less exalted than those of our gentlemen, this was not the late-nineteenth-century view: as Crothers wrote, morphinism "produces a pathologic condition demanding a repetition of the dose until the disease impulse for more is finally uncontrollable. . . . [T]he higher the brain culture and development, the more certain and persistent are the disastrous effects produced by it" (45). These effects would have been particularly problematic given the Marquesas' other claim to fame in the late nineteenth century: the island's degenerate appetites were not limited to aliment legitimized, however problematically, by science, medicine, and trade.

The Marquesas are volcanic, with famously craggy, inhospitable shorelines, and it is no surprise that "trying a landing" there might produce injuries. But those "wounds" might also result not from the topographical difficulties of going ashore but from the reception the adventurers may have met with: these islands were widely considered the home of "barbaric cannibals" (as the American missionary Titus Coan wrote in his 1882 *Life in Hawaii*). The island's indigenous people were, at least according to European adventure-travel writers, legendary anthropophagists, much given to killing and eating members of other tribes and, on occasion, white-skinned voyagers and colonialists. Melville wrote of cannibalism among the Marquesans[24]—as did Stevenson, despite his apparent sympathy for the indigenous people of the island. As Nathaniel Philbrick writes in *In the Heart of the Sea*,[25] "the Essex men had heard that [the Marquesas'] native inhabitants had a reputation for cannibalism. 'In time of famine,' insisted [a] visitor, 'the men butcher their wives, and children, and aged parents.' Georg von Langsdorff, whose ship touched at the Marquesas in 1804, claimed that the natives found human flesh so delicious 'that those who have once eaten it can [only] with difficulty abstain from it'" (quoted in P. Walton, 18).

The presence of cannibalism on the island recasts the opium dream,[26] making manifest what lies beneath the romance, the "love" of the vampire's bite, at the heart of the authentic, "Nilotic" self: the bloody, atavistic, and addictive appetite that reduces the human to meat, to wine. This is where the men are "wound[ed]" in "trying a landing"—where, that is, their skin is pierced, their veins opened. The cannibalistic craving of the vampire, the reference to the Marquesas suggests, offers a rewriting of De Quincey's "Nilotic" dreams as even darker, more frightening, more degenerated—and productive, in the end, of an erasure, a disappearance of the self, that is far more effective than Seward's chloral hydrate. The gentleman, it suggests, is not only a creature of terrible, disgusting appetites, insufficiently differentiated: he is also nothing more than meat, the animal. If the modern is a state of solipsistic emptiness for the gentleman, *Dracula* suggests, in which true communication fails and commensality is impossible, then the oceanic wholeness of class completion longed for by the protagonists, imbibed by them with vampiric hunger, is no better: rather than a terrible isolation of the self, it offers a Darwinian morass.

The gentleman who takes up this idea most overtly, of course, is Renfield, the asylum inmate who seeks to eat his way up the food chain in order to collect as many lives as possible and in this way to live forever. Renfield's most clearly vampiric behavior involves Seward directly. As the doctor recounts in his phonograph diary,

> I was engaged after dinner in my study. . . . Suddenly the door was burst open, and in rushed my patient, with his face distorted with passion. . . . [H]e made straight at me. He had a dinner-knife in his hand, and . . . before I could get my balance he had struck at me and cut my left wrist rather severely. Before he could strike again, however, I got in my right, and he was sprawling on his back on the floor. My wrist bled freely, and quite a little pool trickled on to the carpet. . . . When the attendants rushed in, and we turned our attention to him, his employment positively sickened me. He was lying on his belly on the floor licking up, like a dog, the blood which had fallen from my wounded wrist. He was easily secured, and, to my surprise, went with the attendants quite placidly, simply repeating over and over again: "The blood is the life! The blood is the life!" (129–30)

It is particularly telling that Renfield's act of vampiric cannibalism is performed not with teeth or claws or hunting weapons but with a dinner knife, the furniture of the gentlemanly table, the marker of gentlemanly civility: with this implement, he turns his doctor into meat, aligning himself with the vampire who sips at the chalice of the human. Renfield, of course, is explicitly affiliated with the vampire he calls "Master" (98), in this way positioning himself not as a gentleman at all but as a servant to that aristocratic force. But class seems, for Renfield, to be costumery, assumed and rejected as it is useful to him; and the act of cannibalism is also an inherent refusal of the notion of selfhood and containment. The identity of the eater is always already transformed and destabilized by the act of taking in the other who is proximate to the self.

Certainly, this is the case with Renfield and Seward. Though Seward calls his patient a madman, Renfield refuses containment in such labeling. When Van Helsing, Arthur, and Quincey accompany Renfield to the interview in which he asks Seward to send him home, for example, Renfield requests a formal introduction to his visitors. Seward recounts, "I was so much astonished that the oddness of introducing a madman in an asylum did not strike me at the moment; and, besides, there was a certain dignity in the man's manner, so much of the habit of equality, that I at once made the introduction" (215). Renfield tells Arthur, "I had the honour of seconding your father at the Windham"; he praises Texas to Quincey; and he expresses his "pleasure" at meeting Van Helsing, whose work he knows. In every case, Renfield speaks like the gentleman he is. When Seward refuses him his immediate liberty, Renfield requests his freedom "not on personal grounds, but for the sake of others," for reasons that "are good ones, sound and unselfish, and springing from the highest sense of duty" (216). The insect-eating, cannibal madman speaks, in other words, in the classic, chivalric language of idealized moral gentlemanliness.

Renfield's behavior in the presence of these gentlemen destabilizes gentlemanliness itself, implying that its appetites are as raw and selfish as his own. Indeed, if this group of men is linked by bravery, nobility of nature, and selflessness, so too are these qualities displayed by the chivalric Renfield, bent only on doing his duty to save Mina, even at the cost of his own life. And if his disgusting habits are full of desire and blood and figure him as an animal/hunter bent only on satisfying his terrible, disgusting hunger, so too are these qualities reflected in his interlocutors: in their desire (for Lucy), their propensity for blood (in their travels and adventures), their willingness to hunt (for the vampire).[27]

Renfield's anthropophagic appetite thus belongs to the gentlemen as well: they seek, in their longing after wholeness, after full gentlemanlihood and an integrated selfhood—not the substitute flavor of wine, as the men in *Dr. Jekyll and Mr. Hyde* do, but the gritty, metallic taste of blood. The vampire's desire is the desire of those around him. In him, the act of drinking blood becomes the act of a depraved Rousseauian natural man, a Darwinian predator in rusty evening dress.[28] Like Dracula crawling down the wall in Jonathan's clothes, like Jonathan crawling down the wall after him, gentlemen are animals underneath civilized trappings, utterly desiring, endlessly thirsty beings. The modern gentlemen of the Band of Light, then, hunt the vampire—fighting for clarity, order, and reason—while always already embodying his terrible appetites, his promiscuous and destabilizing mixing, and his bloody morass.

But this animal depth is not readily apparent. Dracula's acts of feeding and being fed upon involve draining the inside matter of the body and the self without displacing the outer shell, the signifier of selfhood. Dracula looks like a man; his victims look like themselves through their illnesses and even in the grave. In fact, the vampire's bite in some ways seems to make the body *more* whole: except for the mark of the teeth (hidden away by Lucy under the black band she wears around her neck, the gift of her fiancé; unseen by Jonathan on Mina's neck), the body grows more complete, more classical; like the classical statue, the body will never age. "Adamantine" (187) Lucy in the grave is "more radiantly beautiful than ever" (178); Dracula himself grows ever younger.[29] The seemingly perfect body hides an entirely liquid self beneath the skin. This, too, is of a piece with the "pains" of opium and morphinism: the "degeneration" of the disease is "concealed. . . . The early use of morphin, and sometimes its continued use for years, may exhibit little physical impairment, but in all cases the will and moral forces suffer from the beginning" (Crothers, 45). One of the most insidious effects of morphinism, Crothers claims, is "[t]he possibility of concealing its use for many years," making "it a most seductive addiction" (29), so that "not one-tenth of the cases of morphinism are known to any except their most intimate friends" (Crothers, 31). This has serious implications for our gentlemanly heroes: like Dracula, they cannot be recognized until viewed from close up; the moral results of their cravings are not written on their faces; they hide, beneath the skin, the horror and danger of the vampiric addiction to class and place, which is the addiction to the impossible, the morass, the endless autophagic appetite of gentlemanliness in the modern age.

The end of the novel makes an attempt to reposition the gentleman: introducing a child to demonstrate the return of the productive middle-class narrative; marrying off Seward and Arthur; and giving Quincey a hero's death, in which he is recast as a Christ figure. But this recuperative conclusion rings false; and the child's uncertain parentage ("[h]is bundle of names links all our little band of men together; but we call him Quincey" [326]) and his rebirth from death (his "birthday is the same day as that on which Quincey Morris died" [326], which is, of course, also the death date of the vampire) hardly solve the problem of liminality, of the morass, in the collective body of our gentlemanly heroes. If the gentleman, in the old-fashioned nineteenth-century imagining, is made of rarefied blood, is immune to social forces, is beyond the bodily and yet entirely of the body (by bloodlines and birth), then here his late-century self is made manifest in the vampire: a sloshing repository of bloody appetites, covered over with a shell of perfect respectability and enabled by professionalism. And if Renfield can put on and take off gentlemanliness like a costume—if blood and "weeps" and "healths" can be transferred from body to body—if, at bottom, the gentleman is no different than the "teeming millions" of London—then gentlemanliness itself, like Mr. Hyde, does not even exist.

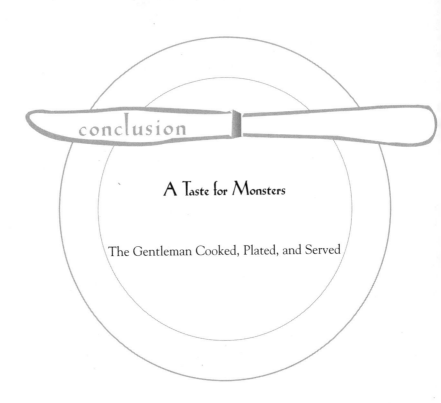

conclusion

A Taste for Monsters

The Gentleman Cooked, Plated, and Served

I began working on this project by first attempting to define my terms: that is, to pin down this question of what the gentleman *is*. I amassed definitions, made lists of basic requirements, consulted scholarly and popular texts, sketched and resketched—but no matter how much I sweated over the question, I couldn't get it right. The gentleman seemed to shape-shift every time I pinned him down: to transform himself, to undergo radical surgery, sometimes to disappear completely. But when I turned to the table, I began to see glimmerings of a transactional gentlemanliness, a selfhood taken in by mouth, a hungry creature of class and gender and power made and remade by the sociocultural, economic, and political world of which he had (he would like us to believe) taken charge. The process of writing *Making a Man* taught me that the definition is not only impossible but also beside the point: it is the endless project of trying to define gentlemanliness that drives the gentleman himself to sip or swallow, to eat ravenously or shut his mouth against the world, and these acts, in turn, make him visible as he shifts and changes across the century.

Aliment is a means of reading the gentleman's character at any given moment, of understanding his relations to others, to himself, and to the social body; when the fictional gentleman sits down to dinner, he is illuminated as a creature of his particular time and place, his particular imagining. And alimental analysis of the gentleman in English literature of the nineteenth century makes clear a set of recurring traits and issues regarding this problematic figure. In each of the novels that I discuss in this volume, the gentleman—whether putatively benign or overtly dreadful—is clearly a force that is in some way fundamentally threatening to the health of the nation. He may, like Mr. Woodhouse, threaten to close down the renewal and fecundity of the society around him, trapping his community in a moment of endless liminality with his improperly bounded alimental concerns; he may, like Arthur Clennam, become a closed figure of sterility and starvation, depleting the body politic through his withdrawal from the project of community and nation in an attempt to repudiate an endlessly ravenous economic gentlemanliness; or he may, like Arthur Huntingdon, attempt to keep class in its place, obviating social movement, through his bodily inscription. Like Miserrimus Dexter, he may seek to swallow the core of the social realm, devouring the very possibility of social regeneration in his quest for self-perpetuation; like Mr. Hyde, he might, in seeking place for himself, prey on his own kind. Or like Stoker's Band of Light, he may attempt to swallow himself, discovering in the process the extent of his own bloody appetites. In every case, however, he is a force to be reformed or excised, and the novel must direct its energies toward correcting the problem that he becomes—regardless of whether or not the ruin of the society around him is his intention. Aliment reveals, encapsulates, and embodies this threat.

The alimental gentleman is hardly a creature apart from the society that struggles to contain and rewrite him: he is intimately imbricated in the sociocultural, political, economic, technological, and scientific movements and notions that swirl around him. But while the gentleman is unquestionably a creature of his time, built and rebuilt by these varied (and often competing) discourses, he is hardly a controlling force. The gentleman might certainly be a creature of great fear and loathing, a swallower of the nation; but rather than standing as the figure in charge of the social order, he is a reactive, relational character, less an actor than one who responds to being acted upon. He seems to care very little about the social realm on its own terms—rather, he is, in every case, selfish in the more profound sense. Though his self-interest may be manifested through a discourse of benevolence or disinterest, he is, at bottom, concerned only about feeding himself in order to perpetuate or to preserve himself. His sole aim is survival; and his appetite for that particular dish is insatiable and indiscriminate.

In this sense, he may be called, despite the traditionalism to which he may adhere, a remarkably modern figure: alienated from the world around him (despite or because of his tendency to swallow others whole), self-absorbed, self-serving, and self-protective, he above all insists on his own primacy. Claude Lévi-Strauss, writing of the effects of eating behaviors on others, sees this attitude as a mark of Western modernity; alimentary ritual, he contends, is used in Western society to protect not the community (as it is in more "primitive" societies, which he explores through the use of myth) but the self. "If the origin of table manners . . . is to be found . . . in deference towards the world—good manners consisting precisely in respecting its obligations—it follows that the inherent ethic of the myths runs counter to the ethic we profess today," Lévi-Strauss writes. "It teaches us, at any rate, that the formula 'hell is other people' . . . is not so much a philosophical proposition as an ethnographic statement about our civilization. For, since childhood, we have been accustomed to fear impurity as coming from without" (Origin, 505). Discourses of fear and loathing about food and appetite; notions of appropriately or inappropriately gendered or classed fare; insistence on the primacy of one's own aliment or refusal of the offerings of the world; attempts to replace food and drink with synthesized, self-generated, or medically defined fare— all work to protect the would-be self-controlled body from the dangerous incursions of socially imbricated food. Such efforts are often coded as "good" or "bad," weighted with moral baggage: as Lupton writes, in modernity, "It is the individual body that makes decisions on what is taken into the body and the self and this judgement of 'taste' becomes crucial to self-formation. Moral and medical discourses guide individuals in how best to use food for the individual rather than the collective good" (18).

In some of the novels I have addressed here, as in many others throughout the century, gentlemanly consuming, of course, is often predicated on large meals eaten in the company of others—a set of rituals that seems to belie the notion of the self-serving gentleman alienated from the communal, since, as Barbara Kirshenblatt-Gimblett writes, "[f]easts are prominent in rites of incorporation, where commensality, the act of eating together, is an archetype of union" (23). But in these settings, the act of eating together often showcases precisely the lack of such union. The ritual of the formal gentlemanly Victorian table, after all, begins not in the dining room but in the drawing room, where drinking, not eating, is engaged in (the Victorians pioneered the cocktail hour); the group is fragmented, unsettled, possibly shifting, and the potentially sacramental quality of imbibing is undermined by these factors. The guests go in to dinner in accordance with a strict hierarchy, reinforcing the notion of rule and submission and tamping down possibilities of transactional democracy through shared aliment. Commensality at the Victorian table is further disrupted by the introduction of "Russian" service, in which servants deliver food and drink to each guest in place of a general sharing of sustenance. The group is fragmented once again at the end of the meal by the departure of the women. The very rites and rituals of the gentlemanly table, then, discourage a sense of communal consumption and defeat the notion of eating as socially transubstantiating.

But even this troubled notion of commensality is obviated in the later novels, as the gentleman turns resolutely from the communal, becoming increasingly ambitious in his quest for self-preservation as he perceives himself to be more and more under attack—from class movement, from professionalization, and from modernity itself. He is a striver, using his appetites to defeat or contain the forces around him and thus to protect, to perpetuate, and even to strengthen himself. These largely middle-class narratives infuse the gentleman with all of the anxieties that the middle class carries regarding the relative weights of the competing discourses of tradition and innovation, of ambition and of community: he is the unresolved, the site of the issues that will not go away, the locus of striver self-contradiction. The gentleman becomes the force to be excised, the abject, the thing to be cast out: an anxious, inventive projection of the inhabitants of the putatively bounded middle-class social order. In this regard, he is not a historical figure at all, though he is narratively reactive to history. Instead, the alimental gentleman in nineteenth-century fiction is in every sense a fiction: an imaginative force created to embody the fears and apprehensions of an endlessly shifting society that seeks, impossibly, to codify itself even as it insists upon its own inexhaustible capacity for innovation and self-invention. For this reason, the monstrously swallowing gentleman always remains.

The making and unmaking of the alimental gentleman, then, is a battle of the would-be community against itself, as it is delineated in these texts: marriage is pitted against celibacy, fecundity against stasis and barrenness, the communal table against the starver and the solitary binger, the ordered appetite against the terrible morass of anthropophagy. The gentleman is a site and a symbol for these battles, necessarily a monstrous and perpetually unresolved creature. And though the novels express a longing for resolution, they are also taken with the glamour of the dark side: they cannot bring themselves to expurgate the ravenous, terrible appetites of the gentleman, because the fare of the gentleman is secretly longed for, even by the novels' most recuperative forces. The community, then, is a utopian entity that is always already unreachable, always already imbricated in the marketplace, corrupted by desire, hungry. The alimental gentleman, that problematic creature of hideous cravings and appetites, is a crucial force in the project of national definition, despite his removal from and insistence on feeding upon the social; the alienated sign of the endless, possibly fortunate fall into the marketplace of desire, he can never be cast aside. He is—in his bloated body, his starving self, his rapaciousness and refusal—the essence of the longings and fears, the problematic appetites, of the middle-class readers and writers whose autophagic appetites center on his consumption. And, thus, the nineteenth-century gentleman (deglazed, reduced, baked, cooled, blanched, and endlessly rewarmed) is served up at table, for our delectation.

NOTES

INTRODUCTION

1. See Mary Douglas's pivotal *Purity and Danger* (for instance, 35–40).
2. See Rozin and Fallon, 26, on the valences of the mouth as transitory site.
3. See also Priscilla Walton's *Our Cannibals, Ourselves*, especially chapter 1. Margaret Visser has written, particularly in *The Rituals of Dinner*, about the development of the rites of the table as a social defense against the panic and desperation of hunger—that is, as a means of avoiding the horror of the rawest of atavistic appetites.
4. See, for instance, Mennell, 26.
5. See, for instance, Davidoff, 48.
6. See, for instance, Burnett, 70.
7. Wilson, xvi.
8. Tannahill, 307.
9. See, for instance, Freud, "Uber Coca," 68.

CHAPTER I

1. Austen, *Emma*, 7. Further references to this text (the 1988 Oxford edition) throughout this chapter will be indicated only by page number.
2. Marvin Mudrick, for instance, refers to Woodhouse as "an idiot" (192), "a *tour de force*—nothing else" (196). Mark Schorer describes Emma's father as "a destructive (though comic, of course) malingering egotist" (108–9). Mr. Woodhouse's gastronomic peculiarities have not been completely ignored, however. Stephen Mennell, for instance, declares, "Of the faddy, anxious eater, Mr. Woodhouse . . . can stand as a literary archetype" (295); Mennell goes on to attribute our hero's eating habits to bad English nursery training.
3. Christine Roulston, for instance, sees the novel as "an inverted world," and she asserts that Emma and Mr. Woodhouse have "an inverse father-daughter relationship. In a pointed parody of the powerful father figure . . . Mr. Woodhouse has the distinctive characteristic

of gossiping like a woman and never being listened to" (44–45). Roulston casts Mr. Woodhouse in "the role of the mother rather than that of the patriarch" (51).

4. See Lupton, 109–10.

5. See, for instance, Lupton, 133–35.

6. The art of canning had been invented by Nicholas Appert in France at the end of the eighteenth century; John Hall probably pioneered the use of tinned iron containers in England. By 1814, sailors on long sea voyages had begun to carry canned goods on board ship, and the practice of large-scale importing of perishable foods to England was well under way (Drummond and Wilbraham, 355).

7. The exigencies of industrial life also played a central role in the creation of a ready-made market for canned and prepared foods: as factory-driven economies led to accelerated urbanization, fewer people had access to adequate kitchen facilities (ovens, for instance, were hard to come by in the overcrowded and heavily subdivided tenements of the big cities).

8. Because heat, not absence of air, was believed to be the salient factor in preserving food, the technique remained imperfect until Louis Pasteur's discoveries became widespread, so that people continued to sicken from the effects of eating inadequately preserved canned foods.

9. Even the redoubtable Eliza Acton, writing some thirty years later, emphasized the importance of light-colored bread. She advised the home cook: "When only porter-yeast—which is dark-coloured and bitter—can be procured, use a much smaller proportion than usual, and allow *much* longer time for it to rise. Never let it be sent to the oven until it is evidently *light*" (Ray, 259).

10. See Burnett, 81–82, for a sustained discussion of the removal of government regulation over foodstuffs.

11. David Cannadine's *Lords and Landlords* offers a particularly cogent discussion of the belief on the part of the upper classes that society was fundamentally threatened by middle-class mobility and enterprise, as well as by working-class agitation (see 26–32).

12. While the foreign was clearly dangerous, the home front was hardly safe ground. As J. C. Drummond and Anne Wilbraham note,

> To the ill effects of war and financial and trade disturbances were added the grave consequences of . . . indifferent harvests; in 1812 the country came very near real famine. A bumper crop in 1813 brought the price of wheat down, but . . . farmers protested that cheap corn would ruin agriculture

and the Corn Law of 1815 was passed to placate them. This measure hit the poor very severely, keeping up the price of wheat by authorizing the suspension of imported grain when the price fell below 80s. a quarter. The Peace of 1815 found England in a thoroughly exhausted condition, with distress and discontent rife among the labouring classes and even spreading to the middle class. . . . Peace brought . . . a sharp fall in prices but it was offset by a considerable increase in unemployment. (331)

13. See, for instance, Mennell, 206–8.

14. Such anxieties often lie half buried in Austen's text, cropping up in unexpected little narratives about the horrors of poverty and the ever-looming threat of invasion. These stories are quickly contained and resolved, so that the threat is seen as minor or marginal. The dangers of incursion, for instance, are signaled by the gypsies who attack Harriet; but she escapes with her purse intact, and her attackers flee the neighborhood. Though the invaders themselves disappear, however, their brief presence signifies the danger of strangers, foreigners, outsiders who seek to destroy the staid, self-satisfied order of the town. The very containment of these threats signals the need to dispose of them quickly.

15. See Joseph Ritson's *Essay on Abstinence from Animal Food* (1802); Nicholson's "On Food" (1803); Lambe's *Medical and Experimental Inquiry* (1805); Newton's *Return to Nature* (1811); and Shelley's *Vindication of Natural Diet* (1813).

16. See Morton, *Shelley*, 19.

17. See Drummond and Wilbraham, 474.

18. Lévi-Strauss in *The Raw and the Cooked* posits that food and technology are linked in the delineation of the social realm: "Food presents itself to man in three main states: it may be raw, cooked or rotten. . . . [T]he raw state constitutes the unmarked pole, whereas the other two are strongly marked, although in opposite directions: the cooked being a cultural transformation of the raw, and the rotten its natural transformation. Underlying the main triangle, there is, then, a double opposition between *processed/non-processed,* on the one hand, and *culture/nature,* on the other" (478). Further, "the boiled [can be placed] on the side of culture. Literally, since boiled food necessitates the use of a receptacle, which is a cultural object; and symbolically, in the sense that culture mediates between man and the world, and boiling is also a mediation, by means of water, between the

food which man ingests and that other element of the physical world: fire" (480).

19. See Mennell, 301–2.

20. See, for instance, Gilmour's *Idea of the Gentleman.*

21. See Gallagher's "Body versus the Social Body."

22. See Mennell, 55–57, for an extended discussion on nineteenth-century neochivalry.

23. "A good deal of Victorian romanticism lingers on in the popular view of the manorial community dining together in [the] hall . . . under the paternal eye of their lord" (Mennell, 57). Medieval feasts were "a means of asserting social rank and power . . . which [had] perhaps [become] more attractive and significant for the nobility as the process of internal pacification . . . progressively [limited] their opportunities to resort to warfare as a means of establishing their standing over their fellow noble subjects of the king" (58). The onrushing industrial age, with its diminished role for the country gentry, created a similar need for the gentleman to affirm his powerful position in the community.

24. Mr. Woodhouse's lack of real benevolence is clearly marked, for instance, on the occasion of Mr. Knightley's unexpected trip to London: "In the hope of diverting her father's thoughts from the disagreeableness of Mr. Knightley's going to London; and going so suddenly; and going on horseback, which she knew would be all very bad; Emma communicated her news of Jane Fairfax, and . . . it supplied a very useful check—interested without disturbing him. He had long made up his mind to Jane Fairfax's going out as a governess, and could talk of it cheerfully, but Mr. Knightley's going to London had been an unexpected blow" (387). Mr. Woodhouse's anxiety is clearly not directed toward the good of others here: his beneficence and care grow from his anxieties and fears, and he blithely ignores the real tragedies and struggles of those around him when they are removed from his special area of expertise.

25. See, for instance, Mennell, 26.

26. Cannadine notes that

> the interests of the English aristocracy were never limited to farms, fields and agriculture. However much they may have affected to despise trade, they were rarely averse to increasing their income from non-agricultural sources. . . . The participation of the English aristocracy in ventures as varied as docks and harbours, mines and markets, urban estates and East In-

diamen, canals, turnpikes and railways, is a platitude of English social history for all periods since the time of Elizabeth. Indeed, during the century from the 1780s . . . their involvement was greater than ever before. . . . [T]he East India Company and a host of similar trading ventures beckoned. . . . So, at one and the same time, the English landed classes were downwardly mobile, entrepreneurially adventurous, and also well integrated into the London money market. (*Lords and Landlords*, 30)

27. John Cordy Jeaffreson notes in his 1875 *A Book about the Table*,

A man should not be too thoughtful for his health when he is satisfying his hunger. "Everything agrees with you until it has disagreed with you," Abernethy remarked to the valetudinarian who troubled himself overmuch as to what he should eat, drink and avoid. The *malade imaginaire*, who creates dyspepsia for himself out of nervous fancies about his food, should take the surgeon's counsel to heart. Whilst dishes are usually wholesome to the eater who takes their wholesomeness for granted, the best fare is apt to avenge itself on the man who regards it with suspicion. Enjoyment is impossible at the dinner-table without proper confidence in the caterer and cook; and the man with a mischievous habit of mistrusting them has travelled some way on the road that leads to the hell of hypochondria and ends in madness. Of all the monomaniacs, there are none more truly pitiable than the few wretched people who sniff poison in every culinary savour, and fear death from a sauce. (107–8)

28. Mr. Elton is fundamentally lacking in discernment. Roland Barthes writes of Brillat-Savarin's notion of fine dining that "it is *discernment* which allows one to make a fine distinction between Good and Bad; there exists a casuistry of taste: taste must always be on the alert, practicing subtlety and meticulousness" (66).

29. Joseph Litvak, in *Strange Gourmets*, takes up the issue of the indiscriminate eater in Austen's work. Discussing slimness and gluttony in *Pride and Prejudice*, Litvak argues that "moral superiority" adheres to control over one's appetites, in contrast to characters who "betray both an excessive appetite and an inability or an unwillingness to control it." Such characters, "[r]educed—or, rather, expanded—to comic types . . . paradoxically, can never really 'grow': they can only repeat themselves" (23). Though Mr. Elton is not portrayed as an outright

glutton, he certainly evinces a less-than-refined interest in the pleasures of the table, and his character is accordingly stunted, as though he is caught in some infantile stage of stupid desire and lack of control over the body and its whims.

30. His wife is no better than Mr. Elton: "Every body . . . was disposed to pay [Mr. Elton] attention on his marriage. Dinner-parties and evening-parties were made for him and his lady; and invitations flowed in so fast that she had soon the pleasure of apprehending they were never to have a disengaged day. 'I see how it is,' said she. . . . 'We really seem quite the fashion.' . . . No invitation came amiss to her. Her Bath habits made evening-parties perfectly natural to her, and Maple Grove had given her a taste for dinners" (290).

31. Harriet, of course, is the other problematic eater here: she threatens to take Emma's place at the side of Mr. Knightley.

32. In Julia Kristeva's terms (esp. 3–4), Mr. Woodhouse is the putrefying corpse that refuses either to revive itself as a living being or to melt away decently into a safely buried body.

33. See Elias's *History of Manners: The Civilizing Process*, vol. 1.

CHAPTER 2

1. Alisa M. Clapp, for instance, argues that *Tenant* "is an astonishingly feminist novel, with few counterparts in nineteenth-century literature" (113–14). Elizabeth Langland concurs: "*The Tenant of Wildfell Hall* rewrites the story of the Fallen Woman as a story of female excellence. In so doing, it takes on a radical feminist dimension" (119). Elizabeth Hollis Berry writes that "Brontë . . . recognized the personal diary as a potentially subversive expression of women's experience, its forbidden authority offering the sole outlet for those imprisoned by repressive social structures. . . . Brontë unerringly grasped the radical implications of allowing her heroine to speak for herself within the thoughtful confines of the written page" (72).

2. Arthur Huntingdon is "[t]he centre of the novel—the structural pivot of the main story, the moving power of the plot . . . the nadir of self-indulgence, [he] decrees the rest of the characters and events" (Craik, 38).

3. The young and innocent Helen, smitten with the dashing Mr. Huntingdon, seems to believe at first that Arthur drinks simply because he has never learned to refrain from indulging himself in any way that he pleases, as a result of his bad upbringing by "a bad, selfish, miserly father, who . . . restricted him in the most innocent enjoyments of child-

hood and youth, and so disgusted him with every kind of restraint;—and a foolish mother who indulged him to the top of his bent . . . doing her utmost to encourage . . . germs of folly and vice" (190–91). Helen believes that marriage will cure him—more specifically, that, as the domestic angel she will be, "his wife shall undo what his mother did" (191). But her faith in her own zeal is soon shown to be misplaced: blood is certainly stronger than water, or circumstance, or even love here.

4. See, for instance, Annette Federico's reading of Huntingdon's drinking as evidence of his "modern" existential nature: "His moodiness represents his moral restlessness, as well as the fluidity of human psychology and the dangerous depths of personality. . . . Brontë emphasizes her character's radical and monstrous duality. Attention is repeatedly given to the fact that Huntingdon has fundamentally, spiritually changed, that he is able to 'call evil good, and good evil.' . . . [H]is addiction is an aspect of his general lassitude, of a weariness of life and a terror of death which emerges suddenly and startlingly when he receives a fatal injury" (19). She adds, "Far from being just a vicious habit, his alcoholism has been his means of coping with a universe empty of meaning, an extension of his own moral despair" (20).

5. The novel's preoccupation with drink and its attendant horrors is not altogether surprising, given its author's background. The novel is not simply an imagining of the evils of drink: the sin she chooses to witness is particularly well known to her. As many commentators have noted, the famous story of Branwell Brontë's descent into drink took a powerful hold over his sisters—particularly Anne. In her case, these events took on religious significance: she was a great supporter of the Low Church, a follower of John Wesley's dictates, and a reader of *Methodist* magazine; all of these institutions were deeply opposed to drink and drunkenness. Her sense of Christian duty in undertaking her story is made manifest in the foreword to the second edition, in which, writing in the persona of Acton Bell, she declares that she seeks to warn young people away from the wrongs she depicts, adding, "[W]hen I feel it my duty to speak an unpalatable truth, with the help of God, I *will* speak it, though it be to the prejudice of my name and to the detriment of my reader's immediate pleasure as well as my own" (30). But Huntingdon is not simply an embodiment of Branwell Brontë, and the biographical explanation for the character's drinking is not particularly satisfying. Branwell was hardly a man of power and wealth, and the novel travels far beyond the biographical in its scope, its concerns, and its implications, taking up issues and questions that resonate in a larger sociocultural sense.

6. In *Drink and the Victorians,* Brian Harrison notes that "the word alcoholism . . . appeared only about 1860. . . . Not till the 1860s and 1870s did American experiments convince Englishmen that habitual drunkards required voluntary or compulsory asylum treatment, and that alcoholism was, as Chamberlain argued in 1877, 'more a disease than a crime'" (22–23).

7. Gin, the scourge of the working-class drinker, was the lowest and most debased of nineteenth-century alcoholic drinks. The term referred generically to a range of hard alcohols, including the drink presently known as gin, usually taken in shots. Gin was a cheap, fast intoxicant, consumed for no reason other than to get drunk. It was widely regarded as a destroyer of community pub life, a drink considerably worse for the social body than any other (see, for instance, Harrison, 69; see also chapter 5).

8. . . . as did brewers, who opposed spirits on economic grounds and used the temperance movement as a convenient political lobby.

9. Harrison makes this point: "[T]he propaganda of early anti-spirits societies explicitly sought to confirm the higher ranks in their superior station now threatened by the progress of mass education; their social position would be secure only if they took the lead in morally reforming their social inferiors" (115).

10. For a more thorough discussion of this topic, see Cannadine, *Decline,* esp. 37–39.

11. Frederic Lawrence, Helen's landlord and supposed paramour (in fact, he is her brother), is one version of this superannuated gentleman. He is, Gilbert tells us,

> gentlemanly and inoffensive to all. . . . Essentially of reserved habits, and but seldom quitting the secluded place of his birth, where he . . . lived in solitary state[,] . . . he had neither the opportunity nor the inclination for forming many acquaintances. . . . [H]e was . . . cold, and shy, and self-contained . . . [with] excessive reserve upon all his own concerns . . . originat[ing] . . . in a certain morbid feeling of delicacy, and a peculiar diffidence, that he was sensible of, but wanted energy to overcome. His heart was like a sensitive plant, that opens for a moment in the sunshine, but curls up and shrinks into itself at the slightest touch of the finger, or the lightest breath of wind. . . . Mr. Lawrence was like a new garment, all very neat and trim to look at, but so tight in the elbows that you would fear to split the seams by the unrestricted motion

of your arms, and so smooth and fine in surface that you scruple to expose it to a single drop of rain. (61–62)

Lawrence is the gentleman as disappearing act: quiet, polite, and reserved. Gentlemanly in the nostalgic, chivalric sense but without the knight-errant bravery to go with it, he is fading away, as outdated as the crumbling ancestral hall he leases to Helen. Unable to summon the energy and fire necessary to the striver era, he is reduced to just another sipper of wine at Mrs. Markham's table, desired for his nominal status only by social climbers like Jane Wilson.

12. These are also the behaviors that the middle classes most feared as disruptive to the social order: "The bourgeois ideal enshrined a highly articulated body with all its parts functioning in harmony, controlled by the 'higher' faculties of reason, 'taste,' refinement, spirit, and, by analogy, the 'higher' authorities and social classes, especially the bourgeoisie itself. . . . What would occur if the 'higher' faculties were overwhelmed by the 'lower'? . . . [T]he result would be a grotesque body driven by base desires and impure appetites" (Kasson, *Rudeness*, 195). This could have dire consequences for the new social order that the middle class sought to build, because, as Marianna Adler writes, referencing Jean Baudrillard, "[T]he political economy of consumption entails the creation of specific subjects with needs appropriate for the reproduction of the generalized form of capitalist political economy" (389).

13. See chapter 1.

14. Appropriate eating advances the pursuit of gentlemanliness by demonstrating gender, as well: rich foods, strong flavors, many meats, and a variety of alcoholic beverages had long been considered incompatible with femininity (Lupton, 109–10; also see chapter 1). By eating widely and well at table, Arthur distances himself from the feminization with which his leisure, like Helen's list of projects, threatens him.

15. See Gilmour.

16. See Kasson, *Rudeness*, 118–19. Elias's work in *The Civilizing Process* also draws on and reaffirms this notion; see esp. xii–xiii.

17. Of Huntingdon's understanding of his gendered role, Lydia Shires writes that "to be a man is equated with an imperious will, 'spirit,' and disdain for those qualities associated with women: piety, abstinence, selflessness, and dependence" (161). Similarly, Brontë's novel is judged to engage with the issue of "what happens to a marriage and to the innocent partner when one partner (specifically, the male) leads a solipsistic life, where personal pleasures are seen as deserved,

where maleness and the role of husband is tied to the freedom to do as one wants" (Jackson, 203).

18. As Cadogan writes,

> the greatest ascescent [sic], or rather bane of all . . . whoever they are that take it constantly, is wine: wine alone produces more diseases than all the other causes put together. All men allow that wine taken to excess is hurtful. . . . And though it be often taken with a view to promote digestion and assist the operations of the stomach, it manifestly does harm to both. Instead of digesting and dissolving, it hardens, and prevents dissolution, and curdles and corrupts the milky chyle and first juices produced from our food. It warms indeed and stimulates the stomach to greater exertion than is natural or necessary, and thereby enables it to discharge it's [sic] contents the sooner; whence that agreeable feeling of warmth and comfort from it's [sic] immediate action. But by this extraordinary action it forces our food out of the stomach too soon, before it is softened, dissolved, and properly prepared, and sends it into the bowels crude, hard, and austere, in that state to be carried into the blood, there to produce every kind of disease. (65–66)

19. For more on the shape of productive versus unproductive bodies and theories of burning off what is taken in, see Gallagher.

20. Helen's uncle demonstrates both the longstanding tradition of gentlemanly excess and the absorption of that excess into the body of the useful socially, economically, and politically integrated gent. He was, as he tells Helen, "a sad wild fellow . . . when he was young"; the phrase, Helen's aunt says, "means destitute of principle, and prone to every vice that is common to youth" (153). His gout is a subject of remark from the beginning of Helen's narrative, appearing on the first page of her story as a "slight attack" (148). In London, his gout reasserts itself and intensifies: the illness "had been gradually increasing upon him ever since we came to town," Helen explains, and by this time it has caused him to retain a physician, who joins his wife in urging him to leave town—the seat, presumably, of everything that feeds and inflames the disease. Tellingly, Helen's uncle lives to a reasonable old age before succumbing to the fruits of his "sad wild" career. An old-fashioned member of the last useful generation of gentlemen, he seems to have burned off the effects of his excess for many years through attention to his estate and his finances; only in the last years of his life,

in the age of the useless gentleman, does he fall prey to the gout that kills him.

21. Sarah Freeman notes that "what people drank was strictly limited by circumstance, i.e. class and place. In England, the basic lower-class drinks were beer, ale (which was not hopped), and gin. . . . The upper and middle classes confined themselves chiefly to wine and imported brandy. . . . [A]s they had become accustomed to it at school, men quite often favoured beer, but never gin, which had disreputable associations ever since it was first introduced into this country" (97). For a discussion of the perceived obscenity and danger of the poor body without orderly employment, see Gallagher.

22. See Shiman, 20–22.

23. There were two types of pledges: short and long. The short pledge required abstinence from most drink except in cases of medicinal requirement and, in line with the moderate temperance movement, permitted some beer and wine drinking; the long pledge allowed no drinking at all and was the hallmark of the hard-line teetotalers (Shiman, 21).

24. See Kristeva, 4.

CHAPTER 3

1. See chapter 2 for further discussion of the effects of coffee on the construction of the middle-class industrial body.

2. Invalid food was generally the softest, most easily digested, well-cooked, and flavorless fare (see chapter 1). Note, for instance, the recommended dishes for invalids in Miss E. Briggs's School Board for London Cookery Book and General Axioms for Plain Cookery: she suggests gruel (37), steamed fish with butter ("[a] sprinkling of lemon juice is a great improvement, when the invalid can take it" [55]); an "Invalid's Jelly" (55) composed of gelatin, sugar rubbed with citrus, and egg; arrowroot (arrowroot mixed with boiling water or milk, salt, and sugar and boiled thoroughly); and rice water (rice is stewed for three or four hours and strained, after which the invalid drinks the strained water, perhaps flavored with orange or lemon juice and sugar if his or her stomach is particularly strong) (56). The recovering invalid who needs building up rather than intense caregiving might try beef tea, in which beef is left to stand in cold water for an hour, then brought to a boil within another dish of cold water and simmered for another hour. The resulting liquid is loosely strained and skimmed to remove fat: "Foods for invalids should never be greasy" (Briggs, 34).

Meats and strong liquors were to be avoided, as they were believed to have an inflaming effect; any food with a hard surface was thought to damage the inner organs; and rich foods were to be avoided at all costs. Mrs. Clennam's invalid meals hardly seem to fit the bill: they are rich, inflaming, and hard-surfaced. But all of this, of course, is more easily assimilated than the fare Flintwinch accuses her of craving: "[Y]ou wanted to swallow up everybody alive," he declares (850–51).

3. For a discussion of Amy Dorrit's own refusal to eat at this feast, see Houston, *Consuming Fictions*, 144–46.

4. Robin Gilmour, writing of "the powerful link between the idea of liberal education and the gentlemanly ideal" (97), summarizes the Victorian bias against real-world preparation that created scores of Dorrit-like gentlemen: "[A] study of the classics familiarized a man with the cultural achievements, social, political, legal, literary, philosophical, of the most highly developed civilisations of antiquity; it not only offered access to a still-relevant body of inherited wisdom, but also freed the mind . . . to range beyond the narrowly technical and utilitarian to contemplate the complex interrelationships of civilisation itself. It was thus an education for . . . leadership. . . . Training was for the professionals who would do the ordinary business of society, liberal education was for the gentleman amateurs who would govern it" (97). Dorrit's education, his musical training, his fluency in many languages, and indeed all of his accomplishments are evidence that this man has no business running a business; thus, he must de facto be destined for gentlemanliness. According to Gilmour, not until the last two decades of the century did people begin to become aware of the folly of bringing up the sons of merchants as gentlemen: a generation or so of leaders had been lost, not formed. Gilmour observes that "in the long run British society . . . paid a heavy price to have the sons of its entrepreneurs educated alongside the traditional elite, for it meant the alienation of the new men from the business, and particularly the technology, necessary for the continued advance of an industrial civilisation. . . . The sons of the trading classes were taught by the system to despise the origins of their parents' wealth, and they learnt little to equip them for the modern world" (96).

5. Dorrit, like Rigaud (and like Mrs. Clennam), prefers to dine on dainties: witness, later in the novel, the feast of tea cakes, fresh butter, eggs, ham, and shrimp that he hosts with Clennam's money (423), a tableful of little luxuries made more luxurious by their perishable nature in the summer heat of the prison. Like Rigaud, he seeks out the finest fare as a marker of his rank.

6. Barbara Weiss notes that when "Dickens was engaged in the writing of *Little Dorrit*, an epidemic of sordid financial scandals seemed to be shaking the confidence of the public" (67). "To a public outraged by each new revelation of dishonesty, it must have seemed as if mercantile life in the mid-Victorian years had been overwhelmed with a corruption which threatened to poison the moral life of the whole community" (Weiss, 71).

7. On Victorian affection for the feudal image of the lord of the manor at the head of the table, with his loyal subjects ranged around him, see Mennell, 57; on the romance of a nostalgic feudal past and the growth of neofeudalism in Victorian England, particularly at mid-century, see Mennell, 116; see also chapter 1 for a discussion of the issue of the nostalgic feudal ideal.

8. Of this scene, Jeff Nunokawa has written that "[t]he proprietor appears to consume nothing that lies outside the confines of his estate, instead relying on his own excretions. This mirage operates to render Casby's acquisition covert even when he dines at home" (24).

9. Gail Houston's reading of this scene in *Consuming Fictions* takes up the most common view of Casby: that he is the emblem of a closed system of capitalism, in which, as Houston puts it, aliment and excrement are one.

10. For a discussion of the implications of benevolence, see Dvorak.

11. On the role of sugar in nineteenth-century England, see Mintz, esp. 120–30.

12. In this sense, Casby is evocative of Judith Halberstam's all-consuming monsters, wrought from the charnel house of the social (16–23).

13. Gail Houston writes extensively of the role of the anorexic girl in Dickens's fiction (see, for instance, *Consuming Fictions*, 139–40). Clennam in many ways fits into this paradigm, as he starves himself, sacrificing his own body while he feeds others around him. But gender is a crucial difference here: I argue that Clennam seeks not self-control and empowerment through his self-starvation, as the anorexic girl does, but rather the complete elision of the self. Further, as Deborah Lupton notes, "[m]ost people experience [the] ontological split between the 'self' and the 'body,' particularly when they are ill or in pain. But where anorexics differ is in their need to isolate the self from the body, in a certain fear and anxiety about the hold the body has over the self" (134–35). Arthur again fails to fit into this paradigm: he is not anxious to separate the body from the self but instead seeks to obliterate the self through obliteration of the body.

14. "The rigors of Clennam's childhood repression create in his imagination the sense of an indefinable guilt and an abiding sense of personal responsibility that are the foundations of his moral being" (Holoch, 337).

15. Indeed, Mr. Merdle seems to be physically absent from his own clothing on more than one occasion, as when he shakes Fanny's hand on parting from her, with her penknife, on his last evening among the living: "The illustrious visitor . . . put out his coat-cuff, and for a moment entombed Mrs Sparkler's hand: wrist, bracelet, and all. Where his own hand had shrunk to, was not made manifest, but it was as remote from Mrs Sparkler's sense of touch as if he had been a highly meritorious Chelsea Veteran or Greenwich Pensioner" (767).

16. It is telling that on the evening of his suicide, Merdle skips dinner and drinks a bottle of wine alone at his club: alcohol is a liminal food, and "[i]ts consumption signals escape from the 'civilized' body into self-indulgence and physical and emotional release" (Lupton, 31–32). At this moment, the man who can swallow nothing but greed turns entirely from the social, spurning society (and Society) in favor of a complete turn inward. See chapter 2 for more on the valences of alcohol.

17. In *Consuming Fictions*, Gail Houston reads Merdle's body as filled with excrement, and she aligns excrement with money in a capitalist system, asserting that capitalists "[confuse] . . . the alimental with the excremental" (134). Referring to the denizens of Bleeding Heart Yard who invoke the great man's name, she writes, "In this Dickensian image, confusing aliment with excrement, all the would-be capitalists have Merdle in their mouths" (135). While I agree that the Merdle diet is decidedly unnutritious, I contend that Merdle is not stuffed full of money; rather, he feeds on greed, giving up the cash as soon as it comes in. The Bleeding Hearts, like the most grasping members of Society, feed on this vampirelike creature. No wonder they are poisoned: what they imbibe is the worst and most antisocial part of themselves.

18. *Little Dorrit* was first published in serial form in 1857, and the novel is set, as its opening words put it, "[t]hirty years ago" (39)—that is, in 1827. Though the Oxford Movement essentially came to an end in 1845, when J. H. Newman embraced Catholicism, its beliefs lingered in several High Church sects through the middle decades of the century.

19. Martin Meisel reads Little Dorrit as a "daughter-mother [who] has figuratively given [Clennam] her loving breast." He writes that

"[i]n recreating the configuration [of the Roman Daughter story], Little Dorrit and Clennam have achieved a point of fulfillment and rest, a perfect union, and in the most important sense Clennam has already been given his release. . . . [T]he capacity for adult union has been achieved by a redeeming recapitulation of the heart, repairing an original starvation of the senses and affections that left the grown Arthur Clennam with the miserable sense of his own impotence, deprivation, unspecified guilt, and paralysis of the will" (314).

20. This is slightly different from, though certainly related to, Jeff Nunokawa's formulation regarding the circulation of property: "The novel literalizes and intensifies the iron law of equivalent exchange that governs the marketplace, generally, according to most accounts of it: in Dickens's novel, the acquisition of property does not merely require payment; such payment must consist of the very property acquired in the first place. Thus, when property is acquired in *Little Dorrit*, it must be relinquished" (20–21).

21. The novel opens in the "burning" wastes of mid-1820s Marseilles, a place of deserted streets under a "fervid" sun, in which "[e]verything that lived or grew, was oppressed by the glare" (40). In these opening moments, the town seems to have entered some purgatory beyond the reach of human desires, bodily or otherwise. The opposite of that dreamed-of decadent foreign port where all appetites may be supplied, Marseilles is "a fact to be strongly smelled and tasted" as it lies "broiling in the sun" (39). Parched, overcooked, it feels (not to put too fine a point on it) too hot to eat.

22. See, for instance, Philpotts, 273; Holoch, 336; and Herst, 90–91.

CHAPTER 4

1. Though many critics of the day—as well as a legion of later writers—were appalled by Dexter, it is not clear that ordinary Victorian readers were terribly shocked by Collins's creature. As Nuell Pharr Davis ruefully notes, "When [the novel] was published in June of 1875 some of the newspapers denounced its bizarre extravagance and some wearily called it 'just Wilkie Collins.' It sold very well and was immediately translated into French, German, Italian, Russian, and Dutch" (282). The later critical reception of Dexter has not been particularly warm. Widely ignored in contemporary critical discourse, Dexter bears the dubious distinction of being misunderstood where he is not neglected. Some critics, while acknowledging him to be the most compelling character in the novel, have nevertheless dismissed him as a

lecherous freak; they bemoan Collins's apparent compulsion to create such a horrible creature, blaming his seemingly bizarre sense of aesthetics, his desire to generate buzz through shock value, or his inability to read the effects of his own overheated imagination. Julian Symons, for instance, dismisses Dexter as "one of [Collins's] more unsuccessful grotesques, [a] self-styled poet . . . a sort of legless Quilp" (49). Pharr Davis complains that "[t]o appreciate [the novel] . . . one must have sympathies that extend to a legless, lustful lunatic in a wheelchair" (282). And Gavin Lambert neatly dismisses Dexter as "a dime novel maniac[,] . . . the legless poet lurching and plotting in his wheelchair, crazed with impotent lust" (29).

2. See chapter 2 for a discussion of Arthur Huntingdon's troubled and troubling relationship to the aliment that marks his gentlemanly status even as it inevitably leads to his fatal degeneration. For a discussion of degeneration, see Taylor, "Introduction," xiv.

3. For a discussion of masculine versus feminine foods, see Lupton, 31.

4. Kathleen O'Fallon writes that "Dexter appears to be the androgynous figure of [Collins's] earlier novels taken to its maddest extreme" (237), and she claims that "Collins uses his androgynous villain in this novel to parody the traditional power structure of the male-female relationship" (238). Sue Lonoff calls Dexter a figure of Freudian libidinal energy, "a wayward child who has never had to curb his impulses" (166).

5. For a discussion of the rise of tea as a midafternoon collation, see Freeman, 183-84.

6. See Mary Douglas, "Deciphering a Meal," esp. 66-69.

7. See Pollard, esp. 235-80; see also McCloskey, 94-111; Aldcroft, 111-15; Crafts, 126-31; Capie et al., 251-84; and Tames, 123-25.

8. See, for instance, Cannadine, *Decline*, 35-222; Tames, 15-25, 47-68; and Pollard, 227-56.

9. See, for instance, *Little Dorrit*; Lord Vane in *East Lynne*; and, of course, that famous depraved gentleman, Dracula.

10. The effect is not merely further displacement of this apparently out-of-place creature: by defining himself as "melancholy," the "poor cripple" moves himself into language, transforming his body from a locus of overwrought overdetermination into a subject for serious, rational study, for a preoccupation leading the thinker to despair over his place in the world. This discourse is very specifically classed and gendered—melancholy is a noble disease of the mind specifically associated with educated men, who, unlike their counterparts of the weaker sex, are capable of the sort of overanalytical, obsessive rationality that

leads to despair. On this subject, I am indebted to Elizabeth Dolan's paper, "Rationality, Sensibility and Genius: Romantic Woman Poets and the Melancholy Body."

11. This is not an unimaginable process in the late nineteenth century, as David Cannadine discusses in *Lords and Landlords*, though certainly the upper class limited its imagined alliances to the middle class: "Embourgeoisement was not a process limited to certain groups within the working class. Many of the aristocracy succumbed with equal commitment to this new and essentially urban idea. In the triumph of the creed of 'Godliness and Good Learning,' the counting house vanquished the country house as the arbiter of morality" (29). Cannadine notes that "at one and the same time, the English landed classes were downwardly mobile, entrepreneurially adventurous, and also well integrated into the London money market" (30).

12. Dexter-the-cook and his tidy little kitchen also point toward the mix of old and new, of the modern and the traditional, that Dexter encompasses. His drink is served up in "ancient" goblets; his wine is appropriately rich with age; and his fare is densely luxurious, evoking the old-fashioned world of the gentleman of leisure. But Dexter cooks up "the new vegetable" (as Valeria calls the truffle [248]) for his guest, and he does so using that most contemporary of inventions, "a neat little gas stove" (245). As Reay Tannahill observes, "The solid-fuel iron range came into general use in middle-class homes in the 1860s, and the gas version twenty years later. (Gas ovens had in fact been used in the Reform Club as early as the 1830s, but people remained suspicious of gas, especially of its smell, for some time.)" (322). In this sense, Dexter is an intrepid pioneer, unafraid to take on the volatile new machines—secure, as he is, in his knowledge of himself as an equally volatile, equally modern, and equally "boiling" piece of industrial equipment.

Even Dexter's indulgence in women's work fails to inscribe him as a man who lacks. His embroidery (235–36), his cooking, and his peculiarly colorful clothes and showy jewelry (232) only enhance his unsettling power: Dexter seems a creature who can shift between identities as he sees fit, making use of the tropes of femininity while never lessening his overwhelming sense of his own maleness. He seems, indeed, to move beyond the limits of gendered behavior, refusing such limits not as a sort of nineteenth-century gender pioneer but as an adaptive creature who is able to make use of whatever comes to hand to advance his own interest. Seated in his chair with the pretty little workbasket on the arm, he is the lady made uncanny; busily working in his kitchen, transforming the lumps that are truffles into an unnerving repast, surrounded by his collected "horrors" (247), he is a wicked witch preparing a questionable feast. He seems to encompass femaleness in his very virility, using feminine behaviors by turns to calm his rages and ardors and to accent the breadth of his strange, unmistakable power. In fact, Dexter becomes more threatening and more fascinating precisely because he can indulge in embroidery without losing any of his authority. Similarly, his participation in the distinctly servile, often feminized act of cooking serves not to lessen his power but, rather, to accentuate his upper-class status: his freedom to play-act in this way demonstrates that he is above the class concerns and petty strivings of the bourgeoisie.

13. See Rozin and Fallon, 27.

14. As Maggie Kilgour writes of Stoker's later model, "Vampirism is the gothic definition of symbiosis and communion. . . . Dracula . . . consumes others by offering himself to them; the reciprocity of exchange is thus shown to be an illusion, for he is an alien who possesses those who have let him into their bodies" (173).

15. On her second visit to Dexter, Valeria finds the legless gentleman dressed with "inveterate oddity": "His jacket . . . was of pink quilted silk. The coverlid which hid his deformity matched the jacket in pale sea-green satin. . . . [H]is wrists were actually adorned with massive bracelets of gold, formed on the severely-simple models which have descended to us from ancient times!" (232). Dexter explains, "I have dressed, expressly to receive you, in the prettiest clothes I have. . . . I like to be bright and beautiful" (232).

16. See chapter 3 for a discussion of the disinterested gentleman in reference to Arthur Clennam.

17. Judith Halberstam, in *Skin Shows*, argues that the power of Gothic monstrosity lies precisely in this ability to attain proximity to the normative, the domestic: "The monster . . . will find you in the intimacy of your own home; indeed, it will make your home its home (or you its home) and alter forever the comfort of domestic privacy. The monster peeps through the window, enters through the back door, and sits beside you in the parlor; the monster is always invited in but never asked to stay. . . . The figure of the parasite becomes paramount within Gothic precisely because it is an internal not an external danger that Gothic identifies and attempts to dispel" (15). For Halberstam, in other words, the danger of the monster is that he is both familiar and not-so, both proximate and foreign, and this shape-shifting ability al-

lows the monster to penetrate the boundaries of the protected sphere of the domestic.

18. For a discussion of the role of the knife in the competition for food and the subsequent development of table rituals, see Visser. For gentlemanly hunger, see chapter 3.

19. Freeman notes that in England, "attempts had been made to cultivate truffles . . . [and] a white variety known as 'summer' truffles were found in the woods . . . [but] English truffles were not usually bought and sold. . . . [B]lack French ones . . . [were] extremely dear" but were imported in large numbers to satisfy the appetites of the rich (73).

20. Major Fitz-David's latest "Queen of Song," Miss Hoighty, similarly refuses to be fed upon, and the effects on the Major are similarly dire. She makes it abundantly clear to Valeria that she is only interested in the Major's money: "Not that I care . . . about the old fool. But I've lost my situation at the railway," she confides, "and I've got my own interests to look after, and I don't know what may happen if I let other women come between him and me" (91). Miss Hoighty, then, is feeding not on the Major's dainties but on the Major himself: she seeks to swallow him whole and thus to remake herself by taking on his position and, more important, his money. The gentleman's role as devourer is supplanted by this forthright gold digger. The transformation of the Major is striking:

> The ordeal of marriage had so changed my gay and gallant admirer of former times, that I hardly knew him again. He had lost all his pretensions to youth; he had become, hopelessly and undisguisedly, an old man. Standing behind the chair on which his imperious young wife sat enthroned, he looked at her submissively between every two words that he addressed to me, as if he waited for her permission to open his lips and speak. Whenever she interrupted him . . . he submitted with a senile docility and admiration, at once absurd and shocking to see. (408)

The Major's quality control over his food, it seems, has deteriorated significantly. What he swallows when he devours Miss Hoighty is precisely the sort of fare that his ladylike diet is meant to avoid: she is the picture of coarse pragmatism, of businesslike transactions, of the hard world outside of the Major's soft little nest. She operates on need, not on desire; what she needs from the Major is monetary sustenance, not chivalrous speeches. She is a distinctly unedifying meal, the round-eyed Queen of Song; and her refusal to swallow his narrative whole has brought an abrupt end to his magical cannibalistic meals: he has poisoned himself.

21. For a discussion of the gentlemanly valences of wine, see chapter 2.

CHAPTER 5

1. Indeed, Utterson's narrative function here appears of a piece with his willingness to tolerate and support "down-going men." His notion of allowing such men to "go to the devil" seems to contradict his apparently religious austerity, but it is of a piece with both his character and his profession: as a lawyer, Utterson's work is not to "reprove" or to improve or to create or destroy. He is only a repository of tales and secrets, a safe space in which stories can be hidden away as safely and easily as Dr. Jekyll's extraordinary will (written in "holograph, for Mr. Utterson . . . had refused to lend the least assistance in the making of it" [12], since "[i]t offended him both as a lawyer and as a lover of the sane and customary sides of life, to whom the fanciful was immodest" [13], though as a professional, "he took charge of it now that it was made" [12]).

2. This view, most famously taken up by Elaine Showalter in *Sexual Anarchy* (110), has been built upon by commentators working specifically on issues of gentlemanliness or of drink in the novella. Karen Volland Waters, for instance, calls Utterson "a man who is so controlled that he seems to be a parody of Victorian gentlemanly control," explaining, "Utterson represses tendencies toward pleasure by being 'austere with himself': he drinks gin rather than the fine wines which he prefers and he denies himself the pleasure of attending the theater" (105). Lisa Butler, in her examination of *Dr. Jekyll and Mr. Hyde* as an exploration of the anxieties of degeneration as taken up by the temperance movement, sees Utterson as "a man whose surface control hides the reality of a sensuality coded dangerous intemperate. . . . Utterson's vital energy . . . released by wine, is . . . imagined in terms of an inner light . . . that shines through his customary shroud of self-control" (25). "Utterson's extreme temperance," she writes later, "seems to mask the illicit and excessive elements of his character" (27). Yet she reaffirms that repression of appetites is what Utterson's gin drinking is all about: "Lurking underneath [the] veneer of self-control . . . is a definite sense of sensual energy not always successfully repressed. . . .

Stevenson's representation of Utterson as 'austere' and 'undemonstrative' is undercut by numerous tantalizing contradictions: Utterson might consume gin to 'mortify a taste for vintages,' for instance, but this strategy clearly fails him on some level, as he is deemed by the narrator to be . . . a 'judge[] of good wine'" (24).

3. The movement was, as Marianna Adler notes, a socially useful tool for the middle class, providing "a moral platform legitimating the demand for security of property, a disciplined labor force, and an expanded home market" (386). See chapter 2 for more on this subject.

4. Sundays were of particular importance to radical teetotalers in particular. As Norman Longmate details in *The Water-Drinkers*, leaders in the movement fought for years against the serving of Sunday drink, in the face of protest and full-fledged riots on the part of working-class men and women who, not surprisingly, were passionately and sometimes violently opposed to the loss of the pub on their one weekly day of leisure (164). The teetotal cause was continually hampered by the fact that drinking in private gentlemen's clubs continued to be legal under every proposed and enacted piece of Sunday-closing legislation across Great Britain, reinforcing the divide between working men who drank and gentlemanly imbibers.

5. Interestingly, the failure of barriers to the business world in the domestic realm is the opposite of the failure of barriers that Dickens writes into *David Copperfield*, in which the lawyer Traddles lives with his new bride, Sophy, and her six sisters in his rooms at Gray's Inn, hiding the women (and the tea things) away in a back room when a client comes calling: "[O]ur domestic arrangements are, to say the truth, quite unprofessional altogether," Traddles explains to Copperfield (804). For Dickens, the professional life is, for right-reasoning men, a means of achieving the longed-for end of modest prosperity, family, community, domesticity, and productive, right-reasoning involvement with the world; great wealth, as I explore in my discussion of *Little Dorrit* in chapter 3, is never healthy, nor is a life dedicated to the acquisition of wealth. (See also, for instance, Frank Nickleby in *Nicholas Nickleby* and, of course, Scrooge in *A Christmas Carol*.)

6. Mary Douglas argues in *Purity and Danger* that the autonomous self is defined and differentiated from the threatening, unbounded morass of the outside world through the creation of boundaries dividing the "clean" from the "dirty," the acceptable from the unacceptable. "[D]irt," she declares, is "matter out of place. . . . It implies . . . a set of ordered relations and a contravention of that order. . . . Dirt is the by-product of a systematic ordering and classification of matter, in so

far as ordering involves rejecting inappropriate elements. . . . [P]ollution behaviour is the reaction which condemns any object or idea likely to confuse or contradict cherished classifications" (36). On the notion of disgust in relation to dirt, see W. I. Miller's *Anatomy of Disgust* and Menninghaus's *Disgust*.

7. For a more thorough discussion of the role of the upper classes vis-à-vis the rising bourgeois professional class, see Cannadine, *Decline*, esp. 37–39.

8. On *Dr. Jekyll and Mr. Hyde* and temperance, see Reed; see also L. Butler.

9. The echoes of this form of drink in Jekyll's experience are apparent in the text, as Linda Dryden notes: "The location of Hyde's abode is seemingly a living hell surrounded by gin palaces, 'a low French eating-house,' ragged children and 'many women of many different nationalities passing out, key in hand, to have a morning glass'" (93–94).

10. See Gilman.

11. See Schivelbusch, 38.

12. Stevenson famously composed his novella in three days, then burnt the manuscript (in response to his wife's critique) and rewrote it in three days more. Daniel Wright and others have hypothesized, reasonably enough, that the chronically ailing author worked on *Dr. Jekyll and Mr. Hyde* not under the influence of the depressing opiates he had become accustomed to but, rather, with the help of cocaine. Myron G. Schultz explores the idea that Stevenson may have been under cocaine treatment for catarrh during the time he was writing his novella. Explaining that Fanny Stevenson often read medical journals hoping to find a cure for her husband's pressing physical ills, Schultz notes that "the use of a cocaine solution to be applied to the larynx was described in *Lancet*, in September 1885, about a month before Stevenson wrote *Jekyll and Hyde*" (94). The use of cocaine in "catarrh snuffs and nasal sprays" (Schultz, 93) was common in the mid-1880s, and given his physician's worries about Stevenson's risk of hemorrhage (a fragile patient, he was ordered to speak only in a whisper and to avoid all excitement), it is not unlikely that the author was acquainted, to paraphrase Thomas De Quincey, with the pleasures and pains of cocaine. Schultz argues that Stevenson's story "about a respectable physician . . . transformed into a diabolical creature by a powerful new drug" (92) draws directly on the author's cocaine experience. "[T]here is a striking parallelism between cocaine habituation and 'the business of the powders,'" Schultz asserts, adding, "There are

hardly more definitive transformations of personality than can be worked by cocaine."

13. Tales of its miraculous effects were legion: Karl Fredrich Philip von Martius, a South African explorer, for instance, retailed stories of Indians who "subsisted on only a few spoons of maize and water each day, and never complained, as long as they also had coca leaves to chew on" (Karch, 29).

14. The interest of nineteenth-century scientists and military planners across Europe and in America was piqued, in particular, by a monograph entitled *On the Hygienic and Medicinal Virtues of Coca*, published in in 1859 by an Italian doctor named Paolo Mantegazza. The monograph detailed Mantegazza's encounters with coca-chewing Indians in Argentina and his own subsequent, and extensive, first-hand experiments in chewing vast quantities of the leaves (Jay, 150). The medical community was less intrigued by Mantegazza's detailed and vivid stories of hallucinations (he chewed truly heroic quantities of the leaf in service to science) than by his accounts of vastly increased endurance and muscular strength and of his ability, when chewing coca, to go for long periods of time without food or sleep. Showy experiments soon abounded. One American investigator dosed a team of "lady racewalkers" with the stuff to see how it helped their performance, and another climbed mountains at top speed and with little sustenance well into his seventies, with the aid of the coca leaves tucked into his cheek. Another American, in an early performance-enhancing doping move, won an endurance racewalking competition in England with the help of coca leaves—much to the outrage of his hosts and the general public.

15. In late 1859, Niemann, a young German researcher, isolated a white, crystalline substance, which he named "cocaine." In 1860, Niemann published his dissertation, entitled (in English) *On a New Organic Base in the Coca Leaves*, detailing his methods and his discovery.

16. In 1863, a Corsican chemist living in Paris named Angelo Mariani began selling a tonic, a mixture of sweet Burgundy and coca leaves, called Vin Mariani. Its inventor was a master marketer, and his wine became hugely popular across Britain, Europe, and the United States as a general cure for any number of ills. The tonic spawned many imitators, the most famous of which, as Mike Jay notes, was Coca-Cola in the United States (a tonic that originally copied Mariani's blend but substituted cocaine for coca and later, in the face of an early bout of American prohibition, was reworked as a blend of cocaine, caffeine, and cola nut, which contains caffeinelike properties—

the Real Thing indeed). Mariani's testimonials from satisfied customers included paeans from presidents and popes, but doctors shunned it.

17. Niemann's method was difficult to reproduce, particularly given the unreliability of coca leaves, which often arrived overdried and inert after their long voyage (and frequently, in the grand tradition of British food adulteration, were not coca leaves at all); see Karch, 17. Doctors disagreed over whether there was anything to the stuff at all, with many concluding that the Indians who chewed coca leaves derived benefit chiefly from their primitive belief in the magic of the substance (and that Europeans who believed likewise had more or less gone native). Niemann died shortly after his breakthrough discovery, leaving his work without a champion.

18. Tim Madge notes, for instance, that "Frederick Schroff, in 1862, thought that cocaine's after-effects (in his case, a deep depression) more than outweighed its initial benefits of making a person feel cheerful, so much that he warned against any use of it at all" (2).

19. Though there was some scant evidence that cocaine was in fact addictive and could have negative consequences, the vast majority of reports on the white powder were overwhelmingly positive, tempered only by the occasional inefficacy of inert powder (a complaint that became less and less common as the big pharmaceutical companies stepped up production). As late as 1887, in "Craving for and Fear of Cocaine," Freud battled the perception that cocaine was dangerous, insisting that only those with a previous history of overuse of morphine were susceptible to the drug (though he conceded that the effects of the substance were so variable in different individuals that it was impossible to know when "cocaine poisoning" ["Craving," 173] occurred).

20. This essay is rarely cited by experts on Freud and is difficult to find: its English translation seems limited to a 1974 collection of essays by Freud on cocaine, Cocaine Papers, edited by Robert Byck and with essay introductions by Anna Freud. Byck posits that Freud's uncritical work on cocaine is an embarrassment to the psychoanalytic community, particularly given Freud's enthusiastic self-experimentation—common enough in the period, but seen, of course, as uncomfortably unscientific in the twentieth and twenty-first centuries.

21. The lecture was a great success and was published to much acclaim in the Medico-Chirurgische Centralblatt on August 7 of that year and abstracted in The Lancet soon after. It is reprinted in Byck's edition, Cocaine Papers.

22. Researchers like Justus von Liebig (the inventor of bouillon cubes) theorized that human exertion used up muscle mass and "wasted" the body and that dietary components existed that could restore the body to health in the face of such labor-driven wasting, if only they could be identified. Scientists were determined to find substances that could replace the materials they saw disappearing from the body. As Steven B. Karch notes, "von Liebig's theory of nutrition . . . had many adherents in the 1870s and 1880s. There was a general feeling, shared by physicians and their patients, that many ailments were the result of 'tissue wasting,' and that 'tissue wasting' occurred when certain vital, but uncharacterized, compounds were absent from the diet" (29). Referring to this same notion, Freud argues that although a cocaine diet could not be proved to nourish the body (laboratory animals subjected to such a diet by other experimenters had "succumbed to inanition just as soon [as]—perhaps even sooner . . . than those which had received no cocaine" ["Uber Coca," 69]), cocaine did seem effective at reducing human hunger, perhaps through the workings of the mind. "The excitation of nerve centers by cocaine," Freud concludes, "can have a favorable influence on the nourishment of the body afflicted by a consumptive condition, even though that influence might well not take the form of a slowing down of metabolism" ("Uber Coca," 69).

23. The nature of the elixir reinforces this notion of nostalgic longing for authenticity and place. Jekyll calls his white powder a "salt"— that is, a substance that may be food and chemical at the same time. Salt both brings out the flavor of food and preserves it, a telling set of abilities in light of the story of *Dr. Jekyll and Mr. Hyde*. The potion's salt certainly brings flavor out, allowing Hyde to shine forth; but it also "preserves" the gentleman on the shelf of the pantry of selfhood. The potion also evokes the patent medicine Vin Mariani—coca leaves and sweet Burgundy—which in turn brings together the gentlemanly self-indulgence of drink and the speedy new worlds of work, medicine, and the mechanization of the body.

24. See L. Butler. As Wright notes, *Dr. Jekyll and Mr. Hyde* is fraught with the language of habitual inebriation, literally and figuratively. Jekyll takes his first dose because, despite the risks, he cannot resist "the temptation" (50); his "new power," he recalls, "tempted me until I fell into slavery" (51). As control over the transformation passes out of his hands, he begins "to spy a danger that . . . the balance of [his] nature might be permanently overthrown, the power of voluntary change be forfeited" (55). He notes that he "had been obliged on

more than one occasion to double, and once, with infinite risk of death, to treble the amount" and that "whereas, in the beginning, the difficulty had been to throw off the body of Jekyll, it had of late, gradually but decidedly transferred itself to the other side" (55). Faced with the choice of a life as Jekyll or as Hyde, he "chose the better part and was found wanting in the strength to keep to it" (55). He is "tortured by throes and longings" (56). The idea of an involuntary physical and psychological enslavement to a drug, beyond the realm of will and control, was problematic to the medical profession, which had in the 1880s only recently begun to use the language of addiction and which continued to grapple with these unexpected side effects of its miracle cures, particularly in the case of cocaine. Doctors themselves struggled mightily—and publicly—with their own drugs.

25. This notion makes Hyde's trampling of the little girl read more clearly: she is nothing, she is less than nothing, because no one else can be anything to Hyde, who is complete in and of himself.

CHAPTER 6

1. See Gilman.

2. I have excluded Van Helsing from my discussion of gentlemanliness here because, it seems to me, the learned doctor is less a gentleman than a genteel superhero, an entirely different breed, and a rank foreigner to boot. I have, on the other hand, included Quincey Morris because although he is American, he is clearly of the same kind, so to speak, as Seward, Harker, and Arthur, and his gentlemanliness is never in question: as Lucy puts it, "[H]e is really well educated and has exquisite manners" (59).

3. Even Arthur Holmwood rejects his aristocratic naming ("No, no, not that, for God's sake!" he corrects Van Helsing [153] when Van Helsing would call him "Lord Godalming") to put his hand in, offering both his money and his pure, Arthurian heart to the cause. (It is interesting that he is revealed to be "an amateur fitter" [311], capable of restoring the injured launch as it travels upriver: here the aristocratic melding with the working man is put in service to the cause, just as the aristocrat uses his money and title to obtain goods and services in the battle against the vampire.)

4. As early as 1880, "[a] report on chloral produced by the Clinical Society of London . . . drew attention to the possibility of misuse" of the drug (Berridge and Edwards, 143). Dante Gabriel Rossetti spent the last years of his life as a chloral inebriate (dying in 1882); as Griffith

Edwards notes, in 1889, Norman Kerr, a pioneering activist on the study of addiction in late-Victorian England, began "reporting on cases he was beginning to encounter of 'chloral inebriety' . . . [and] warned of the dangers attached to the burgeoning prescription of sedatives and hypnotics he saw going on around him" (35).

5. It is not Mina who finds oblivion but Jonathan—no longer a gentlemanly protector of his wife, reduced to an unconscious body in the bed beside her as Dracula ravishes her.

6. Though injection had been practiced for centuries (albeit not with great success), medical historians tend to attribute the popularization of the modern hypodermic needle to Alexander Wood, who published papers on his successful experiments with injected morphia in neuralgia patients in 1855 and 1858 (Berridge and Griffiths, 139).

7. A process thought at first to obviate the risk of addiction, though of course the error of this notion was soon made apparent.

8. The state that the drug induces seems very much to mimic the effects of the vampire's bite. Under the influence, breathing slows, the pulse drops, and the body cools. This is made manifest in *Dracula* when Van Helsing injects Lucy with morphine as she lies in a vampire-induced swoon: as the drug takes effect, "[t]he faint seemed to merge subtly into the narcotic sleep" (119). His needle, too, of course, is evocative of the monster's fang, which injects the stuff of vampirism into its victim even as it draws the blood out.

9. De Quincey makes a point of speaking to his relatively lowly roots and, by inference, his striver's tale:

> [B]ecause I have had occasion incidentally to speak of various patrician friends, it must not be supposed that I have myself any pretensions to rank or high blood. I thank God that I have not:—I am the son of a plain English merchant, esteemed during his life for his great integrity . . . [who] left no more than about 30,000£ among seven different claimants. . . . These are my honours of descent; I have no others: and I have thanked God sincerely that I have not, because, in my judgment, a station which raises a man too eminently above the level of his fellow-creaturs is not the most favourable to moral, or to intellectual qualities. (35–36)

A legacy of £4,000 or so, of course, was nothing to sneeze at: De Quincey was hardly a man facing starvation, though he was certainly not rich. In this way, he is typical of our gentlemen here.

10. Perhaps England's most famous user of opium before De Quincey was the young writer's idol, friend, and sometimes-employer, Samuel Taylor Coleridge (Jay, 59–60), whose 1798 *Rime of the Ancient Mariner*, of course, is evoked in a host of references throughout *Dracula*, both directly and in the story of death-in-life, of corpses walking.

11. See Arata, "Occidental Tourist."

12. See Moretti.

13. In 1883, for instance, Dr. Danelson wrote a book of popular medicine that suggested a home remedy for cholera in which opium plays a central and unremarkable role. But Danelson's book also lists opium as a poison, providing instructions for treating an overdose that include the forced marching of an opium-intoxicated patient up and down in a warm room, unclothed. Elsewhere, Danelson classifies the "opium-eating habit" under "dietic diseases" and comments that "[t]he indiscriminate administration of opium and morphine for the relief of pain, places much of the blame for this habit upon physicians' shoulders" (299).

14. The Opium Wars in China (1839–42 and 1856–60) in particular led to a transformation in public perception of the drug. There was a great public outcry against the British government's heavy-handed colonialist policies in China, which sought to open markets and create profits for Britain by forcing the Chinese to allow importation of Britain's lucrative Indian opium. The effect was twofold and apparently contradictory: as Virginia Berridge and Griffith Edwards explain, when the British colonial opium trade to China was blocked, there was a sense in England that the overflow had come home, to ill effect; at the same time, missionary reports of the terrible effects of opium addiction in China were matched with growing medical concern about the drug (174–75).

15. According to Berridge and Edwards, "[i]n 1861, there were an estimated 147 Chinese in the whole country, by 1881, 665" (195).

16. "[T]he idea began to form that the Chinese, still burning with hate from the wrongs they had suffered at Western hands, were laying plans to reduce the populations of America and Europe to opium slavery in reprisal" (Jay, 71).

17. See, for instance, the opening of Arthur Conan Doyle's story "The Man with the Twisted Lip" (306–27), in which Watson sets out to rescue the gentlemanly Isa Whitney from an opium den at the behest of Whitney's sobbing wife. Whitney, as Watson recounts,

> was much addicted to opium. The habit grew upon him, as I understand, from some foolish freak when he was at college;

for having read De Quincey's description of his dreams and sensations, he had drenched his tobacco with laudanum in an attempt to produce the same effects. He found, as so many more have done, that the practice is easier to attain than to get rid of, and for many years he continued to be a slave to the drug, an object of mingled horror and pity to his friends and relatives. I can see him now, with yellow, pasty face, drooping lids, and pin-point pupils, all huddled in a chair, the wreck and ruin of a noble man. (306–7)

18. This idea is evoked, for instance, by Dickens's racinated Princess Puffer in *The Mystery of Edwin Drood*.

19. The suitors have focused on Lucy as a site of connection and completion, and their approaches to her are certainly vampiric. Seward "play[s] with a lancet in a way that made [Lucy] nearly scream" (58) during his proposal; Quincey asks for a kiss, "something to keep off the darkness now and then," which literally brings forth the blood in Lucy's face (60).

20. The editors' notes to *Dracula* by Nina Auerbach and David J. Skal offer another possibility: the Korea as "[a]n imperialist hot spot in the 1890s, when Europe and the United States tried unsuccessfully to counter Japan's growing commercial control" (62). Auerbach and Skal are presumably referring to the Sino-Japanese War of 1894–95, when the two countries fought over control of the Korean peninsula. But although this war was closer to the period of writing in terms of chronology, the role of the United States was relatively limited in a military capacity (some of the new Japanese gunships were headed by American naval officers) and the British were not involved, so this seems a less likely reference. Furthermore, because Jonathan tells us that the events of the story took place "[s]even years ago" (326), the events of the mid-1890s are an unlikely reference, given the text's 1897 publication date.

21. This is a situation appropriate to the end of the century, when, despite a strong economy, the landed gentry were in economic freefall, industrialism was in retreat, and the future was uncertain. The relative status of inherence and acquisition in the formation of selfhood was also being questioned—as was the role of class.

22. William Ian Miller quotes Gordon Allport's thought experiments on the subject of the consumption of bodily fluids: "Think first of swallowing the saliva in your mouth, or do so. Then imagine expectorating it into a tumbler and drinking it! What seemed natural and

'mine' suddenly becomes disgusting and alien. Or picture yourself sucking blood from a prick in your finger; then imagine sucking blood from a bandage around your finger! What I perceive as separate from my body becomes, in the twinkling of an eye, cold and foreign" (quoted in Miller, 97). What belongs on the inside of the body, what is natural to that realm, becomes instantly disgusting when it is reconfigured as aliment. The vampire, of course, takes things a step further: it is not the blood from his own pricked finger that he sucks on.

23. The letters that made up this collection were widely read in serial form (1891) well before their publication as a collection in 1896 and can thus plausibly be seen as a source for Stoker.

24. For an exploration of the topic in Melville's work, see Crain.

25. Melville modeled his vessel in *Moby Dick* on the whaler *Essex*.

26. H. L. Malchow, writing on the vampire and "racial gothic" (12), contends,

> The savage cannibal and the gothic vampire, a species of cannibal, have much in common. . . . Both are types of the primitive: the vampire appropriates the vitality, the life-blood, of his victim, just as the cannibal wished, it was thought, to absorb the physical strength and courage of the enemy upon whose body he feasted. Together they share a kind of unholy communion, taking the body and blood of the innocent and transmuting them into their own identities. That which the cannibal performs by the machinery of his digestive system, the vampire accomplishes by a supernatural parasitism and pollution. (11)

27. All of the novel's medical interventions are distinctly vampiric, illustrating the problematic rewriting of body and selfhood that modern technology has brought about. Medicine is figured as a corrective to the ugly insides of the human: modern, speedy, and technological, it posits that the human can be controlled and repaired and thus is no longer prey to the horror of dissolution. The novel begins to fight the vampire by positing medicine as the cure to the biting disease: Drs. Van Helsing and Seward will save Lucy with their skill, their expertise, their transfusions, and their laudanum. But the insistence on the centrality of medical knowledge and its bloody repetitions in the novel refute the idea that the body holds some sort of higher selfhood. Van Helsing explains the process of blood transfusion as the "transfer from full veins of one to the empty veins which pine for him" (113–14)—a process not unlike the drinking of the vampire, whose

empty veins "pine" for the blood of his victim. Seward says of his donation to Lucy's veins, "No man knows till he experiences it, what it is to feel his own life-blood drawn away into the veins of the woman he loves" (119). The self drains away into the longed-for other-self; the boundaries between body and body are made immaterial by the technology of medicine.

The addiction of blood, then—the appetite for a Romantic, liminal, atavistic consciousness—is hardly beaten back by the bright light of science, knowledge, and modernity. Instead, the technological and the modern collude in this search for completeness and obscure this longing through medical machinations and technologies of forgetting and self-erasure, of alienation from self and from community. In its turn to synthetic drugs like chloral hydrate, in its enclosure of the body, the medical, alienating discourse of science and the modern creates a dangerous radical individualism, in which the self is distanced from community and lost to its own understanding. But in its acts of opening the body, of intervening, of cutting, of playing in blood, it beckons the morass and erases boundary, even as it reveals the interior as lacking interiority, a soul—as meat.

28. In the face of Dracula's liminality—his status as old and new, archaic and modern, self and other, human and not—language fails. Mina and Lucy cannot speak of their experiences; Jonathan, too, becomes silent, unable to recount his experiences even to himself. When the female vampires disappear and he is left with Dracula, he recounts that "the horror overcame me, and I sank down unconscious," and he adds in the opening to the next chapter, "I awoke in my own bed. If it be that I had not dreamt, the Count must have carried me here. I tried to satisfy myself on the subject, but could not arrive at any unquestionable result" (44). Under the influence of the vampire, Jonathan, like Mina and Lucy, seems to lose the power of telling—to lose even the power of knowing what it is that he knows. The experience of the vampire is at once "nineteenth century up-to-date with a vengeance" (Stoker, 40) and somehow beyond, before language. It is a return to the primordial—to the uncivilized, prelinguistic self.

29. This beautiful eternal youth is, however, horrible in its uncanniness: as Winfried Menninghaus posits, youth is idealized not as a state of stasis but as "perfection qua imperfection, Being qua promise. Its forms correspond to the rule of the fruitful moment precisely in not yet being fully articulated, unfolding precisely in a withholding of their completion" (59). The beauty of youth, then, lies in its promise of possibility—and the "adamantine" youth of the vampire, with its

promise only of more of the same (see, for instance, the three vampire sisters, locked forever in the suspended animation of their dusty rooms and dusty costumes), is in no way so lovely. The act of growing younger makes the vampire not only more virile but also more horrible: his youth is the youth of the new world, of course, but it is also an utter reversal of nature, a promise turned on its head.

BIBLIOGRAPHY

Accum, Frederick. *A Treatise on Adulterations of Food, and Culinary Poisons, Exhibiting the Fraudulent Sophistications of Bread, Beer, Wine, Spirituous Liquors, Tea, Coffee, Cream, Confectionary, Vinegar, Mustard, Pepper, Cheese, Olive Oil, Pickles, and Other Articles Employed in Domestic Economy; and Methods of Detecting Them*. London: Longman, Hurst, Rees, Orme and Brown, 1820.

Adams, James Eli. *Dandies and Desert Saints: Styles of Victorian Masculinity*. Ithaca, NY: Cornell University Press, 1995.

Adler, Marianna. "From Symbolic Exchange to Commodity Consumption: Anthropological Notes on Drinking as a Symbolic Practice." In *Drinking: Behavior and Belief in Modern History*, edited by Susanna Barrows and Robin Room, 376–98. Berkeley: University of California Press, 1991.

Aldcroft, Derek H. "McCloskey on Victorian Growth: A Comment." In *Enterprise and Trade in Victorian Britain: Essays in Historical Economics*, edited by Donald N. McCloskey, 111–15. London: George Allen and Unwin, 1981.

Alderson, David. "An Anatomy of the British Polity: *Alton Locke* and Christian Manliness." *Victorian Identities: Social and Cultural Formations in Nineteenth-Century Literature*, edited by Ruth Robbins and Julian Wolfreys, 43–61. London: Macmillan, 1996.

Alexander, Anna, and Mark S. Roberts, eds. *High Culture: Reflections on Addiction and Modernity*. Albany: State University of New York Press, 2003.

Ambrosini, Richard, and Richard Dury, eds. *Robert Louis Stevenson: Writer of Boundaries*. Madison: University of Wisconsin Press, 2006.

Arata, Stephen D. *Fictions of Loss in the Victorian Fin de Siècle*. Cambridge: Cambridge University Press, 1996.

———. "The Occidental Tourist: *Dracula* and the Anxiety of Reverse Colonization." *Victorian Studies* 33 (Summer 1990): 627–34.

———. "The Sedulous Ape: Atavism, Professionalism, and Stevenson's *Jekyll and Hyde*." *Criticism* 37, no. 2 (Spring 1995): 233–60.

Armstrong, Francis. *Dickens and the Concept of Home*. Ann Arbor: UMI Research Press, 1990.

Aron, Jean-Paul. *The Art of Eating in France: Manners and Menus in the Nineteenth Century*. Translated by Nina Rootes. New York: Harper and Row, 1975.

Ashley, Robert P. "Wilkie Collins." In *Victorian Fiction: A Guide to Research*, edited by Lionel Stevenson, 223–29. Cambridge, MA: Harvard University Press, 1964.

Austen, Jane. *Emma*. 1816. Oxford: Oxford University Press, 1988.

———. *Pride and Prejudice*. 1813. Edited by James Kinsley. Oxford: Oxford University Press, 1990.

Bakhtin, Mikhail. *Rabelais and His World*. Translated by Helene Iswolsky. Bloomington, IN: Indiana University Press, 1984.

Barthes, Roland. "Reading Brillat-Savarin." In *On Signs*, edited by M. Blornsley, 62–75. Baltimore, MD: Johns Hopkins University Press, 1985.

Baudrillard, Jean. *Simulacra and Simulation*. Translated by Sheila Faria Glaser. Ann Arbor: University of Michigan Press, 1995.

Beaumont, Thomas. *An Essay on the Nature and Properties of Alcoholic Drinks*. London: Simpkin, Marshall, 1838.

Bédarida, François. *A Social History of England, 1851–1990*. London: Routledge, 1990.

Benthien, Claudia. *Skin: On the Cultural Border between Self and the World*. 1999. Translated by Thomas Dunlap. New York: Columbia University Press, 2002.

Berridge, Virginia, and Griffith Edwards. *Opium and the People: Opiate Use in Nineteenth-Century England*. London: Allen Lane; New York: St. Martin's, 1981.

Berry, Elizabeth Hollis. *Anne Brontë's Radical Vision: Structures of Consciousness*. Victoria, BC: University of Victoria Press, 1994.

Berry, Laura C. "Acts of Custody and Incarceration in *Wuthering Heights* and *The Tenant of Wildfell Hall*." *Novel* 30, no. 1 (Fall 1996): 32–55.

Bevan, David, ed. *Literary Gastronomy*. Amsterdam: Rodopi, 1988.

Biasin, Gian-Paolo. *The Flavors of Modernity: Food and the Novel*. Princeton, NJ: Princeton University Press, 1993.

Block, Ed, Jr. "James Sully, Evolutionist Psychology, and Late Victorian Gothic Fiction." *Victorian Studies* 25, no. 4 (Summer 1982): 443–67.

Bloom, Harold, ed. *The Brontës: Modern Critical Views*. New York: Chelsea House, 1987.

Botting, Fred. *Gothic*. New York: Routledge, 1996.

Bourdieu, Pierre. *Distinction: A Social Critique of the Judgement of Taste*. 1979. Translated by Richard Nice. Cambridge, MA: Harvard University Press, 1984.

———. *The Field of Cultural Production: Essays on Art and Literature*. Edited by Randal Johnson. New York: Columbia University Press, 1993.

Briggs, E. *Cookery Book and General Axioms for Plain Cookery*. London: School Board for London; Frederick Tarrant and Son, 1890.

Brillat-Savarin, Jean Anthelme. *The Physiology of Taste, or Meditations on Transcendental Gastronomy*. 1825. Translated by M.F.K. Fisher. 1949. San Francisco: North Point, 1986.

Brodie, Janet Farrell, and Marc Redfield, eds. *High Anxieties: Cultural Studies in Addiction*. Berkeley: University of California Press, 2002.

Brontë, Anne. *The Tenant of Wildfell Hall*. 1848. London: Penguin, 1985.

Brooks, Peter. *Body Work: Objects of Desire in Modern Narrative*. Cambridge, MA: Harvard University Press, 1993.

Brown, Kate E. "The Half Life of Bachelors in Wilkie Collins' *The Law and the Lady*." Paper presented at the MLA Convention, Washington, DC, December 1996.

Brumberg, Joan Jacobs. *Fasting Girls: The Emergence of Anorexia as a Modern Disease*. Cambridge, MA: Harvard University Press, 1988.

Burgan, Mary. "Bringing Up by Hand: Dickens and the Feeding of Children." In *Diet and Discourse: Eating, Drinking and Literature*, edited by Evelyn J. Hinz, 69–88. Winnipeg: University of Manitoba Press, 1991.

Burnett, John. *Plenty and Want: A Social History of Diet in England from 1815 to the Present Day*. London: Thomas Nelson and Sons, 1966.

Butler, Erik. "Writing and Contagion in Dracula." *Iowa Journal of Cultural Studies* 2 (Fall 2002): 14–32.

Butler, Judith. *Bodies That Matter: On the Discursive Limits of "Sex."* New York: Routledge, 1993.

Butler, Lisa. "'That damned old business of the war in the members': The Discourse of (In)Temperance in Robert Louis Stevenson's *The Strange Case of Dr Jekyll and Mr Hyde*." *Romanticism on the Net* 44 (November 2006): http://www.erudit.org/revue/ron/2006/v/m44/014000ar.html.

Bynum, W. F. "Chronic Alcoholism in the First Half of the Nineteenth Century." *Bulletin of the History of Medicine* 42 (1968): 160–85.

Cadogan, William. "A Dissertation on the Gout, and all Chronic Diseases, jointly considered, as proceeding from the same causes, what those causes are; and a rational Method of Cure Proposed. Addressed to all Invalids." London, 1771. Reprinted in John Ruhräh, ed., *William Cadogan [His Essay on Gout]*. New York: Paul B. Hoeber, 1925.

Cannadine, David. *The Decline and Fall of the British Aristocracy*. New Haven, CT: Yale University Press, 1990.

———. *Lords and Landlords: The Aristocracy and the Towns, 1774–1967*. Leicester: Leicester University Press, 1980.

Capie, Forrest H., Terence C. Mills, and Geoffrey E. Wood. "Money, Interest Rates and the Great Depression: Britain from 1870 to 1913." In *New Perspectives on the Late Victorian Economy: Essays in Quantitative Economic History, 1860–1914*, edited by James Foreman-Peck, 251–84. Cambridge: Cambridge University Press, 1991.

Carter, Margaret L. *Specter or Delusion? The Supernatural in Gothic Fiction*. Ann Arbor: UMI Research, 1987.

Castricano, Jodey. "Much Ado about Handwriting: Countersigning with the Other Hand in Stevenson's *The Strange Case of Dr. Jekyll and Mr. Hyde*." *Romanticism on the Net* 44 (November 2006). http://www.erudit.org/revue/ron/2006/v/n44/014001ar.html.

Cavallaro, Dani. *The Gothic Vision: Three Centuries of Horror, Terror, and Fear*. London: Continuum, 2002.

Chamberlin, J. Edward, and Sander L. Gilman, eds. *Degeneration: The Dark Side of Progress*. New York: Columbia University Press, 1985.

Clapp, Alisa M. "The Tenant of Patriarchal Culture: Anne Brontë's Problematic Female Artist." *Michigan Academician* 28, no. 2 (March 1996): 113–22.

Clemens, Valdine. *The Return of the Repressed: Gothic Horror from The Castle of Otranto to Alien*. Albany: State University of New York Press, 1999.

Coan, Titus. *Life in Hawaii: An Autobiographic Sketch of Mission Life and Labors, 1835–1881*. New York: A.D.F. Randolph and Co., 1882.

Cohen, William A., and Ryan Johnson, eds. *Filth: Dirt, Disgust and Modern Life*. Minneapolis: University of Minnesota Press, 2005.

Collins, Wilkie. *Armadale*. 1866. Edited by John Sutherland. London: Penguin, 1995.

———. *The Haunted Hotel*. 1878. New York: Collier.

———. *The Law and the Lady*. 1875. Edited by Jenny Bourne Taylor. Oxford: Oxford University Press, 1992.

———. *The Moonstone*. 1871. Edited by Carolyn G. Heilbrun. New York: Modern Library, 2001.

———. *No Name*. 1862. Edited by Virginia Blain. Oxford: Oxford University Press, 1986, 1990.

Cookson, Gillian. "Engineering Influences on *Jekyll and Hyde*." *Notes and Queries* 46, no. 4 (December 1999): 487–91.

Corbin, Alain. *The Foul and the Fragrant: Odor and the French Social Imagination.* 1982. Translated by Alain Corbin. Cambridge, MA: Harvard University Press, 1986.

Counihan, Carole, and Penny Van Esterik, eds. *Food and Culture: A Reader.* New York: Routledge, 1997.

Craft, Christopher. "'Kiss me with those red lips': Gender and Inversion in Bram Stoker's *Dracula.*" *Representations* 8 (Fall 1984): 107–33.

Crafts, N.F.R. "Victorian Britain Did Fail." In *Enterprise and Trade in Victorian Britain: Essays in Historical Economics,* edited by Donald N. McCloskey, 126–31. London: George Allen and Unwin, 1981.

Craik, W. A. *The Brontë Novels.* 1968. Reprinted in *The Brontës: Modern Critical Views,* edited by Harold Bloom, 37–56. New York: Chelsea House, 1987.

Crain, Caleb. "Lovers of Human Flesh: Homosexuality and Cannibalism in Melville's Novels." *American Literature* 66, no. 1 (March 1994): 25–53.

Crothers, Thomas Davison. *Morphinism and Narcomanias from Other Drugs.* Philadelphia: Saunders, 1902. Reprint, Manchester, NH: Arno, 1981.

Dallas, E. *Kettner's Book of the Table: A Manual of Cookery, Practical, Theoretical, Historical.* London: Dulau and Co., 1877.

Dalrymple, Theodore. "Mr. Hyde and the Epidemology of Evil." *New Criterion* (September 2004): 24–28.

Daly, Nicholas. *Modernism, Romance, and the Fin de Siecle: Popular Fiction and British Culture.* Cambridge: Cambridge University Press, 1999.

Danelson, J. Edwin, M.D. *Dr. Danelson's Counselor with Recipes: A Practical and Trusty Guide for the Family and A Suggestive Hand-Book for the Physician.* New York: A. L. Burt, 1883.

Davidoff, Leonore. *The Best Circles: Society, Etiquette and the Season.* 1973. London: Century Hutchinson, 1986.

Davis, Michael. "Incongruous Compounds: Re-reading *Jekyll and Hyde* and Late-Victorian Psychology." *Journal of Victorian Culture* 11, no. 2 (Autumn 2006): 207–25.

Davis, Nuell Pharr. *The Life of Wilkie Collins.* Urbana: University of Illinois Press, 1956.

Dellamora, Richard. *Masculine Desire: The Sexual Politics of Victorian Aestheticism.* Chapel Hill: University of North Carolina Press, 1990.

De Quincey, Thomas. *Confessions of an English Opium-Eater and Other Writings*. Edited by Barry Milligan. New York: Penguin, 2003.

Dickens, Charles. *A Christmas Carol*. 1843. Edited by Robert Douglas Fairhurst. New York: Oxford University Press, 2007.

———. *David Copperfield*. 1850. New York: Oxford University Press, 2000.

———. *Hard Times*. 1854. Edited by Paul Schlicke. Oxford: Oxford University Press, 1989.

———. *Little Dorrit*. 1857. Edited by John Holloway. London: Penguin, 1985.

———. *Nicholas Nickleby*. 1839. Edited by Paul Shicke. New York: Oxford University Press, 1998.

———. *The Mystery of Edwin Drood and Other Stories*. 1870. Ware, UK: Wordsworth, 1998.

Dillon, Patrick. *Gin: The Much-Lamented Death of Lady Geneva*. Boston: Justin, Charles and Co., 2003.

Dingle, A. E. *The Campaign for Prohibition in Victorian England: The United Kingdom Alliance, 1872–1895*. New Brunswick, NJ: Rutgers University Press, 1980.

Dolan, Elizabeth A. "Rationality, Sensibility and Genius: Romantic Woman Poets and the Melancholic Body." Paper presented at "By Body Bound," Nineteenth Century Studies Association 17th Annual Conference, University of Alabama in Huntsville, April 2–4, 1998.

Dollimore, Jonathan. "Perversion, Degeneration, and the Death Drive." In *Sexualities in Victorian Britain*, edited by James Eli Adams and Andrew Miller, 96–117. Bloomington: Indiana University Press, 1996.

Douglas, Mary. "Deciphering a Meal." *Daedalus* 101, no. 1 (Winter 1972): 61–81.

———. *Purity and Danger: An Analysis of Concepts of Pollution and Taboo*. New York: Praeger, 1966.

Dowling, Andrew. *Manliness and the Male Novelist in Victorian Literature*. Aldershot, UK: Ashgate, 2001.

Doyle, Arthur Conan. *Sherlock Holmes: The Complete Novels and Stories*, vol 1. New York: Bantam, 1986.

Driscoll, Lawrence. *Reconsidering Drugs: Mapping Victorian and Modern Drug Discourses*. New York: Palgrave, 2000.

Drummond, J. C., and Anne Wilbraham. *The Englishman's Food: A History of Five Centuries of English Diet*. London: Jonathan Cape, 1939.

Dryden, Linda. *The Modern Gothic and Literary Doubles: Stevenson, Wilde and Wells*. Houndmills, UK: Palgrave Macmillan, 2003.

Dvorak, William. "The Misunderstood Pancks: Money and the Rhetoric of Disguise in *Little Dorrit*." *Studies in the Novel* 7 (1975): 538–51.

Edwards, Griffith. *Matters of Substance: Drugs—And Why Everyone's a User*. New York: St. Martin's, 2004.

Eigner, Edwin M. "Dogmatism and Puppyism: The Novelist, the Reviewer, and the Serious Subject: The Case of *Little Dorrit*." *Dickens Studies Annual* 22 (1993): 217–37.

Elias, Norbert. *The History of Manners*. Vol. 1, *The Civilizing Process*. 1939. Translated by Edmund Jephcott. New York: Pantheon, 1978.

Ellwanger, George H. *Meditations on Gout*. 1897. Cambridge: John Wilson and Son, 1929.

Falflak, Joel. "De Quincey Collects Himself." In *Nervous Reactions: Victorian Recollections of Romanticism*, edited by Joel Falflak and Julia M. Wright, 23–45. Albany: State University of New York Press, 2004.

Federico, Annette. "'I must have drink': Addiction, Angst, and Victorian Realism." *Dionysus* 2, no. 2 (Fall 1990): 11–25.

Ferris, Ina. "Thackeray and the Ideology of the Gentleman." In *Columbia History of the British Novel*, edited by John Richetti, 407–28. New York: Columbia University Press, 1994.

Finkelstein, Joanne. *Dining Out: A Sociology of Modern Manners*. New York: New York University Press, 1989.

Foster, Dennis. "'The little children can be bitten': A Hunger for Dracula." In *Dracula*, Case Studies in Contemporary Criticism series, edited by John Paul Riquelme, 483–99. Boston: Bedford; New York: St. Martin's, 2002.

Foust, Ronald. "Rite of Passage: The Vampire Tale as Cosmogonic Myth." In *Aspects of Fantasy: Selected Essays from the Second International Conference on the Fantastic in Literature and Film*, edited by William Coyle, 73–84. Westport, CT: Greenwood, 1986.

Freeman, Sarah. *Mutton and Oysters: The Victorians and Their Food*. London: Victor Gollancz, 1989.

Freud, Sigmund. "Craving for and Fear of Cocaine." 1887. Reprinted in *Cocaine Papers by Sigmund Freud*, edited by Robert Byck, 171–76. New York: Stonehill, 1974.

———. "On the General Effects of Cocaine." 1885. Reprinted in *Cocaine Papers by Sigmund Freud*, edited by Robert Byck, 111–18. New York: Stonehill, 1974.

———. *Three Essays on the Theory of Sexuality*. Translated by James Strachey. New York: Basic, 1962, 1975.

———. "Uber Coca." 1884. Reprinted in *Cocaine Papers by Sigmund Freud*, edited by Robert Byck, 47–74. New York: Stonehill, 1974.

Gagnier, Regenia. "Evolution and Information, or Eroticism and Everyday Life, in *Dracula* and Late Victorian Aestheticism." In *Sex and Death in Victorian Literature*, edited by Regina Barreca, 140–57. Bloomington: Indiana University Press, 1990.

Gallagher, Catherine. "The Body versus the Social Body in the Works of Thomas Malthus and Henry Mayhew." In *The Making of the Modern Body: Sexuality and Society in the Nineteenth Century*, edited by Catherine Gallagher and Thomas Laqueur, 83–106. Berkeley: University of California Press, 1987.

Garrett, Peter K. *Gothic Reflections: Narrative Force in Nineteenth-Century Fiction.* Ithaca, NY: Cornell University Press, 2003.

Gaughan, Richard T. "Mr. Hyde and Mr. Seek: Utterson's Antidote." *Journal of Narrative Technique* 17, no. 2 (Spring 1987): 184–97.

Gay, Peter. *Education of the Senses*, vol. 1, *The Bourgeois Experience: Victoria to Freud.* New York: W. W. Norton, 1984.

Gelder, Ken, ed. *The Horror Reader.* New York: Routledge, 2000.

Gérin, Winnifred. *Anne Bronte.* London: Thomas Nelson and Sons, 1959.

Gigante, Denise. *Taste: A Literary History.* New Haven, CT: Yale University Press, 2005.

Gilman, Sander. *The Jew's Body.* New York: Routledge, 1991.

Gilmour, Robin. *The Idea of the Gentleman in the Victorian Novel.* London: George Allen and Unwin, 1981.

Girouard, Mark. *Life in the English Country House: A Social and Architectural History.* New Haven, CT: Yale University Press, 1978, 1984.

Goodman, Jordan, Paul E. Lovejoy, and Andrew Sherratt, eds. *Consuming Habits: Drugs in History and Anthropology.* New York: Routledge, 1995.

Goody, Jack. *Cooking and Class: A Study in Comparative Sociology.* Cambridge: Cambridge University Press, 1982.

Gordon, Joan, and Veronica Hollinger, eds. *Blood Read: The Vampire as Metaphor in Contemporary Culture.* Philadelphia: University of Pennsylvania Press, 1997.

Greenstein, Michael. "Liminality in *Little Dorrit*." *Dickens Quarterly* 7, no. 2 (June 1990): 275–83.

Grindrod, Ralph Barnes. *Bacchus: An Essay on Intemperance.* New York: Langley, 1840.

Grudin, Peter D. *The Demon-Lover: The Theme of Demonality in English and Continental Fiction of the Late Eighteenth and Early Nineteenth Centuries.* New York: Garland, 1987.

Haggerty, George E. "'The end of history': Identity and Dissolution in Apocalyptic Gothic." *Eighteenth Century: Theory and Interpretation* 41, no. 3 (Fall 2000): 225–48.

Halberstam, Judith. *Skin Shows: Gothic Horror and the Technology of Monsters*. Durham, NC: Duke University Press, 1995.

Haley, Bruce. *The Healthy Body and Victorian Culture*. Cambridge, MA: Harvard University Press, 1978.

Hall, Jasmine Yong. "Solicitors Soliciting: The Dangerous Circulations of Professionalism in *Dracula*." In *The New Nineteenth Century: Feminist Readings of Underread Victorian Fiction*, edited by Barbara Leah Harman and Susan Meyer, 97–116. New York: Garland, 1996.

Haraway, Donna. *Simians, Cyborgs, and Women: The Reinvention of Nature*. New York: Routledge, 1991.

Harrison, Brian. *Drink and the Victorians: The Temperance Question in England, 1815–1872*. Pittsburgh: University of Pittsburgh Press, 1971.

Hayter, Alethea. *Opium and the Romantic Imagination*. Berkeley: University of California Press, 1970.

Heath, Stephen. "Psychopathia Sexualis: Stevenson's *Strange Case*." *Critical Quarterly* 28, nos. 1–2 (Spring/Summer 1986): 93–108.

Hendershot, Cyndy. *The Animal Within: Masculinity and the Gothic*. Ann Arbor: University of Michigan Press, 1998.

Herst, Beth F. *The Dickens Hero: Selfhood and Alienation in the Dickens World*. New York: St. Martin's, 1990.

Hirsch, Gordon, and William Veeder, eds. *Dr. Jekyll and Mr. Hyde after One Hundred Years*. Chicago: University of Chicago Press, 1988.

Hoffman, Emily. "Dickens' 'Misrepresentation of the Real': The Ideological Influence of Food and Its Consumption in *Pickwick Papers* and *Little Dorrit*." Unpublished paper, 1997.

Holden, Philip. "Castle, Coffin, Stomach: *Dracula* and the Banalities of the Occult." *Victorian Literature and Culture* (2001): 469–85.

Holoch, George. "Consciousness and Society in 'Little Dorrit.'" *Victorian Studies* 21, no. 3 (Spring 1978): 335–51.

Houston, Gail Turley. *Consuming Fictions: Gender, Class, and Hunger in Dickens's Novels*. Carbondale: Southern Illinois University Press, 1994.

———. *From Dickens to Dracula: Gothic Economies and Victorian Fiction*. Cambridge: Cambridge University Press, 2005.

Howlett, Caroline J. "Writing on the Body? Representation and Resistance in British Suffragette Accounts of Forcible Feeding." In *Bodies of Writing, Bodies in Performance*, edited by Thomas Foster,

Carol Siegel, and Ellen E. Berry, 3–41. New York: New York University Press.

Hughes, William. *Beyond Dracula: Bram Stoker's Fiction and Its Cultural Context.* Houndmills, UK: Macmillan; New York: St. Martin's, 2000.

Hunter, Lynette. "Proliferating Publications: The Progress of Victorian Cookery Literature." *Luncheon, Nuncheon and Other Meals: Eating with the Victorians,* edited by C. Anne Wilson, 51–70. Dover, NH: Alan Sutton, 1994.

Hurst, Beth F. *The Dickens Hero: Selfhood and Alienation in the Dickens World.* London: Weidenfeld and Nicolson, 1990.

Jackson, Arlene M. "The Question of Credibility in Anne Brontë's *Tenant of Wildfell Hall.*" *English Studies* 63, no. 3 (June 1982): 198–206.

Jacobs, N. M. "Gender and Layered Narrative in *Wuthering Heights* and *The Tenant of Wildfell Hall.*" *Journal of Narrative Technique* 16, no. 3 (Fall 1986): 204–19.

James, Allison. "Piggy in the Middle: Food Symbolism and Social Relations." *Food, Culture and History* (London Food Seminar) 1 (1993): 29–48.

Jann, Rosemary. "Saved by Science? The Mixed Messages of Stoker's *Dracula.*" *Texas Studies in Literature and Language* 31, no. 2 (Summer 1989): 273–87.

Jay, Mike. *Emperors of Dreams: Drugs in the Nineteenth Century.* Sawtry, UK: Dedalus, 2000.

Jeaffreson, John Cordy. *A Book about the Table.* London: Hurst and Blackett, 1875.

Jefford, Andrew. "Dr. Jekyll and Professor Nabokov: Reading a Reading." In *Robert Louis Stevenson,* edited by Andrew Noble, 47–72. London: Vision; Totowa, NJ: Barnes and Noble, 1983.

Johnson, Claudia L. *Jane Austen: Women, Politics and the Novel.* Chicago: University of Chicago Press, 1988.

Joyce, Simon. *Capital Offenses: Geographies of Class and Crime in Victorian London.* Charlottesville: University of Virginia Press, 2003.

Karch, Steven B. *A Brief History of Cocaine.* Boca Raton, FL: CRC, 1998.

Kasson, John F. "Rituals of Dining: Table Manners in Victorian America." In *Dining in America, 1850–1900,* edited by Kathryn Grover, 114–41. Amherst: University of Massachusetts Press and Margaret Woodbury Strong Museum, 1987.

———. *Rudeness and Civility: Manners in Nineteenth-Century Urban America.* New York: Hill and Wang, 1990.

Kilgour, Maggie. *From Communion to Cannibalism: An Anatomy of Metaphors of Incorporation*. Princeton, NJ: Princeton University Press, 1990.

Kirshenblatt-Gimblett, Barbara. "Playing to the Senses: Food as a Performance Medium." *Performance Research* 4, no. 1 (1999): 1–30.

Koestenbaum, Wayne. "The Shadow on the Bed: Dr. Jekyll, Mr. Hyde, and the Labouchere Amendment." *Critical Matrix* 1, no. 35 (March 1988): 35–46.

Korsmeyer, Carolyn, ed. *The Taste Culture Reader: Experiencing Food and Drink*. Oxford, UK: Berg, 2005.

Kramp, Michael. *Disciplining Love: Austen and the Modern Man*. Columbus: Ohio State University Press, 2007.

Kristeva, Julia. *Powers of Horror: An Essay on Abjection*. 1980. Translated by Leon S. Roudiez. New York: Columbia University Press, 1982.

Lacan, Jacques. *Feminine Sexuality*. Edited by Juliet Mitchell and Jacqueline Rose, translated by Jacqueline Rose. New York: W. W. Norton, 1982.

———. "The Mirror Stage as Formative of the *I* Function as Revealed in Psychoanalytic Experience." In *Écrits: The First Complete Edition in English*, translated by Bruce Fink, Héloise Fink, and Russell Grig, 75–81. New York: W. W. Norton, 2006.

Lambe, William. *A Medical and Experimental Inquiry, into the Origin, Symptoms, and Cure of Constitutional Diseases; Particularly Scrophula, Consumption, Cancer, and Gout*. 1805.

Lambert, Gavin. *The Dangerous Edge*. London: Barrie and Jenkins, 1975.

Lambert, W. R. *Drink and Sobriety in Victorian Wales c. 1820–c. 1895*. Cardiff: University of Wales Press, 1983.

Lane, Maggie. *Jane Austen and Food*. London: Hambledon, 1995.

Langland, Elizabeth. *Anne Brontë: The Other One*. London: Macmillan, 1989.

Lawson, Nigella. *How to Eat: The Pleasures and Principles of Good Food*. New York: Wiley, 2002.

Le Fanu, Sheridan. *Uncle Silas*. 1864. Edited by Victor Sage. New York: Penguin, 2000.

Leffler, Yvonne. *Horror as Pleasure: The Aesthetics of Horror Fiction*. Translated by Sarah Death. Stockholm: Almquvist and Wiksell, 2000.

Levine, George. "*Little Dorrit* and Three Kinds of Science." In *Dickens and Other Victorians: Essays in Honour of Philip Collins*, edited by Joanne Shattock, 3–24. London: Macmillan, 1988.

Levenstein, Edward. *Morbid Craving for Morphia: Die Morphiumsucht*. 1878. Edited by Gerald Grob, translated by Charles Harrer. Manchester: Ayer, 1981.

Lévi-Strauss, Claude. *The Origin of Table Manners*, vol. 3 of *Introduction to a Science of Mythology*. 1968. Translated by Doreen Weightman and John Weightman. New York: Harper and Row, 1978.

———. *The Raw and the Cooked*, vol. 1 of *Introduction to a Science of Mythology*. 1964. Translated by Doreen Weightman and John Weightman. New York: Harper and Row, 1969.

Liggins, Emma, Antony Rowland, and Eriks Uskalis, eds. *Signs of Masculinity: Men in Literature, 1700 to the Present*. Atlanta: Rodopi, 1998.

Lilienfeld, Jane, and Jeffrey Oxford, eds. *The Languages of Addiction*. New York: St. Martin's, 1999.

Litvak, Joseph. *Strange Gourmets: Sophistication, Theory, and the Novel*. Durham, NC: Duke University Press, 1997.

Long Hoeveler, Diane. "Objectifying Anxieties: Scientific Ideologies in Bram Stoker's *Dracula* and *The Lair of the White Worm*." *Romanticism on the Net* 44 (November 2006). http://www.erudit.org/revue/ron/2006/v/n44/014003ar.html.

Longmate, Norman. *The Water-Drinkers: A History of Temperance*. London: Hamish Hamilton, 1968.

Lonoff, Sue. *Wilkie Collins and His Victorian Readers: A Study in the Rhetoric of Authorship*. New York: AMS, 1982.

Lung, Roger D. "Genteel Fictions: Caricature and Satirical Design in *Little Dorrit*." *Dickens Studies Annual* 10 (1982): 45–66.

Lupton, Deborah. *Food, the Body and the Self*. London: Sage, 1996.

MacEachen, Dougald. "Wilkie Collins and British Law." *Nineteenth Century Fiction* 5 (September 1950): 121–36.

MacGregor, Catherine. "'I cannot trust your oaths and promises: I must have a written agreement': Talk and Text in *The Tenant of Wildfell Hall*." *Dionysus* 4, no. 2 (Fall 1992): 31–39.

Madge, Tim. *White Mischief: A Cultural History of Cocaine*. Edinburgh: Mainstream, 2001.

Malchow, Howard L. *Gothic Images of Race in Nineteenth-Century Britain*. Stanford: Stanford University Press, 1996.

Marin, Louis. *Food for Thought*. Baltimore, MD: John Hopkins University Press, 1997.

Markels, Julian. "Toward a Marxian Reentry to the Novel." *Narrative* 4, no. 3 (October 1996): 197–217.

Mars, Valerie. "Parsimony amid Plenty: Views from Victorian Didactic Works on Food for Nursery Children." *Food, Culture and History* (London Food Seminar) 1 (1993): 152–62.

Mattison, J. B. "Opium Addiction among Medical Men." *Medical Record* 23 (June 9, 1883): 621–23.

Matus, Jill L. *Victorian Representations of Sexuality and Maternity.* Manchester: Manchester University Press, 1995.

Mayhew, Henry. *London Labour and the London Poor.* 1861. Edited by Victor Neuburg. London: Penguin, 1985.

Maynard, John. *Victorian Discourses on Sexuality and Religion.* Cambridge: Cambridge University Press, 1993.

McCloskey, Donald L. *Enterprise and Trade in Victorian Britain: Essays in Historical Economics.* New York: Routledge, 1981.

McCormack, Kathleen. *George Eliot and Intoxication: Dangerous Drugs for the Condition of England.* London: Macmillan; New York: St. Martin's, 2000.

McCormick, Mairi. "First Representations of the Gamma Alcoholic in the English Novel." *Quarterly Journal of Studies on Alcohol* 30 (1969): 957–80.

McDonald, Beth E. *Spiritual Journey with the Undead in British and American Literature.* Jefferson, NC: McFarland and Co., 2004.

McMaster, Juliet. "'Imbecile Laughter' and 'Desperate Earnest' in *The Tenant of Wildfell Hall.*" *Modern Language Quarterly* 43, no. 4 (December 1982): 352–68.

Meisel, Martin. *Realizations: Narrative, Pictorial, and Theatrical Arts in Nineteenth-Century England.* Princeton, NJ: Princeton University Press, 1983.

Mennell, Stephen. *All Manners of Food: Eating and Taste in England and France from the Middle Ages to the Present.* 1985. 2nd ed. Urbana: University of Illinois Press, 1996.

———. "On the Civilizing of Appetite." In *Food and Culture: A Reader,* edited by Carole Counihan and Penny Van Esterik, 315–37. New York: Routledge, 1997.

Menninghaus, Winfried. *Disgust: Theory and History of a Strong Sensation.* Translated by Howard Eiland and Joel Golb. Albany: State University of New York Press, 2003.

Michie, Helena. *The Flesh Made Word: Female Figures and Women's Bodies.* New York: Oxford University Press, 1987.

Mighall, Robert. *A Geography of Victorian Gothic Fiction: Mapping History's Nightmares.* Oxford: Oxford University Press, 1999.

Miller, D. A. *Narrative and Its Discontents: Problems of Closure in the Traditional Novel.* Princeton: Princeton University Press, 1981.

———. *The Novel and the Police.* Berkeley: University of California Press, 1988.

Miller, Elizabeth. "Coitus Interruptus: Sex, Bram Stoker, and *Dracula*." *Romanticism on the Net* 44 (November 2006). http://www.erudit.org/revue/ron/2006/v/n44/014002ar.html.

Miller, William Ian. *The Anatomy of Disgust*. Cambridge, MA: Harvard University Press, 1997.

Milligan, Barry. "Morphine-Addicted Doctors, the English Opium-Eater, and Embattled Medical Authority." *Victorian Literature and Culture* 33 (2005): 541–53.

———. *Pleasures and Pains: Opium and the Orient in Nineteenth-Century British Culture*. Charlottesville: University Press of Virginia, 1995.

Mills, Kevin. "The Stain on the Mirror: Pauline Reflections in *The Strange Case of Dr. Jekyll and Mr. Hyde*." *Christianity and Literature* 53, no. 3 (Spring 2004): 337–49.

Mintz, Sidney. *Sweetness and Power: The Place of Sugar in Modern History*. New York: Penguin, 1985.

Moore, Grace. "Something to Hyde: The 'Strange Preference' of Henry Jekyll." In *Victorian Crime, Madness and Sensation*, edited by Andrew Maunder and Grace Moore, 147–61. Aldershot, UK: Ashgate, 2004.

Moretti, Franco. *Signs Taken for Wonders: Essays in the Sociology of Literary Forms*. Translated by Susan Fischer, David Forgacs, and David Miller. New York: Verso, 1988.

Morton, Peter. *The Vital Science: Biology and the Literary Imagination, 1860–1900*. London: George Allen and Unwin, 1984.

Morton, Timothy, ed. *Cultures of Taste/Theories of Appetite: Eating Romanticism*. New York: Palgrave/Macmillan, 2004.

———. *Shelley and the Revolution in Taste: The Body and the Natural World*. Cambridge: Cambridge University Press, 1994.

Mudrick, Marvin. *Jane Austen: Irony as Defense and Discovery*. Princeton, NJ: Princeton University Press, 1952.

Newton, John Frank. *The Return to Nature; or, A Defence of the Vegetable Regimen; with Some Account of an Experiment Made during the Last Three Years in the Author's Family*. London: Cadell and Davies, 1811.

Nicholson, George. "On Food." *The Literary Miscellany; or, Selections and Extracts, Classical and Scientific, in Prose and Verse*. Ludow: Nicholson, 1803.

Nordau, Max. *Degeneration*. 2nd ed. New York: D. Appleton, 1895.

North, Julian. "The Opium-Eater as Criminal in Victorian Writing." In *Writing and Victorianism*, edited by J. B. Bullen. New York: Longman, 1997.

Novak, Daniel. "If Re-Collecting Were Forgetting: Forged Bodies and Forgotten Labor in *Little Dorrit*." *Novel* 31, no. 1 (Fall 1997): 21–44.

Nunokawa, Jeff. *The Afterlife of Property: Domestic Security and the Victorian Novel.* Princeton, NJ: Princeton University Press, 1994.

Oates, Joyce Carol. "Jekyll/Hyde." *Hudson Review* 40, no. 4 (Winter 1988): 603–8.

O'Fallon, Kathleen. "Breaking the Laws about Ladies: Wilkie Collins' Questioning of Gender Roles." In *Wilkie Collins to the Forefront: Some Reassessments,* edited by Nelson Smith and R. C. Terry, 227–40. New York: AMS, 1995.

Parsinnen, Terry M. *Secret Passions, Secret Remedies: Narcotic Drugs in British Society, 1820–1930.* Philadelphia: Institute for the Study of Human Issues, 1983.

Pendleton, Robert W. "The Detective's Languishing Forefinger: Narrative Guides in *Bleak House* and *Little Dorrit* (Part II)." *Dickens Quarterly* 7, no. 4 (December 1990): 371–78.

Persack, Christine. "Spencer's Doctrines and Mr. Hyde: Moral Evolution in Stevenson's 'Strange Case.'" *Victorian Newsletter* (Fall 1994): 13–17.

Philpotts, Trey. "'To Working Men' and 'The People': Dickens's View of Class Relations in the Months Preceding *Little Dorrit*." *Dickens Quarterly* 7, no. 2 (June 1990): 262–75.

Pollard, Sidney. *Britain's Prime and Britain's Decline: The British Economy, 1870–1914.* London: Edward Arnold, 1989.

Porter, Roy, and G. S. Rousseau. *Gout: The Patrician Malady.* New Haven, CT: Yale University Press, 1998.

———, and Mikulas Teich, eds. *Drugs and Narcotics in History.* Cambridge: Cambridge University Press, 1994.

Pruitt, Amy. "Approaches to Alcoholism in Mid-Victorian England." *Clio Medica* 9, no. 2 (1974): 93–101.

Punter, David. "*Dracula* and Taboo." In *Dracula: New Casebooks,* edited by Glennis Byron, 22–29. New York: St. Martin's, 1999.

Rance, Nicholas. "'Jonathan's great knife': *Dracula* Meets Jack the Ripper." *Victorian Literature and Culture* (2002): 439–53.

Ray, Elizabeth, ed. *The Best of Eliza Acton: Recipes from Her Classic Modern Cookery for Private Families, First Published in 1845.* London: Longmans, Green and Co., 1968.

Reed, Thomas L., Jr. *The Transforming Draught: Jekyll and Hyde, Robert Louis Stevenson and the Victorian Alcohol Debate.* Jefferson, NC: McFarland, 2006.

Reid, Julia. *Robert Louis Stevenson, Science, and the Fin de Siecle.* Houndmills, UK: Palgrave Macmillan, 2006.

Reynolds, David S., and Debra J. Rosenthal, eds. *The Serpent in the Cup: Temperance in American Literature.* Amherst: University of Massachussetts Press, 1997.

Rice, Anne. *Interview with the Vampire.* New York: Ballantine, 1976.

"Richardson." "Abuse of Chloral Hydrate." *Quarterly Journal of Inebriety* 4, no. 1 (January 1880): 53–54.

Ritson, Joseph. *An Essay on Abstinence from Animal Food, as a Moral Duty.* London: Richard Phillips, 1802.

Robinson, Kenneth. *Wilkie Collins: A Biography.* New York: Macmillan, 1952.

Ronell, Avital. *Crack Wars: Literature Addiction Mania.* Lincoln: University of Nebraska Press, 1992; repr., Urbana: University of Illinois Press, 2004.

Rosenberg, Brian. *Little Dorrit's Shadows: Character and Contradiction in Dickens.* Columbia: University of Missouri Press, 1996.

Rosner, Mary. "'A total subversion of character': Dr. Jekyll's Moral Insanity." *Victorian Newsletter* (Spring 1998): 27–31.

Roulston, Christine. "Discourse, Gender, and Gossip: Some Reflections on Bakhtin and *Emma.*" In *Ambiguous Discourse: Feminist Narratology and British Women Writers,* edited by Kathy Mezei, 40–65. Chapel Hill: University of North Carolina Press, 1996.

Rozin, Paul, and April E. Fallon. "A Perspective on Disgust." *Psychological Review* 94, no. 1 (1987): 23–41.

Ruderman, Anne. "Moral Education in Jane Austen's *Emma.*" In *Poets, Princes, and Private Citizens: Literary Alternatives to Postmodern Politics,* edited by Joseph M. Knippenberg and Peter Augustine Lawler, 271–88. Lanham, MD: Rowman and Littlefield, 1996.

Russert, Margaret. "De Quincey, Nerves, and Narration." *Review* 22 (2000): 192–97.

Rymer, Malcolm. *Varney the Vampire; or, The Feast of Blood.* New York: Dover, 1972.

Sadrin, Amy. *Parentage and Inheritance in the Novels of Charles Dickens.* Cambridge: Cambridge University Press, 1994.

Scapp, Ron, and Brian Seitz, eds. *Eating Culture.* Albany: State University of New York Press, 1998.

Schaffer, Talia. "'A wild desire took me': The Homoerotic History of *Dracula.*" *ELH* 61, no. 2 (1994).

Schivelbusch, Wolfgang. *Tastes of Paradise: A Social History of Spices, Stimulants, and Intoxicants.* 1980. Translated by David Jacobson. New York: Pantheon, 1992.

Schofield, Mary Anne, ed. *Cooking by the Book: Food in Literature and Culture*. Bowling Green: Bowling Green University Press, 1989.

Schorer, Mark. "The Humiliation of Emma Woodhouse." In *Jane Austen: A Collection of Critical Essays*, edited by Ian Watt, 547–63. Englewood Cliffs, NJ: Prentice Hall, 1963.

Schultz, Myron G. "The 'Strange Case' of Robert Louis Stevenson." *Journal of the American Medical Association (JAMA)* 216, no. 1 (April 5, 1971): 90–94.

Schwartz, Hillel. *Never Satisfied: A Cultural History of Diets, Fantasies and Fat*. New York: Macmillan, 1986.

Senf, Carol A. *Dracula: Between Tradition and Modernism*. London: Twayne; New York: Prentice Hall, 1998.

———. *Science and Social Science in Bram Stoker's Fiction*. Westport, CT: Greenwood, 2002.

Shadwell, Arthur. *Drink, Temperance and Legislation*. 3rd ed. New York: Longmans, Green, and Co., 1915.

Shaw, George Bernard. *Shaw on Dickens*. Edited by Dan H. Lawrence and Martin Quinn. New York: Frederick Ungar, 1985.

Shelley, Mary. *Frankenstein*. 1816. New York: Signet, 1963.

Shelley, Percy Bysshe. *A Vindication of Natural Diet*. 1813.

Shiman, Lilian Lewis. *Crusade against Drink in Victorian England*. London: Macmillan, 1988.

Shires, Lydia M. "Of Maenads, Mothers, and Feminized Males: Victorian Readings of the French Revolution." In *Rewriting the Victorians: Theory, History, and the Politics of Gender*, edited by Lydia M. Shires, 147–65. New York: Routledge, 1992.

Showalter, Elaine. "Guilt, Authority and the Shadows of *Little Dorrit*." *Nineteenth Century Fiction* 34 (1979): 20–40.

———. *Sexual Anarchy: Gender and Culture at the Fin de Siècle*. New York: Viking, 1990.

Smith, Andrew. *Victorian Demons: Medicine, Masculinity and the Gothic at the Fin-de-Siecle*. Manchester: Manchester University Press, 2004.

Snyder, Katherine V. *Bachelors, Manhood, and the Novel, 1850–1925*. Cambridge: Cambridge University Press, 1999.

Soyer, Alexis. *The Gastronomic Regenerator: A Simplified and Entirely New System of Cookery, with Nearly Two Thousand Practical Receipts Suited to the Income of All Classes*. London: Simpkin, Marshall, and Co., 1846.

Sparks, Tabitha. "Medical Gothic and the Return of the Contagious Diseases Act in Stoker and Machen." *Nineteenth-Century Feminisms* 6 (Fall/Winter 2002): 87–102.

Spear, Jeffrey L. "Gender and Sexual Dis-Ease in *Dracula*." In *Virginal Sexuality and Textuality in Victorian Literature*, edited by Lloyd Davis, 179–92. Albany: State University of New York Press, 1993.

Spencer, Kathleen L. "Purity and Danger: *Dracula*, the Urban Gothic, and the Late Victorian Degeneracy Crisis." *ELH* 59 (1992): 197–225.

Stallybrass, Peter, and Allon White. *The Politics and Poetics of Transgression*. Ithaca, NY: Cornell University Press, 1986.

Stein, Gertrude. *Everybody's Autobiography*. 1937. New York: Random House, 1971.

Stevenson, Robert Louis. *In the South Seas*. 1896. Charleston, SC: BiblioBazaar, 2006.

———. *Strange Case of Dr. Jekyll and Mr. Hyde*. 1886. Edited by Katherine Linehan. New York: Norton, 2003.

Stoker, Bram. *Dracula*. 1897. Edited by Nina Auerbach and David J. Skal. New York: Norton, 1997.

Stone, Lawrence, and Jeanne Fawtier Stone. *An Open Elite? England, 1540–1880*. Oxford: Clarendon, 1984.

Sussman, Herbert. *Victorian Masculinities: Manhood and Masculine Poetics in Early Victorian Literature and Art*. Cambridge: Cambridge University Press, 1995.

Symons, Julian. *Mortal Consequences: A History—From the Detective Story to the Crime Novel*. New York: Harper and Row, 1972.

Tambling, Jeremy. "Opium, Wholesale, Resale, and for Export: On Dickens and China," pt. 1. *Dickens Quarterly* 21, no. 1 (March 2004): 29–43.

———. "Opium, Wholesale, Resale, and for Export: On Dickens and China," pt. 2. *Dickens Quarterly* 21, no. 2 (June 2004): 104–15.

Tames, Richard. *Economy and Society in Nineteenth-Century Britain*. London: George Allen and Unwin, 1972.

Tannahill, Reay. *Food in History*. 1973. Rev. ed. London: Penguin, 1988.

Taylor, Jenny Bourne. *In the Secret Theatre of Home: Wilkie Collins, Sensation Narrative, and Nineteenth-century Psychology*. London: Routledge, 1988.

———. "Introduction." In *Wilkie Collins, "The Law and the Lady,"* edited by Jenny Bourne Taylor. Oxford: Oxford University Press, 1992.

———. "Obscure Recesses: Locating the Victorian Unconscious." In *Writing and Victorianism*, edited by J. B. Bullen, 137–79. London: Longman, 1997.

Thomas, Ronald R. "Specters of the Novel: *Dracula* and the Cinematic Afterlife of the Victorian Novel." In *Victorian Afterlife: Post-*

modern Culture Rewrites the Nineteenth Century, edited by John Kucich and Diane F. Sadoff. Minneapolis: University of Minnesota Press, 2000.

Thompson, Deborah Ann. "Anorexia as a Lived Trope: Christina Rossetti's 'Goblin Market.'" In *Diet and Discourse: Eating, Drinking and Literature*, edited by Evelyn J. Hinz, 89–106. Winnipeg: University of Manitoba Press, 1991.

Thompson, F.M.L. *English Landed Society in the Nineteenth Century*. London: Routledge and Kegan Paul, 1963.

———. *The Rise of Respectable Society: A Social History of Victorian Britain, 1830–1900*. Cambridge, MA: Harvard University Press, 1988.

Thormahlen, Marianne. "The Village of Wildfell Hall." *Modern Language Review* 88, no. 4 (October 1993): 831–41.

Tracy, Robert. "Loving You All Ways: Vamps, Vampires, Necrophiles and Necrofilles in Nineteenth-Century Fiction." In *Sex and Death in Victorian Literature*, edited by Regina Barreca, 32–59. Bloomington: Indiana University Press, 1990.

Trollope, Anthony. *He Knew He Was Right*. 1869. Edited by John Sutherland. Oxford: Oxford University Press, 1990.

Tropp, Martin. *Images of Fear: How Horror Stories Helped Shape Modern Culture (1818–1918)*. Jefferson, NC: McFarland Classics, 1990.

Tucker, Robert C., ed. *The Marx-Engels Reader*. New York: Norton, 1978.

Vance, Norman. *The Sinews of the Spirit: The Ideal of Christian Manliness in Victorian Literature and Religious Thought*. Cambridge: Cambridge University Press, 1985.

Visser, Margaret. *The Rituals of Dinner*. New York: Penguin, 1992.

Waldron, Mary. "Men of Sense and Silly Wives: The Confusions of Mr. Knightley." *Studies in the Novel* 28, no. 2 (Summer 1996): 141–57.

Walkowitz, Judith R. *Prostitution and Victorian Society: Women, Class, and the State*. Cambridge: Cambridge University Press, 1980.

Walton, Priscilla J. *Our Cannibals, Ourselves*. Urbana: University of Illinois Press, 2004.

Walton, Stuart. *Out of It: A Cultural History of Intoxication*. New York: Harmony, 2002.

Warde, Alan. *Consumption, Food and Taste: Culinary Antimonies and Commodity Culture*. London: Sage, 1997.

Waters, Catherine. *Dickens and the Politics of the Family*. Cambridge: Cambridge University Press, 1997.

Waters, Karen Volland. *The Perfect Gentleman: Masculine Control in Victorian Men's Fiction, 1870–1911*. New York: Lang, 1997.

Watt, Ian P., and Bruce Thompson. *The Literal Imagination: Selected Essays*. Stanford: Stanford University Press, 2002.

Weinsheimer, Joel C. "In Praise of Mr. Woodhouse." *Ariel* 6, no. 1 (1975): 81–95.

Weiss, Barbara. "Secret Pockets and Secret Breasts: *Little Dorrit* and the Commercial Scandals of the Fifties." *Dickens Studies Annual* 10 (1982): 67–76.

Wells, H. G. *The Island of Dr Moreau*. 1896. Edited by Brian Aldiss. London: J. M. Dent, 1993.

Williams, Anne. "*Dracula*: Si(g)ns of the Fathers." *Texas Studies in Literature and Language* 33, no. 4 (Winter 1991): 445–63.

Wilson, C. Anne. "Introduction." In *Luncheon, Nuncheon and Other Meals: Eating with the Victorians*, edited by C. A. Wilson. Dover, NH: Alan Sutton, 1994.

Wood, Ellen. *East Lynne*. 1861. London: Dent, 1984.

Wood, Robin. "An Introduction to the American Horror Film." In *Movies and Methods*, vol. 2, edited by Bill Nichols, 195–219. Los Angeles: University of California Press, 1985.

Wood, Roy C. *The Sociology of the Meal*. Edinburgh: Edinburgh University Press, 1995.

Wright, Daniel. "'The prisonhouse of my disposition': A Study of the Psychology of Addiction in *Dr. Jekyll and Mr. Hyde*." *Studies in the Novel* 26, no. 3 (Fall 1994): 254–68.

Young, Arlene. *Culture, Class and Gender in the Victorian Novel: Gentlemen, Gents and Working Women*. London: Macmillan; New York: St. Martin's, 1999.

Youngquist, Paul. "De Quincey's Crazy Body." *PMLA* 114, no. 3 (May 1999): 346–58.

———. "Romantic Dietetics! Or, Eating Your Way to a New You." In *Cultures of Taste/Theories of Appetite: Eating Romanticism*, edited by Timothy Morton, 237–56. Houndmills, UK: Palgrave Macmillan, 2004.

INDEX

abjection, 83, 246
abstinence, 59, 61–62, 80–81, 257n23.
 See also teetotal movement
Accum, Frederick, 24
Acton, Eliza, 32, 248n9
addiction, 214–15, 227–28, 238,
 240–41, 273n7; drinking as, 58,
 59; to vampires, 229
Adler, Marianna, 177, 255n12,
 267n3
adulteration, of food, 8–9, 23–25, 26,
 270n17
agriculture, 49, 138
alcohol: gentlemanliness and, 176–77,
 181–83, 196, 245; liminality of,
 260n16; upper-class social relations
 and, 79. *See also* ale; beer; drunkenness; gin; wine
alcoholism, 58, 254n6
ale, 63, 257n21
aliment: bodily control and, 188;
 constitution of self by, 132;
 fetishization of, 106; healthy, 22,
 27–28, 210; nationalism and Englishness in, 8; pleasure and, 177;
 as political barometer and social
 prod, 125; purity in, 28, 29; self-
 construction and, 5; status and,
 69; as threat, 3–4; and understanding of character in, 22. *See
 also* alcohol; coffee; food; *specific
 types of aliment*
alimentary practices, Mr. Woodhouse
 and obsession with, 17–19, 22
alimentary ritual, 244–45, 247n3
allochronistic space, 223–26, 228, 232
Allport, Gordon, 275–76n22
alum, 23, 24
anorexia, 259n13; male, 22
anthropophagy, 107, 127, 148–53, 246

anti-industrialism, radical, 28–30
Appert, Nicholas, 248n6
appetite, 182, 185, 196; cocaine and
 suppression of, 193–94; disciplining
 of, 4, 6, 114, 179 (*see also* body,
 control over); of gentleman of
 leisure, 178; lack of, 110–23,
 154, 176, 210, 214, 259n21;
 middle class, 209–10; obscuring
 of, 115–16; sexual, 112; of vampires, 208, 209, 217
apples, 20, 24, 32, 40, 49
aristocracy, 145, 201, 239, 272n3;
 Dexter's collection and, 145; gentleman and, 42, 55, 66, 203, 226,
 229; seen as parasitic, 205, 207,
 208, 211; teetotal movement and,
 79–80
Assizes of Bread and Ale, 24
atavism, 199, 203, 238. *See also* degeneration
Auerbach, Nina, 275n20
Austen, Jane, 8, 12, 13–14, 17–22,
 24, 26–53, 57, 90, 98, 130, 176,
 184, 197, 205, 208, 210, 235, 243,
 247–52nn1–33. *See also* Woodhouse, Mr. (char., *Emma*)
Australia, food imported from, 22
autophagy, 84, 107–8, 111, 148, 185,
 197, 201, 231, 241, 246

Bakhtin, Michel, 235
Band of Light, 205, 207–10, 243
Barthes, Roland, 28, 251n28
Baudrillard, Jean, 211, 255n12
beef, imported, 22
beer, 59, 61, 257n21; adulteration of,
 25
beer soup, 9, 58, 62
behavior modification, 80, 84

299